UNDERSTANDING THE BUSH DOCTRINE

PSYCHOLOGY AND STRATEGY
IN AN AGE OF TERRORISM

UNDERSTANDING THE BUSH DOCTRINE

EDITED BY

STANLEY A. RENSHON AND PETER SUEDFELD

Routledge
Taylor & Francis Group
New York   London

Routledge
Taylor & Francis Group
270 Madison Avenue
New York, NY 10016

Routledge
Taylor & Francis Group
2 Park Square
Milton Park, Abingdon
Oxon OX14 4RN

© 2007 by Taylor & Francis Group, LLC
Routledge is an imprint of Taylor & Francis Group, an Informa business

Printed in the United States of America on acid-free paper
10 9 8 7 6 5 4 3 2 1

International Standard Book Number-10: 0-415-95504-1 (Softcover) 0-415-95503-3 (Hardcover)
International Standard Book Number-13: 978-0-415-95504-1 (Softcover) 978-0-415-95503-4 (Hardcover)

Library of Congress Cataloging-in-Publication Data

Understanding the Bush doctrine : psychology and strategy in an age of terrorism /
    edited by Stanley A. Renshon and Peter Suedfeld.
        p. cm.
    ISBN 0-415-95503-3 (hb) -- ISBN 0-415-95504-1 (pb)
        1. United States--Politics and government--2001- 2. Bush, George W. (George
Walker), 1946- 3. Iraq War, 2003- 4. War on Terrorism, 2001- 5. United
States--Foreign relations. I. Renshon, Stanley Allen. II. Suedfeld, Peter, 1935-

JK276.U55 2006
363.325'15610973--dc22   2006021851

Visit the Taylor & Francis Web site at
http://www.taylorandfrancis.com

and the Routledge Web site at
http://www.routledge.com

Contents

Acknowledgments

Every published book owes a debt to the dedicated people who helped make it a reality, and this book is no exception.

The support and encouragement of Robert Tempio, then politics acquisitions editor at Routledge, was instrumental in bringing this book to the Taylor and Francis Group. When he left to pursue another major publishing challenge, the book was placed in the extremely capable hands of Charlotte Roh, who made sure that not a beat was missed on the way to completion. Michael Kerns, recently appointed politics editor at Routledge, has continued to be exceptionally supportive of this project.

Michael Davidson has handled all of the many aspects of the production process with effectiveness and dispatch, and Joanne Yang did excellent work copyediting the manuscript.

In the process of the finding a good home for this book, a number of anonymous reviewers offered their views on a detailed proposal and chapter outline. The book and its editors are much appreciative of the very helpful and thoughtful observations.

We are also extremely indebted to our contributors. They all gave their time and insights in the service of analyzing a controversial policy and helping it become more understandable. In the process, they had to contend with two editors, each reviewing their chapters several times. The ensuing discussions were enormously helpful to us as editors and students of the many issues this book addresses. We thank them for their time and willingness to engage our questions and observations.

It has been a real pleasure for the two editors to work together. We share a long friendship and history of mutual interests that was only strengthened by our work on this book.

Finally, Stanley Renshon would like to acknowledge Judith, a warm, loving, and thoughtful wife, who was together with him in this work, as always. Peter Suedfeld thanks his beloved wife, Phyllis Johnson, who combines her own academic career with being his best editor, ally in the face of political controversy and moderator of his arguments.

Preface

The Bush Doctrine is one of the most consequential statements of national security policy in contemporary American history. It is also one of the most controversial. Not surprisingly, given the scope of its importance and its association with a very controversial president, understanding of the Doctrine—its strategic foundations, its psychological premises, and its development—as it has and continues to unfold in practice, is widely misunderstood and under-examined. It has been variously and erroneously equated with the doctrine of preventive war, imperious unilateralism, and American empire. It is true the Doctrine lends itself to these overly broad and bold characterizations; however, its premises are more thoughtful and its implementation more nuanced than the critics allow.

Certainly, the Bush Doctrine is much wider in scope than any of the singular elements for which it is criticized. It is rather a set of policies that reflect five interconnected strategic elements*:

American Preeminence—The reality and consequences of the fact that America is the most powerful country in the world, but that power has its limits.

Assertive Realism—Central to the Bush Doctrine is the judgment that when it comes to catastrophic terrorism, the best defense is a strong offensive, including the use, when necessary, of preemption and preventive war.

Strategic Stand-Apart Alliances—The Bush administration understands the lesson that every administration eventually learns: few allies are supporters on every matter, and all have their own interests, which may or may not coincide with ours on particular matters, as well as the understanding that allies have differing levels of sympathy with and commitment to American national security policies.

The New Internationalism: Selective Multilateralism—The Bush administration believes that international institutions are not currently structured or operating in a way that allows the United States to fully depend on them for vital national security issues. It follows that these institutions must be reformed before they can be depended upon, if ever.

Democratic Transformation—Here the Doctrine presents a twist by using an old solution to solve a new problem. President Bush is not the first president to want to make the world safe for democracy, but he is the first to explicitly voice the strategy of using democracy as a tool to transform or neutralize now-dangerous countries.

These five elements provide a general, though not inflexible, framework for this book, housed in four major sections: The Foundations of the Bush

ix

Doctrine; the Bush Doctrine in the Post-9/11 World; The View from Abroad; and The Bush Doctrine in Perspective. Any assessment of the Doctrine, for example, must consider its future (S. Renshon, Chapter 12), which is obviously related to the five elements, but not strictly speaking one of them. So, too, the response to the Bush Doctrine abroad (Moens, Chapter 10; Stein, Chapter 11) is an important aspect of the assessment of the Doctrine, but not one its five general elements. Other aspects of the relationship between the Doctrine's elements and this volume's chapters are more straightforward. The chapters on democracy (Zonis, Chapter 9) and strategic alliances (Suedfeld, Tetlock, and Jhangiani, Chapter 4) follow directly from the general framework. The same is true of the *assertive realism* and *American preeminence* elements that are taken up in chapters on strategic debates (Alexander, Chapter 2), American and world public opinion (Foyle, Chapter 3; Moens, Chapter 10; Stein, Chapter 11), and the psychology of strategic response (Curtis, Chapter 5; Post, Chapter 6; Levy, Chapter 7; J. Renshon, Chapter 8).

Given its centrality to American national security, and the fact that the premises of the Doctrine raise questions that are going to be essential to address well into the twenty-first century, it is important to have a fair and balanced assessment of the Doctrine. It is also crucial to have the same kind of appraisal for its consequences and prospects, as it is being applied. This means both criticizing its shortcomings and acknowledging its accomplishments, where appropriate. These are the primary goals of this volume.

The five domains of the Bush Doctrine rest on diverse conceptual foundations, including traditional international relations theory, the psychology of conflict, strategic analysis, and national security policy. Theoretically, the Doctrine reflects concerns at the intersection of risk, uncertainty, and consequence, as well as strategic theories of deterrence, preemption, and prevention in relation to both state and nonstate actors. All of these concepts rest on a foundation of psychology and political analysis—hence the importance of political psychology. Furthermore, any assessment of the Doctrine must take into account the fact that it must function within the current international structure, which is still to a great extent anarchical. Consequently, it will be perceived and received very differently by the widely varying regimes and leaders who must take it into account and respond to it. Questions of international structure and its consequences are the traditional domains of international relations theory. The Bush Doctrine blends these disciplinary strands at their intersection with American national security policy. It is well to always keep in mind that national security policy requires that steps be taken, most often in the absence of validated theory from any of the disciplinary perspectives that this book examines.

Because the perspectives that frame this book intersect at the overlapping disciplines of international relations theory, national security policy, and political psychology, it is appropriate that the contributors to this volume represent a mix of interdisciplinary perspectives. Some are primarily trained in political science, some in history, others in psychology. Most have interests that span several perspectives. In their training, interests, and perspectives, they are a diverse group.

Given that the Bush Doctrine is controversial both domestically as well as internationally, with strongly held feelings on both sides of the political spectrum, an inescapable question arises about the position of this book and its contributors. The answer is straightforward. The invited contributors have been carefully chosen on the basis of their expertise and academic accomplishment, not their political viewpoints. This volume makes no attempt to present a consensus of views, one way or the other, about the Bush Doctrine. Nor have we asked the contributors to try and find one.

What does unite the authors is a record of substantive interest in the questions at hand and a demonstrated ability to identify and thoughtfully address the psychological and strategic issues that the Bush Doctrine presents in their areas of knowledge.

Finally, there is the issue of geographical perspective. The Bush Doctrine is, in a number of ways, quintessentially American. Yet its effects are clearly felt worldwide. This being the case, shouldn't a volume concerned with the impact of this Doctrine attempt to represent the range of international responses? The question is fair, but misses the point. The purpose of this volume is not to sample the world's views on the Doctrine itself. Geographical diversity was less a concern to us than bringing together diverse disciplinary and intellectual perspectives coupled with substantive quality. As the chapters in the volume demonstrate, you don't have to be French to have significant questions about the Bush Doctrine.

The best measure of how well the volume addresses the diverse range of issues raised by the Doctrine is not how evenly balanced each individual chapter is but the extent of useful understanding that the chapters, individually and collectively, provide about the nature, implications, and operation of this important doctrine.

Stanley A. Renshon
Peter Suedfeld

---

* The formulation of the five basic elements outlined here is the work of the first editor and the basis of a forthcoming book. See Stanley A. Renshon, *The Bush Doctrine and the Future of American National Security.* (New Haven, CT: Yale University Press, 2008).

1

The Bush Doctrine Considered

STANLEY A. RENSHON

On a crisp early September morning, four groups of Muslim terrorists boarded the planes they would use as instruments of destruction, aimed symbolically and literally at the heart of America's economic, political, and military institutions. Two planes targeted and demolished the World Trade Towers, icons of American entrepreneurial spirit. A third plane struck the South Wing of the Pentagon, headquarters and worldwide symbol of America's military primacy. The third plane, aimed at either the White House or Congress, hearts of American democracy, crashed in Pennsylvania after heroic passengers recaptured control of the plane from the terrorists.

The targets were chosen with care. The plan was ruthlessly and effectively carried out. And it succeeded beyond the wildest dreams of the perpetrators. The chief architect of the slaughter, Osama bin Laden, was recorded boasting to friends that the total collapse of the World Trade Center Towers surpassed anything he had expected, in his phrase, "Allah be praised."

The immediate result of the attack could be counted in the thousands killed, the tens of thousands more deprived of their husbands, wives, fathers, mothers, sisters, and brothers. It could also be tallied in the billions of dollars lost in actual physical destruction and the many billions more lost in economic consequences. It was also a devastating psychological blow.

The 9/11 attacks demonstrated that the United States was vulnerable. Oceans were not enough to protect it. Nor, seemingly, was the most prodigious military in the world's history. Americans awoke on September 11 to discover that they were personally vulnerable at home and at work, as well as abroad. They soon learned that this country is the primary target of individuals and groups that would like to deliver a mortal or crippling blow to it, preferably with weapons of mass destruction. September 11 demonstrated that they have the intent, the capacity, and the will. They only lack the means, and they are striving with every ounce of their ambition to acquire it.[1] Thus was born the highly contentious "Bush Doctrine."

A Controversial and Misunderstood Policy

To say the Bush Doctrine is controversial is a little like breathing air; we have become so used to the fact that we hardly notice it. Critics on the left have equated the Bush Doctrine with preemptive and preventive war, imperious unilateralism, and American empire. Critics on the right have focused on the adminisration's mistakes after the overthrow of Saddam Hussein and its insistence that the Middle East must be transformed. The argument advanced here, however, is that the Bush Doctrine has been, but should not be, confused with just one of its elements, preventive war; it is an option, but not a doctrine by itself.[2] Nor should it be confused with its single most visible application, the war in Iraq. Clearly that war is a direct consequence of the Doctrine's assertive stance and assumptions about risk. However, while the war in Iraq is a consequence of the Bush Doctrine, it does not itself represent the whole strategy.

The Bush Doctrine is best understood as a conceptual and strategic response to a set of important national security issues that the United States faces in the post-9/11 world.

- How can the United States avoid being the victim of anther major terrorist attack, this time with weapons of mass destruction (WMDs)?
- What roles do the doctrines of prevention, preemption, containment, and deterrence play in the range of threats with which the United States and its allies must contend?
- How can the United States resolve the dilemma of needing the cooperation of allies to address common threats, while having to deal with allies' different priorities and understandings of these very threats that may require the United States to act alone?
- How can the United States resolve the dilemma of needing international institutions to further develop a liberal democratic world order and its own legitimacy with the fact that the "international community" is sometimes not democratic, liberal, nor supportive of basic American national security concerns?

The Bush Doctrine's answers to these questions have drawn strong views from both sides of the political spectrum. Liberals (exemplified by the The Daily Kos Blog) and their allies in the Democratic party (exemplified by Howard Dean and John Kerry) have constantly hurled a stream of harsh invective at both the Doctrine and President George W. Bush. At every step, be it the invasion of Afghanistan, whether 9/11 could have been prevented, what the United States should (and should not) do to protect itself, the "misuse" of intelligence data, and post-Saddam strategy in Iraq, the Bush Doctrine has been critiqued and second-guessed by the "left," but rarely fairly analyzed.

Less appreciated is the fact that contrary to conventional perceptions, conservatives have not marched in lockstep behind Bush. A November 2005 *Commentary* symposium entitled "Defending and Advancing Freedom" contains comments from 36 academic and political commentators, most but not all conservatives of the Bush Doctrine.[3] Among numerous things conservative writers criticized in that symposium is the Doctrine itself (William F. Buckley), "bungling: the Iraq War" (Max Boot), and the Doctrine's "bleak" long - range prospects" (Niall Ferguson). Francis Fukuyama opined in the *New York Times* that the Doctrine was "now in shambles."[4] The Cato Institute, a conservative libertarian think tank, published a paper by its director of defense policy studies arguing that Bush's National Security Strategy (NSS) was a misnomer for a set of policies that resulted in national *insecurity*.[5] Gerhard Baker, a sympathetic columnist for the *London Times*, after listening to the President's 2004 State of the Union Address, wrote, "The Wild Ride Is Over, The Days of an Aggressive US Policy Are Gone."[6] In other venues, some of the President's allies went much further. Paul Craig Roberts, a conservative commentator, penned an article about the administration's new doctrine entitled "Is the Bush administration certifiable?" and began the pundit piece by asking, "Has President Bush lost his grip on reality?"[7]

It is difficult to sort out the portions of disagreements over the Doctrine that come from partisan views, dislike of President Bush and his agenda, the difficulties of the Iraq occupation, and the specifics of the policies themselves. A number of the more general, less shrill criticisms come from scholars who appear truly taken aback by the assertive stance of the Doctrine, especially when compared to what is clearly their preferred stance toward foreign policy—multilateralism, international institutionalism, and extensive search in almost all circumstances for foreign policy options other than force.

The result has been a certain amount of confusion and selectivity in criticisms of the Doctrine. So, two senior international relations specialists (Ivo H. Daalder and James M. Lindsay) who worked in the Clinton administration, one of whom served as a foreign policy advisor to Senator Kerry in the 2004 presidential campaign, characterized the Doctrine as "revolutionary" and "radical."[8] They subtitled their book "The Bush Revolution in Foreign Affairs." The word *revolution* conjures up historic institutions and practices swept away, yet any fair assessment of the Doctrine would need to account for some fairly conventional elements within it. Its assumptions in some key respects are perfectly compatible with traditional "realism."

What exactly is it about Mr. Bush's foreign policy that makes it a "revolution," and "potentially even radical"? Not the goals of American foreign policy, since Daalder and Lindsay agree that these are fully consistent with the goals of many of the presidents who preceded him.[9] Indeed, these critics argue, somewhat paradoxically, that the goals are thoroughly conventional,[10] and that, surprisingly, Mr. Bush could be considered a "status quo" president![11]

It is quite a neat conceptual feat to be both revolutionary, almost radical, yet thoroughly conventional and an upholder of the status quo.

The Bush Doctrine: Theory vs. Practice

It is important at the outset to distinguish between the Bush Doctrine in theory and in practice. Just as no battle plan survives the first skirmish, no doctrine escapes modification, except perhaps in its critics' minds. The Bush Doctrine is no exception.

There are at least four reasons for this. Most obviously and importantly, principles are declarations of preference and intent. They are not robotic mandates that must be carried out regardless of circumstances. The same critics who believe they have uncovered something profound in the fact that Mr. Bush treats members of the "axis of evil" differently would be legitimately aghast if he treated them all the same.

The common principle of the "axis of evil" was that all three regimes were tyrannical, dangerous, and illegitimate. What to do about them is quite another matter. President Bush has invaded Iraq, supports six-nation talks with North Korea, and deferred to the European Union lead in referring Iran to the United Nations for its clandestine efforts to develop nuclear weapons. The reasons for the separate policies are to be found in their different strategic circumstances and the nature of the problem in each of the three countries. Kim Jong Il and Saddam Hussein, to take but one difference, were both dangerous, but in different ways. Saddam aspired to regional conquest and hegemony, while Kim Jong Il could not invade South Korea successfully or survive the attempt, and he has shown no hint of regional hegemonic aspirations.

Second, doctrines, and this is true of the Bush Doctrine, do not spring forth fully developed like Athena from Zeus' head.[12] The worldview foundations of the Bush Doctrine were in place well before 9/11. I characterize it later in this chapter as *nationalist realism*. However, that foundation was only that, and 9/11 brought new circumstances, new understandings on the part of senior administration officials and, as a result, new policies. That the administration would not tolerate the transfer of WMD components or technical information from or to dangerous countries was certainly a by-product of Bush's realist view; since the world is a dangerous place, it is best to be prudent. September 11 added to that foreign policy stance the understanding that WMDs and ruthless tyrants and groups were a recipe for destruction. Still, general doctrinal statements, such as "some governments will be timid in the face of terror. And make no mistake about it: If they do not act, America will,"[13] must be translated into policy as it meets specific circumstances. What steps define "timid" and which are "bold"? What do countries have to do to forestall American action and what action, exactly, may they expect if they don't?

Or again, "I will not wait on events, while dangers gather. I will not stand by, as peril draws closer and closer."[14] What events? What specific dangers?

How long can one wait, if at all? To simply ask these questions is to underscore just how far doctrine by itself carries one toward actual policy. The issue is not so much, as some critics frame it, of one policy *versus* another (for example, multi-versus unilateralism), but rather the more nuanced requirment to calibrate policy in the face of divergent possibilities (how much of each is necessary and possible in these circumstances).

Third, even when the worldviews of a grand strategy are in place, major news events can have a dramatic effect on what then becomes expressed as the doctrine. One example is the change in foreign policy from President Bush's pre-9/11 worldview to the actual formulation of the Bush Doctrine after 9/11. Another example is the Doctrine's stress on democratization. It was not mentioned during Bush's 2000 presidential campaign and was not in evidence in the months before 9/11. Its first mention by the president was during his West Point speech in June 2002, nine months after 9/11.[15]

It was brought up again in the administration's official National Security Strategy document, in Mr. Bush's September 2002 speech at the United Nations, and again in an October 2002 speech by Condoleezza Rice at the Manhattan Institute.[16] After the invasion of Iraq and the failure to date to find WMDs, it became a staple of the President's and his senior advisors' rhetorical emphasis.[17] It is now officially an indelible part of the Bush Doctrine, despite its late arrival.

Fourth, doctrines, policies, and the infrastructure that supports them may and should change, particularly in response to the lessons learned while applying and refining the doctrine. For example, consider the force structure of the American armed forces. In the past, it was oriented toward fighting *two* conventional wars. The new Quadrennial Defense Review (QDR) has clearly been revised in accord with the lessons of post-9/11 conflicts and the threat of catastrophic terrorism.[18] In the 2001 version, the Pentagon envisioned being able to "swiftly defeat" two adversaries in overlapping military campaigns, while perhaps overthrowing a hostile government in one. In the new strategy, one of those two campaigns can be a large-scale, prolonged "irregular" conflict, such as the counterinsurgency in Iraq. The strategy also envisions conducting combat operations, if necessary, in countries with whom we are *not* at war and operating as necessary on a worldwide, rather than a limited regional basis.[19]

Refining doctrines in practice also can lead to reconceptualization. Consider the concept of deterrence. That doctrine was developed and refined as American national security policy during a Cold War that featured two nuclear-armed and ideologically opposed superpowers. Of course, deterrence and its variants (coercive diplomacy, compellence) were applied outside the American–Soviet confrontation, but the basic idea was still the same. Deterrence involved the actual or implied threat to take action if an adversary did not refrain or desist from certain actions.

The new defense review anticipates "tailored deterrence,"[20] to develop doctrine and capabilities that aid deterrence in at least three different domains: advanced military competitors (read China), regional WMD states (for example, Syria, Iran, North Korea), and nonstate terrorist threats. The *Quadrennial Review* is a strategic concept document, not a fully refined operational theory. It therefore provides little in specifics beyond some general statements of the capacities needed to address these three separate domains. Nonetheless, conceptualizing three different deterrence domains raises the important theoretical questions of what is similar and what is different about the three areas, and how these understandings affect the development and application of deterrence in each.

Or, consider the second revised iteration of the administration's National Security Strategy, issued March 16, 2006.[21] That document reaffirms many of the major elements of the 2002 version, but it also refines them. The 2002 version extolled democracy, presenting it as key of domestic stability and international order. It devoted considerable attention to the administration's views and policies on the subject.[22] The 2006 version, coming after the election victory of Hamas (officially designated as a terrorist organization) in the Palestinian territories, forced the administration to draw an important distinction between being democratically voted into office and continuing an avowed policy of "armed conflict including terrorism." The focus in this new iteration is on "effective democracy"; in the case of Hamas, any government that does not honor these principles (renouncing violence and terror) "cannot be considered fully democratic, however, it may have taken office."[23]

The revised National Security Strategy also incorporates a lesson bitterly learned in Iraq. Post-conflict stabilization matters a great deal. It has become clear from a variety of assessments, that postwar planning for the aftermath of the Iraq War was deeply flawed.[24] The failures to adequately anticipate and prepare for post-Saddam security seem particularly critical. Iraq has proven a bloody and very difficult lesson in the failure to anticipate the brutal mix of suppressed interethnic conflict, the psychological consequences of decades of brutal dictatorship, severely damaged economies and infrastructure, the development and consolidation of governmental institutions of repression and domestic terror, and the powerful effects of nationalism.

How much these failures to anticipate were a by-product of Mr. Bush's well-known aversion to "nation building" is unclear. However, the 2003 National Security Strategy document did not mention the term "post-conflict stabilization and reconstruction." The 2006 revision does and specifically touts the development of the Office of Coordinator of Reconstruction and Stabilization, located in the Department of State—an explicit transfer of these responsibilities from the Department of Defense, which was given responsibility for post-Saddam security and redevelopment.

The 2002 NSS mentioned public diplomacy only twice, in passing.[25] The 2006 version takes seriously the fact that the United States is both at war and also engaged in a "battle of ideas"[26] and an attempt to limit "sub-cultures of conspiracy and misinformation."[27] The policies for addressing these issues are not only "public diplomacy," but also "transformational diplomacy" that includes "actively engaging foreign audiences" and "enlisting the support of the private sector."[28] The catchiness of the concept phrasing is much less important than the fact that it reflects recognition of a key strategic element in future American national security policy.

Finally, the 2006 NSS strategy rearranged the foreign policy universe of allies, rivals, and enemies. Al-Qaeda remains a principal enemy.[29] North Korea is a power that destabilizes its region.[30] Russia appears to have moved from friend to strategic partner, but, on the issue of democracy, a disappointment.[31] India has moved from a standoffish, possible ally to a more fully functional strategic partner.[32] China has gone from a strategic competitor to global player with an important role to play, *if* it acts as a "responsible stakeholder that fulfills its obligations and works with the United States and others to advance the international system that has enabled its success."[33]

The NSS restates the doctrine of preventive attacks on terrorists groups[34] and elsewhere refers to "anticipatory action to defend ourselves."[35] These policies renew preemption and preventive force without so naming them. In this context, no one should fail to notice the following sentence: "We face no greater challenge from a single country than from Iran."[36]

The 2006 NSS also makes another subtle, but important language shift. Gone are the political theological references in which the President stated that it was the responsibility of America to "rid the world of evil."[37] In its place is a focus on tyrants and tyranny,[38] two terms that bring to mind America's earliest indictment against King George III. The focus on tyranny and tyrants replaces the language of primal religious categories with a much more politically familiar and acceptable terms. Thus, in such subtle phasing, reconceptualization and refinement, does a doctrine evolve.

The Bush Doctrine: Myth and Reality

Controversy heightens emotional responses. Extreme controversies generate strong, sometimes narrow, views that lose sight of important facts. The Bush Doctrine is controversial and, not surprisingly, has evoked a number of strongly held, but not necessarily accurate views.

The Neoconservative "Cabal"

One of the most widely held myths is that the Bush Doctrine is the result of, and that the real powers in the administration are, a small, highly influential group of neoconservatives. They had been supposedly agitating for Bush Doctrine-like policies years before the Bush presidency.[39] Limited evidence for this view is to be found in the pre-Bush administration views of several administration officials. Among them are Paul Wolfowitz and Douglas Feif, both of whom served in the Department of Defense. Others who are ordinarily included as "influential" outside advisors include Richard Perle and William Kristol, neither of whom has ever served in the administration.

The standard critical narrative runs somewhat as follows: "An intellectually lightweight president, unschooled in foreign affairs, was led by a highly motivated cabal of foreign policy advisors and mysterious connected outsiders to embrace their controversial doctrines."[40] A particularly egregious and muddled recent addition to this mistaken view adds that the group is primarily Jewish and beholden to the State of Israel.[41] Francis Fukuyama, a neoconservative critic of the Bush Doctrine, says of these accusations, "Much of this literature is factually wrong, animated by ill-will, and a deliberate distortion of the record of both the Bush Administration and its supporters."[42]

Another version of this criticism is found in an allegation by Lawrence B. Wilkerson, Chief of Staff to Secretary of State Colin Powell, that "in President Bush's first term, some of the most important decisions about U.S. national security—including vital decisions about postwar Iraq—were made by a secretive, little-known cabal…made up of a very small group of people led by Vice President Dick Cheney and Defense Secretary Donald Rumsfeld."[43]

There are a number of difficulties with this view however. Yes, when he entered the presidency, Mr. Bush was unschooled in foreign affairs. However, he is no dunce, and is by no means a policy pushover.[44] Indeed, the usual criticism of his leadership style is that it is "arrogant" and "imperious," two traits inconsistent with being a pushover.

Moreover Secretary of State Colin Powell, Vice President Dick Cheney, National Security Advisor Condoleezza Rice, and Secretary of Defense Donald Rumsfeld were, if anything, conservative nationalists and maybe even "realists," but not neoconservatives. The same was true of the President before 9/11. As James Mann makes clear in his magisterial history of the Bush war cabinet, "labels are sometimes not very useful."[45] In any event, the dramatic impact of 9/11 throughout the Bush administration swept away many preconceptions that had anchored previous views among a number of senior foreign policy advisors.

What of Wilkerson's "cabal"? The evidence is that Bush foreign policy principals came to agree on many things, but strongly disagreed on many others. All the administration's foreign policy principals had their way on some, but by no means all, policy issues. Rumsfeld wanted to include Iraq immediately on the post-9/11 target list along with Afghanistan, but the President overruled him. Powell insisted the President go to the UN for approval. He got his way, but not exactly in the way he had envisioned. Bush coupled his request to the UN with a suggestion that it show some backbone.

On some occasions, the administration foreign policy principals agreed, only to run into opposition from Paul Bremmer, Chief Presidential Envoy to Iraq from May 2003 to June 2004.[46] On the issue of quickly putting together a "Provisional Council" to supersede the original Governing Council without elections, they lost.

The question of whether to delay the first interim election (January 30) after the Hussein regime fell produced a spirited debate. The *Washington Post* reported that "[a] powerful debate was raging, officials now acknowledge, among the president's top advisers over postponing the January 30 interim election in hopes of first tamping down the flaring insurgency and bringing disaffected factions to the table." National Security Advisor Steven Hadley acknowledged, "There was a good debate in front of the president.... It was a close question and if it had gone to consensus, I don't know how it would have come out."[47] Ultimately, it did not go to a consensus decision but to Bush, who opted to stick with the election. This was not the first time that Bush's views settled a debate with a decision.[48]

In the end, Bush's foreign policy advisors came to agree on many things and diverge on others. It is not surprising that smart, principled, and experienced policy makers would have disagreements, sometimes strong ones. The fate of those advisors' policy preferences, like those in other administrations, can best be described by the adage: win some, lose some.

Unilateralism?

Torrents of criticism have been directed at the Doctrine's "unilateralism."[49] The usual criticism is that President Bush ignores and alienates important allies, not to mention the rest of the world because "He prefers to build an empire on American power alone rather than on the greater power that comes from working with friends and allies."[50] This is usually accompanied by complaints about the President's "disdain for the sorts of formal multilateral arrangements," and the "arrogance of American power."[51]

Such analyses ignore a great deal of contrary evidence. There is no evidence that Mr. Bush is interested in building an "empire" in the traditional understanding of that term. Moreover, there is no evidence that he "prefers" not to work with friends and allies. The evidence is quite the contrary. Mr. Bush has been on an extended search during his presidency for allies. Among these one might count are new and closer relationships with India,[52] Pakistan, Japan,[53] among others, and attempts to bring China and Russia into the international institutional community.

The criticism of Bush's "disdain" for international agreements is premised on the assumption that these agreements accomplish their stated purposes with no significant damage to American economic or strategic interests, and that there are no better ways to accomplish these purposes. In each of the cases ordinarily presented as evidence for "disdain" (e.g., the Kyoto

Protocol, the Anti-Ballistic Missile Treaty, the International Criminal Court, and the Nuclear Test Ban Treaty), the administration has raised reasonable and legitimate arguments for its views. It would be fairer and more appropriate for critics to deal with the substance of these arguments rather than to issue blanket condemnations.

Few critics recall that it was the Clinton Administration that began the process that led to the scraping of the ABM treaty, and that it did so in response to the launching of a powerful North Korean missile in 1999. Or, consider the widely criticized decision of the administration to not sign the Kyoto accords. At the time these were negotiated, during the Clinton administration, the Senate went on record 95-0 opposing them, and President Bill Clinton never submitted them for ratification. One reason was that the treaty would have had a substantial adverse impact on the U.S. economy. Another was that it exempted two major polluting countries, China and India, from its provisions. Those reasons are still valid.

Isn't global warming a problem about which something should be done? Apparently, although exactly how much of a problem it is, what causes it, and whether the Kyoto agreement adequately addresses it in a timely, cost-effective manner are issues of genuine debate. The Bush administration has not simply rejected the Kyoto accords and done nothing else. It has proposed an alternative climate warming-reduction policy. This includes an agreement among six nations (the United States, Japan, Australia, China, India, and South Korea) that "will build on existing bilateral agreements on technology sharing to control emissions, but will not set mandatory targets."[54] That agreement envisions the use of technology, not mandatory caps to reduce warming, and "cap and trade" methods to further that process. Interestingly, a recent international panel on global warming "called for a broader version of the Kyoto Protocol, one that might include the Bush administration's voluntary approach to combating global warming," and a "gradual and voluntary reduction of carbon-dioxide emissions, in proportion to economic output."[55]

I am not sufficiently versed in the science involved to make an informed judgment on these matters. However, it does seem clear that the administration's position has found some backers among those who previously excoriated it for its failure to sign on to the mandatory controls involved in the original agreement. Fair-minded assessments of the Doctrine and the administration's "unilateralism" in this area and others would address these developments and the substantive concerns that led to them.

Finally, the charge of unilateralism reflects a less than nuanced understanding of the complexities of international relationships. Consider America's equivocal ally, France. The French clearly opposed the United States' invasion of Iraq and stymied American attempts at the United Nations to gain a resolution specifically adding force to the consequences for Iraqi noncompliance. Yet, at the same time, France has helped the U.S. in counterterrorism operations,[56] and both have worked effectively together at the UN to pressure Syria to withdraw from Lebanon.[57]

Another recent report notes, "The CIA has established joint operation centers in more than two dozen countries where U.S. and foreign intelligence officers work side by side to track and capture suspected terrorists and to destroy or penetrate their networks."[58] While Germany and the United States were at loggerheads over the decision to invade Iraq, the German Secret Service's information aided the invasion.[59] Moreover, if the Bush Doctrine is synonymous with unilateralism, how does one explain the administration's Proliferation Security Initiative? It is designed to intercept WMD materials and was signed by over 40 countries, including France and Germany.[60]

Many assessments of the Bush Doctrine contain both a political and partisan dimension. Disagreements with France on Iraq are emphasized; agreements with France on fighting terrorism, helping them quell rebel violence in the Ivory Coast, and containing Iran's nuclear program are downplayed or forgotten. Disagreements with Germany (before the 2005 election of Chancellor Angela Merkel) are emphasized; new and improved relationships with India, Eastern European countries, and Japan are ignored or dismissed.

Even when the administration allows its European or Asian partners to take the lead or work with the United States as part of a team, the administration is criticized. Hillary Clinton has criticized the President for his multilateral efforts with Iran and North Korea, saying, "I believe that we lost critical time in dealing with Iran because the White House chose to downplay the threats and to *outsource the negotiations*.... I don't believe you face threats like Iran or North Korea by *outsourcing it to others* and standing on the sidelines."[61] Such criticisms leave the impression that no matter what the administration does, or doesn't do, it will be subject to criticism by some.

The post-9/11 world of alliances is complicated because old allies like France are competitors and spoilers on some issues, while they cooperate with the United States on others. Russia has both helped and stymied the United States in dealing with Iran's nuclear ambitions,[62] and has also been implicated in passing on American intelligence to Saddam Hussein at the start of the Iraq War.[63] The testiness of France and the limited alliance with Russia is really a pre-9/11, not a post-9/11, story.

New to the post-9/11 world are the partnerships that have developed and the added strains on old ones. It is a world in which new nations in Eastern Europe have become allies out of shared historical experiences and perspectives, and others like Pakistan have become allies because of military necessity. Other alliances of economic, political, and strategic necessity, such as those with Saudi Arabia and Egypt, are troubling in a number of ways, but important enough to merit continued efforts on our part.

It is certainly true that the administration has taken tough stands regarding what it considers to be the security interests of the United States. It has also done so in a sometimes brusque, impatient, and provocative way.[64] And it has certainly, in the aftermath of 9/11, relied less on diplomatic "give and take" than in stating its positions and following through on them; this stance seems to have shifted as it has confronted the dangers of a nuclear-armed Iran.[65] Perhaps this adds up to a "disdain" for allies, a thrust for "empire," or the "arrogance of power." Or, perhaps it reflects understandable and realistic concerns born out of the 9/11 attacks and the implications that the administration drew from them.

Worldview Origins of the Bush Doctrine

The intellectual origins of the Bush Doctrine can be traced to a conservative-leaning group nicknamed the "Vulcans." They were concerned with the drift of U.S. foreign policy during the Clinton administration.[66] Their statement of principles included increasing defense spending and strengthening relationships with democratic allies. They further wanted to "*challenge* regimes hostile to our interests," "*promote* political and economic freedom abroad," and accept responsibility for "America's unique role in preserving and *extending* an international order friendly to our security, our prosperity, and our principles."[67]

The next year, this same group sent an open letter to President Clinton warning that "[t]he policy of 'containment' of Saddam Hussein has been steadily eroding over the past several months." They argued, "If Saddam does acquire the capability to deliver weapons of mass destruction, as he is almost certain to do if we continue along the present course, the safety of American troops in the region, of our friends and allies like Israel and the moderate Arab states, and a significant portion of the world's supply of oil will all be put at hazard." And they ended by urging Clinton to act decisively by "implementing a strategy for removing Saddam's regime from power."[68]

The Vulcans, it is easy to see, favored a "forward-leaning" national security policy. *Promoting* freedom and democracy, *challenging* hostile regimes, *extending* our preferred international order, and of course *removing* Saddam Hussein from power sound remarkably prescient and predictive of elements that were to become the Bush Doctrine. The only thing missing from this mix was Bush himself and those he surrounded himself with once in office. Rumsfeld, Rice, Cheney, and Powell were, as already noted, Cold War realists, not neoconservatives. Before 9/11 Bush himself was a nationalist, not a Vulcan. He was certainly not a neoconservative. After 9/11 he remained a nationalist,[69] but adapted many of the positions associated with neoconservatives.

The first view of Bush's foreign policy inclinations is found in a 1999 speech he gave at the Reagan Ranch while running for president.[70] The themes reflecting his worldview are helpful in understanding the impact 9/11 had in cementing them. Here are some key phrases: "The empire [Soviet Union] has passed, but evil remains"; "America has determined enemies who hate our values";

"We must protect our homeland and our allies against missiles and terror"; "in defense of our nation, a president must be a clear-eyed realist"; "armies and missiles are not stopped by stiff notes of condemnation, [but] by strength and purpose and the promise of swift punishment"; "unless a president sets his own priorities, his priorities will be set by others"; the Comprehensive Test Ban Treaty…is not verifiable…it would stop us from ensuring the safety and reliability of our deterrent…. It is not enforceable…it offers only words and false hopes and high intentions—with no guarantees whatsoever."

They are the words of an American nationalist. However, these phases also clearly reflect a worldview that that any international relations "realist" would agree with. Bush sees the world as dangerous; realists would say it is anarchic.[71] Bush seems to favor a forward-looking offensive stance toward national security. This is entirely consistent with realist-in-chief John Mearsheimer's major premise that "the best defense is a good offense."[72] Even so-called "defensive realists insist that states must be prepared for the worst even if they hope for the best."[73] Bush believes national security concerns take precedence over international agreements; realists detail "the false promise of institutions."[74] Many "realists" have complained about the Bush Doctrine via the advocacy group, The Coalition for a Realistic Foreign Policy. Their full-page ad in the *New York Times* ultimately seems to be a case of disowning one's progeny.[75]

There is one further point worth noting here. Realists research the state of the international system with theories that aspire to explain how states act. Other international relations theorists look at the same world, with different theories and different questions and arrive at different conclusions. The ensuing academic debates are rarely fully resolved. Debates arise and fade away without any particular theory being able to claim decisive victory or an agreed upon metric to adjudicate conflicting claims.[76] In the meantime, in Mr. Bush's words, we hear a candidate for the presidency whose principal concern is the United States, and who does not have the luxury to await settled theory, should it ever arrive.

It was then Bush's worldview and his stance toward that understanding that is the constant in both pre- and post-9/11. The 9/11 attacks reaffirmed and strengthened those views; they did not bring them into existence. The key elements of the Bush Doctrine grew very comfortably out of the President's basic foreign policy premises.

The Bush Doctrine, in Reality

Both the left and right have roundly criticized the Bush Doctrine, though for vastly different reasons. The left has been critical of the Doctrine's assertive posture, preferring the comfort of traditional allies, international institutions, and treaty agreements. They have not addressed what happens when allies don't support you, institutions don't protect you, and treaties don't deter your sworn enemies.

Paradoxically, given conventional wisdom about the Doctrine, some conservatives have criticized the Bush administration's lack of assertiveness. Their plea is: unleash the Bush Doctrine! They want to know why the Bush administration has not militarily confronted the other charter members of the "axis of evil," and has let Syria get away with encouraging terrorist infiltration into Iraq.[77] They are, apparently, not bothered by the prospect of having more than one war at a time when the public is barely supporting a major and critical test of the Bush Doctrine in Iraq. Nor do they seem to accept the facts that limit what the United States can accomplish in some circumstances, good doctrine or not.

Other conservatives have abandoned the Bush Doctrine primarily because of the costly postwar errors that became clear after the regime of Saddam Hussein had been toppled. George Will has criticized the President's rhetoric on progress in Iraq as "unrealistic."[78] William F. Buckley has stated boldly, "our mission has failed."[79] Francis Fukuyama, as noted, has asserted that the Doctrine is now "in shambles," and it "is not surprising that in its second term, the administration has been distancing itself from these policies and is in the process of rewriting the National Security Strategy document."[80] In this, Fukuyama proved mistaken. As already noted, the administration did not distance itself from the basic tenets of the Doctrine in its 2006 revision—quite the contrary.

A major problem with assessing the Doctrine is that critics focus on one element of it (say, trying to spread democracy or preventive war) or one flawed attempt to implement it (Iraq), and conclude that the whole Doctrine has been discredited. Yet, the Bush Doctrine is not one single policy. It is, rather, a set of policies that reflect five related strategic elements.

American Preeminence   The Bush Doctrine's primary formal explication, the National Security Strategy of the United States, makes quite clear both the premise and the fact of American primacy.[81] It has been amply documented by Joseph Nye.[82] President Bush is often credited or criticized for the view that America should be the dominant country in the world. However, that view was clearly articulated as policy in 1992 during the Clinton administration. During that period the Pentagon drafted a new grand strategy designed to prevent the emergence of any possible global rival.[83] When that idea ran into criticism, the administration began to describe the United States as the "indispensable" country. Being indispensable of course is not the same as being dominant. Bush did appear to share that view, although in his debate with presidential rival Al Gore and in his 1999 major foreign policy speech at the Reagan Ranch, he did mention the word "humble." Yet, that is hard to reconcile with what else he said in that same speech. He talked quite directly of his vision, "in which no great power, or coalition of great powers dominates or endangers our friends."[84] One possible implication of that statement is that it wouldn't happen because the United States would be stronger than the threatening powers or groups of powers. That view receives confirmation from a speech given in 2002 by Condoleezza Rice at the Manhattan Institute. In it, she bluntly stated, "We will seek to dissuade any potential adversary from pursuing a military build-up in the hope of surpassing, or equaling, the power of the United States."[85]

At least for now, the reality is that America is the most powerful country in the world, although, as Huntington notes, all this power doesn't necessarily translate to effective influence.[86] America's preeminence and unique position as the most powerful country in the world raises a number of critical issues. Chief among them: For what purposes will, and ought, the United States use its preeminent position? Must hegemony equal empire? Critics think so, and accuse the United States of seeking one.[87] Others ask: What's so bad about an American empire?[88]

Madeline Albright called the United States an "indispensable power."[89] That may be, but the United States certainly appears to spur contradictory impulses in the world (see Foyle, Chapter 3; Moens, Chapter 10; Stein, Chapter 11). American primacy reassures some, scares others, and angers more than a few. For a country of people who want to be liked and belong, this is a difficult and paradoxical position.

There are in fact many roles that the United States can and does play, but not all of them are compatible with the Bush Doctrine's primary purpose, to keep American from being devastated by a WMD attack. What role the United States chooses to play and how well that role fits with its now primary national security purpose are key issues for the future of the Doctrine (see Renshon, Chapter 12).

Assertive Realism   The second tenet of the Bush Doctrine is the judgment that when it comes to catastrophic terrorism, the best defense is a strong offense (Alexander, Chapter 2). In the past, the advance of military technology fueled an "ideology of the offensive"[90] in aggressive nation states. Importantly, this is not the case for the Bush Doctrine. It is not assertive because of a "use it or lose it" window of opportunity psychology generated by technological advances. Rather, it is assertive because the United States was successfully attacked by a group that would like to repeat their success, the next time with catastrophic weapons. The strategic origin of the administration's posture is found in Rumsfeld's observation that "[i]t is not possible to defend ourselves against every conceivable attack, in every conceivable location at every minute of the day or night, [therefore] the best, and in some cases, the only defense is a good offense."[91]

Jervis writes, "Offensive realism perhaps provides the best explanation for what the US is doing because it sees states as always wanting more power in order to try to gain more security for an uncertain future."[92] It is true that higher levels of power, whether military or economic, can be translated into more security. After all, deterrence, a policy that many Bush critics prefer to his Doctrine, is premised upon it. However, it is also true, as 9/11 demonstrated, that there is no such thing as absolute security, even if you are the world's reigning "hegemon."

However, Jervis' criticism misses an important point. Yes, the Bush Doctrine translates into support for high military budgets, more attention to domestic security, forceful rhetoric and, in several notable cases, the use of military force. Yes, the Bush Doctrine has elevated preventive action to an important role, while not neglecting to prepare for preemptive strikes, if necessary (see Levy, Chapter 7; J. Renshon, Chapter 8) and making use of more traditional deterrence where possible (see Curtis, Chapter 5). However, the Doctrine's vigor is not some fear-fed attempt to provide illusionary security from equally illusionary perceptual threats. It is a direct result of America's post-9/11 national security circumstances. Americans had been savagely and effectively attacked by terrorists who want to do it again, if possible with WMDs. Such an attack, if successful, would severely damage the political, economic, cultural, and psychological fabric of the country.

The Bush Doctrine was not proposed to support a *pax America*. It was not proposed to acquire an empire. It was proposed to protect the United States from leaders and groups who would like to inflict catastrophic harm on this country, and had already demonstrated the desire, intention, and will to do so.

Realists point out that as countries gain more power, they gain more interests.[93] It therefore stands to reason, critics assert, that the United States as *the* most powerful country has expanded its interests. Those new interests now include Iraq, the development of democracy in critical states and areas, and the war on terror. Thus Jervis writes, "American policy towards Iraq and the Bush Doctrine in general conforms to the *standard Realist generalization* that a state's definition of its interests will expand as its power does."[94] So while Jervis, himself a realist, states quite directly that his article is "partially motivated by my opposition to American policy,"[95] in this respect at least the President's behavior is just what he as a realist would expect and predict.

We are therefore faced with a somewhat confusing situation wherein a realist criticizes a president for behaving exactly as realist theory predicts he will. The implication of the criticism is that the President ought not to act in accordance with the theory. In taking this position, Jervis both affirms realism's explanatory power while decrying the policies that in his view lead to the theory's confirmation.

Actually, the dilemma runs somewhat deeper because Jervis also points to a difference between "what the deterrent relationship is and can appear between the US and Iraq and how we can explain what Bush and his colleagues appear to believe." He goes on to say that "the divergence between the two, and the ways in which the actors' beliefs affect the use and impact of threats, raises questions about how we theorize about actors who are themselves thinking about deterrence."[96] Indeed they do.

One question that immediately arises is why the actors' own views of their circumstances, risks, and choices as they struggle with questions of threats and deterrence should be accorded any less weight than the views of the theorists who are analyzing their choices. Jervis answers this question rather decisively. He says that "when states behave 'badly,' general claims may be embarrassed." More specifically, "We are theorizing about actors that have their own explanations, which may be different than ours, and we have a problem explaining behavior we think is foolish when our theories do not incorporate foolishness."[97] The problem with this view is that it makes the theorist the final arbiter of what is wise or foolish, impetuous or prudent, or pragmatic rather than overly ambitious. Not only does the president have to live up to the tenets of a particular theoretical perspective, but he must also do so in a way consistent with the theorist's views of exactly how he should do it.

Why are the actors' view of his circumstances and options not a crucial focus of a theory called realism? The president, or any other leader, may or may not act in accord with the principles of the theory, but the reasons why he does or doesn't do so are valuable data for the refinement of the theory. Instead of criticizing the leader for not adhering to the theory as the theorist defines it, why not ask whether a leader's behavior outside of the critic's theoretical box doesn't offer new avenues of analysis or understanding?

That question arises directly with the invasion of Iraq. Bush decided to invade Iraq primarily because he thought Saddam Hussein was dangerous to vital American national interests. He supported that contention with a list of Hussein's past behaviors and WMD aspirations.

Yet, in truth Bush never made clear why Hussein was more dangerous than Kim Jong Il, or why he might be more (or less) dangerous than Mahmoud Ahmadinejad, the hard-line mayor of Tehran who won the Iranian presidency in 2005.[98] Both the 2002 and 2006 National Security Strategies have been noticeably silent on the circumstances in which preventive action should be considered and used.[99] This is a gap in the Doctrine that needs to be addressed.

What of deterrence? In the desire to avoid another worse 9/11, the administration has declared that theory of limited usefulness in dealing with terrorists. Historically, the fact is that deterrence has both failed and succeeded for reasons that are still debated. Terrorists committed to getting their heavenly rewards may embrace martyrdom, but many who enable and support them don't.[100] So, while deterrence has failed, it can also succeed. The question for the Bush Doctrine, and any competing doctrine, is just what role deterrence can and should play. Indeed, it is possible to read the specific concerns regarding Iran in the 2006 NSS as establishing one element in the deterrence chain,[101] namely that the United States is very concerned and might have to take action if Iran does not change its behavior.

Whether the Osama bin Ladens of the world or their associates can be deterred (see Post, Chapter 6) is an important element in assessing the Bush Doctrine. However, catastrophic terrorists are not the only enemy that the United States faces. What about others who simply crave a little more territory or regional hegemony rather than the destruction or crippling of the United States?

Some worry whether it is possible to deter "madmen," and that is a legitimate question. However, many ruthless dictators are not so much crazy as insulated, isolated, and ill-informed. A recent Department of Defense after-action analysis (Iraqi Perspective Project) found that Saddam Hussein had so isolated himself, both structurally and psychologically, from the realities of his decaying position that it was impossible to use his military assets to save his rule.[102] In such circumstances, misjudgments are not only possible, but also highly likely.

Strategic, Stand-Apart Alliances   The issue of strategic, stand-apart alliances raises in direct terms the differences between American international relationships of convenience, necessity, and true friendship (see Suedfeld, Tetlock, and Jhangiani, Chapter 4). The post-9/11 alliance landscape has rearranged the traditional groupings of ally, competitor, and enemy, as the examples of France, Germany, India, Pakistan, Saudi Arabia, Yemen, among others, make clear. Some Americans give iconic status to the European countries we rescued from Nazi occupation, rebuilt after World War II, and made our allies during the Cold War. They forget that fighting Nazi world domination submerged other policy differences and that even during the Cold War ally was not synonymous with unanimity.

Moreover, as Mead points out, changes in the relationships between the United States and France and Germany have been gathering steam for some time. The reasons transcend the Bush administration's direct response to their attempts at political "balancing" against American security interests in Iraq.[103] French President Jacques Chirac had pretensions of international grandeur; Germany was one the leading advocates of enmeshing national power into international institutions. Before 9/11, as a practical matter, no American president could go very far in responding favorably to these developments. After 9/11, it was impossible to do so.

Americans have ambivalent feelings when it comes to alliances. They want to be liked, respected, and part of a larger community, but they have also been historically skittish about putting too many of their national security eggs in others' baskets. The Bush administration understood from the start the lesson that every administration eventually learns: allies have different levels of sympathy with and commitment to American national security policies; few allies are supporters on every matter, and every ally has interests that may or may not coincide with ours on particular matters.

It is certainly true that the administration's assertive stance has carried over to foreign policy more generally, as can be easily seen in its views on the Kyoto Protocol, the International Criminal Court, and the ABM Treaty. To the administration such a stance simply reflects the realities of the international system and its assessment of what it needs to do to protect American national security. Others see it as unnecessarily unilateral. While the administration might have done more to "package" its attitude in a soft wrapper, the fact of distinct interests cannot be easily disguised.

Alliances are, at base, associations of mutual interests and compatible values. That fact has led to a dramatic, but little commented upon, shift. Europe, the traditional focus of our attention during the Cold War, has receded to the periphery of our geopolitical focus. Asia—the Near, Central, and Far East, along with South East and South Asia and, of course, the wider Middle East—now looms much larger in the calculation of American national security interests. Interestingly, this new focus may be a point of security congruence between "Old Europe" and the United States. At this point, Europe has more to fear from both Middle East migration and long-range missiles than the United States. Shared threats, as well as shared values, may yet help to overcome differences in the use and projection of power.

The New Internationalism and Selective Multilateralism   The fourth element of the Bush Doctrine raises the question of how, exactly, American national security policy should engage international institutions. The easy criticism of the Bush Doctrine is that it "disdains" international institutions. A more accurate analysis would focus on the Bush administration's view that these institutions are not currently structured or operating in a way that allows the United States to fully depend on them for vital national security issues. It seems clear, given domestic and world public opinion, that it is necessary to take the United Nations and other international organizations into account. Could they, however, be developed into a helpful vehicle for managing the risks the United States and other allied countries face? Is the development of alternative, or most likely supplemental, international institutions a viable national security alternative? Bush clearly thinks so. Critics hardly take notice of administration attempts to transform existing institutions and their practices. The list includes the UN, World Bank, foreign aid,[104] and NATO,[105] to name just a few. Why attempt to reform these institutions if you are committed, as critics charge, to doing without them?

The obvious answer is that the Bush administration would like to see these institutions operate effectively and helpfully. They would then help shoulder the burden that the United States carries as the chief defender of the liberal international order. Critics miss the irony of the fact that their nemesis Bush is actually defending their institutional preferences.

Bush's attempts to reform international institutions have led to the development of new international institutional initiatives: the Proliferation Security Initiative;[106] (a new international climate pact among the United States, Japan, Australia, China, India, and South Korea that bypasses the Kyoto accords)[107], and possible alternative multilateral structures such as the recent Community of Democracies. I term this the "New Internationalism." It is a little noticed but important part of the Bush Doctrine. What critics see as American "unilateralism" is in fact the first stage of an attempt to build a new international institutional order or at least modernize the old one.

Democratic Transformation   Finally, there is the issue of spreading democracy. The Bush Doctrine is rhetorically front and center behind the idea of expanding democracy, often in difficult and inhospitable places (see Zonis, Chapter 9). However, its democratic impulse is hardly altruistic. Contrary to careless critics who characterize the Doctrine's emphasis on democracy as reflecting "the president's belief that democracy and elections solve everything,"[108] Bush has said and believes no such thing. Indeed, he has made it very clear, repeatedly, that "[e]lections are only the beginning of democracy, not the end."[109]

What Bush has signed onto is the closest finding we have in political science to a validated law. Mature democracies do not fight wars with each other. They don't terrorize each other either. Why this is so remains a matter of some debate,[110] but the fact remains.

In championing democracy, the Bush Doctrine presents a twist on the "root causes" of political instability argument by using an old solution to solve a new problem. It takes an innovative conceptual step of redefining the issue of "root causes" by suggesting that at their core, the ills of "failed" and "rogue" states alike is that they lack freedom and democracy. In this view, problems of poverty, infrastructure failure, authoritarianism, and dictatorship would all benefit from a healthy dose of democracy. President Bush is not the first president to want to make the world safe for democracy. He is, however, the first to use democracy to make the world safe for America.

Like other aspects of the Bush Doctrine, the administration's support of democracy has not been entirely consistent with either its general principles or its rhetoric. As noted at the outset of this chapter, this is to be expected.

Some critics aruge that democracy cannot be imposed.[111] However, it can and has been. Yet, the conditions for doing so are quite distinctive. In Germany and Japan it took a devastating military defeat, long years of allied occupation, and the building up over time of democratic institutions and practices. At the same time, it is clear that invasion and occupation is an expensive route to democratization.

Other paths are even slower and more fraught with difficulties because they must deal with legitimate, if not always praiseworthy, governments and institutions. Thus, an international conference intended to advance democracy in the Middle East was derailed because Egypt demanded the right to control which groups would get funding from a new aid fund.[112] Yet, another analyst noted, "Washington has stepped up pressure on repressive regimes in countries such as Belarus, Burma and Zimbabwe—where the costs of a confrontation are minimal—while still dealing gingerly with China, Pakistan, Russia and other countries with strategic and trade significance."[113] Yet, when Egyptian opposition leader Ayman Nour was sentenced to a five-year prison term on what the administration felt were bogus charges, it suspended important trade talks.[114]

The New American Calculus of Risk

The 9/11 attacks reinforced the administration's realist view that the world was a dangerous place. They also did something more. They changed the way policy makers looked at risk. It is not possible to understand the Bush Doctrine without understanding that this was one of the most fundamental changes in national security decisions. Catastrophic terrorism introduced a new primary frame into the American national security decision process. In doing so it altered both traditional baselines and assumptions.

In the past "hegemons" could rest comfortably, somewhat assured that their size and power provided a protective buffer. Waltz notes, "Strong states can be inattentive, they can afford not to learn; they can do the same dumb things over and over again. More sensibly, they can act slowly and wait to see if the threatening acts of others are truly so.... They can hold back until the ambiguity of events is resolved without fearing that the moment for effective action will be lost."[115] No longer.

This complacency ended dramatically, certainly with respect to the dangers of catastrophic terrorism. So, when Litwak argues, "Although the 11 September attacks did not alter the structure of international relations, they did usher in a new age of American vulnerability," he misses the insight that his coupling of these two matters provides. It is precisely because the United States is, and feels, more vulnerable that the international system has changed.

Anxious hegemons will be less likely, in Waltz's words, to be inattentive, act slowly, or await developments. Nor in such circumstances does their size necessarily give them a margin of safety and limit their vulnerability[116] As a consequence, they will calculate and act differently. Being both the most powerful nation in the world and the chief defender of the liberal international system, these changes are bound to have consequences for the United States and how it views its foreign policy options.

The Consequences of Framing: "We're at War"

Bush's immediate framing judgment after the 9/11 attacks, "We're at war,"[117] repositioned almost every domestic and foreign policy initiative. The boundary line between "the two presidencies" faded,[118] and almost every policy now had to be reconsidered through the lens of national vulnerability and security. The implications of this frame shift are substantial.

As a result of the 9/11 attacks, one problem has been catapulted into the role of primary framing issue for American national security policy, and a good deal of domestic policy as well. The third report of the 9/11 Public Discourse Project, a successor to the 9/11 Commission, bluntly stated, "Preventing terrorists from gaining access to weapons of mass destruction *must be elevated above all other problems of national security because it represents the gravest threat to the American people.*"[119] The President clearly shares this view.

Obviously, this does not mean that there are no other problems for the United States to deal with; on the contrary, the world is full of them. There is the issue of managing our relationships with China and Russia; there are the problems of poverty and development; regional issues; specific country issues; genocidal civil wars; the reform (if possible) of international institutions—there is no shortage of issues facing the United States.

However, as important as each or all of these issues may be, 9/11 imposed an instant hierarchy on the American national interest. There may still be arguments about which problems make the B or C list,[120] but the major A-list problem is very clear, at least to the Bush administration. This means that for the first time since World War II and the Cold War there is a single central issue that organizes our national security focus, understanding, and frameworks. The advantage of such a focus is that it prioritizes threats. The disadvantage is that there is a world that requires attention beyond this focus.

The intersection of terrorism and WMD technology is not a single issue. It involves the United States and its allies in a wide range of issues and geographical regions. It has also rearranged policy priorities, perspectives, and frames. Issues that were central have now moved toward the periphery; areas that were on the periphery are now more central. Before 9/11, immigration was primarily framed as a cultural and political issue. It has now been reframed as a national security one.

What had previously been disparaged has now been embraced. The Bush administration started out being skeptical of "nation building." It is now involved in two major efforts to do exactly that in Iraq and Afghanistan. While it is still not interested in Haiti, it might well reconsider elsewhere if the linkage to the WMD problem was clear.

Another example of the decision focus rearrangement post-9/11 is that a number of previously peripheral problems in other countries now impact the WMD problem. Before 9/11, integrating Muslim immigrants in France and

England was an issue of modest importance within these countries; since 9/11 it has become part of America's terrorism problem. Or consider, the mundane bureaucratic issue of international airlines rules governing, say, flights between Bonn and New York. After 9/11, the Bush administration insisted that foreign airlines flying into the United States provide this country with passenger information that could be run through terrorist databases.[121] Many European Union countries objected because of their own rules regarding privacy. What might have been considered a minor dispute has, in the wake of 9/11, become considerably more complicated and central.

Losses, Gains, and Risks

It is hard to overstate the consequences of having a single primary prism as the calculus of post-9/11 national security decisions. In the past, a number of concerns competed for attention, but there was no single overarching decision framework. Each issue was decided on a case-by-case basis, conditioned by specific cost-benefit calculations; many had established probabilities of loss and gain associated with them. These standard operating procedures are no longer wholly viable.

During the Cold War, and especially after the Cuban missile crisis, tensions between the United States and Soviet Union never reached apocalyptic levels because each side had so much to lose. Both had an investment in preserving their respective countries, their citizens, and their way of life, all of which would have been destroyed by a nuclear exchange. So, while the prospect of a nuclear exchange had to be prepared for, the risk of such an exchange was made smaller by the commitment of both sides to avoid it and the awful consequences of not doing so successfully.

Paradoxically, during the Cold War, the higher risks of catastrophic loss in nuclear exchanges appear to have heightened the risks of regional competitions and conflict between the two superpowers. The prospect of certain loss generally weighs more heavily than the possibility of gain.[122] But what happens once the prospect of extreme loss, as represented by a mutual assured destruction nuclear exchange, drastically recedes in probability? The possibility of coveted gains arises, especially for a nation that has an ideology of expansion, or has at its helm a leader whose psychology and self-image accentuates rather than minimizes risk taking.

It is true that in laboratory experiments many people are cautious regarding risks for small or modest gains, while being willing to take larger risks to keep from suffering certain losses. Political scientists have applied this model to nations.[123] But here the question of real life looms large. The average college sophomore is a long way psychologically, politically, and experientially from Saddam Hussein.

In the real world of national security policy some dictators take dangerous risks, repeatedly, because of miscalculation or ignorance. Other actors on the world scene, like Osama bin Laden and his senior associates, are willing to risk death to accomplish their catastrophic purposes. The "normal" model of risk aversion does not seem highly applicable in these circumstances.

Moreover, in most of the work on experimental risk assessments, people are asked to choose between preferences that are, to say the least, not life and death matters. When college experiments do raise life and death issues, these are purely hypothetical. President Bush's daily CIA briefings on threats are no hypothetical matter. It is 100% certain that there are people out there who want to destroy this country. It is 100% certain that these people would do so if they could. And it is 100% certain that they are trying to obtain the means to do so.

What are the chances of their success? The answer to that question depends in part on American strategic behavior. If the United States does little, nothing, or bungles, the chances are then high. If it does everything that can be done within reason, we just don't know the answer to the question.

That is the meaning behind Vice President Cheney's assertion that "deliverable weapons of mass destruction in the hands of a terror network, or a murderous dictator, or the two working together [are unacceptable]…the risks of inaction are far greater than the risk of action."[124] It is a small step conceptually (but a large one politically) to the view that "[t]o forestall or prevent such hostile acts by our adversaries, the United States will, if necessary, act pre-emptively."[125] This is the new calculus of risk.

Now, imagine you are the president. Every day you are being updated on worldwide efforts to destroy the country that you have taken an oath to preserve and protect. Even leaving your official responsibilities aside, you love this country, and you experienced the 9/11 attacks as a deep personal wound, as well as a national trauma.[126] Imagine further that the attack, while not your fault, happened on your watch. And last, factor in the realization that the consequences of another intelligence or defensive failure on your part could be catastrophic. If you have done all this, you have now arrived at Bush's decision calculus framework.

Imminence and Uncertainty   In his 2003 State of the Union Address Bush argued, "Some have said we must not act until the threat is imminent. Since when have terrorists and tyrants announced their intention, politely putting us on notice before they strike? If this threat is permitted to fully and suddenly emerge, all actions…would come too late."[127] Earlier at West Point he had said, "given the intersection of technology and catastrophic terrorism…if we wait for threats to fully materialize, we will have waited too long."[128] In these (and in similar other administration) statements, Bush raised, but did not really answer a very profound strategic question: How long, in any particular circumstance, can the United States afford to wait, before taking decisive action? The answer to that question has enormous significance for the national security of the United States. It also has profound implications for American international legitimacy. International law has always recognized a right to self-defense. The question regarding catastrophic terrorism is: How far before an attack occurs does that umbrella of legitimacy extend?

Using "imminence" as a justification for self-defense has a long history. American reliance on that source of legitimacy goes back to the *Caroline* case in 1842. Daniel Webster argued for the right of "anticipatory self-defense" in cases in which there was "a need for self-defense, instant, overwhelming, leaving no choice of means, and no moment for deliberation."[129] Webster's formulation provides a "right then and there" quality to the understanding of imminence, which has usually led to "armies massing" and "countdown to missile launch" as examples relevant to contemporary circumstances.

These examples sound more useful than they are. Kenneth Pollack points out that when Saddam Hussein's armies massed on the border of Kuwait, intelligence was still unclear whether this was a form of coercive diplomacy or the prelude to an attack.[130] It proved to be the latter. So too, countdowns may well be too late in the sequence of attack events to be a useful strategic Rubicon.

Like much else surrounding the invasion of Iraq, the debate about imminence has both a political and a strategic element. The political element involved accusing the President of saying that Hussein was an imminent threat while his critics argued that he was not. As late as December 2005, House Minority Leader Nancy Pelosi was arguing that "President Bush asserted that Saddam Hussein presented an imminent threat to the security of the United States.... The president was wrong."[131] Actually, Bush never used the word "imminent" in this context. However, in a somewhat ironic twist, the term was actually used by Democratic Senator Jay Rockefeller in an October 10, 2002 speech.[132]

The fact that Bush did not actually use the word "imminent" is, of cocurse, tangential to the more basic problem at hand. He thought that time was not on the side of the United States; his critics thought he had a great deal more of it. As it turned out, at least given what we know at this point, his critics were right; there was more time. Yet, this was a fact that only emerged *after* the invasion. Furthermore, it does not necessarily follow from this that time was on the side of American security concerns.

Critics rest their anti-invasion case on their view that Saddam Hussein could have either been deterred[133] or disarmed.[134] Both cases are flawed. The deterrence case is a plausible one, but falters on several grounds: the underestimates of regional intimidation that a nuclear-armed Iraq under Hussein would have generated,[135] the degree of self-restraint and appeasement that a nuclear-armed enemy encourages,[136] and the degree of Hussein's dangerousness and its implications for United States security interests.[137] As Pollack documents, the sanctions regime was slowly crumbling under the weight of short memories, a desire by several European countries in the UN Security Council (that governed the fate of the sanctions) to rehabilitate Iraq as a market, and a general fading of will and resolve on the part of American allies.

The case for "disarming" Hussein rests on the assumption that he would "come clean" about the extent of his WMD programs, or that we would be able to pinpoint and detail them. Neither seems consistent with Hussein's psychology or past behavior, or with the level of information that was available about his programs. Moreover, even if we had this information, it is not clear what would have induced Hussein to come clean and disarm. Inspections had not done it. Sanctions had not done it. Threats had not done it. Indeed, in the most recent Libyan example of a country giving up its WMD programs, Jentleson and Whylock conclude that the U.S. use of force in Iraq had a "demonstration effect," and "U.S. credibility on the use of force was a factor."[138] They do not think it was the most important sufficient factor, but it is hard to see from their analysis how it could not be considered necessary.

It is often forgotten that the "we had more time" argument took on added weight only because the invasion succeeded in revealing the extent of Hussein's plans and what he actually had on hand. Intelligence agencies worldwide believed that Hussein very much wanted to acquire WMDs and that he had actually done so. As it turned out, the first was certainly true; the second is, to this point, largely undocumented—except for the chemical weapons he had already used. Critics cannot legitimately use postinvasion information about the failure to find WMDs as the basis of suggesting what the United States should have done before having such information.

The same issue of uncertainty arises with regard to Iran's acquisition of nuclear weapons. Leaving aside the debate on what it would mean for United States security interests in the region and elsewhere if Iran developed a nuclear bomb stockpile and the missiles to deliver it, and what to do about that, consider the question of *when* they will be in that position. It clearly makes a difference to discussions concerning what to do about it.

It was of great significance when "[a] major U.S. intelligence review has projected that Iran is about a decade away from manufacturing the key ingredient for a nuclear weapon, roughly doubling the previous estimate of five years, according to government sources with firsthand knowledge of the new analysis."[139] The implications of such a review are obvious. Ten years would provide some time for negotiation and regime moderation. Whatever threat a nuclear-armed Iran would present to the United States, it would certain not be in any sense of that word, imminent.

An alternative timetable was provided by International Atomic Energy Agency chief Mohamed ElBaradei in an interview with *The Independent* of London. He said that once Iran got its uranium enrichment plant at Natanz up and running it would be months away from having a nuclear weapon. Estimates were that it would take two years for that plant to become fully operational.[140]

Two years does not seem "imminent," but it is in the very near future, perhaps impending. The Iran example raises the question of exactly what imminence actually means in a post-9/11 context. The term generally refers to something "ready to take place," or "hanging threateningly over one's head."[141] William Safire, in his column "On Language" says, "'Overhanging' is its essence—an immediate threat, a sinister event close at hand—unlike *impending*, which is not so near in time."[142] Imagine your adversaries practicing their marksmanship on the hair that holds the Sword of Damocles over your head, and you have an idea of the dictionary meaning of the term.

Of course, assessments of imminence depend partly to knowing what is taking place and the pace of its unfolding. That requires intelligence. Yet, the places where it is most needed are often the places where it is hardest to obtain. The United States had few strategic intelligence assets within the Iraq government. As a result, assessments were forced to depend on presumption and extrapolation, which proved deficient. North Korea, al-Qaeda, and Iran are all entities where the United States is forced to make critical strategic decisions without the benefit, so far as we know, of that kind of information.

Nor is the issue one of solely gaining access to inside information via informants or spies. Consider again, Iran's quest for nuclear weapons. U.S. intelligence officials have had in their possession, for some time, complete sophisticated drawings of a deep subterranean shaft designed for underground nuclear tests. However, this and other evidence according to the report is "Often circumstantial, usually ambiguous and always incomplete, the evidence has confounded efforts by policymakers, intelligence officials and U.S. allies to reach a confident judgment about Iran's intentions and a diplomatic solution to the crisis."[143]

Ultimately, given the uncertainty that is likely to accompany any such assessments, it comes down to a matter of judgment and the willingness to act on it. At least the first part of this twosome was recently on display when French Foreign Minister Philippe Douste-Blazy said bluntly, "No civilian nuclear program can explain the Iranian nuclear program, so it is a clandestine military nuclear program."[144] His British counterpart Jack Snow disagreed, saying," We do not have *absolute proof*, we do not have *conclusive evidence* of this. There are strong suspicions."[145]

Absolute proof? Conclusive evidence? What form would that take? A regime announcement? Spikes on a seismograph accompanied by a surge of radiation-level readings? The problem often is that by the time the evidence is conclusive or absolute, options have narrowed and strategic risks have dangerously increased.

Consider Rumsfeld's thought experiment: "Go back before September 11th and ask yourself this question, was the attack that took place on September 11th an imminent threat the month before, or two months before, or three months before, or six months before? When did the attack on September 11th become an imminent threat? When was it sufficiently dangerous to our country that had we known about it that we could have stepped up and stopped it and saved 3,000 lives?"[146]

Good questions. And they point to the primary national security dilemma in this age of catastrophic terrorism. A mortal threat that is gathering is no less lethal because it is not immediate. As a result of the experiences of 9/11, it seems very likely that the time frame alluded to by the word "imminent" has been pushed backwards in the time line and may also be fading as a matter of practicality. The massing armies or the impending missile launch may have been replaced in the minds of decision makers with the clandestine gathering of terrorist planning cells.

Conclusion

While the January 2005 national election in Iraq has been recognized as an important event in that country's transition, it resulted in an equally astounding first in the American domestic debate about Iraq. For the very first time a liberal pundit has allowed in print that Bush's strategy may have been right, and those of his critics wrong.[147] At the same time, two other critics have done what amounts to an abrupt about-face.

In a 2004 opinion piece entitled, "The Preemptive-War Doctrine Has Met an Early Death in Iraq," Daadler and Lindsay boldly stated, "Bush's doctrine of preemption is, to all intents and purposes, dead."[148] Aside from the elementary mistake of confusing the doctrine of preemption with that of prevention, their death notice proved premature. Just one year later they suggested that preventive war may be a "useful tool."[149] If such miracles can happen regarding liberal assessments of the war in Iraq and in the preventive war debates, perhaps the time really has come to have a serious, honest discussion about the Bush Doctrine.

Notes

I am indebted to Peter Suedfeld, Gerhard Alexander, Jonathan Renshon, and Nick Petaludis for their comments on this chapter. Research support for this chapter was also provided by a City University of New York Research Award (No: 68018-00-37). I wish to thank the anonymous external reviewers for their comments.

Endnotes

1. Ashton B. Carter, John Deutch, and Philip Zelikow, "Catastrophic Terrorism: Tackling the New Danger," *Foreign Affairs* November/December (1998); see also, *The 9/11 Commission Report: Final Report of the National Commission on Terrorist Attacks upon the United States* (New York: Norton, 2004).

2. In a debate with Ashton Cater, John Bolton had this to say, "I don't consider what was said about preemption to constitute a doctrine…it is an element in an overall approach to the geostrategic state of the world today…the issue is not whether preemption has somehow assumed a higher place—or a different place—than before in the range of options that the U.S. has, but whether the nature of the threat posed by terrorists or terrorist-supporting states and WMD means that preemption necessarily fits into that difference context." See "Interview with Under Secretary of State John R. Bolton," *The Fletcher Forum on World Affairs* 29 (2005): 5-6; see also M. Elaine Bunn, "Preemptive Action: When, How, and to What Effect?" *Strategic Forum* 200 (July 2003): 7.

3. For an equally diverse set of "right-center" spectrum views on the Iraq War, see Gary Rosen, ed., *The Right War; The Conservative Debate on Iraq* (New York: Cambridge University Press, 2005).

4. Francis Fukuyama, "After Neoconservatism," *New York Times*, February 19, 2006; see also, Francis Fukuyama, *America at the Crossroads* (New Haven, CT: Yale University Press, 2006).

5. Charles V. Pena, "Bush's National Security Strategy Is a Misnomer," *The Cato Institute, Policy Analysis*, no. 496 (October 30, 2003), http://www.cato.org/pubs/pas/pa496.pdf.

6. Gerhard Baker, "The Wild Ride Is Over, The Days of an Aggressive US Policy Are Gone," *The Times* [UK], February 17, 2006.

7. Paul Craig Roberts, "Is the Bush Administration Certifiable?," *The Washington Times*, December 8, 2004, www.washingtontimes.com.

8. Ivo H. Daalder and James M. Lindsay, *America Unbound: The Bush Revolution in Foreign Policy* (Washington, DC: Brookings Institution Press, 2003), 2.

9. Ibid., 36.

10. Ibid., 39.

11. Ibid., 40.

12. Stephen L. Harris and Gloria Platzner, *Classical Mythology: Images and Insights*, 3rd ed. (Mountain View, CA: Mayfied, 2001), 5.

13. George W. Bush, "State of the Union Address", January 29, 2002, http://www.whitehouse.gov/news/releases/2002/01/20020129-11.html.

14. Ibid.

15. "[W]e will extend the peace by encouraging free and open societies on every continent" in George W. Bush, "President Bush Delivers Graduation Speech at West Point," June 1, 2002, www.whitehouse.gov/news/releases/2002/06/20020601-3.html.

16. Condoleezza Rice, "A Balance of Power That Favors Freedom," Wriston Lecture, Manhattan Institute, October 1, 2002, http://www.manhattan-institute.org/html/wl2002.htm.

17. Condoleezza Rice, "Promise of Democratic Peace," *Washington Post*, December 11, 2005, B07.

18. Department of Defense, Quadrennial Defense Review Report, February 6, 2006, http://www.comw.org/qdr/qdr2006.pdf.

19. Ibid., vi.

20. Ibid., 49-51.

21. The National Security Strategy of the United States, March 16, 2006, http://www.whitehouse.gov/nsc/nss/2006/nss2006.pdf; hereafter, 2006 NSS.

22. The National Security Strategy of the United States, September 17, 2002, 4, http://www.whitehouse.gov/nsc/nss.pdf; hereafter, 2002 NSS.

23. 2006 NSS, 10.

24. George Packer, *The Assassins' Gate: America in Iraq* (New York: Farrar, Straus & Giroux, 2005); see also, Michael R. Gordon and Bernard E. Trainor, *Cobra II: The Inside Story of the Invasion and Occupation of Iraq* (New York: Pantheon, 2006); Thomas E. Ricks, *Fiasco: The American Military Adventure in Iraq* (New York, Penguin, 2006); Bob Woodword, *State of Denial: Bush at War*, Part III (New York: Simon & Shuster, 2006); and L. Paul Bremmer (with Malcolm McConnell), *My Year in Iraq: The Struggle to Build a Future of Hope* (New York: Simon & Schuster, 2006).

25. 2002 NSS, 12, 34.

26. 2006 NSS, 9.

27. Ibid., 14, 15.

28. Ibid., 33, 45.

29. Ibid., 9-10, 19.

30. Ibid., 19.

31. Ibid., 39.

32. Ibid., 35, 39.

33. Ibid., 41.

34. Ibid., 12.

35. Ibid., 18.

36. Ibid., 20.

37. 2002 NSS, 5.

38. 2006 NSS, 3-4, 33, 34.

39. Stephan Halper and Jonathan Clarke, *America Alone: The Neoconservatives and the Global Order* (New York: Cambridge University Press, 2004).

40. Gerard Baker, "Neo-Conspiracy Theories," *The Public Interest* (Winter 2004/05).

41. John J. Mearsheimer and Stephen Walt, "The Israel Lobby and U.S. Foreign Policy," Faculty Working Paper No. RWP06-011, submitted March 13, 2006, Harvard University, John F. Kennedy School of Government, http://ksgnotes1. harvard.edu/Research/wpaper.nsf/rwp/RWP06-011. This paper has sent off a storm of criticism on many grounds; see Alan Dershowitz, "Debunking the Newest—and Oldest—Jewish Conspiracy: A Reply to the Mearsheimer-Walt "Working Paper," submitted April 5, 2006, Harvard University, John F. Kennedy School of Government, April 5, 2006, http://www.ksg.harvard.edu/research/working_papers/facultyresponses.htm.

42. Fukuyama, *America at the Crossroads*, 13.

43. Lawrence B. Wilkerson, "The White House Cabal," *Los Angeles Times*, October 25, 2005.

44. I take up these and other misconceptions about the President's psychology and leadership style elsewhere. See Stanley A. Renshon, *In His Father's Shadow: The Transformations of George W. Bush* (New York: Palgrave/St. Martin's, 2005).

45. James Mann, *Rise of the Vulcans: The History of Bush's War Cabinet* (New York: Viking, 2004).

46. Bremmer, *My Year in Iraq*, 188.

47. Peter Baker and Robin Wright, "Iraq, Bush Pushed for Deadline Democracy," *Washington Post*, December 11, 2005, A01.

48. Bob Woodward, *Bush at War* (New York: Simon & Schuster, 2002).

49. Stephan Halper and Jonathan Clarke. *America Alone.*

50. Ivo H. Daalder and James M. Lindsay, "Bush's Flawed Revolution," *The American Prospect* 14/10 (November 1, 2003).

51. Ibid.

52. William S. Cohen, "The U.S. and India: A Relationship Restored," *Wall Street Journal*, December 22, 2005.

53. Thom Shanker, "U.S. and Japan Agree to Strengthen Military Ties," *New York Times*, October 30, 2005.

54. Reuters, "Bush Administration Unveils Alternative Climate Pack," *New York Times*, July 28, 2005.

55. John J. Fialka, "Panel Calls for Flexible Climate Treaty," *Wall Street Journal*, November 16, 2005, A16.

56. Dana Priest, "Help From France Key in Overt Operations," *Washington Post*, July 3, 2005, A01.

57. Robin Wright, "U.S. to Put New Pressure on Syria Initiative Also Has Goal of Helping Lebanon Rebuild Politically," *Washington Post*, September 2, 2005, A06.

58. Dana Priest, "Foreign Network at Front of CIA's Terror Fight," *Washington Post*, November 18, 2005, A01.

59. Richard Bernstein and Michael R. Gordon, "Berlin File Says Germany's Spies Aided U.S. in Iraq," *New York Times*, March 2, 2006, A1.

60. Announced by the White House on May 31, 2003; included the following original signing countries: Australia, France, Germany, Italy, Japan, the Netherlands, Poland, Portugal, Spain, the United Kingdom, and the United States. See Editorial "The New Multilateralism," *Wall Street Journal*, January 8, 2004; see also Erin E. Harbaugh, "The Proliferation Security Initiative: Counterproliferation at the Crossroads," *Strategic Insights* 3/7 (2004).

61. Quoted in John O'Neil, "Hillary Clinton Says White House Mishandled Iran," *New York Times*, January 19, 2006.

62. Peter Finn, "Iran, Russia Reach Tentative Nuclear Deal," *Washington Post*, February 27, 2006, A09; Evelyn Leopold and Irwin Arieff, "Russia Said to Still Object to UN Iran Statement," *Reuters*, March 20, 2006.

63. Thom Shanker, "U.S. Inquiry Finds Russia Passed Spy Data on to Iraq," *New York Times*, March 25, 2006; Robert Collier and Bill Wallace, "Iraq-Russia Spy Link Uncovered, SECRET FILES: Documents Reveal Iraqi Agents Trained in Moscow," *San Francisco Chronicle*, April 13, 2003.

64. At his press conference on May 26, 2006, Bush expressed regret for some of his more provocative language, like the taunt to insurgents attacking American troops in Iraq, "bring it on." See "President Bush and Prime Minister Tony Blair of the United Kingdom Participate in Joint Press Availability," May 25, 2006, http://www.whitehouse.gov/news/releases/2006/05/print/20060525-12.html. **Q:** Mr. President, you spoke about missteps and mistakes in Iraq. Could I ask both of you which missteps and mistakes of your own you most regret? **PRESIDENT BUSH:** —saying "bring it on," kind of tough talk, you know, that sent the wrong signal to people. I learned some lessons about expressing myself maybe in a little more sophisticated manner—you know, "wanted dead or alive," that kind of talk. I think in certain parts of the world it was misinterpreted, and so I learned from that.

65. Glenn Kessler, "Shift in U.S. Stance Shows Power of Seven-Letter Word," *Washington Post*, June 1, 2006, A13.

66. Mann, *Rise of the Vulcans*; see also, Fukuyama, *American at the Crossroads*, 12-65.

67. Project for the New American Century, Statement of Principles, June 3, 1997 [emphasis mine], http://www.newamericancentury.org/statementofprinciples. htm. The statement was signed by a number of people who would play prominent roles in the administration, among them: Elliott Abrams, Dick Cheney, Zalmay Khalilzad, I. Lewis Libby, Donald Rumsfeld, and Paul Wolfowitz.

68. Project for the New American Century, Letter to President Clinton on Iraq, January 26, 1998, http://www.newamericancentury.org/iraqclintonletter.htm. Two years later Robert Kagan and William Kristol published a book that surveyed the array of threats facing the United States and offered strong policy prescriptions to deal with them; see Robert Kagan and William Kristol, eds., *Present Dangers: Crisis and Opportunity in American Foreign and Defense Policy* (San Francisco: Encounter Books, 2000).

69. Steven Hurst argues that the pre-9/11 group of White House senior foreign policy advisors are best considered as "conservative nationalists," rather than neoconservatives; see Steven Hurst, "Myths of Neocons," *International Politics* 42 (2005): 75-96.

I think "nationalist realism" is a better, more descriptive term, since Bush and his advisors would, and have argued, that they are being clear-eyed and realistic about what needs to be done, even if accomplishing their purposes is a large reach. However, in any event, the use of the term "neoconservative" for this early group is a misnomer.

70. George W. Bush, "A Distinctly American Internationalism," Ronald Reagan Presidential Library, Simi Valley, CA, November 19, 1999 (http://www.fas.org/news/usa/1999/11/991119-bush-foreignpolicy.htm)

71. Joseph Grieco, "Anarchy and the Limits of Cooperation: A Realist Critique of the Newest Liberal Institutionalism," *International Organization* 42 (1988): 485-507.

72. John J. Mearsheimer, *The Tragedy of Great Power Politics* (New York: Norton, 2001), 36.

73. John H. Herz, "Idealist Internationalism and the Security Dilemma," *World Politics* 2 (1950): 157-180; see also, Robert Jervis, "Cooperation Under the Security Dilemma," *World Politics* 30 (1978): 167-214.

74. John J. Mearsheimer, "The False Promise of International Institutions," *International Security* 19 (1994/95): 5-49.

75. See, "The Perils of Empire," and "The Perils of Occupation," both at http://www.realisticforeignpolicy.org.

76. Robert Jervis notes, "Although it is easy to see that various kinds of research wax and wane, explaining the pattern is more difficult. Indeed, there is an element of circularity in determining what constitutes a successful research program. In the absence of some arguably objective measure, a research program succeeds when many scholars adapt it." Robert Jervis, "Realism in World Politics," *International Organization* 52 (1998): 972.

77. David Frum and Richard Perle, *An End to Evil: How to Win the War on Terrorism* (New York: Random House, 2003); see also, Angelo M. Codevilla, "No Victory, No Peace: What Rumsfeld's Memo Reveals...and Other Lessons from the War So Far," *Claremont Review of Books*, November 26, 2003.

78. George Will, "Rhetoric of Unreality," *Washington Post*, March 2, 2006, A21; see also George F. Will," The Triumph of Unrealism," *Washington Post*, August 15, 2006, A13.

79. William F. Buckley, Jr., "It Didn't Work," National Review online, February 24, 2006, http://www.nationalreview.com/script/printpage.p?ref=/buckley/buckley200602241451.asp.

80. Fukuyama, "After Neoconservatism."

81. 2002 NSS.

82. Joseph Nye, Jr. , Soft Power: *The Means to Success in World Politics* (New York: Public Affairs, 2004), Chapter One

83. William C. Wohlforth, "The Stability of a Unipolar World," *International Security* 24 (1999): 5; see also, Patrick Tyler, "The Lone Superpower Plan: Ammunition for Critics," *New York Times*, March 10, 1992, A12; "Excerpts from Pentagon's Plan: 'Prevent the Re-Emergence of a New Rival'," *New York Times*, March 8, 1992, A14. Substantial excerpts from the plan may be found at: http://www.pbs.org/wgbh/pages/frontline/shows/iraq/etc/wolf.html.

84. Bush, "A Distinctly American Internationalism."

85. Rice, "A Balance of Power that Favors Freedom."

86. Samuel P. Huntington, "The Erosion of American National Interest," *Foreign Affairs* (September/October, 1997): 43.

87. Arthur Schlesinger, Jr., "An American Empire? Not so Fast," *World Policy Journal* (Spring 2005): 43-46.

88. Sebastian Mallaby, "For a New Imperialism," *Washington Post*, May 10, 2004, A25.

89. Madeleine Albright, "Interview," *New Perspectives Quarterly* (Summer 2004), http://www.digitalnpq.org/archive/2004_summer/albright.html.

90. Jack L. Snyder, *The Ideology of the Offensive: Military Decision Making and the Disasters of 1914* (Ithaca, NY: Cornell University Press, 1989).

91. Donald Rumsfeld, "21st Century Transformation" of U.S. Armed Forces; remarks as delivered at the National Defense University, Fort McNair, Washington, DC, January 31, 2002, http://www.defenselink.mil/speeches/2002/s20020131-secdef.html.

92. Robert Jervis, "The Confrontation between Iraq and the US: Implications for the Theory and Practice of Deterrence," *European Journal of International Relations* 9 (2003): 316.

93. Fareed Zakaria notes, "The classical standard realist hypothesis can be formulated as follows: *Nations expand their political interests when their relative power increases* [emphasis in original]." Fareed Zakaria, *From Wealth to Power: The Unusual Origins of American's World Role* (Princeton, NJ: Princeton University Press, 1998), 19.

94. Jervis, "The Confrontation between Iraq and the US," 316 [italics added].

95. Ibid., 315.

96. Ibid., 316.

97. Ibid.

98. Karl Vick, "Hard-Line Tehran Mayor Wins Iranian Presidency," *Washington Post*, June 25, 2005, A01.

99. Robert S. Litwak, "The New Calculus of Pre-Emption," *Survival* 44 (2003-03): 53.

100. Paul K. Davis and Brian Jenkins, *Deterrence & Influence in Counterterrorism: A Component in the War on al Qaeda* (Santa Monica, CA: Rand, 2002); see also, Daniel Whiteneck, "Deterring Terrorists: Thoughts on a Framework," *Washington Quarterly* 28 2005: 197-199.

101. 2006 NSS, 20.

102. Kevin Woods, James Lacey, and Williamson Murray, "Saddam's Delusions: The View from the Inside," *Foreign Affairs* (May/June 2006).

103. Walter Russell Mead, *Power, Terror, Peace, and War: America's Grand Strategy in a World at Risk* (New York: Knopf, 2004), 141-146.

104. Guy Dinmore, "Bush Plans Overhaul of US Foreign Aid System," *Financial Times*, December 11, 2005; See also Editorial, "Fixing Foreign Aid," *Washington Post*, May 24, 2004, A22.

105. David Sanger, "Bush Sees Need to Expand Role of NATO in Sudan," *New York Times*, February 18, 2006, A1; see also Editorial, "NATO's New Threat," *Los Angeles Times*, February 5, 2006.

106. Carla Anne Robbins, "Why U.S. Gave U.N. No Role in Plan to Halt Arms Ships," *Wall Street Journal*, October 23, 2003, A1.

107. "Sayonara Kyoto," *Wall Street Journal*, July 29, 2005, Review & Outlook section.

108. Martin Indyk, quoted in Steven R. Wesimann, "Rice Admits U.S. Underestimated Hamas Strength," *New York Times*, January 30, 2006.

109. George W. Bush, "President Discusses Global War on Terror Following Briefing at CENTCOM," Tampa, Florida, February 17, 2006 (http://www.whitehouse.gov/news/releases/2006/02/20060217-4.html).

110. David Kinsella, "No Rest for Democratic Peace," *American Political Science Review* 99 (2005): 453-458. This issue also contains several additional responses to the "democratic peace" debate.

111. Chris Patton, "Democracy Doesn't Flow From the Barrel of a Gun," *Foreign Policy* (September/October 2003).

112. Robin Wright, "U.S. Goals Are Thwarted at Pro-Democracy Forum," *Washington Post*, November 13, 2005, A24.

113. Peter Baker, "The Realities of Exporting Democracy," *Washington Post*, January 25, 2006, A01.

114. Ibid.

115. Kenneth N. Waltz, *Theory of International Politics* (New York: McGraw-Hill, 1978).

116. Ibid., 194.

117. Actually, in 1998 George Tenet, then director of the CIA, had sent a memo after a major terrorist attack declaring, "We're at war." But not much came of it at the presidential level. See Scott Shane and James Risen, "C.I.A. Report Said to Fault Pre-9/11 Leadership," *New York Times*, August 26, 2005.

118. Aaron Wildavsky has postulated the existence of two presidencies, one domestic, the other foreign, with different rules governing the use of presidential power in each. See Aaron Wildavsky, "The Two Presidencies," *Trans-Action* 4 (1966): 5-15.

119. "Report on the Status of 9/11 Commission Recommendations, Part III: Foreign Policy, Public Diplomacy, and Nonproliferation," November 14, 2005, 5 [italics added], http://www.9-11pdp.org/press/2005-11-14_report.pdf.

120. The terminology of lists is borrowed from Joseph S. Nye, Jr., "Redefining the National Interest," *Foreign Affairs* 78 (July/August 1999): 22-35.

121. Robert Pear, "U.S. Pressures Foreign Airlines Over Manifests," *Washington Post*, November 27, 2001.

122. Daniel Kahnenman and Amos Tversky, "Prospect Theory: An Analysis of Decision Under Risk," *Econometrica* 47 (1979): 263-291; see also, Daniel Kahnenman and Amos Tversky, "Choices, Values, and Frames," *American Psychologist* 39 (1984): 341-350.

123. See Rose McDermott, "Prospect Theory in Political Science: Gains and Losses From the First Decade," *Political Psychology* 25 (2004): 291, 294. For some problems of measurement and conceptualization in applying prospect theory to international politics, see Barry O'Neill, "Risk Aversion in International Relations Theory," *International Studies Quarterly* 45 (2001): 617-640.

124. Quoted in Linda D. Kozaryn, "Cheney Says Grave Threats Require Pre-Emptive Action," *American Forces Press Service*, August 26, 2002.

125. 2002 NSS.

126. "Prospect theory has been limited by its failure to incorporate notions and models of emotion into its analysis of decision-making." See McDermott, "Prospect Theory in Political Science," 306.

127. George W. Bush, "State of the Union Address", January 28, 2003, http://www.whitehouse.gov/news/releases/2003/01/20030128-19.html.

128. Bush, "President Bush Delivers Graduation Speech at West Point."

129. Quoted in Terence Taylor, "The End of Imminence?" *Washington Quarterly* (Autumn 2004): 4-5.

130. Kenneth Pollack, *The Threatening Storm: The Case for Invading Iraq* (New York: Random House, 2002).

131. Quoted in John D. Mckinnon and Yochi J. Dreazen, "Bush Concedes Intelligence Flaws Played Part in War," *Wall Street Journal*, December 15, 2005, A1.

132. "There has also been some debate over how 'imminent' a threat Iraq poses. I do believe that Iraq poses an imminent threat, but I also believe that after September 11, the question is increasingly outdated. It is in the nature of these weapons, and the way they are targeted against civilian populations that documented capability and demonstrated intent may be the only warning we get. To insist on further evidence could put some of our fellow Americans at risk. Can we afford to take that chance? We cannot!" Jay Rockefeller, *Fox News Sunday*, October 12, 2003, transcript.

133. John J. Mearsheimer and Stephen M. Walt, "Can Saddam Be Contained? History Says Yes," Balfour Center for Science and International Affairs, Occasional Paper, November 12, 2002.

134. "The U.N. wanted more time. And there was no great immediacy, there was no great imminence of a threat that should have caused this president to cut off those inspections, begin the attack before the inspections could be completed." Carl Levin (D-MI), *CNN's Late Edition with Wolf Blitzer*, February 8, 2004.

135. Countries like Kuwait, the United Arab Emirates, Qatar, Oman, Bahrain would have been immediately under severe pressure, and through them pressure on other Middle Eastern countries would have arisen. Bringing one after another of these countries into Hussein's political orbit would have given him enormous economic and thus military and political reach.

136. Invading a country with nuclear weapons is extremely dangerous. In these circumstances regime change would be a dangerous option. Moreover, what would the United States do if a nuclear-armed Hussein manufactured a pretext for war and invaded Kuwait, letting it be known that he would use his weapons if any state interfered? Would we be able to assemble another grand alliance? Would the United States think twice, or more, in such a circumstance? Surely it would.

137. Hussein need not be a "madman" in order to be extremely dangerous. Mearsheimer and Walt ("Can Saddam Be Contained?") count on Hussein's concern with being found out if he ever helped terrorists gain nuclear materials to attack the United States. They have a robust confidence in the capacity of our intelligence agencies to penetrate Hussein's regime and terrorist operational cells. The former was not true before the invasion and the latter does not seem like a safe bet.

Furthermore, these critics fail to mention that Hussein was proven complicit in the attempted assassination of George H. W. Bush. Consider the audacity of that act, and the seething wish for vengeance it represents. Would a person with that psychology be beyond crippling his sworn enemies through proxy parties? No.

138. Bruce W. Jentleson and Christopher Whytock, "Who 'Won' Libya?," *International Security* 30 (2005/06): 78.

139. Dafna Linzer, "Iran Is Judged 10 Years From Nuclear Bomb," *Washington Post*, August 2, 2005, A01.

140. Review and Outlook, "Ticking Tehran Bomb," *Wall Street Journal*, December 7, 2005.

141. *Webster's New Ninth Collegiate Dictionary* (Springfield, MA: Merriam-Webster, 1991), 602.

142. William Safire, "On Language; Imminent," *New York Times*, February 8, 2004.

143. Dafna Linzer, "Strong Leads and Dead Ends in Nuclear Case Against Iran," *Washington Post*, February 8, 2006, A01.

144. Molly Moore, "Iran Working on Nuclear Arms Plan, France Says," *Washington Post*, February 17, 2006, A1.

145. Ariane Bernard, "France Alleges Iran's Nuclear Plan Is for Military Use," *New York Times*, February 17, 2006 [italics added].

146. Donald Rumsfeld, *CBS Radio*, November 14, 2002.

147. "*If* the election does begin a process whereby Iraqis, like Nicaraguans, Salvadorans, and so many others before them, opt for the political rather than the military arena, the Bush team *could* claim vindication on more than one count. There have always been two schools about democratizing Iraq. The Bush approach was to hold elections quickly; but the other school, whose adherents include *Newsweek* editor Fareed Zakaria, former Coalition Provisional Authority advisor Larry Diamond, and this writer, has long argued that the administration was in such a rush to establish electoral democracy in Iraq that it mostly ignored the requisites of liberal democracy in Iraq—ignoring, for instance, that the advantages of democracy routinely get lost in societies divided along ethnic and religious lines. But if the elections truly jolt Iraq's civic arena, then the rush will have been justified. And not just on the grounds of political expedi-

ency: Maybe the principle of consent that lies at the heart of liberalism really does mean putting elections first [italics added]." Lawrence F. Kaplan, "Climate Change: In Iraq, Reasons For Hope—Finally," *The New Republic* online, posted December 16, 2005.

148. Ivo H. Daalder and James Lindsay, "The Preemptive-War Doctrine Has Met an Early Death in Iraq," *Los Angeles Times*, May 30, 2004.

149. Ivo Daalder and James Steinberg, "Preventive War, A Useful Tool," *Los Angeles Times*, December 4, 2005.

2

International Relations Theory Meets World Politics

The Neoconservative vs. Realism Debate

GERARD ALEXANDER

The Bush Doctrine has been defined very differently by different scholars and commentators. The Bush administration itself has used the term narrowly, to describe "the policy that nations harboring terrorists would be treated as if they were guilty of terrorist acts."[1] Others define it almost exclusively in terms of preventive war.[2] Robert Jervis and Robert Lieber identify the Doctrine with four more or less comparable components: the belief that domestic regimes—democracy vs. authoritarianism—drive a country's foreign policy and thus a goal of democratizing other countries, especially in the Middle East; the perception that grave threats are best dealt with by vigorous measures like preemptive and preventive war; a commitment to multilateralism conditional on efficacy, as such, a stated willingness to act unilaterally; and a goal of maintaining U.S. primacy based on the belief that America has a unique role in causing international peace and stability.[3] For the purposes of this volume, the Bush Doctrine consists of four similar themes: the maintenance of U.S. primacy, selective multilateralism, stand-apart alliances, and democratization, especially in the Middle East. The doctrine was laid out in the administration's 2002 National Security Strategy (NSS), President George W. Bush's 2002 speech at West Point, and his 2003 speech at the National Endowment for Democracy (the 2006 NSS amplifies and updates, rather than revises, the 2002 NSS).[4]

However it is defined, the Bush Doctrine and neoconservative thinking are said to diverge sharply from the other major schools of foreign policy thought, especially realism.[5] This chapter argues, in contrast, that the Bush Doctrine is not nearly so radical a departure. The Bush Doctrine foreign policy shares core ontological assumptions with major streams of realist thought, varies in several subassumptions, and adds a very small number of supplementary assumptions to the mix. As in all theoretical matters, devils can easily lurk in these details, but details are the measure of the distance separating these approaches within the broad realist tradition. Specifically, the neoconservative foreign policy thinking embodied in the Doctrine is a variant of realism, specifically a variant of a variant of realism, "balance-of-threat" realism.

Mounting this rebellious argument is made difficult by the fact that the Doctrine has been the target of much overheated analysis. And an impression of rupture with the past is encouraged by an understandable focus on those aspects of the Bush administration's foreign policy that are especially innovative, a focus that obscures or ignores outright the overwhelming continuities in U.S. foreign policy. The major continuities include the persistent emphasis on traditional deterrence, basic post-1945 immigration policy, foreign trade policy, foreign aid, membership and activism in numerous international organizations, and the broad contours of workaday policy toward Russia, China, India, South East Asia, sub-Saharan Africa, and Latin America (countries representing more than half the world's population). Much of the talk about a "revolution" in foreign policy is much ado about nothing. In particular, the departure from the realist tradition is overblown.

The Varieties of Realism

Realism is a powerful analytic perspective, made up of a series of assumptions about how states and the international system work. By varying major and minor assumptions, scholars have produced many distinct variants of this intellectual tradition. A few major assumptions seem definitional to realism.[6] First, realists assume that the international system lacks a central authority and that individual states are the system's primary actors. Second, in this anarchic context, all states are centrally concerned with their safety and survival, and set about trying to secure them in the most efficient way they know how. Third, whether for that security-seeking reason or as the result of predatory agendas, states sometimes have territorial ambitions on other states and are prepared to use force to act on them.

These core assumptions go a long way to establishing a way of seeing the world. But they do *not* specify a number of things. Among other issues, this "minimalist realism" does not specify exactly how countries do or should measure levels of threat to their safety or survival. It does not identify the most effective strategies for addressing a given level of threat. It does not specify exactly how states do or should feel about interstate cooperation. It does not identify all the effects of international institutions, concerning for example whether they can solve coordination problems or can develop emergent properties. And minimalist realism explains virtually nothing about the behavior of nonstate actors.

Different variants of realist thinking are distinguished by the supplementary assumptions they add to minimalist realism to address these and other issues. The most familiar debates are between neorealists, liberal institutionalists, balance-of-threat realists, and neoconservatives. Variations in subassumptions ensure that many thinkers are not easily contained by one or another of these schools. But we can usefully, if crudely, summarize major cleavage lines on the issues of threat assessment and regime type; deterrence and preventive use of force; and U.S. primacy and international institutions.

Neorealism. Neorealists like Kenneth Waltz, John Mearsheimer, and Robert Gilpin add several assumptions to minimalist realism.[7] They assume that states best judge threats by measuring the relative power of other states. States will try to deter potential expansionists by balancing against power, through mobilization or alliances, or both. Because states fear power, they fear powerful states regardless of domestic regime characteristics. No "democratic peace" is to be expected, and even fellow democracies are prone to balancing against the United States (though Waltz and Mearsheimer differ somewhat on the U.S. case for reasons discussed below). Because states jealously guard power and sovereignty, international institutions can provide a useful forum for states already committed to cooperation, but cannot, as creatures of states, become reliable independent sources of security.[8] Finally, neorealism does not have "a whole heck of a lot" to say about terrorism because it is carried out by nonstate actors on whom realism sheds no particular analytic light.[9]

Balance-of-Threat Realism. Stephen Walt crafted a variant of realism when he argued that threats to a given state are better measured by measurement of other states' intentions as well as their capabilities.[10] This balance-of-threat (as opposed to balance-of-power) assumption generates the distinctive prediction that states may balance as much against, say, the aggressive agenda of a middling state as the less threatening behavior of a larger one. Since perceived intentions matter, a state might influence how it is perceived, for example, by convincing others that it harbors no expansionist ambitions. Like neorealism, balance-of-threat realism offers no analytic tools for deducing what generates threats from nonstate actors.

Balance-of-threat realism is compatible with certain "liberal" and institutional claims about international relations (though much liberal and institutionalist thought is nonrealist in nature). First, the empirical record appears to indicate that states governed democratically manifest less threatening intentions toward one another, creating the basis for the "democratic peace."[11] By this standard, democracies should be unlikely to balance against a fellow democracy like America. Similarly, international institutions might influence outcomes by helping to create or signal less threatening intentions. For example, Walt and G. John Ikenberry argue that institutions can be an effective method of restraining—and signaling the restraint—even of powerful states like the post-Cold War United States, reducing the chances that others will fear and balance against them.[12]

Neoconservatism. Finally, neoconservatives also believe that threats arise from intentions as well as capabilities. For this reason they steer security concerns away from states that are powerful but deemed nonhostile (Japan, Western Europe, India) and toward states with perceived hostile intentions, whether large (China) or middling (Iran). Specifically, neoconservatism adopts the assumption that domestic regime type is the best indicator of intentions, with democracies judged more peaceful. After 9/11, neoconservatives added the claim that nondemocracies threaten other states not only directly but also indirectly, by incubating terrorism. To deal with threats, neoconservatism adopts neorealist assumptions about international institutions. And neoconservatives argue, distinctively, that not only nonstate actors but also certain states may not be responsive to traditional deterrence.[13]

In sum, neoconservatives are balance-of-threat realists with several supplementary assumptions: that institutions exert negligible independent effects (shared with neorealists); that domestic regime type profoundly shapes a state's intentions (shared with democratic-peace liberals); that regime type affects whether a state generates terrorists; and that certain states might not be easily deterrable (the latter two being claims on which the other approaches do not pronounce). The remaining sections draw four major themes from this summary: how the Bush Doctrine measures threats; how it proposes to deal with threats; what role international institutions play in its strategies; and its long-term strategy of democratization.

Measuring Threats by Regime Type

Measuring Threats and Risks

The Bush Doctrine is said to assess threats to U.S. security in ways that sharply diverge from traditional methods, above all by tracing threats to nondemocratic regimes. This section elaborates the Doctrine's approach to this foundational aspect of national security policy.

For all variants of realism, how to identify and measure threats is a nonobvious and controversial task. Neorealists measure potential threats by measuring each country's power. As Waltz puts it, "State behavior varies more with differences of power than with differences in ideology, in internal structure of property relations, or in governmental form."[14] But how should we measure power? We could measure a state's mobilized military forces, but more often scholars measure total latent power resources. In many studies, latent resources are measured parsimoniously by each country's population and economic wealth.[15] So a given state could be less threatened by a large poor country than by a medium-sized rich one. Mearsheimer adds a geographic feature to this short list of measures of latent power, on the grounds that power-projection is profoundly affected by the "stopping power of water."[16] In this thinking, a state could be more threatened by a nearby, medium-sized poor country than by a large rich one an ocean away.

While many realists take it for granted, this focus on power alone is a striking analytic choice. It is informed by the assumption that a country should base its security strategy on an assessment of how dangerous another country would be were the two to find themselves at war, without explicit concern for the probability of war breaking out. In this, realism is very different from most other applications of rational choice theory (of which realism has become a kind). These other forms (whether parametric or game theoretic), assume instead that actors base strategies on their assessment of risks, which are measured by both the *effects* of a given event (say, a war, drought, or election defeat) were it to occur and the *probability* that that event will occur. Applied to the case at hand, this would mean that a state, to assess the threat posed by another, would assess both how powerful that potential adversary is *and* the likelihood that the two states will come to blows. The latter at least partly involves the other state's intentions, though the two are not coterminous. Neorealists assume that "states can never be certain about other states' intentions."[17] The implication is that states should accordingly prepare for the worst at all times, virtually regardless of the short- and medium-term costs of this form of "insurance." But uncertainty characterizes most of political, social, and economic life, and yet most rational choice theorists nonetheless assume that actors select strategies in part by making their best guesses about what others are likely to do. If actors could not and did not make such guesses, game theory would make no sense, at least outside games of chance with fixed odds.[18]

This alternative and common practice within the rational choice tradition is more consistent with balance-of-threat realism's measurement of threats based on a mix of a state's intentions and capabilities. But can the intentions half of this mix be measured, and can it be measured as parsimoniously as power? Walt does not provide simple measures of intentions, arguing instead that contexts vary in the degree to which credible information about other states' intentions is available and offering ad hoc coding of certain regimes (like Nasser's in Egypt) as threatening.[19] Such coding has a lengthy history. Many have traced security threats disproportionately to a subset of governments distinguished by expansionist militarism. This approach has analytic risks. If we identify regimes as "threatening" based on their expansionist behavior, we cannot know whether this behavior is better explained by domestically derived "intentions" or by the systemic factors proposed by neorealists (for example, an imbalance of power favorable to a bid for regional hegemony). The best way of sorting these competing predictions is to control for distributions of power and then ask if a given country behaves substantially differently under successive domestic regimes. Balance-of-threat realism is meaningful only if the answer is "yes," at least sometimes.

U.S. Foreign Policy and the Democratic Peace

If domestic factors help explain why some countries are more threatening than others, then which domestic factors matter? The Bush Doctrine is understood to distinctively emphasize domestic regime types. But in fact, regime-based analyses of threats have been invoked repeatedly in the making of modern U.S. foreign policy.[20] U.S. policy in both World War II and the Cold War was not centrally to reduce the latent power of Germany, Japan, or the Soviet Union (say, by dismembering them) but to change their intentions by transforming their domestic political orders. This assumed that new regimes could be less threatening, including because different regimes would mobilize less latent power. Thus, major Cold War documents traced the threat posed by the USSR at least as much to the nature of its regime—"ideology" for George Kennan; "fanatic faith" in NSC-68—as to Russia's innate capabilities. In this spirit, later Cold Warriors generally coded threats by distinguishing between states with totalitarian regimes and all others, with the "free world" containing many authoritarian regimes. For example, Jeane Kirkpatrick famously warned of totalitarian regimes while suggesting that the U.S. could view many other nondemocratic regimes relatively benignly. And Ronald Reagan's celebrated 1982 Westminster speech cast the global struggle not as between all democracies and all nondemocracies, but as one between "free" countries and expansionist totalitarianism in particular.[21]

After the Cold War, the United States under George H. W. Bush and Bill Clinton continued to scrutinize countries by their intentions as much as their capabilities. This took two forms. The first invested special concern in an especially violence-prone subset of nondemocracies labeled "rogue states." The second was quite different. Claims of a "democratic peace" shifted threat assessment regarding interstate conflicts to a new cut-point: the one separating all democracies from all nondemocracies. This, alongside deeper philosophical roots, is the most immediate ancestor of neoconservative thinking about measuring threats.[22]

Of course, U.S. foreign policy since 2001 makes important short-term distinctions between less vs. more hostile nondemocratic regimes, as seen in America's antiterrorist cooperation with nondemocratic Pakistan, Saudi Arabia, Kuwait, and North African countries such as Algeria in the Trans-Sahara Counter-Terrorism Initiative. But more generally, neoconservatives adopt the same cut-point as democratic peace theorists, and the Bush Doctrine reflects this. It does so in part by echoing the democratic-peace thesis about the sources of interstate threats. But al-Qaeda's 2001 attack also elevated threats from nonstate actors, and neoconservatives and some neoliberals have proposed a complementary thesis that might be called the "authoritarian radicalization" thesis.[23] This argues that nondemocratic regimes are additionally problematic to U.S. national security because they, often inadvertently, incubate violent extremism among their citizens.[24] In a 2003 speech, Bush said that nondemocratic regimes in the Middle East bred "stagnation, resentment, and violence ready for export."[25] His 2004 State of the Union speech was even more specific: "As long as the Middle East remains a place of tyranny and despair and anger, it will continue to produce men and movements that threaten the safety of

America and our friends."[26] While the Bush administration also emphasizes the causal importance of terrorist organizations and their emergent properties, the idea of radicalization under authoritarianism is a "root causes" theory of terrorism in all but name. As traditional realists David Hendrickson and Robert Tucker put it, "Now it is the 'being' and not the 'doing' of autocratic states that creates the security threat to the United States."[27]

This version of balance-of-threat realism basically codes states' intentions by the proxy of a state's democratic vs. nondemocratic status. Like all methods of coding threats, this creates categories of states deemed both threatening and nonthreatening. For neorealists, less threatening states are ones with limited capabilities, that is, ones with small populations and/or small economies and perhaps ones located a body of water away. For balance-of-threat realists, nonthreatening states are ones with status quo intentions. The post-Cold War version of balance-of-threat realism, as expressed in the democratic-peace and authoritarian-radicalization theses, identifies democracies as the quintessential status quo powers. This is reinforced by the unusual post-Cold War spectacle of the world's major powers—mostly democracies—being durably at peace with one another. It is in that spirit that Secretary of State Condoleezza Rice wrote in 2005 that "the fundamental character of regimes matters more today than the international distribution of power."[28] For that matter, terrorists are considered threatening only because their very limited capabilities are harnessed to very aggressive intentions. And "failed states" are of concern not because of their (minimal) capabilities, but because of the violent intentions of substate and nonstate actors who can flourish in them.

By measuring threats based on actors' intentions as well as their capabilities, and by using democratic status to code intentions, the Bush Doctrine adopts the central insight of balance-of-threat realism and adds to it the supplementary assumption that regime type crucially structures the behavior of both states and nonstate actors.

Deterrence, Preemption, and Prevention

Whatever the sources of security threats, the perennial question remains: What should the United States do about threats that arise in the foreseeable future? Neorealism and balance-of-threat realism provide ample grounds for relying on traditional strategies such as power-balancing and deterrence. It is a common perception that the Bush Doctrine instead proposes to deal with threats preventively. Certainly the Bush administration's discussion of preventive war has been the Doctrine's most controversial feature. At first blush, the preventive use of force seems to be a major innovation. But closer inspection shows that the role that the Bush Doctrine assigns to prevention does not constitute such a radical departure from realism after all. This is the case for two reasons.

The Durability of Deterrence

First, the Doctrine does not suggest that all, most, or even many threats should be dealt with preventively. Some scholars, like Daalder and Lindsay, say that Bush's security strategy elevated prevention as a central new tool and "effectively abandoned a decades-long consensus that put deterrence and containment at the heart of American foreign policy."[29] But Lindsay and Daalder had earlier concluded that "[d]eterrence features prominently" in the 2002 NSS, that "[p]reemption has a total of three paragraphs in a 31-page document," and that "the strategy, for all the talk publicly about preemption, in addition is a fairly narrow goal for preemption."[30] These earlier observations are closer to the mark. The 2002 NSS notes that deterrence both has worked and does work against states, so long as they are risk-averse, and twice says specifically that the U.S. can "deter" certain states already in possession of weapons of mass destruction (WMDs). It concludes only that the United States can "no longer *solely* rely" on deterrence (or in the 2006 NSS, "no longer *simply* rely" on it). The 2002 NSS thus proposes that preventive force is not needed against all emerging threats, only against risk-tolerant rogue states and stateless terrorist groups.[31] Rice has insisted that the number of cases to which preemption or prevention applies "will always be small," while more traditional tools remain highly appropriate. So, she insists, the 2002 NSS "does not overturn five decades of doctrine and jettison either containment or deterrence."[32]

This emphasis seems not simply rhetorical since it is consistent with the architecture of U.S. security policy since 2001. The 2004 U.S. "National Military Strategy" refers over two dozen times to the core U.S. strategy of "deterring" or "dissuading" aggression.[33] America has continued to invest heavily in the military capabilities required by such a strategy. It is fairly evidently pursuing a policy of deterrence toward specific potential adversaries such as North Korea (with U.S. troops in South Korea) and China (with the shift of U.S. forces from the Atlantic to the Pacific, the rapprochement between the U.S. and regional counterweight India, and talk of "containing" China). Against this expensive and extensive backdrop, the U.S. has used preventive coercion in only one case so far. In all these ways, the Bush administration's workaday policies appear to rely heavily on traditional practices.

There is a second reason to conclude that discussion of the use of preventive force in a minority of cases does not represent a radical departure from traditional realist thought. Many find the proposal of any preventive use of force controversial because they believe that it is either unnecessary or inadvisable. The remainder of this section argues that even a realist can conclude that this might not be true under certain very limited circumstances. If deterrence makes compelling sense in most circumstances but not in some very limited ones, then considering the use of preventive force in those few exceptions does not seem especially radical.

The Presumption Against Preventive Use of Force

Several assumptions underpin the proposition that traditional security strategies like deterrence are preferable to the preventive use of force. These assumptions rest on the durable realist language of costs and benefits. In sum, preventive war is understood to have several important disadvantages and few obvious advantages. Prevention has three main disadvantages. First, the preventive use of force could initiate a war that was unnecessary, since a given adversary might never have ended up attacking after all. Because wars are costly and risky, unnecessary ones are a highly undesirable type 1 error (a false positive). Second, even if an adversary *has* entertained plans for an attack, it might successfully be deterred. Since deterrence appears to be routinely effective in international politics, preventive war seems a costly alternative. Third, a state that uses force preventively risks an additional cost beyond that of the war itself: it risks being seen (or mistaken) as an aggressor, and thus risks provoking balancing behavior against itself. Often, better that the other side fires the first shot.

Moreover, despite discussion of "the cult of the offensive," the advantage of preventive war (being the first to strike) may not be especially valuable, especially to a power as secure as the United States. Even if an adversary does wish to attack and cannot successfully be deterred, it may still be preferable to absorb the initial blow since the costs of doing so are usually limited. The attacked state is usually able to respond. It goes without saying that it knows against whom to retaliate. And initial attacks are unlikely to be devastating because they are unlikely to come as complete surprises. Most countries can suffer a major attack only at the hands of a relatively small number of other states, whose preparations for war are typically evident even if not transparent in every detail. In Richard Betts' words, "Pure bolts from the blue do not happen. Sudden attacks occur after prolonged political conflict."[34] For all these reasons, it is usually preferable to eschew preventive use of force.

But what if circumstances arise such that one or more of these underlying assumptions does not hold? In other words, how should a cost-benefit analysis judge the preventive use of force if two actors are already at war or an adversary is manifestly bent on attack; or if a specific adversary does not seem to respond to normal methods of deterrence; or if other countries seem uninterested in balancing against oneself; or if absorbing an attack might not leave a state fully capable of responding effectively?

Let us consider these possibilities. First, concerns about initiating an unnecessary war are moot if a conflict is already under way. That now applies to any attack directly on al-Qaeda, even if in a new form or venue. The Bush administration argues that it may also apply in some form to a case like Iraq, because the line between a new vs. already-existing conflict has been unusually blurred since 9/11. Certainly the United States is involved in an unusual conflict. Because of the stateless and loosely organized nature of violently anti-American Islamists, their attacks can emanate from a remarkably diffuse geography; such attacks can take on many forms, and they could acquire weapons and other assistance from a very wide array of sources, not limited only to states. This explains why Western countries have engaged in such an unusually wide range of policies since 9/11, from military action in Afghanistan and the continued securing of ex-Soviet nuclear materials to enhanced computer security and stepped-up defenses against biological weapons. So in this unusually diffuse struggle, what is a new conflict? This is not a novel situation. Consider whether Allied military action against Francoist Spain during World War II would have initiated a new war or would simply have opened a new front in a war already under way against the Axis. The answer is not self-evident. In that light, was an attack on Saddam's regime an entirely innovative act, or a new front in an already-initiated war between America and extremism emanating from the Mideast, including Saddam's brand of it?[35] For that matter, which would an attack on Iran's nuclear facilities be?

"Nondeterrability"

Second, what if an adversary is bent on attack and seemingly cannot be deterred? The arguments that follow concerning "deterrability" have been rehearsed elsewhere by others, but are worth repeating and developing. International relations scholars have long debated what is required for deterrence to be effective.[36] At the very least, it requires a credible threat of costly retaliation and a sufficiently cost-sensitive adversary. Realism generally assumes the second condition is fulfilled, and attributes any failures (to deter) to the absence of the first.[37] This appears to describe accurately a great many situations. But since 9/11, both assumptions may be experiencing not general but "spotty" failures. Recognizing this merely updates rather than repudiates realism's analytic assumptions.

The first condition for effective deterrence—that a state like the U.S. can credibly threaten retaliation—may not be holding in all instances. This is not because America lacks sufficient military resources, but because it could now be attacked and not know against whom to retaliate. This is rarely a problem when one country directly attacks another. It has also not been a problem with terrorists who leave fingerprints or claim credit for attacks. But it has already proven problematic when terrorists strike without leaving much of a trail. Al-Qaeda appears to have a policy of not claiming credit. This does not necessarily prevent its actions from being traced. But the possibility of anonymity is not fanciful. The 2001 anthrax attack in America lacks a single publicly identified suspect, and a number of major bombings remain not just unclaimed but unattributed. Consider the number of groups that might happily detonate a nuclear device in Tel Aviv without claiming credit. Proliferation lengthened the list of actors potentially armed with WMDs to more states and also to nonstate actors. Historically, attacks could be (relatively) unexpected; now they could be mysterious.

Related but distinct is the much-imagined scenario in which a rogue state "hands off" a WMD, especially a nuclear or radiological weapon. Then, an attacked country might retain ample retaliatory capacities and identify its terrorist attackers, but not know with a high level of confidence which state provided the weapon. As the columnist Charles Krauthammer has said, deterrence "does not work against…undetectables: nonsuicidal enemy regimes that might attack through clandestine means."[38] Some consider a WMD handoff unlikely because it would be highly risky for the rogue state involved.[39] This skepticism assumes, first, that a weapon will be traceable to its source. But we are still asking: where did the 2001 anthrax come from? It also assumes that rulers are, broadly speaking, risk-averse. Is that the case?

The second condition for effective deterrence is adversaries who are sensitive to costs and risks. This condition might usually be borne out and yet fail in certain narrow instances. In that minority of cases, deterrence could fail not because of the (inadequate) credibility or preparations of the would-be deterrer but because of the nature of the attacker. It is obviously not clear that "cost-sensitivity" describes all terrorist groups. It surely describes some, who can be deterred at least sometimes and in some regards.[40] But it may well not describe others. Even a traditional realist like Owen Harries says that compared, for example, to the cautious, calculating rulers of the Soviet Union, "[f]lying two aircraft into those towers in New York is an animal of a different breed."[41]

Some "rogue states" may also be of a different breed. The claim here is not that rogue state leaders are psychotic or suicidal, only that there is no a priori reason to assume that leaders are homogenous in their cost-sensitivity and risk-tolerance. They may well vary on those dimensions. Stalin, Hitler, Kim Jong-Il, and Saddam Hussein seem especially unpreoccupied by the deaths of hundreds of thousands (or millions) of their own citizens. And Napoleon, Hitler, and some other rulers manifest high-risk tendencies in their foreign policies.[42] This might be because they are prone to perceiving other states as unlikely to display resolve or as unlikely to prevail in a conflict. And tyrants with such proclivities may have few effective checks on their personal decision making. Lieber argues that such high risk-tolerance may make a small number of regimes not easily susceptible to deterrence.[43]

We can briefly consider two cases. The most extensively debated is Saddam Hussein.[44] The claim that Hussein was deterrable is difficult to reconcile with several of his major decisions. Why was he alone in taking military advantage of Iran's vulnerability in 1980 and Kuwait's in 1990? Regardless of what Hussein stood to gain through control of Kuwait, including possibly deflecting domestic challenges to his regime, why was he confident the world would not react with overwhelming force to his 1990 threat to major oil supplies? Why did he refuse to withdraw from Kuwait once that reaction became apparent?

Withdrawal at that time may have posed risks to his rule, but why was he confident his regime could better survive the confrontation? And above all, regardless of theories about 1980 and 1990–91, why was Hussein unwilling to do whatever was needed to save his throne in 2002–03, whatever domestic and international risks he would have had to run to do so? Many proffered answers to these questions remain unpersuasive.[45]

Another, woefully understudied, case is the Taliban. If that regime's rulers were bent on survival, why did they allow the 9/11 plot against the world's most powerful state to proceed from their territory? And why did they not accept the ultimatum offered by Bush immediately after the attack?[46] Conceivably, the Taliban did not know about the 9/11 plot beforehand and/or lacked the coercive capacity either to stop it then or to turn over al-Qaeda's leaders afterward. In any of those cases, though, classic deterrence faces a new problem: How is deterrence supposed to work if some states cannot control threatening events originating in their territories?[47]

Jervis makes the more general point that the Bush administration's strategy (of coercive diplomacy against rogue states that might hand off WMDs) is based on the assumption that the U.S. understands how its adversaries think. He argues that this assumption is flawed, since adversaries often make decisions that U.S. decision makers find puzzling. This is a fair point. But its prescriptive teeth are drawn the moment we realize that it applies just as much to a strategy of deterrence, a strategy that also assumes we know how our adversaries think. If the adversaries are unpredictable or puzzling, then deterrence may be as risky or ineffective a strategy as a more intrusive one. In the end, deterrence appears to be effective against most actors. But there are legitimate questions about how effective it is against a very narrow set of them.

Against some of these actors, a policy of deterrence may be doomed from the start. If certain "rogue" rulers are especially risk-tolerant or convinced of the weakness or lack of resolve of major democracies, then status quo states may have to resort to strategies other than deterrence, at least deterrence as traditionally practiced. This might mean preventive use of force. But it could instead mean flamboyant displays of resolve, ostentatiously and overwhelmingly favorable constellations of forces or, as Jacques Chirac's France has mounted, threats to respond with highly disproportionate force.[48]

Let Them Fire the First Shot?

But even if certain adversaries can't be deterred, wouldn't it still be wiser for the United States to absorb an initial blow than to engage in provocative behavior that might scare others? Neorealists and balance-of-threat realists have argued that America's power and muscular behavior could easily or will inevitably provoke—or indeed already have provoked—balancing against itself. It hardly furthers U.S. national security goals to provoke balancing behavior against itself by persuading other states that America is an aggressor.

This is not a concern for neorealism, which predicts that others will inevitably balance against the U.S. because of its power and regardless of its behavior.[49] But balance-of-threat realism suggests that a power would be wise not to be seen as threatening, and Walt and Robert Pape argue that U.S. behavior after 9/11 risks just that.[50]

But to be persuasive, these critiques have to pass two tests. First, it is a core realist proposition that avoiding balancing behavior is not a state's overriding goal. Consider an action that advances a state's security vis-à-vis a given threat but provokes a certain amount of balancing by third parties. Whether the action is advisable is still up for debate, subject to the cost-benefit analysis emphasized by realism. Different members of the realist family can legitimately assess such a situation somewhat differently.[51]

Second, whether a given strategy *is* even provoking balancing behavior is an empirical question. As it happens, claims that the Bush Doctrine is threatening to other states and provoking them to balance against the U.S. are unpersuasive. Since 9/11, most major powers, although they have the material resources to do so, have not responded to U.S. policies with the defensive military buildups characteristically pursued by states that perceive an acute threat. Instead, they have maintained pre-9/11 spending levels or even continued to reduce them. Alliance patterns have remained similarly stable rather than rearranging into new coalitions designed to block Washington. And claims of "soft balancing" have so far not revealed truly new behavior beyond historically routine diplomatic friction. For example, displays of anti-Americanism do not seem much different from those of the early 1980s, when scholars are agreed that other states were *not* balancing against the U.S. This lack of balancing might be because America is an "offshore balancer" an ocean away from other major powers, or because the vast majority of states seem to believe that the United States harbors no aggressive intentions toward them to begin with. Whichever it is, the evidence suggests that balancing behavior is being foregone except by isolated states like Iran and North Korea.[52]

I am not arguing here that other major powers *ought* not to see the U.S. as threatening. I am saying that they are acting as if they *do* not see it as threatening. It is a strange hegemon that regularly urges other great powers to spend more, not less, on their militaries. It is an even stranger set of fearful other states that spend no more, and often less, on their militaries as time goes on.

Finally, it is normally tolerable to absorb an initial attack rather than act preventively because the attacked state typically retains retaliatory capabilities. To revisit the issue: What happens if this is not the case? To repeat, this would not be because America would be overwhelmed. Tiny Israel risks being annihilated by a surprise attack, explaining why it has resorted to preventive and preemptive strikes. But as Francis Fukuyama insists, "Unlike Israel, the United States has a substantial margin of strategic depth."[53] Indeed, the 2002 NSS noted that rogue states and terrorists do not "rival the sheer destructive power that was arrayed against us by the Soviet Union."[54] Islamist extremists do not possess the ability to occupy even a sliver of Western territory. And we now know that even an attack like 9/11 leaves intact America's capabilities of response.

Instead, the new risk is twofold. We have already considered the first: the possibility that terrorists could strike anonymously or with untraceable weapons. When this is the case, absorbing an initial blow, even a catastrophic one, could be the prelude not to effective retaliation but instead to simply absorbing further blows. The second compelling danger is that an attack, instead of mimicking 9/11, will involve a biological or especially nuclear weapon. Waltz argues that one of "the two biggest changes in international politics" after World War II was the dramatic shift in "the extent and rapidity with which some states can hurt others" as a result of the development of nuclear weapons.[55] That change has only accelerated with further proliferation, and John Lewis Gaddis observes that "terrorists can now inflict levels of destruction that only states wielding military power used to be able to accomplish."[56] We can consider scenarios in which cities like Chicago or Washington, DC, are severely damaged by actors against whom the U.S. did not act sufficiently.

While false positives in these matters (unnecessary wars) are costly, type 2 errors (false negatives) have become much more costly with the development of nonconventional weapons. This has hardly gone unnoticed by the Bush administration: "weak states and small groups could attain a catastrophic power to strike great nations."[57] It is no coincidence that the leading previous example of American preventive use of force, the 1962 "quarantine" of Cuba, was directed against nuclear weapons. The downside to letting the other side take the first shot, then, is that the shot might be much more severe than 9/11 and leave the U.S. to retaliate against an unknown target.

If any of these exceptional circumstances arise, or some combination of them, then even a realist perspective emphasizing the cautious calculation of costs and benefits might conclude that in one or more of these narrow circumstances, preventive use of force is in fact advisable. In other words, the broad realist tradition does not seem to offer grounds for rigorously eschewing a highly selective preventive use of force if an adversary has already attacked you, is exceedingly difficult to deter, and could do severe damage in ways that make retaliation difficult, and balancing behavior is unlikely to result. In that sense, the Bush Doctrine's proposal that prevention be used in just such circumstances does not obviously represent the violation of realist thinking that some of its critics suggest. Above all, the Doctrine suggests that deterrence is appropriate when conventional circumstances are present. Gaddis' conclusion appears apt: the "Bush Doctrine does not reject deterrence and containment. It does, however, insist upon the need to supplement these familiar strategies with preemption."[58] If neoconservatives depart from realists in these matters, it is primarily at the level of area of focus rather than of analytic principles. For example, neoconservatives do not consider possible deterrence failures in ways that repudiate realist assumptions so much as they consider whether deterrence might fail for reasons that most neorealists have not focused on.

American Primacy, Multilateralism, and Unilateralism

The Bush Doctrine's emphasis on the maintenance of U.S. primacy and its orientation toward international institutions both fit within the realist tradition. The Bush Doctrine shares ground with many, not all, realists regarding U.S. primacy. Most obviously, realism assumes that a country in a position of primacy will want to maintain it, and the Bush Doctrine prescribes as realism predicts. As for the *desirability* of U.S. primacy, neorealists are unusually divided. Waltz and some others assume that any state with primacy will provoke balancing and is likely to become domineering to boot.[59] In contrast, Mearsheimer emphasizes that America's oceanic separation from other great powers makes any U.S. territorial ambitions implausible and thus makes America appear both objectively and subjectively less threatening to others. Neoconservatives share this last characterization, but trace it to domestic U.S. sources of benevolence such as democracy.

The result is that neoconservatives differ with those neorealists who see the U.S. as broadly interchangeable with other great powers in history, while converging with other neorealists who characterize the U.S. role in the world not merely as unusually benevolent by historical standards but even pacifying in its broadest brushstrokes. Specifically, both these camps have argued that the United States plays a broadly pacifying role by (1) maintaining "offshore" support for allied states in northeast Asia and Western Europe, deterring bids for regional hegemony there, and (2) merely being so relatively powerful, since other major states do not bother to compete for primacy, avoiding arms races and other potentially destabilizing aspects of active rivalry.[60] Parallel claims can be made about America's stabilizing and progressive role in the world economy. The neoconservative assumption is not that other states will bandwagon with the United States out of a desire to share in its loot. It is that other status quo states have nothing to fear from America and thus have no incentive to balance against it but instead have many reasons to cooperate in the crafting of mutually beneficial interstate peace and growing world trade.

The Bush Doctrine's stance on international institutions has similarly scant disagreements with neorealists, though sharp ones with liberal-institutionalists. Most noticeably, the Doctrine is not beholden to the notion that international cooperation is desirable in and of itself. This is visible in the Bush administration's disregard for the International Criminal Court, the Kyoto climate accord, and other treaties. This is probably related to the fact that the Doctrine shares neorealists' skepticism that international institutions and treaties can reliably deliver security, not only because these entities logically depend on the uncertain compliance of signatory states but also because of the ample empirical record of noncompliance and lackadaisical enforcement.[61] In this, the Doctrine and neorealism are consistent with a great deal of U.S. foreign policy history. In Gaddis' succinct conclusion, evidence of a "unilateralist 'turn'" after the Cold War and after 9/11 "reflects a return to an old position, not the emergence of a new one."[62]

As with neorealists, however, the Doctrine's strategy is nonetheless to seek allies for many initiatives, even if the resulting coalitions fall short of worldwide or even all-Western unanimity.[63] Thus Bush's America remains active in such institutions as the Organization of American States, the World Trade Organization, the United Nations and its affiliates, and durable alliances, especially NATO. Since 9/11 the Bush administration has launched two new security-related international organizations, the Proliferation and Container Security Initiatives. Its policies toward North Korea, Iran, Libya, and Syria (especially regarding Lebanon) have been consistently multilateral. In matters of trade, America arguably has remained more consistently "multilateralist" than many of its European allies.[64] It is not a reach, despite the skepticism of some, for Keir Lieber and Robert Lieber to say that the 2002 NSS "is clear about the necessity and benefits of multilateral cooperation, especially with other great powers."[65]

Perhaps the neoconservative position is most distinctive concerning two implications of U.S. primacy and international cooperation. First, unlike most neorealists, neoconservatives frequently detect in U.S. primacy a concurrent responsibility to intervene in humanitarian crises, especially genocides. But, to a degree many liberal-institutionalists are not, they have been willing to intervene with force and multilaterally if possible but unilaterally if necessary, especially when international institutions seem ineffective.[66] Second, many neoconservatives share realists' preference to approach rising China with caution and deterrence. But this may largely be because China is nondemocratic; were that to change, neoconservatives might converge with "liberal optimists" on this subject.[67]

Democratization

In one way more than any other, the Bush Doctrine strategy and the neoconservative thinking it is said to instantiate are distinct from other major approaches to U.S. foreign policy. Neorealism assumes that security threats emanate from particular distributions of power, and mutual fears about those distributions, in the case of "security dilemma" thinking within neorealism. A state can largely address such threats by engaging in balancing behavior: mobilizing military resources, seeking allies, and offering assurances that it does not harbor aggressive agendas, in the case of security dilemmas. As a result, neorealism offers a country only two avenues for addressing threats of war: either changing the objective balance of power (through a military buildup or alliance-formation) or offering a fearful adversary assurances that you do not harbor aggressive intentions.

Balance-of-threat realism brings into the equation variation in other states' intentions, and a major variant of it traces that variation to the other states' domestic regime types. This adds an additional possible avenue for addressing a security threat: a country can seek to alter the domestic politics of adversary states. As we have seen, the United States pursued just such a strategy in World War II and the Cold War. The Bush Doctrine, by tracing both interstate and terrorist threats to nondemocratic regimes, identifies an even more ambitious transformative agenda of this kind: Western security through global democratization.

The democratic-peace thesis inspired the Clinton administration to talk about "democratic enlargement." That thesis and especially the post-9/11 authoritarian-radicalization thesis inspired the Bush administration actively to pursue that goal. The 2002 NSS seeks "modern government, especially in the Muslim world" to undermine the "fertile ground" that exists for "the conditions and ideologies that promote terrorism."[68] Critics and defenders have debated to what extent this project is feasible or reckless.[69] It is worth noting that the Bush administration has not pursued the strategy single-mindedly. It rhetorically champions the causes of pro-democratic dissidents, has dramatically increased the National Endowment for Democracy's budget, and has supported democratic initiatives in Iraq, Afghanistan, Lebanon, the Palestinian territories, and former Soviet republics. But it has used force only in two countries and works closely in the war on terror with nondemocratic regimes such as Saudi Arabia, Kuwait, and Pakistan.

What is more controversial about the democratization strategy is the reasoning underpinning it, which concerns comparative politics more than international relations. The strategy poses two questions concerning feasibility and efficacy: Does democratic practice effectively diminish violent anti-Western intentions? And can stable democracy be induced in all settings? Democratization is a pressing national security strategy if nondemocratic regimes are determined to be an important generator of aggressive state behavior and an incubator of terrorists. Simply put, the record is mixed. Regarding interstate security, it is true that the greatest twentieth century security threats to Western democracies have been nondemocratic states like Nazi Germany and the Soviet empire. But many nondemocratic regimes have also been durable allies, including those in NATO. It is symbolic that the United States shared demilitarized borders through most of the twentieth century with both democratic Canada and authoritarian Mexico. As for threats from nonstate actors, the majority of al-Qaeda rank-and-file come from nondemocratic states, and many authoritarian regimes have a record of provoking extremist opposition. But many nondemocratic regimes, including many in majority-Muslim central Asia and sub-Saharan Africa, have produced little extremism.

In sum, the democratic-peace thesis suggests at most that nondemocratic regimes are *more* likely to be interstate threats than democracies are, not that many of either category are. And for now, the authoritarian-radicalization thesis lacks the level of empirical support enjoyed by the democratic-peace thesis.[70] Perhaps nondemocratic regimes are a necessary but not sufficient condition for generating security threats: while not all nondemocracies pose threats, only nondemocracies do so. One option then is to focus security concerns on some subset of nondemocratic regimes. Another is the blunt but potentially effective instrument of gradual, global democratization. This seems to be the long-term strategy of the Bush Doctrine. In the words of the 2006 NSS, the "advance of freedom and human dignity through democracy is the long-term solution to the transnational terrorism of today."[71]

Is this feasible? Realists are often portrayed as skeptics, though it is worth noting that realist assumptions offer no theoretical grounds for any particular stand on this subject; realism assumes nationalism, not authoritarian predilections. The record is mixed on this score, too. Democracy has flourished in previously hostile contexts such as post-1945 Japan and Germany. And events in Iraq could have a "contagion" effect on other countries, as Bush envisions.[72] But democracy has also serially failed in many countries, including in several European cases pre-1945. This suggests that certain structural conditions are required for democracy to stabilize, even if not the cultural ones that were once the focus of research and despair. External assistance might best be targeted at encouraging propitious conditions for democracy.[73]

Does the Bush Doctrine Have Staying Power?

This chapter has argued that Bush Doctrine neoconservatism is a variant of realism, specifically balance-of-threat realism, characterized by the supplementary assumption that nondemocratic regimes generate interstate, and incubate nonstate, threats to Western democracies in general and America in particular. In these ways, the strategy outlined by the Doctrine is better understood not as a radical departure from modern U.S. foreign policy, which is substantially realist in nature, but as an adaptation of that tradition to the novel circumstances of the post-9/11 world. For example, the supposedly radical innovation of preventive use of force can, and I think should, be understood not as a rejection of deterrence but simply as a supplementary tool intended for very narrow circumstances in which deterrence might be prone to fail at great cost.

This point has one important implication. If the core elements of the Bush Doctrine are not the precarious product of a single foreign policy team, they are likely to endure under successor administrations. Observers should expect wholesale abandonment only if they conceive of the Doctrine in caricatured terms, for example as allergic to all international cooperation and bent on a policy of constant preventive war (or even "periodic preventive wars").[74] Such a strategy would be unsustainable. But that does not accurately represent the Doctrine. We can consider sustainability regarding the preventive use of force, periodically "narrow" coalitions of the willing, threat assessment, and democratization. The point of the analysis below is not that each of these elements is likely to remain unaltered after the Bush administration, only that their broad features are unlikely to be abandoned.

There is little evidence that any U.S. government is likely to renounce the option of *preemptive* force as a supplement to America's durable reliance on deterrence, though it might return discussion of that option to a classified annex of its National Security Strategy. Clinton certainly did not renounce this option when president. And in the 2004 presidential campaign, the Democratic party platform promised action if an attack with WMDs "appears imminent" (that is, before it materializes) and John Kerry pointedly retained the "right to preempt in any way necessary to protect" the U.S.[75] It is a distinct question whether future administrations would exercise the *preventive* option. Incoming U.S. governments of both parties may well be chastened by how difficult Iraq proved. Many now conclude that further preventive use of force is highly unlikely.

But substantial evidence suggests otherwise. Both of America's major political parties, and for that matter, the European Union, have identified as their top security priority to ensure that terrorists do not acquire WMDs—a task that is entirely preventive in nature.[76] The Bush team is not unique in doubting whether all adversaries can effectively be deterred.[77] Moreover, what appears most chastening about Iraq has been the experience of the U.S.-U.K. project *after* the original military strike, a project of political reconstitution that is not a necessary feature of a preventive attack on WMDs. This may explain the striking fact that even amidst problems in Iraq, Americans (and Europeans) have been calmly discussing the pros and cons of preventive military action against Iran's nuclear facilities. And it is suggestive that the two U.S. politicians leading in public opinion polls for the 2008 presidential race, Hillary Clinton and John McCain, both continue to insist that the preventive action against Iraq was appropriate. There is a good case to be made that the idea of the limited preventive use of force has been mainstreamed rather than made anathema.[78]

Future U.S. governments are especially unlikely to abandon the Bush Doctrine's emphasis on maintaining U.S. primacy, either by deliberately squandering the U.S. lead in mobilized military resources or by ending a policy of seeking to deflect China, the most plausible peer competitor in coming decades, from achieving military parity with America. The Doctrine's "unilateralism" is more likely to be contested, but quite possibly rhetorically more than operationally. Alongside the U.S.'s extensive ongoing engagements in international institutions, several Bush policies have been most heatedly discussed on this matter: relations with Europe; the Kyoto Protocol, Anti-Ballistic Missile (ABM) Treaty, and other treaties; and the willingness to use force without UN Security Council approval. On each count, a Democratic administration is likely to act more multilaterally than a Republican one. But as Stephen Walt notes, post-Cold War diplomatic relations between America and Europe began to fray in the 1990s, not after 2001.[79] America under Clinton joined a Kosovo operation that lacked UN approval. Both Democrats and Republicans under Clinton made clear they would not ratify the Kyoto climate change treaty. Leading Democrats even now do not call for Kyoto's implementation nor for restoration of the ABM Treaty. Leading Democratic foreign policy intellectuals discuss multilateralism, but at the same time champion U.S. primacy, describe the UN as frequently ineffectual, and support aggressive anti-WMD policies.[80] The debates between these thinkers and many conservatives are not distinctions without a difference. But they are differences of degree and not of kind. Certainly mainstream U.S. Democratic approaches do not approximate the principled and strict multilateralism to which many European social democrats are at least rhetorically committed.

Is it regarding democratization that change is most likely after Bush? Are future U.S. governments likely to trace threats to nondemocratic regimes? The Clinton administration called for "democratic enlargement"; the 2004 Democratic platform argued that "Americans will be safer in a world of democracies"; and John Kerry broadly endorsed the notion that lack of democracy and political reform are among the root causes "breeding this virulent new form of anti-American terrorism."[81] But this has not been translated into a comparable emphasis in policy making. Democratic "enlargement" was not a major priority under Clinton. And since the Iraq invasion, Democrats have not emphasized democratization to nearly the same degree as Bush.

This caution regarding democratization may be traced not to issues of efficacy but of feasibility. Realists are not the only observers who have concluded that the creation of stable democracies, however desirable, is a complex process, many of whose moving parts are unknown to us, at least for now.[82] Iraq and Afghanistan have been humbling not only because recalcitrant armed adversaries have proven difficult to defeat but also because it has proven difficult to create effective democratic processes on whose durability we are ready to rely. On the one hand, the Bush administration has continued to champion democratization in many other countries. On the other, time has not noticeably diminished the Bush administration's willingness to work with many nondemocratic regimes, including a post-WMD Libya. It is too soon to know if this reflects a realistic sense of democratization's plausible pace or a grudging conclusion that nondemocratic regimes are pervasive, both historically and today, for complicated reasons. Perhaps America will seek more regime change through socioeconomic change, as it has been crossing its fingers will occur in China. The rigorous assumption that nondemocratic regimes are the source of security threats, both interstate and substate, is the most "radical" departure of the Bush Doctrine from preexisting thinking about international relations. It may be unsurprising that it is on this score that the Doctrine looks most vulnerable. But this only brings into sharp relief the durability of its other major features.

NOTES

1. Fred Barnes, *Rebel-in-Chief* (New York: Crown Forum, 2006), 54. Vice President Dick Cheney has said that the "Bush Doctrine asserts that states supporting terrorists, or providing sanctuary for terrorists, will be deemed just as guilty of crimes as the terrorists themselves"; see "Vice President's Remarks at the U.S. Military Academy Commencement," May 31, 2003, http://www.whitehouse.gov/news/releases/2003/05/20030531-7.html.

   In his January 2006 speech at Kansas State University, President Bush three times referred to the "doctrine" that "if you harbor a terrorist, you're equally as guilty as the terrorists"; see "President Discusses Global War on Terror at Kansas State University," January 23, 2006, http://www.whitehouse.gov/news/releases/2006/01/20060123-4.html.

2. Ivo Daalder and James M. Lindsay, *America Unbound* (Washington, DC: Brookings Institution Press, 2003), 15; Peter Dombrowski and Rodger A. Payne, "Global Debate and the Limits of the Bush Doctrine," *International Studies Perspective* 4 (2003): 395-408.

3. Robert Jervis, "Understanding the Bush Doctrine," *Political Science Quarterly* 118 (2003): 365-88, 365; Robert Lieber, *The American Era: Power and Strategy for the 21st Century* (New York: Cambridge University Press, 2004), 43-44.

4. The National Security Strategy, of the United States, September 17, 2002, p. 4, http://www.whitehouse.gov/nsc/nss.pdfpassim; hereafter, 2002 NSS. George W. Bush, "President Bush Delivers Graduation Speech at West Point," June 1, 2002, www.whitehouse.gov/news/releases/2002/06/20020601-3.html. George W. Bush, "President Bush Discusses Freedom in Iraq and Middle East," November 6, 2003, http://www.whitehouse.gov/news/releases/2003/11/20031 106-2.html. The National Security Strategy of the United States, March 16, 2006, http://www.whitehouse.gov/nsc/nss/2006/nss2006.pdf; hereafter, 2006 NSS.

5. Charles Krauthammer remarks that "the Bush Doctrine is, essentially, a synonym for neoconservative foreign policy" in "The Neoconservative Convergence," *Commentary* (July-August 2005): 22. Neoconservatism diverges sharply from constructivist theorizing in international relations, but that analytic approach for now plays no prominent role in policy debates and is not discussed here.

6. For a basic definition of realism, see John J. Mearsheimer, *The Tragedy of Great Power Politics* (New York: Norton, 2001), 17-18.

7. Kenneth N. Waltz, *Theory of International Politics* (Reading, MA: Addison-Wesley, 1979); Mearsheimer, *The Tragedy of Great Power Politics*; Robert Gilpin, *War and Change in World Politics* (New York: Cambridge University Press, 1981).

8. John Mearsheimer, "The False Promise of International Institutions," *International Security* 19 (Winter 1994/95): 5-49.

9. John Mearsheimer, "Conversation with John Mearsheimer," interviewed by Harry Kreiseler, April 8 p://globetrotter.berkeley.edu/people2/Mearsheimer/mearsheimer-con5.html.

10. Stephen Walt, The Origins of Alliances (Ithaca, NY: Cornell University Press, 1987).

11. See, for example, John Owen, *Liberal Peace, Liberal War* (Ithaca, NY: Cornell University Press, 1997).

12. G. John Ikenberry, *After Victory* (Princeton, NJ: Princeton University Press, 2001); Stephen Walt, *Taming American Power* (New York: Norton, 2005).

13. There is a substantial academic literature identifiable as neoconservative. Analysis fruitfully focuses on such works as Lieber, *The American Era*; William Kristol and Robert Kagan, "Toward a Neo-Reaganite Foreign Policy," *Foreign Affairs* 75/4 (July-August 1996); and other works discussed below.

14. Kenneth Waltz, "Reflections on Theory of International Relations: A Response to My Critics," in ed. Robert Keohane, *Neorealism and Its Critics* (New York: Columbia University Press, 1986), 329.

15. It is worth observing that populations and especially levels of wealth can also fluctuate substantially across time.

16. Mearsheimer, *Tragedy*, chapters 3-4.

17. Mearsheimer, *Tragedy*, 3.

18. In the economic and decision-theoretic tradition, "risk" refers to an event with a known probability of occurrence (as in a game of chance) and "uncertainty" to one with no quantified probability. But many studies emphasize the difference between uncertainty as a total unknown and uncertainty as, in effect, ranges of unquantified likelihood such as "highly unlikely" or "very likely," ranges that seem to inform a great deal of real-world decision making. For two applied examples, see Dale Copeland, *The Origins of Major War* (Ithaca, NY: Cornell University Press, 2001) and Gerard Alexander, *The Sources of Democratic Consolidation* (Ithaca, NY: Cornell University Press, 2002).

19. Walt, *The Origins of Alliances*; Stephen Walt, "Revolution and War," *World Politics* 44 (April 1992): 321-368.

20. This section draws on Gerard Alexander, "The Authoritarian Illusion," *National Interest* (Fall 2004): 79-83.

21. Jeane Kirkpatrick, "Dictatorships and Double Standards," *Commentary* (November, 1979), http://www.reagan.utexas.edu/archives/speeches/1982/60882a.htm.

22. For a different interpretation of the deeper roots, see Michael C. Williams, "What Is the National Interest? The Neoconservative Challenge in IR Theory," *European Journal of International Relations* 11 (2005): 307-37.

23. Alexander, "The Authoritarian Illusion," 80.

24. Some states also deliberately encourage terrorist activity. See Daniel Byman, *Deadly Connections: States That Sponsor Terrorism* (New York: Cambridge University Press, 2005).

25. George W. Bush, "President Bush Discusses Freedom in Iraq and Middle East," November 6, 2003, http://www.whitehouse.gov/news/releases/2003/11/20031106-2.html.

26. George W. Bush, State of the Union Address, January 20, 2004, http://www.whitehouse.gov/news/releases/2004/01/20040120-7.html.

27. David C. Hendrickson and Robert W. Tucker, "The Freedom Crusade," *The National Interest* 81 (Fall 2005): 12-13.

28. Condoleezza Rice, "The Promise of Democratic Peace," *Washington Post*, December 11, 2005, B7.

29. Daalder and Lindsay, *America Unbound*, 125.
30. Ivo Daalder and James M.Lindsay's contributions to "Brookings Forum: Brook-ings Scholars Evaluate and Analyze President's National Security Strategy Paper," http://www.brook.edu/comm/events/20021004.pdf.
31. 2002 NSS, 14-15; 2006 NSS, 8; italics added. In these discussions, "deterrence" often includes compellance and other strategies.
32. Condoleezza Rice, "Dr. Condoleezza Rice Discusses President's National Secu-rity Strategy," October 1, 2002, http://www.whitehouse.gov/news/releases/2002/ 10/20021001-6.html. Long before 9/11, Kristol and Kagan took pains to note that "[d]uring the Cold War, the strategies of deterrence and containment worked... well" in "Toward a Neo-Reaganite Foreign Policy," 22.
33. Joint Chiefs of Staff, "The National Military Strategy of the United States of Amer-ica," 2004, http://www.defenselink.mil/news/Mar2005/d20050318nms.pdf.
34. Richard Betts, *Surprise Attack* (Washington, DC: Brookings Institution, 1982), 95. See also, John Lewis Gaddis, *Surprise, Security, and the American Experience* (Cambridge, MA: Harvard University Press, 2004).
35. As the Bush administration also pointed out, Iraq had not definitively resolved the 1990–1991 war and continued to fire at allied planes patrolling agreed-to no-fly zones.
36. For recent discussions, see Lawrence Freedman, *Deterrence* (Cambridge, UK: Polity Press, 2004) and Patrick Morgan, *Deterrence Now* (New York: Cambridge University Press, 2003).
37. Some streams of realist thought also trace conflicts to security dilemmas that spiral sufficiently.
38. Charles Krauthammer, "Democratic Realism: An American Foreign Policy for a Unipolar World," Irving Kristol Lecture at the American Enterprise Institute for Public Policy Research, February 10, 2004 [emphasis in original], http://www. aei.org/publications/pubID.19912,filter.all/pub_detail.asp. The issue of uncer-tainty over the origins of an attack might pose a new dilemma for preventive action: If a state doesn't know who to use force against after an attack, how can it possibly know who to use force against *before* one? The answer has been made simpler by the fact that only a small number of rogue states possess the programs of greatest concern: advanced nuclear programs. Eliminating them, alongside securing former Soviet weapons, might deny all terrorists such weapons.
39. For example, see John J. Mearsheimer and Stephen M. Walt, "An Unnecessary War," *Foreign Policy* 137 (January-February 2003): 58.
40. For one partial discussion, see Robert F. Trager and Dessislava P. Zagorcheva, "Deterring Terrorism: It Can Be Done," *International Security* 30 (Winter 2005-06): 87-123.
41. Interview with Owen Harries, "On Prudence and Restraint in Foreign Policy," *Policy* 18 (Autumn 2002): 32, available through http://www.policymagazine. com.
42. Nikita Khrushchev may have been the most risk-tolerant Soviet leader.
43. Robert Lieber, "Are Realists Realistic About Foreign Policy?" Paper prepared for delivery at the 2003 Annual Meeting of the American Political Science Associa-tion, Philadelphia, August 2003.
44. Kenneth Pollack, *The Threatening Storm* (New York: Random House, 2002), 248-271; Mearsheimer and Walt, "Unnecessary War."

45. U.S. Ambassador April Glaspie is said to have assured Saddam Hussein in 1990 that the U.S. would not resist his invasion of Kuwait. But even if true, how often have rulers launched major wars on the unconfirmed assurance of a single diplomat? Robert Jervis reviews the various possibilities that Hussein refused to capitulate in 2002–2003 (for instance by permitting absolutely unrestricted inspections) because he was afraid of loss of face among Iraqis, of assassination attempts by Americans, or of possible invasion by an Iran no longer deterred by his alleged WMDs; or because he suspected the U.S. was irrevocably bent on his overthrow regardless; or because he doubted the U.S. would ultimately attack, even though most observers did not. But in all these cases save the last, Hussein would have been taking a massive risk of losing power in a direct military confrontation with the coalition in order to avoid what seem like smaller risks that he *might* lose power. The last scenario suggests he was ill-informed in ways that made his decisions objectively high-risk anyway. See Robert Jervis, "Why the Bush Doctrine Cannot Be Sustained," *Political Science Quarterly* 120 (Fall 2005): 364, 366-367. And even if Saddam faced domestic challenges to his regime in 1980 and 1990 that might fruitfully be addressed through successful war making, why was Hussein confident his wars *would* be successful? And what domestic risk to his regime could have justified the foreign risk he (again unsuccessfully) ran in 2003? See F. Gregory Gause III, "Iraq's Decisions to Go to War, 1980 and 1990," *Middle East Journal* 56 (Winter 2002): 47-70.

46. George W. Bush, "Address to a Joint Session of Congress and the American People," September 20, 2001, http://www.whitehouse.gov/news/releases/2001/09/20010920-8.html.

47. For a brief discussion of some of these issues, see Daniel Byman, *Deadly Connections: States that Sponsor Terror* (New York: Cambridge University Press, 2005), 210-15.

48. Arguably, the 2003 invasion of Iraq might have constituted just such a display of resolve. Another might be admitting Israel into NATO. On Chirac, see Ariane Bernard, "Chirac Hints at Nuclear Reply to State-Supported Terrorism," January 20, 2006, http://www.nytimes.com/2006/01/20/international/europe/20france.html.

49. Kenneth Waltz, "The Emerging Structure of International Politics," *International Security* 18 (Fall 1993): 44-79.

50. Walt, *Taming American Power*; Robert Pape, "Soft Balancing Against the United States," *International Security* 30 (Summer 2005): 7-45.

51. I thank Stanley Renshon for raising this subject.

52. Keir Lieber and Gerard Alexander, "Waiting for Balancing: Why the World Is Not Pushing Back," *International Security* 30 (Summer 2005): 109-139; William Wohlforth and Stephen Brooks, "Hard Times for Soft Balancing," *International Security* 30 (Summer 2005): 72-108.

53. Francis Fukuyama, "The Neoconservative Moment," *National Interest* 74 (Summer 2004): 66.

54. 2002 NSS, 13.

55. Waltz, "Reflections on Theory of International Relations," 327.

56. John Lewis Gaddis, "A Grand Strategy of Transformation," *Foreign Policy* 133 (November-December 2002): 52.

57. Bush, "President Bush Delivers Graduation Speech at West Point."

58. Gaddis, *Surprise, Security*, 86.

59. Robert Jervis, *American Foreign Policy in a New Era* (New York: Routledge, 2005).

60. William Wohlforth, "The Stability of a Unipolar World," *International Security* 24 (1999): 23-28; Mearsheimer, *Tragedy*, 377, 379-380; Kristol and Kagan, "Toward a Neo-Reaganite Foreign Policy."

61. For neorealist skepticism, see Mearsheimer, "False Promise"; and Randall Schweller, "The Problem of International Order Revisited: A Review Essay," *International Security* 26/1 (Summer 2001).

62. Gaddis, *Surprise, Security*, 26.

63. Then again, given the willingness of many Western liberals to use force with substantially less than global unanimity, the policy debate seems to be not whether "coalitions of the willing" are appropriate, but what number of "willing" is sufficient to endow legitimacy. For a prominent example of such willingness (regarding Kosovo), see Robert Kagan, "America's Crisis of Legitimacy," *Foreign Affairs* 83 (March-April 2004): 73-79.

64. A point made by Francis Fukuyama, "Does the 'West' Still Exist?" in *Beyond Paradise and Power*, ed. Tod Lindberg (New York: Routledge, 2004).

65. Keir Lieber and Robert Lieber, "The Bush National Security Strategy," *U.S. Foreign Policy Agenda* 7/4 (December 2002), http://usinfo.state.gov/journals/itps/1202/ijpe/pj7-4lieber.htm.

66. For example, William Kristol and Vance Serchuk, "End the Genocide Now," *Washington Post*, September 22, 2004, A31, http://www.washingtonpost.com/wp-dyn/articles/A40121-2004Sep21.html.

67. Aaron Friedberg, "The Future of U.S.-China Relations: Is Conflict Inevitable?" *International Security* 30 (Fall 2005): 7-45.

68. 2002 NSS, 6.

69. Defenders insist its ambitiousness should not be exaggerated in either pace or extent. For example, Krauthammer, "The Neoconservative Convergence," 25; and Norman Podhoretz's contribution to "The Bush Doctrine: What the President Said and What It Means," Heritage Foundation Lecture #881, June 2, 2005, http://www.heritage.org/research/nationalsecurity/hl881.cfm.

70. Alexander, "The Authoritarian Illusion"; F. Gregory Gause III, "Can Democracy Stop Terrorism?" *Foreign Affairs* (September-October 2005): 62-76.

71. 2006 NSS, 11.

72. For example, George W. Bush, "President's Remarks on Iraq from the Rose Garden," April 15, 2003, http://www.whitehouse.gov/news/releases/ 2003/04/20030415-10.html.

73. Gerard Alexander, "Making Democracy Stick," *Policy Review* (December 2005–January 2006): 45-57.

74. Francis Fukuyama, "After Neoconservatism," *New York Times*, February 19, 2006, http://www.nytimes.com/2006/02/19/magazine/neo.html.

75. The 2004 Democratic National Platform for America, "Strong at Home, Respected in the World," July 27, 2004, 6, http://www.democrats.org/pdfs/2004platform.pdf; Kerry spoke during one of the presidential debates, Commission on Presidential Debates, "The First Bush-Kerry Presidential Debate," September 30, 2004, http://www.debates.org/pages/trans2004a.html.

76. For example, see the 2004 Democratic Platform, "Strong at Home, Respected in the World," 6; the Republican counterpart, 2004 Republican Platform, "A Safer World and a More Hopeful America," August 26, 2004, http://www.gop.com/media/2004platform.pdf; and the Council of the European Union, European Security Strategy, "A Secure Europe in a Better World," December 12, 2003, http://ue.eu.int/uedocs/cmsUpload/78367.pdf.

77. As late as September 2002, former Vice President Al Gore believed that Saddam Hussein's search for WMDs "has proven impossible to completely deter, and we should assume that it will continue for as long as Saddam is in power." See "Text: Gore Assails Bush's Iraq Policy," speech before the Commonwealth Club of San Francisco, September 23, 2003, http://www.washingtonpost.com/wp-srv/politics/transcripts/gore_text092302.html.

78. For example, see James Steinberg, "The Use of Preventive Force as an Element of US National Strategy," a Working Paper of the Princeton Project on National Security, http://www.wws.princeton.edu/ppns/papers/Steinberg_Preemption.pdf.

79. Stephen M. Walt, "The Ties that Fray: Why Europe and America Are Approaching a Parting of the Ways," *The National Interest* 54 (Winter 1998-99): 3-11.

80. For example, Progressive Policy Institute, "Progressive Internationalism: A Democratic National Security Strategy," October 31, 2003, http://www.ppionline.org/documents/Progressive_Internationalism_1003.pdf. See also, Joshua Micah Marshall, "Kerry Faces the World," *Atlantic Monthly* (July/August 2004): 108-14.

81. 2004 Democratic Platform, "Strong at Home, Respected in the World," 7; http://kerry.Senate.gov/low/record.cfm?id=189831.

82. Neo-conservatives are not immune; see Francis Fukuyama's contribution to "Defending and Advancing Freedom: A Symposium," *Commentary* (November 2005): 30.

3

The Convinced, the Skeptical, and the Hostile
American and World Public Opinion on the Bush Doctrine

DOUGLAS C. FOYLE

Introduction

The Bush Doctrine represents the first new grand strategy since President Harry Truman introduced the containment doctrine in the late 1940s. In its various forms,[1] containment was eventually embraced by both major political parties, favored by American public opinion, and supported, for the most part, by Western public opinion. As a grand strategy, the United States consistently followed containment for the roughly 45 years of the Cold War with the Soviet Union. Will the same ever be said about the Bush Doctrine? Does the Bush Doctrine contain the seeds of sustainability in domestic and world opinion that suggest that it could successfully anchor the United States' war against terrorism for decades hence? My answer, which I'll return to in the conclusion, is that while the Doctrine is facing its share of difficulties, the rough early goings of containment suggest it is too soon to write the Doctrine's obituary.

Because the Bush Doctrine is fundamentally about achieving American foreign policy goals through interactions with other actors in the system, the perceptions of non-Americans will have an important influence on its short- and long-term success. The importance of being liked, or at least feared, has long been recognized. In his classic consideration of "whether it is better to be loved than feared, or the reverse," Machiavelli's recommendation to the prince was clear: fear is better than love. While "one would like to be both the one and the other," the difficulty in having them both led him to conclude that "it is far better to be feared than loved." The reason, he argued, was that "men worry less about doing an injury to one who makes himself loved than to one who makes himself feared."[2]

The same might be said for international politics as well. Joseph Nye's concept of "soft power," which a state uses to "obtain the outcomes it wants in world politics because other countries want to follow it, admiring its values, emulating its examples, aspiring to its level of prosperity and openness," most closely mirrors the concept of "love" that Machiavelli discussed. Conversely, Nye's "hard power," which relies on material assets such as the military and economic power as inducements and threats, lies closer to the concept of fear.[3] Whether or not states decide to comply with American policies associated with the Bush Doctrine might be critically linked to public attitudes around the world. Depending on whether these states decide to support or oppose American goals, they have a range of policy options to assist or hinder America's pursuit of effective foreign policies.[4] The danger that the United States faces is that while the Bush Doctrine has undermined positive international feelings toward the U.S., the failures in Iraq might undermine international respect (fear) for American power. As Eric Frey, editor of the Austrian daily *Der Standard* observed: "In 2002 and 2003 everyone was talking about the American 'Hyperpower.' No one these days is talking about overwhelming American power, and that has even added to the anti-Americanism. Because before you had resentment and respect, and now you have resentment and scorn."[5] The peril that this quotation highlights is that the U.S., through its actions, might be simultaneously undermining international opinion's love and fear of America. As Machiavelli added, "the prince must nonetheless make himself feared in such a way that, if he is not loved, at least he escapes being hated."[6] If negative world opinion translates into changed governmental policies around the world, the United States could find itself in a very difficult international situation.

To evaluate these prospects, this chapter examines the nature of American and international support for the five components of the Bush Doctrine (Renshon, Chapter 1). I make three arguments. First, the American public currently supports the broad war against terrorism and the Bush Doctrine to fight it. In practice, the public favors a more cooperative foreign policy than the current approach; an approach that might best be characterized as acting as a "cooperative hegemon." Second, although world opinion is less supportive of the war on terror than American public opinion, it supports more of the fundamental goals of the Bush Doctrine than commonly believed. Although world opinion rejects President George W. Bush personally, opposes the United States' Iraq policy, and is hostile to the perceived hegemonic means of the Bush Doctrine, there are important aspects of the Doctrine that world opinion supports. This array of opinion suggests that while the "Bush Doctrine" will never be welcomed by world opinion, many of its substantive components could provide the foundation for a sustainable foreign policy much like containment did. Finally, the nature of American and world opinion on the Bush Doctrine makes the 2008 presidential election critically important in determining whether the United States continues to pursue the Bush Doctrine (or some variant).

To evaluate this question, I will first consider non-American attitudes toward the United States and how those attitudes have changed over time.

Then, I will examine domestic and international opinion regarding each of the Bush Doctrine's five elements. Finally, I evaluate the implications of this analysis for the long-term prospects of the Doctrine's success in relation to the containment.[7]

International Opinion on the United States

International attitudes toward the United States changed considerably in the period between 1999 and the end of 2005. The common portrayal suggests that these attitudes shifted from strong favorability toward the United States after the 9/11 attacks to negativity, and even outright hostility, in response to the policies of the Bush Doctrine. The available polling implies that any positive influence on opinion by the 9/11 attack dissipated fairly rapidly while the drop in support after the Bush Doctrine's implementation has lasted and is attributable to the Bush administration's policies.

Unfortunately, the available polling (Table 3.1) does not capture the immediate 9/11 aftermath. The first multination favorability poll after 9/11 took place in summer 2002 and illustrates international sentiment after the American intervention in Afghanistan and the Bush administration's initial declarations concerning the Bush Doctrine. Views of the United States varied considerably across countries, with some remaining relatively steady from the pre-9/11 period (Canada, France, Great Britain), two dropping by double-digits but remaining fairly positive (Germany, Indonesia), one rising dramatically (Russia), one dropping dramatically (Turkey), and one remaining fairly negative (Pakistan). In general, European and Canadian attitudes could be characterized as fairly positive, Southwest Asian attitudes as negative, and Asian views as mixed. With the exception of Russia, favorability levels had roughly returned to their pre-9/11 levels by summer 2002. Except for Russia and Turkey, the available data also suggest more continuity than change.

With the approaching U.S. invasion of Iraq in mid-March 2003, a discernable drop in favorability emerged. The European countries for which there are data registered a plunge from nearly two-thirds favorability to nearly one-third favorability. With the exception of Great Britain, none of the favorability ratings had recovered to their pre-Iraq War levels by June 2005, although all ratings had moved up from their March 2003 low. The same pattern describes the polled countries of Southwest Asia. The Asian countries provide a bit more diversity. Pakistan's favorability rating of the U.S. actually rose in the period of the Iraq War before dropping to previous low levels. Indian support rose between 2002 and 2005. Indonesian support dropped dramatically after 2002 and had only marginally improved by 2005. Overall, the general trend suggests a relative peak of favorability in 2000–2002, followed by a dramatic decline in 2003, and moderate recovery by mid-2005. By mid-2005, the favorability rating suggests rather mixed views of the United States in Europe and Canada

Table 3.1 Favorability of United States

	9/11 Attacks ↓		Iraq War Begins ↓			
	1999/ 2000	Summer 2002	Mid-March 2003	May 2003	March 2004	June 2005
United States	—	—	—	—	—	83
Canada	71	72	63	63	—	59
Europe						
Great Britain	83	75	48	70	58	55
France	62	63	31	43	37	43
Germany	78	61	25	45	38	41
Spain	50	—	14	38	—	41
Russia	37	61	28	36	47	52
Poland	—	79	—	—	—	62
Southwest Asia						
Turkey	52	30	12	15	30	23
Lebanon	—	35	—	27	—	42
Jordan	—	25	—	1	5	21
Asia						
Pakistan	23	17	—	38	25	22
India	—	54	—	—	—	71
Indonesia	75	61	—	15	—	38

Figures are the percentage indicating a very favorable or somewhat favorable opinion of the United States.
Source: PGAP, "American Character," question 5.

(with attitudes roughly 10% above or below the 50% mark) and unfavorable attitudes in Southwest Asia and Asia (with the exception of India).

A "feeling thermometer" measure provides a more sanguine perspective on European attitudes (Figure 3.1).[8] A combined European rating by seven nations (hereafter the "Europe 7": Great Britain, France, Germany, the Netherlands, Italy, Poland, and Portugal) gave the United States a 54 out of 100, a decrease of 10 points from 2002. While this measure is consistent with the trend exhibited in Table 3.1, the extent of the drop is not nearly as dramatic. While the United States is clearly not as widely esteemed as the actors

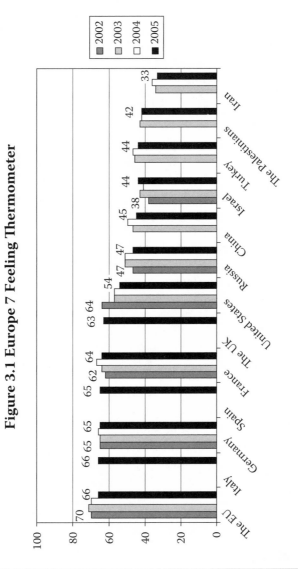

Figure 3.1 Europe 7 Feeling Thermometer

Figure 3.1 Figures are percentages with exact percentage given for 2002 and 2005, if available. Question wording: "Next, I'd like you to rate your feelings toward some countries, institutions, and people, with one hundred meaning a very warm, favorable feeling, zero meaning a very cold, unfavorable feeling, and fifty meaning not particularly warm or cold. You can use any number from zero to one hundred." Source: GMF, "Transatlantic Trends 2005," question 10.

associated with the European Union, outright hostility seems less in evidence by this measure (with a middling U.S. score) and the U.S. scores better than several other actors.

Not surprisingly, President Bush and his policies seem to be the driving force behind the drop in views toward the U.S. (see also Stein, Chapter 11). When those who expressed unfavorable attitudes toward the United States were asked to explain their views, most pointed to President Bush rather than "America" (Table 3.2). In Canada, Great Britain, France, Germany, Spain, and Pakistan, majorities pointed to Bush. Pluralities in Turkey and Lebanon also indicated Bush; India and Indonesia split. On the other hand, Russia, Poland, and Jordan pointed to the United States more broadly.

Compared to May 2003, when the same question was asked in these countries, it appears that in 2005 (to the extent that there were shifts in assigning "blame") the trend among these publics is toward making broader assessments about the United States. In each country in which there was a shift (except for Spain, where the reverse occurred), the percentage identifying America (or both Bush and America) rose, sometimes dramatically. One possible explanation of this pattern is the fact that the American public reelected Bush in 2004. Rather than seeing Bush as an anomaly, his reelection might have been taken to reflect something more enduring about the United States. The significant intensity with which foreign publics disapprove of Bush's foreign policy is illustrated by the pattern in the Europe 7 group, where 56% disapproval in 2002 rose to 70% disapproval by the 2005 survey (Table 3.3). The dismal 2005 figure actually represents an improvement from the post-Iraq War high of 74% disapproval.

Given these sentiments, one might be tempted to blame the Bush Doctrine in its entirety. However, close examination of international attitudes toward the Doctrine's individual components suggests a more complex picture. While there is widespread dissatisfaction regarding some of the policy *means* associated with the Bush Doctrine, significant support exists for many of the Doctrine's *goals*. In particular, the main dissatisfaction with the Doctrine derives from perceptions of American hegemony and unilateralism, while support exists for assertive realism and democratic transformation. This distinction, which I now turn to in relation to the five aspects of the Doctrine, has important implications for the long-term viability of the Bush Doctrine, as discussed in the conclusion.

American Preeminence

Negative perceptions of the United States as a unilateralist hegemon pervade attitudes toward the United States. International attitudes suggest a view of the United States as unconcerned with others' interests at best and a real threat at worst. These attitudes seem to undermine broader support for the American war on international terror. Domestically, the American public shares the perception of the United States as a hegemon, but views this situation less negatively.

European attitudes have consistently supported the EU's rise to rival the U.S., while American attitudes have remained fairly ambivalent, but more

Table 3.2 Unfavorable Because of President George W. Bush or America Generally? Summer 2005

	Mostly Bush	America	Both (volunteered)
Canada	54	37	9
May 2003	60	32	6
Europe			
Great Britain	56	35	8
May 2003	59	31	8
France	63	32	5
May 2003	74	21	4
Germany	65	29	5
May 2003	74	22	3
Spain	76	14	7
May 2003	50	37	12
Russia	30	58	9
May 2003	43	32	15
Poland	27	49	14
Southwest Asia			
Turkey	41	36	17
May 2003	52	33	12
Lebanon	47	32	19
May 2003	51	32	16
Jordan	22	37	41
May 2003	42	28	30
Asia			
Pakistan	51	29	10
May 2003	62	31	2
India	35	35	14
Indonesia	43	42	0
May 2003	69	20	7

Figures are the percentages. Asked of those indicating an unfavorable opinion to the question in Table 1. Question wording: "Why do you have an unfavorable view of the U.S.? Is it mostly because of President George W. Bush or is it more a general problem with America?"
Source: PGAP, "American Character," question 7.

supportive, than Europe (Figure 3.2). In Europe, only about 1 in 10 respondents of the Europe 7 group said that the United States should remain the sole superpower. In the United States, Americans were more favorable toward U.S. superpower status, but this figure has declined over time.[9] In surveys outside

Table 3.3 Europe 7 Approval of Bush International Policies

	2002	2003	2004	2005
Disapprove Very Much	14	28	38	35
Disapprove Somewhat	42	36	36	35
Approve Somewhat	34	24	19	22
Approve Very Much	4	6	4	4

Figures are the percentages. Question wording: "Do you approve or disapprove of the way the President of the United States George W. Bush is handling international policies?"

Source: GMF, "Transatlantic Trends 2005," question 17.

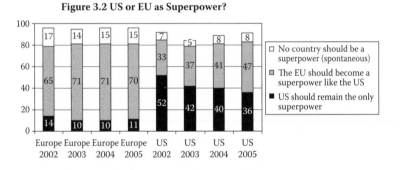

Figure 3.2 US or EU as Superpower?

Figure 3.2 Figures are percentages. Question wording: "In thinking about international affairs, which statement comes closer to your position about the United States and the European Union?" Source: GMF, "Transatlantic Trends 2005," question 3.

Europe, where the question is phrased more broadly, opposition to American hegemony continues, but American support for the idea rises. No country outside the United States expressed majority support for the U.S. as the only superpower and most favored the rise of another power. By contrast, nearly two-thirds of Americans supported United States hegemony (Figure 3.3).[10]

Aside from actual power, European attitudes have a mixed view on whether the U.S. should use its influence. Asked whether the U.S. should "exert strong leadership in world affairs," 41% of the Europe 7 saw it as desirable in a 2005 survey (a significant drop from the 2002 level of 64%). As shown in Table 3.4, the main shift in this group appears to have occurred between the mid-2002 and mid-2003 surveys. The most obvious explanation of this shift, given the timing, lies with perceptions of American leadership associated with the Iraq

Figure 3.3 US as Only Military Superpower?

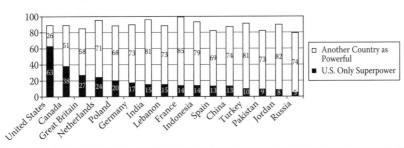

Figure 3.3 Figures are percentages. Question wording: "Right now, the U.S. has the most powerful military capability in the world. Would you like to see the U.S. remain the only military superpower or would it be better if [**Europe** (ask in all countries outside of Europe)/the **EU** (ask in Europe)], China or another country became as powerful as the U.S.?" The American question was slightly reworded asking whether "U.S. policies [should] try to keep it so America is the only military superpower or would it be better if Europe, China or another country became as powerful as the U.S.?" Source: PGAP, "American Character," question 13.

Table 3.4 Desirability of Strong American Leadership

	2002		2003		2004		2005	
	Europe 7	**US**	**Europe 7**	**US**	**Europe 7**	**US**	**Europe 7**	**US**
Very Desirable	17	41	8	—	7	—	8	44
Somewhat Desirable	47	42	37	—	32	—	33	40
Somewhat Undesirable	22	9	33	—	36	—	37	8
Very Undesirable	9	5	16	—	19	—	18	5

Figures are the percentages. Question wording: "How desirable is it that the United States exert strong leadership in world affairs?"

Source: GMF, "Transatlantic Trends 2005," question 2a.

War effort. By contrast, American attitudes remained constant and overwhelmingly favorable toward American leadership. In a different 2005 poll, a plurality of the respondents of 23 surveyed nations indicated that they thought the United States was having a mainly negative (47%) rather than mainly positive influence (38%) on world affairs. Americans overwhelmingly felt the U.S. influence was mainly positive (71%) rather than mainly negative (25%).[11]

Yet, while the American public seems to support the United States being *the* superpower, it has consistently preferred to act with others. Since the early

1990s, the American public has been asked "what kind of leadership role should the United States play in the world? Should it be the single world leader, or should it play a shared leadership role, or shouldn't it play any leadership role?" Despite dramatic changes in the world, the American public's response has been unvarying. In October 2005, 12% preferred the United States act as a single leader, 74% wanted the United States to play a shared leadership role, and 10% felt it had no leadership role to play. Additional surveys in 1993, 1995, 1997, early September 2001, mid-October 2001, 2003, and 2004 found little variation across time, with shifts in the low single-digits.[12] In this question, it appears that roughly three-quarters of the American public consistently prefers that the U.S. act jointly with other nations in foreign affairs. This evidence would seem to suggest that while the public prefers that the United States *be* the hegemon, it should act *with* other nations.

These attitudes have important implications for the war against terrorism. Since summer 2002, the level of support for the U.S.-led effort against terrorism has declined in almost all countries (Table 3.5). Declines of 20% were observed in many countries. Several countries now have populations in which only a thin majority supports the antiterrorist effort (Great Britain, France, Germany, Russia, India) after significant declines. Poland has experienced a large drop, but support still remains relatively high. Notable exceptions to this generalization are Canada, where strong support has turned into a plurality opposing the effort, and Spain, where a significant majority now opposes

Table 3.5 Support for U.S. Fight Against Terrorism

	Favor	Oppose	Don't Know/ Refused
United States 2005	76	18	6
March 2004	81	13	6
Summer 2002	89	8	3
Canada 2005	45	47	8
May 2003	68	26	6
Summer 2002	68	27	6
Europe			
Great Britain 2005	51	40	9
March 2004	63	30	7
May 2003	63	30	7
Summer 2002	69	23	8
France 2005	51	48	1
March 2004	50	47	3
May 2003	60	39	1
Summer 2002	75	12	3

--*continued*

Table 3.5 Support for U.S. Fight Against Terrorism (continued)

	Favor	Oppose	Don't Know/ Refused
Germany 2005	50	45	5
March 2004	55	43	2
May 2003	60	35	5
Summer 2002	70	25	5
Spain 2005	26	67	7
May 2003	63	32	5
Russia 2005	55	34	11
March 2004	73	20	7
May 2003	51	28	21
Summer 2002	73	16	11
Poland 2005	61	29	10
Summer 2002	81	11	9
Southwest Asia			
Turkey 2005	17	71	12
March 2004	37	56	7
May 2003	22	71	7
Summer 2002	30	58	12
Lebanon 2005	31	65	4
May 2003	30	67	3
Summer 2002	38	56	6
Jordan 2005	12	86	1
March 2004	12	78	10
May 2003	21	97	1
Summer 2002	3	85	2
Asia			
Pakistan 2005	22	52	26
March 2004	16	60	25
May 2003	16	74	10
Summer 2002	20	45	35
India 2005	52	41	7
Summer 2002	65	10	25
Indonesia 2005	50	42	8
May 2003	23	72	5
Summer 2002	31	64	5

Figures are percentages. Question wording: "Which of the following phrases comes closer to your view? I favor the U.S.-led efforts to fight terrorism, OR I oppose the U.S. led efforts to fight terrorism?"

Source: PGAP, "American Character," question 9.

the effort. Pakistan, Lebanon, and Jordan have consistently expressed opposition at varying levels. Indonesia provides an interesting exception, in that its opposition has now transformed into a bare majority supporting the war on terrorism. One possible explanation for the shift in Indonesia's sentiment is the American relief effort after the 2004 tsunami.[13] One poll indicates that 79% of Indonesians held a more favorable view of the United States based on American aid efforts.[14]

One of the likely reasons for declining support for the United States antiterrorism effort are doubts about U.S. motivations (which interact with the Iraq War as discussed below). As support for the antiterrorist effort dropped, individuals began to question the "real" motivations behind American efforts. When asked whether they thought "the U.S. led war on terrorism is a sincere effort to reduce international terrorism or don't you believe that," respondents expressed a high degree of skepticism.[15] Of the nine countries surveyed, majorities in only two expressed belief in the sincerity of American intentions (United States 67%, Great Britain 51%). In six, majorities doubted American sincerity (France 61%, Germany 65%, Turkey 64%, Pakistan 58%, Jordan 51%, and Morocco 66%). In Russia, a plurality doubted American sincerity (48% doubting with 35% believing in a sincere effort). Of those who doubted American sincerity, the most popular ulterior motive expressed in each country was "to control Mideast oil," except in Pakistan, where "to dominate the world" was the most popular alternative. Concerns about an American desire "to dominate the world" were cited by majorities in France, Turkey, Pakistan, Jordan, and Morocco and slightly under a majority in Germany (47%) and Russia (44%).

Still, despite concerns about the American power and behavior, European opinion favors the broad American goals even as they question American actions. For example, in a 2005 poll on terrorism[16] asking whether "international terrorism" was an "extremely important threat, an important threat, or not an important threat at all" in the "next 10 years," 94% of the Europe 7 group indicated it was an extremely important (59%) or important (35%) threat. This is roughly the same way that the American public viewed the issue: 96% indicated it is an extremely important (71%) or important (25%) threat. These figures are essentially unchanged since 2002, when 95% of the Europe 7 (64% extremely and 31% important) and 98% of Americans (91% extremely and 7% important) identified international terrorism as a threat to be dealt with.

In general, non-American attitudes could be characterized as opposing American hegemonic aspirations. These suspicions seem to be associated with doubts about American motivations. While Europeans and Americans share a common fear of international terrorism, the Europeans do not approve of how the United States is dealing with the problem. Although Americans support the United States' military supremacy, they want to behave cooperatively.

In sum, this attitude could best be characterized as favoring "multilateral or cooperative hegemony." These aspects will be explored further in the next two sections on selective multilateralism and stand-apart alliances.

The New Internationalism: Selective Multilateralism

Selective multilateralism refers to discriminating engagement with international institutions, such as the United Nations, and intentional flexibility in working with others to solve international problems. Americans express a general favorability toward multilateralism, but are willing to support unilateral action in specific circumstances. International opinion favors multilateralism. However, non-Americans are not willing to justify situational unilateralism, and have been increasingly fearful of American unilateralism.

American attitudes toward the most visible multilateral institution, the United Nations, have remained positive for a long time. However, since the 9/11 attacks, American attitudes toward the UN have eroded to a certain extent (Figure 3.4). The October 2005 poll found the lowest overall support for the United Nations since 1990 (48% favorable), a decrease in those holding very favorable views, and an increase in those holding very unfavorable views when compared to findings from the late 1990s. Clearly, American attitudes toward the UN have changed since the 9/11 attacks, though the cause is unclear. This drop in the United Nations' favorability rating within the United

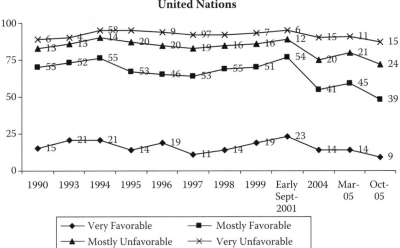

Figure 3.4 U.S. Public Favorability toward the United Nations

Figure 3.4 Question wording: "Is your overall opinion of the United Nations very favorable, mostly favorable, mostly unfavorable or very unfavorable?" Source: Pew/CFR, "America's Place," question 7.

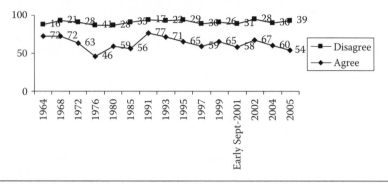

Figure 3.5 Cooperate Fully with United Nations?

Figure 3.5 Question wording: "Please tell me whether you agree or disagree with each of the following statements: "The United States should cooperate fully with the United Nations." Source: Pew/CFR, "America's Place," General Public Survey, question 26.

States has been associated with a moderate drop in American's willingness to work with it to the lowest level in nearly 30 years (Figure 3.5).

Americans have also expressed a greater willingness to act "selectively" regarding the United Nations than have Europeans. When asked in mid-2005 whether "when vital interests of our country are involved, it is justified to bypass the UN," 62% of Americans agreed (35% strongly and 27% somewhat) while only 34% disagreed (16% somewhat and 18% strongly).[17] These findings are essentially unchanged from when the question was asked in 2003 and 2004. This preference for selectivity was not shared by Europeans, whose attitudes might best be characterized as ambivalent. In 2005, 47% of the respondents in the Europe 7 group agreed (18% strongly and 29% somewhat) while 49% disagreed (32% somewhat and 17% strongly).

Part of the problem the United States faces (at least in terms of the favorability rating discussed in previous sections) is that the publics in other nations both doubt that the United States considers their views and they fear American unilateralism. A mid-2005 survey of a diverse set of nations reveals a stark contrast in assessments of U.S. foreign policy (Table 3.6).[18] While 67% of Americans thought that the U.S. considered the attitudes of others, most other publics did not agree. Interestingly, the publics of the United States' closest allies (Canada, Great Britain, France, Germany, Spain, Poland, Turkey) were as prone to express pessimism as others (Russia, Jordan, Pakistan, Lebanon).

Most interesting were the results from India, Indonesia, and China, where majorities believed that the United States thought about their interests. India's and Indonesia's results probably are attributable to specific policy actions taken by the United States in response to tsunami relief.[19] Since previous attitudes in India and Indonesia were more in line with other countries, the large

Table 3.6 Does the United States Take Into Account Your Nation's Interests?

	A Great Deal	A Fair Amount	Not Too Much	Not Much at All
United States 2005	28	39	23	7
March 2004	34	36	21	6
May 2003	28	45	19	6
Summer 2002	31	44	17	3
Canada 2005	4	15	55	25
May 2003	5	23	42	28
Summer 2002	7	18	47	26
Europe				
Great Britain 2005	8	24	44	22
March 2004	7	29	43	18
May 2003	7	37	39	16
Summer 2002	11	33	37	15
France 2005	2	16	51	31
March 2004	3	11	51	33
May 2003	1	13	44	41
Summer 2002	4	17	50	26
Germany 2005	3	35	44	15
March 2004	3	26	47	22
May 2003	3	29	42	24
Summer 2002	9	44	35	10
Spain 2005	7	12	29	47
May 2003	7	15	40	34
Russia 2005	3	18	47	26
March 2004	5	15	43	30
May 2003	7	15	38	33
Summer 2002	3	18	45	25
Poland 2005	2	11	46	28
Summer 2002	4	25	39	20
Southwest Asia				
Turkey 2005	3	11	27	50
March 2004	5	9	35	44
May 2003	3	6	28	58
Summer 2002	5	11	27	47
Lebanon 2005	13	22	27	30
May 2003	5	13	36	45
Summer 2002	4	16	27	50

-- continued

Table 3.6 Does the United States Take Into Account Your Nation's Interests? (continued)

	A Great Deal	A Fair Amount	Not Too Much	Not Much at All
Jordan 2005	5	12	41	41
March 2004	1	15	38	39
May 2003	3	16	44	36
Summer 2002	7	21	35	36
Asia				
Pakistan 2005	12	27	20	21
March 2004	3	15	16	32
May 2003	4	19	22	40
Summer 2002	5	18	9	27
India 2005	21	42	16	10
Summer 2002	13	25	17	14
Indonesia 2005	13	46	31	4
May 2003	5	20	53	17
Summer 2002	12	29	39	10
China 2005	12	41	28	10

Figures are percentages. Question wording: "In making international policy decisions, to what extent do you think the United States takes into account the interests of countries like (survey country)?" U.S. question was "takes into account the interests of other countries around the world."

Source: PGAP, "American Character," question 8.

amounts of American aid after the tsunami seem a likely cause of the dramatic shift in attitudes. Trend data are not available for China, but the economic ties between the two countries provide one possible explanation. Although each of these countries is also facing terrorist challenges of its own, this does not distinguish them from more skeptical publics with similar difficulties such as Pakistan and Russia.

A fear of American unilateralism (the "selective" part of selective multilateralism) reinforces these other concerns (Figure 3.6). A significant portion of the Europeans surveyed in July 2003 indicated that though "U.S. unilateralism" was a threat, it ranked as less important than other possible threats. In addition, Europeans saw unilateralism as the same level of threat as Americans did. When only those who labeled a problem as an "extremely important threat" are considered, differences between Europe and the U.S. on this question remain. However, it is also clear that only a minority in both countries considers unilateralism to be a major problem. Other problems, most notably international terrorism provided a much more urgent threat to both publics.

In the post-9/11 context, the majority of Americans appear willing to cooperate with the UN, but favor "selectivity" if push comes to shove. International

Figure 3.6 Possible International Threats

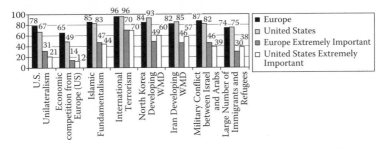

Figure 3.6 Question wording: "I am going to read you a list of possible international threats to Europe ("to the U.S." in the U.S.) in the next 10 years. Please tell me if you think each one on the list is an extremely important threat, an important threat, or not an important threat at all." The U.S. unilateralism was supplemented with "The tendency of the U.S. to 'go it alone,'" if necessary. Figures are percentages indicating the issue is an extremely or important threat. Source: GMF, "Transatlantic Trends 2003," question 7.

survey respondents seem to be concerned about American unilateralism, and fear that the United States does not consider their interests. In this regard, the Bush Doctrine does not appear to be in trouble with American public opinion. In the broader world, the difficulty emerges—especially regarding alliances—which will be discussed next.

Strategic, Stand-Apart Alliances

For this volume, stand-apart alliances refer to the willingness to build alliances anew to meet the challenges of specific problems. In other words, the U.S. might need to build alliances with different partners as it confronts varying challenges around the globe. Although polling on this issue is scarce, what evidence we have suggests that Americans prefer to act with their traditional partners, which seems to move against the Bush Doctrine's conditional alliance framework. Despite Europeans' preferences for multilateralism, their concerns with American hegemony and unilateralism are manifest in their desire not to act with the United States. In other words, while world opinion favors multilateralism, it increasingly prefers not to be multilateral with the United States.

No exact polling on situational alliances appears to exist. However, a series of polls asking the public whether the U.S. should act with alliance partners suggests that the American public does not favor conditional and situational alliances. Instead, they fairly uniformly prefer to act with the traditional alliance partners. Interestingly, the American public seems even more inclined to support working with partners than do some American allies (Table 3.7). Further, as Figure 3.7 indicates, Americans have long thought that their government should consider the views of their major allies in making foreign policy

Table 3.7. U.S. and Western Europe Partnership or More Independent Approach

	Remain as Close	**More Independent**
United States 2005	66	28
March 2004	55	36
May 2003	53	39
February 2003	62	29
Canada 2005	41	57
May 2003	54	43
Great Britain 2005	42	53
March 2004	40	56
May 2003	51	45
March 2003	40	48
April 2002	48	47
France 2005	26	73
March 2004	21	75
May 2003	23	76
March 2003	30	67
April 2002	33	60
Germany 2005	39	59
March 2004	36	63
May 2003	42	57
March 2003	46	52
April 2002	44	51
Spain 2005	43	50
May 2003	28	62
March 2003	24	60
Netherlands 2005	40	59

Figures are percentages. Question wording: "Do you think the partnership between the U.S. and Western Europe should remain as close as it has been or do you think that Western Europe should take a more independent approach to security and diplomatic affairs than it has in the past?" U.S. question "or do you think that the U.S. should take a more independent approach to security and diplomatic affairs than it has in the past?" Canadian question replaced "Western Europe" with "Canada."

Source: PGAP, "16 Nation Survey," questions 36, 37.

decisions. Figures 3.8 and 3.9 indicate that the public prefers not to have the United States "go its own way" in developing foreign policies and would prefer, even more so than its European allies, to act with its closest allies.

Polls on the UN and NATO also shed some light on this subject. In response to questions on whether UN or NATO approval are necessary before using military force, the American public equally preferred authorization from

**Figure 3.7 Should the U.S. Take Into Account Views
of Major Allies**

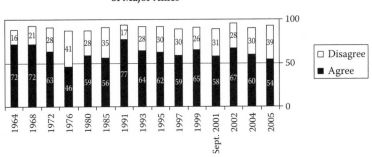

Figure 3.7 Question wording: "In deciding on its foreign policies, the U.S. should take into account the views of its major allies." Source: Pew/CFR, "America's Place," question 26b.

Figure 3.8 U.S. Go Its Own Way

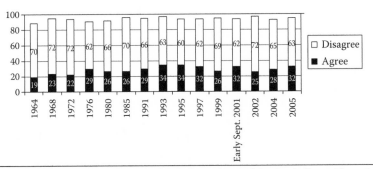

Figure 3.8 Question wording: "Since the U.S. is the most powerful nation in the world, we should go our own way in international matters, not worrying too much about whether other countries agree with us or not." Source: Pew/CFR, "America's Place," question 26c.

**Figure 3.9 Need to Act with Closest Allies on
National Security**

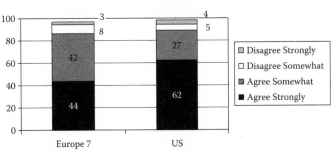
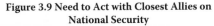

Figure 3.9 Question wording: "When our country acts on a national security issue, it is critical that we do so together with our closest allies." Source: GMF, "Transatlantic Trends 2005," question 22e.

Figure 3.10 Legitimacy and UN and NATO Approval

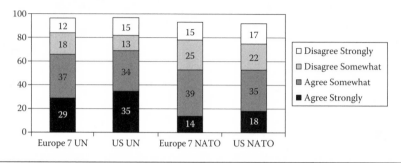

Figure 3.10 Question wording: UN—"The use of military force is more legitimate when the United Nations (UN) approves it." NATO—"NATO approval makes military action legitimate." Source: GMF, "Transatlantic Trends 2005," questions 9a, 14a

either body before acting and at levels comparable to those expressed by the Europe 7 (Figure 3.10).[20]

A series of 2004 questions on Iraq best approximated the stand-apart alliance dynamic in American and European attitudes. Three versions of the same question were asked: "If a situation like Iraq arose in the future, do you think it is essential to secure the approval of *the U.N./NATO/the main European allies* before using military force, or don't you think it is essential?"[21] The majorities of the Europe 7 publics and Americans supported the need for alliance partners. For the UN, 81% of the Europe 7 saw it as essential (14% not essential) and 58% of Americans saw it as essential (38% not essential). On NATO, 72% of the Europe 7 saw its approval as essential (20% not essential) while 58% of Americans saw it as essential (37% not essential). As for the main European allies, 79% of the European 7 saw it as essential (15% not essential) and 66% of Americans saw it as essential (29% not essential). Across all these questions, roughly three-quarters of Europeans thought that international approval was essential, while around two-thirds of Americans felt likewise.

The public's preference discussed here might explain why the Bush administration went to such great lengths to describe the Iraq War in multilateral terms.[22] Still, as discussed in the next section, the public was willing to support the Iraq War even though it was not (in the end) authorized by either the United Nations or NATO. As for the future, the polling does hint that sustained American action in the face of consistent opposition from the main European allies would likely be met with skepticism by a significant portion of the American public. At its base, the public prefers multilateral action and the support of traditional alliance partners (criteria the Bush administration would claim the Iraq War met).

Assertive Realism

The question of public support for assertive realism is the most interesting. Although American action on Iraq was met with opposition in Europe, Europeans seem as supportive as Americans of preemptive and preventive military action regarding weapons of mass destruction (WMDs) and terrorists. This result would seem to suggest that, despite European opposition to the Iraq War, future hostility to this type of action is not automatic.

In Principle

Americans support preemptive and preventive military action to deal with WMDs and terrorists. For a long time, Americans have consistently believed that "preventing the spread of weapons of mass destruction" should be a top priority as a "long range foreign policy" goal (Figure 3.11) with support rising after the 9/11 attacks. In October 2005, 75% of Americans listed it as a "top priority" and an additional 19% believed it should have "some priority."[23] The public also believes that preventive military action is sometimes justified, especially regarding WMDs (Figure 3.12), Although the difficulties with the Iraq War are associated with a slow drop in support for this view, the level of public opposition has never risen above 30%.

Three November 2003 questions directly address the question of preventive and preemptive action.[24] The first question focuses on WMDs as a motivation for action. When asked "when, as a rule, countries have the right to overthrow the government of another country," 31% of the public supported the preventive war option ("countries have the right to overthrow another government if they have strong evidence that the other country is acquiring weapons of mass destruction that could be used to attack them at some point in the future"), 41% supported the preemptive war option ("countries have the right to over-

Figure 3.11 Priority of Preventing Spread of Weapons of Mass Destruction

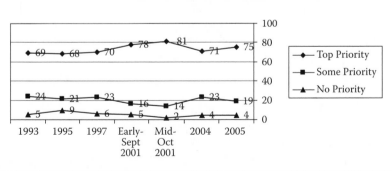

Figure 3.11 Question wording: "As I read a list of possible long-range foreign policy goals which the United States might have, tell me how much priority you think each should be given. Preventing the spread of weapons of mass destruction." Source: Pew/CFR, "America's Place," question 15F2a.

Figure 3.12 Preventive Military Action Justified

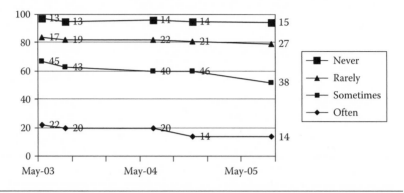

Figure 3.12 Question wording: "Do you think that using military force against countries that may seriously threaten our country, but have not attacked us, can often be justified, sometimes be justified, rarely be justified, or never be justified?" Source: Pew/CFR, "America's Place," question 35F1.

throw another government only if they have strong evidence that they are in imminent danger of being attacked with weapons of mass destruction by the other country"), 9% supported an overthrow after a direct attack, and 15% indicated that an overthrow was never allowed though an attack could be repulsed. This finding suggests that nearly three-quarters of the public supports military action consistent with assertive realism (on the differences preemption and prevention, see J. Renshon, Chapter 8).

A second question focused on the United Nations. When the UN is inserted into the question, responses shift slightly as the public prefers multilateral approval over unilateral action to deal with these threats. When asked, "when countries have evidence that another government is acquiring weapons of mass destruction that could be used to attack them at some point in the future," 39% supported "the right to overthrow the other government even if they do not have UN approval" and 48% only supported "the right to overthrow the other government if they first present their evidence to the UN and the UN determines that such an action is necessary" (8% rejected the right altogether).

The third question asked about the right to overthrow the other government when a nation has "evidence that it is providing substantial support to a terrorist group:" 23% supported action "whenever they deem it necessary, even without UN approval," 44% wanted UN approval "as a general rule" but allowed that "UN approval may not be necessary" if the nation had been attacked, 23% required UN approval, and 6% rejected action altogether.

These data suggest several conclusions. First, roughly 72% of the public supports preventive or preemptive action. Second, 87% of Americans supported the right to overthrow a government acquiring WMDs, though a significant portion wanted UN approval. Third, 90% supported the overthrow of a government that supported terrorism though, again, a significant portion wished to have UN approval. While the American public supports assertive realism when it comes to WMDs and terrorism, a significant portion of the public would prefer, or even require, that UN approval occur first. As with previous questions, the American public's fundamental multilateralist inclination comes through.

Interestingly, European attitudes echo, though to a lesser degree, the American public's inclinations for preventive action. This might come as a surprise given the differences between Americans and Europeans on the Iraq War. As I will discuss below, the differences between Americans and Europeans on Iraq reflect varying assessments of the Iraqi situation rather than the validity of assertive realism as a policy. A 2004 survey found substantial percentages of Europeans supporting preventive action regarding WMD and preemptive action against terrorists.[25] "To prevent the spread of nuclear weapons," 70% of the Europe 7 group approved of the use of their nation's military forces while only 27% disapproved. This figure is only somewhat lower than the survey's 80% of Americans who approved (16% disapproved). "To prevent an imminent terrorist attack," 83% of the Europe 7 publics approved of the use of military forces while 14% disapproved. Americans supported the notion even more strongly, with 92% approving (5% disapproving). To contextualize these figures, they are very similar to the level of public approval of using their nation's military forces "to defend a NATO ally that has been attacked," approved by 76% of respondents from the Europe 7 (19% disapproved) and 87% of Americans (9% disapproved). In other words, Europeans and Americans are almost as willing to support preventive military action against the spread of WMDs and preemptive military action against terrorists as they are to support long-standing treaty commitments to assist an ally that has actually been attacked. In short, European publics do not seem to be opposed to assertive realism in principle.

Iraq and Assertive Realism

What, then, is to be made of the differences between the American and European publics on Iraq? The Bush administration clearly made preemptive and preventive claims about both terrorism and WMDs in relation to Iraq (see Levy, Chapter 7). The main disjuncture between Americans and Europeans emerges because of differing judgments about whether the Iraq War made the world safer and the terrorist threat lower. In 2003, Americans thought it did (and supported the war). They have since begun to question this assessment (and begun to question the war's value). In 2003, Europeans doubted the war's value and opposed it (and still do). The manner in which the United States went to war reinforced underlying European concerns regarding American hegemony and unilateralism. These in turn fed into more negative general assessments about the United States, as discussed earlier.

The majority of Americans supported the Iraq War right before the invasion. In a mid-March 2003 survey, 59% of Americans favored taking military action "to end Saddam Hussein's rule" while 30% opposed it.[26] After the invasion in December 2003, 64% thought the United States did the right thing in taking military action against Iraq" while only 28% thought the U.S. should "have stayed out." With the subsequent difficulties in Iraq, this figure steadily eroded to the point where in May 2006, a minority (39%) thought it was the "right thing" and a majority (56%) thought the nation should have "stayed out."[27]

The basis for the initial American support of the war derived from public assessments regarding Iraqi WMDs. In June 2002, 86% of Americans thought "Iraq developing weapons of mass destruction" was a "critical threat" to "the vital interest of the United States in the next 10 years."[28] After the war, when no WMDs had been found and the occupation costs mounted, American assessments shifted. Although 52% in April 2003 thought the war would leave the United States "in a stronger position in the world" (and only 12% thought the U.S. would be weaker), that figure dropped to 25% by June 2005 (with 39% believing the U.S. had been left in a weaker position).[29] At the same time, while 52% thought the war "had contributed to the long-term security of the United States," 46% thought it had not.[30] Compounding this problem, 59% thought it had "caused long-term damage to US relations with countries that opposed the war, such as France and Germany" (40% thought it had not); 67% believed it had "damaged the United States' image in the rest of the world" (33% thought it had not); 51% believed it "contributed to long-term peace and stability in the Mideast" (40% said it had not); and 49% thought it had encouraged democracy in other Arab nations" (48% thought it had not).[31]

In an October 2005 poll, the public's attitude on the Iraq War's effect on the war on terrorism was mixed. An equal number (44%) thought it had "helped" and "hurt" the effort (this figure is down from May 2003, where 65% said it had helped and only 22% thought it had hurt). A large portion (71%) thought the Iraq War was a "major reason" "why people around the world are unhappy with the U.S."[32]

Non-American attitudes on the war were similar to American attitudes in some ways and different in others. In mid-2002, only 57% of Europeans (compared to 86% of Americans) believed it "extremely important" to prevent "Iraq developing weapons of mass destruction."[33] European and American attitudes about the conditions under which war would be acceptable were rather similar. When asked about a U.S. invasion to "overthrow the government of Saddam Hussein," a similar percentage of Europeans and Americans thought that "the U.S. should only invade Iraq with U.N. approval and the support of its allies" (60% Europe, 65% U.S.). Differences emerged over nonintervention ("U.S. should not invade Iraq": 26% Europe, 13% U.S.), and American unilateralism ("the U.S. should invade Iraq even if they have to do it alone": 10% Europe, 20% U.S.).

None of the publics whose militaries acted with the U.S. favored "joining the U.S. and other allies in military action in Iraq to end Saddam Hussein's rule" at the time of the war (in favor: Great Britain 39%, Italy 17%, Spain 13%, Poland 21%). This contrasts with 59% of Americans who favored American action. Not surprisingly, the publics of the countries that stayed out of the war also did not favor "the U.S. and other allies taking military action in Iraq to end Saddam Hussein's rule" (in favor: France 20%, Germany 27%, Russia 10%, Turkey 12%).[34] Retrospectively, by June 2005, Europeans thought their governments had made the wrong decision "to use military force against Iraq" if they had done so (wrong decision: Great Britain 53%, Spain 69%, Poland 67%) and the right decision if they had not used military force (right decision: Canada 80%, France 92%, Germany 87%, Russia 88%, Turkey 81%).[35]

In addition to the concerns that many of these publics no doubt had about the manner in which the U.S. went to war (unilateral and hegemonic), non-Americans believed that the Iraq War increased the threat of terrorism and made the world a more dangerous place. In mid-2004, 72% of the Europe 7 group (compared with 49% of Americans) thought "the military action in Iraq" had "increased the threat of terrorism around the world," while only 5% (compared with 26% of Americans) thought it had "decreased the threat of terrorism" (20% of the Europe 7 and the United States thought it had "no effect").[36] A broader survey of world opinion in June 2005 found that only in the United States and India did a plurality believe the Iraq War made the world safer.[37] In the rest, pluralities or majorities thought the war had made the world more dangerous (Figure 3.13).

Despite this opposition to the Iraq War, this examination suggests that there might be more support for assertive realism than commonly assumed. Americans and Europeans appear to support the conceptual foundations of

Figure 3.13 Iraq War Makes World Safer or More Dangerous

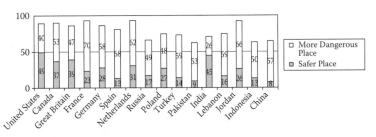

Figure 3.13 Question wording: "Overall, do you think the war with Iraq that removed Saddam Hussein from power made the world a safer place or a more dangerous place?" Source: PGAP, "American Character," question 33.

assertive realism, which implies a potentially broad foundation on which to build support. As the survey data suggest, European opposition to the Iraq War seems to stem from differing substantive conclusions about the situation in Iraq, rather than from an underlying opposition to preventive action per se. Europeans believed that Iraq was not an instance that required the application of preventive action. While Europeans shared American goals, they felt that the United States had misdiagnosed the nature and extent of the Iraq problem. While Americans saw Iraqi WMDs as an important threat and thought the removal of Hussein would benefit American security, Europeans saw the threat as less severe and did not see much advantage to the military action. Retrospectively, both Americans and (to a greater extent) non-Americans saw the Iraq War in a negative light in relation to the war on terror and broader security questions.

Given the underlying support for American goals even after the Iraq War, the declines in support for the war on terror and favorability of the United States could be only temporary downturns associated with the Iraq War, which will fade with time. It is too soon to tell. An American foreign policy that is perceived as less hegemonic and more multilateral could mitigate some of these concerns. Whether it is possible for this substantive shift in policy to occur and have it remain the "Bush Doctrine," as defined in this volume, will be discussed in the concluding section.

Democratic Transformation

The Iraq War provides an example of an attempt at democratic transformation (see Zonis, Chapter 9). Unlike other aspects of the Doctrine, the American public views this goal skeptically, questions its conceptual foundations, and supports only the most minimal of policies to spread democracy. Ironically, this policy goal actually receives much more support from European publics.

The American public holds clear doubts about the value of spreading democracy in the world. A September 2005 poll found that while Americans support the basic "civics course" viewpoint that "democracy is the best form of government" (78% agree and 15% disagree), they have mixed attitudes on whether democracy will find fertile ground in all locales (50% agreed that "democracy is the best form of government for all countries," while 43% thought that "for some countries, democracy is not the best form of government").[38]

They also doubt that the spread of democracy will change international politics. For example, only 26% thought that "when there are more democracies the world is a safer place" while 68% believed that "democracy may make life better within a country, but it does not make the world a safer place." They also question the democratic peace thesis espoused by both Presidents Bill Clinton and Bush. While 46% thought that democracies are "less likely to go to war with each other than are other types of government," the slightly higher figure of 49% felt that democracies are "just as likely to go to war with each other as are other types of government."[39]

These doubts are reflected in the scant support for making democratic transformation a foreign policy goal, wedded with the belief that any transformational efforts are unlikely to have much of an effect. Only 27% of Americans saw "helping to bring a democratic form of government to other nations" as a "very important foreign policy goal" while an additional 49% saw it as a "somewhat important foreign policy goal" (19% thought it was "not important"). The majority of the public expressed a realist sentiment on the practicalities of U.S. policy, rather than a Wilsonian view. Only 38% indicated that "as a rule US foreign policy should encourage countries to be democratic." A majority, 54%, thought that "as a rule US foreign policy should pursue US interests, which sometimes means promoting democracy and sometimes means supporting non-democratic governments."[40]

Consistent with these attitudes, the public takes a minimalist view on the actions to pursue democratic transformation. Given a range of alternatives, majorities (those favoring an action "strongly" or "somewhat") existed only for "helping a government that is having free elections for the first time by giving it aid and technical assistance" (74%: 23% strongly; 51% somewhat), "sending monitors to certify that elections are conducted fairly and honestly" (66%: 24% strongly; 42% somewhat), and "giving more developmental aid to a government that is becoming more democratic" (66%: 15% strongly; 51% somewhat). Given the large percentages of respondents only "somewhat" in favor of these actions, these represent only lukewarm majorities. Majority support did not exist for stronger actions. A plurality opposed "withholding developmental aid from a government that is not democratic or is not moving toward becoming more democratic" (44% favor [12% strongly and 32% somewhat], while 46% opposed it [37% somewhat and 9% strongly]). Majorities opposed "supporting dissidents in [a] non-democratic country" (31% favor [4% strongly and 27% somewhat], while 56% opposed it [39% somewhat and 17% strongly]) and "using military force to overthrow a dictator" (35% favor [8% strongly and 27% somewhat], while 55% opposed [22% strongly and 33% somewhat]).[41]

The majority of Americans also prefer to pursue this foreign policy in a multilateral manner. While only 25% thought "it is better for the US to promote democracy by" "acting on its own because the US can act more decisively and effectively," 68% favored "working through the UN because such efforts will be seen as more legitimate."[42]

In the end, the public doubts that much will come of these efforts. Of eight possible policy mechanisms posited, only two were thought by a majority to do more good than harm. Aid and technical assistance with holding a country's first elections (70%) and educating "students, journalists and political leaders" in the U.S. about democracy (66%) were the only two with a positive net assessment (only 27% on aid and 17% on education said that it did "a lot more good than harm"). The public held mixed attitudes about withholding development aid from countries that are not democratizing (49% more harm to 36% more good), using diplomatic pressure against countries to encourage them to democratize (42% more harm and 44% more good), employing economic sanctions (46% more harm and 40% more good), supporting dissidents in nondemocratic countries (48% more harm and 36% more good), threatening military intervention (63% more harm to 21% more good), and "using military force to overthrow a dictator" (58% more harm to 27% more good).[43]

Ironically, Europeans polled on the question of democratization seem more inclined to support it as a goal and favor foreign policies to help it. To the extent that the Bush Doctrine is attempting to spur democratization, it might actually find broader support for its objectives in Europe than at home.

When asked whether it should "be the role of the European Union [United States in the U.S.] to help establish democracy in other countries," an overwhelming majority in the Europe 7 countries (72%) supported this role (24% opposed); Americans gave 51% support for the idea and 42% opposed.[44] Europeans also expressed strong support for many measures to foster democracy (Figure 3.14). Except for the strongest measures of economic sanctions and military action, Europeans supported democracy efforts as much as, *if not more than*, Americans.

These results are far from definitive. However, they do suggest that democratic transformation itself as a policy objective, and measures to foster it, are widely supported in Europe. The wrinkle in the survey of Europeans, of course, is that the question asked what the "European Union" should do.

Figure 3.14 Action to Help Democracy

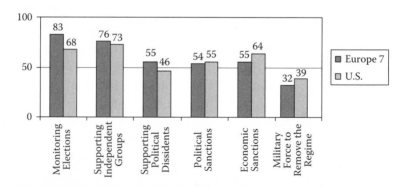

Figure 3.14 Question wording: "Let's imagine an authoritarian regime in which there is no political or religious freedom. To help democracy, would you support the following actions by the [European Union/US]?" Full response options are "monitoring elections in new democracies," "supporting independent groups such as trade unions, human rights associations and religious groups," "supporting political dissidents," "imposing political sanctions," "imposing economic sanctions," and "sending military forces to remove authoritarian regimes." Source: GMF, "Transatlantic Trends 2005," questions 16a–f.

Approaches led by the United States are likely to be met with the same skepticism previously discussed regarding hegemony and unilateralism.

The Survey Process

The potential for bias in surveys resulting from question wording, question order, sampling technique, and interview procedures are well known in the academic literature. The challenges for effective survey design and implementation multiply when undertaking international polls where the political, cultural, and technological environment varies widely.[45] While a full discussion of these issues lies beyond the scope of this chapter, a few issues bear recognition when considering the findings discussed here. First, nonresponse rates ("don't knows" and refusals) vary widely on some questions and across countries. For example, for the question considered in Table 3.3 on support for U.S. antiterrorism efforts, the more typical nonresponse rate was the 6% level found in the U.S. Some countries reached the double-digits such as Russia (11%), Turkey (12%), and Poland (10%), but over one-quarter of Pakistanis (26%) did not give an opinion. No doubt, the controversial nature of these issues in certain political contexts makes some individuals hesitant to respond. To account for this situation, all the figures given in this chapter are presented as a portion of the full sample including the nonrespondents.

Second, the standard sampling technique is now telephone interviewing. However, when conducting surveys outside of developed countries, surveyors have been forced to employ face-to-face questioning, which can add an additional complication. In addition, the logistics of survey research can also lead to an oversampling of urban populations in developing countries. For example, the June 2005 multination Pew Global Attitudes Project survey focused heavily on urban respondents in China, Pakistan, and India. More developed countries were surveyed by telephone (U.S., France, etc.), while developing countries (India, Poland, etc.) were surveyed by face-to-face interviews.

Third, the need to translate surveys into a variety of languages creates an additional potential for bias. For example, the June 2005 Pew survey was conducted in roughly 17 languages and the *Transatlantic Trends 2005* survey was conducted in 10 languages. Fourth, even when the same language is used, changes to question wording might be necessary to account for context. For example, in the question used in Figure 3.3 regarding the U.S. as a military superpower, non-American respondents were asked whether they would "*like to see* the U.S. *remain* the only military superpower or would it be better if [Europe (ask in all countries outside of Europe) /the EU (ask in Europe)] China or another country became as powerful as the U.S." Americans were asked whether "U.S. *policies* [should] *try to keep it* so America is the only military superpower or would it be better if Europe, China or another country became as powerful as the U.S." The non-American question focuses on the situation while the American question focuses on policies to affect the situation. The wide differences between the positive American response and the negative non-American responses might be partly attributed to wording (though it is not clear how much and in what direction attitudes might converge if the same question were asked).

Finally, even questions that might seem to ask the same question might vary subtly in a manner that complicates the comparability of results. For example, the questions in Figure 3.10 on the effect of UN and NATO approval on the legitimacy of the use of force might be interpreted as the Europe 7 and U.S. publics seeing the UN as more important in terms of legitimacy. However, a close reading of the question cautions against this interpretation. The UN question asks whether approval makes action "more legitimate," which implies movement along a continuum. On the other hand, the NATO question asks whether approval "makes military action legitimate" which implies a binary response (legitimate or not legitimate). For this reason, the NATO question could be viewed as granting stronger legitimacy to an action in the eyes of those polled because the respondents who agreed said that the action *was* legitimate with NATO approval. For the UN question, action was just *more* legitimate.

For these reasons, no single poll or question should be read as having pinpointed public opinion on a specific issue. Instead, the analyses, as I have sought to do in this chapter, should seek to discern trends across questions, context, and time. If patterns emerge over time and place, there is good reason to believe that the trends are more real than apparent. As for the surveys themselves, the best practices are to provide transparency in terms of the survey design and method (as have each of the surveys referenced in this chapter).

Looking Forward

Considering these broad trends, the Bush Doctrine would seem to have more American support than opposition, while international attitudes appear mixed. First, on hegemony, the American public favors United States supremacy but would prefer that the United States act in a multilateral manner. International opinion opposes the United States' military supremacy, is suspicious of American motives, and would prefer that American power be balanced by others. Second, Americans, in a somewhat contradictory sense, seem to support selective multilateralism while at the same time favoring a more expansive multilateralism. In other words, they support the current Bush policy while remaining receptive to greater multilateralism. Non-American attitudes perceive selective multilateralism as unilateralism. Even more than Americans, Europeans favor multilateral action to address international problems. The Bush Doctrine's perceived unilateralism has further undermined the willingness of others to want to act *with* the United States. Third, regarding stand-apart alliances, the American public prefers that the United States act with its traditional allies in international affairs. This suggests that sustained efforts in the face of opposition from traditional allies and international organizations are likely to be met with increasing public skepticism. Likewise, European attitudes appear strongly against stand-apart alliances. Fourth, the American public supports assertive realism's goals and means in foreign policy. European attitudes seem to support many of its underlying goals, but remain dubious of the policy's means (especially in its application to Iraq), which are seen as unilateralist. Finally, the American public seems fairly dubious of most aspects of democratic transformation while European attitudes seem more in favor it.

In sum, these attitudes would seem to suggest a fairly supportive American public for most aspects of the Doctrine. More so than commonly realized, while international opinion opposes the Bush administration's application of the Doctrine to Iraq in particular, it agrees with many of its core motivations.

A Cold War Analogy?

What does this array of attitudes imply for the Bush Doctrine's long-term prospects (see also S. Renshon, Chapter 12)? Before turning to this question directly, the experience the United States had with American and world support in the early Cold War regarding the strategy of containment is worth considering. Although the polling data in the late 1940s and early 1950s are not nearly as extensive as in the present day, enough information is available to draw some speculative conclusions. While the containment policy is often viewed favorably in the sense that the United States "won the Cold War," it is often forgotten that, at first, the strategy was highly controversial both domestically and internationally. While it is too soon to tell whether the Bush Doctrine will achieve the same long-term support or success, this historical analogy suggests that the early controversies about the Bush Doctrine do not doom it to failure.

Clear parallels exist between the current war on terrorism and the Bush Doctrine on the one hand and Cold War anticommunism and containment on the other. The goal of the war on terror mirrors the anticommunist goal of American Cold War policy. As a policy means, in both rhetoric and substance, the Bush administration modeled its Doctrine on the Truman Doctrine.[46] What does the early Cold War experience reveal regarding public opinion?

As a foreign policy goal, anticommunism, like the war on terror, was met with overwhelming domestic support and international skepticism. In the United States, large majorities indicated that it was "very important" "for the United States to try to stop the spread of communism in the world." In January 1950, 77% thought it "very important," while only 10% saw it as "only fairly important" and 5% thought it "not important at all." After the United States was well into the (by then-divisive) Korean War, the figure rose to 82% believing anticommunism was "very important" and only 7% "only fairly important," and 4% "not important at all."[47]

No comparable polling exists for international opinion, but polls of both British and French opinion in the early days of the containment policy suggest that international opinion was as equally divided then about the purposes of containment as it is today over the war on terror. In September 1947, French public opinion saw a potential hegemon on the rise—they just were not certain which one. One poll found that 79% of the French believed that there was "one nation which seeks to dominate the world," while 6% thought there was not. Those who saw a rising hegemon were almost equally divided between whether it was the Soviet Union (49%) or the United States (42%). The British were a little more certain by mid-1948. Asked if "any nation seeks to dominate the world," 77% thought there was and 11% thought not. Of those who said yes, 70% believed the Soviet Union was seeking hegemony, while only 14% indicated the United States.[48]

Beyond the goals of American policy, polling on the Truman Doctrine's means found attitudes similar to those of today. The majority of Americans supported the idea, but a significant minority had its doubts. International opinion was decidedly divided. In 1947, the American public supported the notion of aid to Greece, which it favored by a margin of 56% to 32%. Aid to Turkey was slightly more divisive, with 49% favoring aid and 36% opposed. The public also remained somewhat divided over doing more than aid. The public opposed "sending military advisers to train the Greek army" by a ratio of 54% to 37%. And when queried about containment more generally, the public had more mixed attitudes. Asked in March 1947, "if Communists in foreign countries try to seize control of their governments by force, do you think it should or should not be our general policy to help those governments put down such revolts?" only 47% thought it should be the U.S. policy while 37% thought it should not.[49]

Containment itself took nearly a full decade before it was fully embraced by both parties in the American political system. In its early days, critics assailed containment's focus, undefined costs and duration, and reactive nature.[50] The aid program to Greece and Turkey, though passed by Congress, received far from universal support. The Senate passed the aid package 67 to 23, and the House passed it 287 to 107.

After the Korean War engaged the United States, it became the main exhibit in the case against containment rather than, as Korea is widely thought of today, as an example of success given the long-term development of South Korea as a capitalist democracy. Two years after the Korean War began, an assessment of Korea and "the world balance sheet" in the *New York Times* painted a pessimistic picture. The report observed, "we cannot evacuate Korea, or all the suffering has gone for naught, and communism would have won its greatest victory. We cannot attack the enemy's heavily defended lines in Korea without (a) very heavy casualties and (b) more troops…. We are, in other words, fighting a limited war for a compromise peace, and the prospects are for continued stalemate in Korea until time and global events alter the present situation." The parallels between Korea and communism on the one side and Iraq and terrorism on the other are not hard to recognize. Just to illustrate, a little over two years after the start of the Iraq War, a June 2005 *New York Times* assessment of the Iraq situation painted a eerily similar picture as the one of Korea 53 years earlier: "The questions now are how many more times over how many years [Bush] might have to deliver the same message of patience and resolve [regarding Iraq]—and whether the American public confronted with a mounting death toll, an open-ended military commitment, lack of support from allies and a growing price tag, will accept it."[51]

As with Iraq in 2004 (and potentially in 2008), Korea provided a central linchpin in the presidential challenger's 1952 electoral strategy. Republican presidential candidate Dwight D. Eisenhower made Truman's handling of Korea (along with corruption and communism) one of his central indictments of the Democratic administration. As for containment, Republican vice presidential candidate Richard Nixon would charge Democratic presidential candidate Adlai Stevenson as having graduated from Truman Secretary of State Dean Acheson's "Cowardly College of Communist Containment."[52] Eisenhower won the 1952 election in large part because of these criticisms of Truman's foreign policy and his own pledge to "go to Korea."[53]

Containment only became a truly bipartisan policy with the adoption of the New Look in 1954 by President Eisenhower, who modified Truman's version of containment by relying more on the threat of nuclear weapons and more flexibility in the site of containment's application.[54] While Truman pledged to use American conventional forces at the site of a communist incursion, Eisenhower married a pledge to retaliate massively (which implied nuclear weapons) at places and times of his choosing with an emphasis on building up the conventional forces of the threatened nations to resist direct military assaults. The result, in Eisenhower's view, was greater flexibility, lower costs, a stronger deterrent, and better containment of the Soviet Union. By effectively rejecting the option of rolling back communism, the New Look, in promising to achieve Truman's policy aim of deterring communist expansion at a lesser cost, effectively solidified the goal of containing communism as an accepted bipartisan foreign policy.[55] It is this bipartisan consensus that is most prominent in our recollection, rather than the intense policy discord that ruled the early days of containment.

Internationally, the early Truman Doctrine was met with decidedly mixed attitudes. French opinion was sharply divided. A May 1947 poll found that a slight plurality of those who had heard of the Truman Doctrine speech approved of it. Expressed as a percentage of the total sample (76% had heard of the speech and 24% had not), 29% approved of the speech while 26% disapproved of it (21% expressed no opinion). Far from a ringing endorsement. British opinion was equally divided on U.S. policy more generally. Asked in

February 1951 about whether they approved of the "role the United States is now playing in World Affairs," 40% approved while nearly an equal number, 35%, disapproved (25% expressed no opinion). Yet, by 1952, British opinion was of the view that Great Britain and the United States should work together in international affairs. Asked about the relationship that Great Britain should have with the United States, 53% said they should "act together on most things, but Britain should remain independent," 23% indicated they were "natural allies and should always stick together," and 15% thought "relations should be on the same footing as with other countries."[56] To the extent that this information points in any direction, it suggests that the United States' early Cold War policy was not universally lauded by Europe.

Yet, in time, the policy of containing the Soviet Union came to be embraced not only by the governments of Western Europe, but West European publics as well. To be sure, disagreements over specific policies emerged from time to time, but the fundamental support of containment, deterrence, and NATO to implement them continued throughout the Cold War. A full examination of this historical experience is beyond the scope of this chapter. But, in perhaps the most comprehensive study of European attitudes toward national security issues during the Cold War, Richard Eichenberg concluded that European public attitudes in the 1980s reflected a "very strong" "attachment to the NATO Alliance," which was greater than even in the early period of the 1950s. Supportive Western European public opinion toward deterring the Soviet Union and the requisite defense spending also characterized attitudes throughout the Cold War. Despite sharp disagreements on specific policies (such as the deployment of intermediate range nuclear missiles in Europe and a "no first use" pledge regarding nuclear weapons), West European publics remained steadfastly supportive of deterring Soviet aggression in Europe at levels that increased over time.[57] In other words, initial concerns about American strategic policy and sharp disagreements over specific actions did not doom containment to long-term failure.

The Future of the Bush Doctrine in Public Opinion

These experiences during the early Cold War period suggest that it is simply too soon to tell whether the divisions within American public opinion and in the international community doom the Bush Doctrine to failure. Domestically, public opinion then and now seems very similar: majorities supported both the Truman and Bush Doctrines. Yet, significant minorities expressed doubts about both. Internationally, the available opinion data suggest that, even in France which had recently been liberated by American troops and was to receive large amounts of American aid, doubts about American containment policy existed in the early phase.

Domestically, the Bush Doctrine's real test is likely to occur after the transition to a new president following the 2008 presidential elections. American opinion actually favors the fundamental attributes of the Bush Doctrine (minus democratic transformation) to a greater extent today than it did the containment doctrine at a comparable point in time. The public largely agreed with the war on terrorism in the days after the 9/11 attacks, and its support for this broader effort shows no sign of abating. In addition, there is no necessary reason to believe that the Iraq War will undermine broader public support for the war on terror, just as the Korean War did not, in the long term, undermine support for the containment doctrine.

Public support for American hegemony, selective multilateralism, and assertive realism suggests that there is no reason to believe that the next administration would be *compelled* to alter the Bush Doctrine. The 2008 presidential candidates could embrace many of the fundamental notions of the Bush Doctrine and win the office. There is even nothing in American attitudes that would necessitate presidential candidates in the next election to run *away* from the Bush Doctrine. At the same time, there is nothing to indicate that the successful presidential candidate (of either party) would need to adopt the Bush Doctrine as his or her standard to win the 2008 presidential campaign. Just as Eisenhower eventually embraced the fundamental notion of containment but tailored it in a way that he felt better served American interests, the next president has the freedom to embrace the Bush Doctrine or reframe it and maintain domestic support.

Even more, it is equally clear that the Bush Doctrine is not the *only* approach to the war on terror that the public will support making outright rejection of the Doctrine a viable possibility. Public opinion clearly remains skeptical regarding efforts at democratic transformation and the seemingly unilateralist tone of the Bush policy. Since the public wants the United States to act as a multilateral hegemon, it would clearly support a more multilateralist means to the same end as the Bush Doctrine. This preference suggests that a subsequent administration could take the fundamentals of the Bush Doctrine that the public fully embraces (hegemony, assertive realism) and rectify the aspects that the public is slightly more troubled by (the "selective" aspects of the multilateral components) in forming an equally successful grand strategy that does not embrace all the aspects of the Bush Doctrine. For example, a modification of former Secretary of State Madeleine Albright's "assertive multilateralism," which embraced American hegemony and leadership and combined it with assertive realism, greater multilateral efforts through international institutions, and work through traditional alliances, would receive support from the American public.

In short, while the war on terrorism seems firmly embedded in the American political culture (much as anticommunism had become by 1952), the Bush Doctrine clearly has not, at this point, become what containment had achieved by the mid-1950s: the bipartisan strategy to shape American foreign policy. Public attitudes are such that the Bush Doctrine could become like containment if the next administration adopts the policy (especially in the unlikely, though not impossible, circumstance that a Democratic president were to do so). By the mid-1960s, containment had clearly become such a policy, as the electorate decisively rejected presidential candidates who either advocated aggressive rollback of communism (as did Republican Barry Goldwater in 1964) or disengaging from the international obligations of containment (as did Democrat George McGovern in 1972). In other words, domestic public opinion seems convinced by most aspects of the Bush Doctrine and will likely continue to support it though not to the exclusion of other alternatives.

The same cannot be said for international attitudes. While current suspicions of American motives were present at the beginning of the Cold War, the evidence presented here suggests that the Bush Doctrine's continued application will likely enhance these suspicions because they create fears of American unilateralism and hegemony. This aspect makes the Bush Doctrine different than containment. Although the Bush Doctrine has multilateral aspects, containment could be viewed as a fundamentally multilateral strategy because its central foreign policy tenet relied on alliances with states confronting a communist threat. Although disagreements emerged within the alliance framework over specific applications of containment (such as Vietnam), these did not undermine the core perception of containment as a multilateral policy. While some underlying support exists for American goals regarding terrorism and WMDs, the means of the Bush Doctrine heighten not only opposition to American foreign policies but undermine support for the United States more generally. Currently, Iraq and the manner in which the United States went to war are driving much of the anti-Americanism in international public opinion. Iraq reinforced underlying concerns that international opinion held about American hegemony, selective multilateralism, and stand-apart alliances. To the extent that the Bush Doctrine is perceived as embracing these notions, international opinion will continue to react negatively to American foreign policy.

Since international opinion seems to hold Bush, rather than "America" responsible, it is not clear that the growing opposition to the United States' war on terrorism will continue. The specific goals of American policy (such as democratic transformation) and some of its means (assertive realism to deal with terrorism and WMDs) are actually as much, if not more, supported in European opinion than in the United States. The bad news is that American public relations efforts, which assume that other publics oppose the U.S. because of a lack of understanding of American goals and motives, are unlikely to have much influence on international attitudes because international opinion correctly perceives the Bush Doctrine's substance (it just disagrees with it). The good news is that international opinion seems fairly reactive to the substance of American policy. The rapid decline in support for the United States associated with the Iraq War and rapid increases in support for the United

States after specific aid policies (such as in Indonesia after the 2004 tsunami and Pakistan after its 2005 earthquake, where favorability toward the U.S. rose from 23% in May 2005 to 46% in November 2005 following American humanitarian assistance)[58] provide notable negative and positive examples.

The responsiveness of other nations and their publics to American policy provides opportunities as well as dangers. Stephen Walt has suggested that other nations have a range of options to both thwart and assist U.S. foreign policy goals, even with the significant amount of power of the United States.[59] If one thing is clear from this chapter's analysis, it is that the substance of American foreign policy affects how foreign opinions perceive it. Broader assessments of American aid disbursements and UN voting patterns suggest that these positive carrots of support can have a significant influence on state choices on matters that the United States cares deeply about.[60] The recent experience with foreign aid in regions of the world where attitudes toward the U.S. have been decidedly negative suggests that policies that are seemingly not directly connected to the war on terror, but positively affect the lives of ordinary citizens, can have a dramatic affect on improving the perception of the United States around the world.

The policies that the president elected in 2008 pursues will prove decisive in international opinion. If Iraq becomes less of the organizing lens through which international opinion sees American foreign policy, and if the next president adopts a foreign policy that is perceived as more multilateral in nature (i.e., rejecting selective multilateralism and stand-apart alliances), support for the war on terrorism and the United States' standing in international opinion will likely rebound. If the next administration largely pursues the Bush Doctrine without modification, international opposition will likely continue.

While American public opinion seems willing to support the Bush Doctrine (or some variant of it), international opinion seems unlikely to embrace it. While a domestic consensus rivaling the containment policy might still develop around the Bush Doctrine, international support for it comparable to that of containment will not emerge. I began this chapter with reference to Machiavelli's dictum that it is better to be feared than to be loved. Going to war in Iraq undermined the "love" that other nations felt toward the United States. Given the difficulties the U.S. encountered there, it risks losing the "fear" that nations might naturally accord a state with the material resources that the United States currently has. Given the association of the Bush Doctrine with American hegemony, unilateralism, and assertive realism, foreign publics will not accommodate American foreign policy easily if these aspects remain the central components of American policy. At the same time, a preference for multilateralism and shared goals in preventing the spread of WMDs, combating terrorism, and spreading democracy are shared by significant members of non-American publics. If these factors, rather than hegemony and unilateralism, become the primary face of American policy, it is possible that attitudes toward the United States will turn around. However, given the strong negative attitudes toward Bush and the attendant perceptions of hegemony and unilateralism that the Iraq War created, it seems unlikely that Bush or someone embracing the "Bush Doctrine" would be able to achieve this end. Unlike containment, which was a sufficiently flexible concept to accommodate differing policy approaches, it seems unlikely the Bush Doctrine itself could accommodate being stripped of its hegemonic and unilateralist inclinations and still be recognized as the original. While the history of containment and international support for some aspects of the Bush Doctrine suggest the possibility that international opinion will change, the fundamental opposition to American hegemony and unilateralism implies that this transformation might be too much to expect of a skeptical and hostile international community.

Notes

1. John Lewis Gaddis, *Strategies of Containment*, rev. ed. (New York: Oxford University Press, 2005).
2. Niccolò Machiavelli, *The Prince*, trans. George Bull (New York: Penguin Books, 1961), 96.
3. Joseph S. Nye, Jr., *The Paradox of American Power* (New York: Oxford University Press, 2002) 8-9.
4. Stephen M. Walt, *Taming American Power: The Global Response to U.S. Primacy* (New York: Norton, 2005).
5. Quoted in Thomas L. Friedman, "The Post-Post-Cold War," *New York Times*, May 10, 2006, A25.
6. Machiavelli, *The Prince*, 97.
7. Although I will treat international opinion as a single entity, I do not intend to imply unity of belief, since a diversity of attitudes toward the United States exists and is reflected in the data presented. I will also use the terms "international" and "world" opinion interchangeably.
8. German Marshall Fund (hereafter, GMF), "Transatlantic Trends 2005," question 10, http://www.transatlantictrends.org.
9. GMF, "Trends 2005," question 3.
10. Pew Global Attitudes Project (hereafter, PGAP), "American Character Gets Mixed Reviews," June 23, 2005, question 13, http://pewglobal.org/reports/display.php?ReportID=247. Differing results in the U.S. sample on the questions reported in the previous two paragraphs are likely due to the different question wording. The reference to Europe as the other power in the first question and China as one potential other power in the second question likely caused the American public to be more supportive of hegemony in relation to China.
11. Program on International Policy Attitudes (hereafter, PIPA), "23 Nation Poll: Evaluating the World Powers," April 6, 2005, http://www.pipa.org/archives, 6.
12. Pew Research Center and Council on Foreign Relations (hereafter, Pew/CFR), "America's Place in the World 2005," November 2005, question 9, http://people-press.org.
13. Terror Free Tomorrow (hereafter, TFT), "Major Change of Public Opinion in Muslim World," February 2005, http://www.terrorfreetomorrow.org/articlenav.php?id=56.

14. PGAP, "American Character," question 10c. The October 2002 Bali terrorist bombing seems an unlikely candidate to explain Indonesian attitudes, as the 2003 figure after the bombing indicated a drop in Indonesian support for the war on terror.

15. PGAP, "A Year After Iraq War: A Nine-Country Survey," March 2004, question 11, http://www.people-press.org.

16. GMF, "Trends 2005," questions 7a-c.

17. Ibid., question 22.

18. PGAP, "American Character," question 8.

19. TFT, "Major Change."

20. GMF, "Trends 2005," questions 9a, 14.

21. GMF, "Transatlantic Trends 2004," questions 21a-c, http://www.transatlantic-trends.org.

22. Douglas C. Foyle, "Leading the Public to War? The Influence of American Public Opinion on the Bush Administration's Decision to Go to War in Iraq," *International Journal of Public Opinion Research* 16 (Autumn 2004): 269-294.

23. Pew/CFR, "America's Place," question 15F2a.

24. PIPA, "Americans Reevaluate Going to War With Iraq," November 2003, questions 21-23, http://www.pipa.org/archives.

25. GMF, "Trends 2004," questions 15agh.

26. PGAP, "America's Image Further Erodes," March 18, 2003, question 4a, http://pewglobal.org/reports/display.php?ReportID=175.

27. New York Times/CBS News Poll, May 4-8, 2006, www.nytimes.com/polls.

28. GMF, "Worldviews 2002," question 14j, http://www.transatlantictrends.org.

29. In both surveys, around one-third thought the war would not make any difference. Washington Post/ABC News Poll, *Iraq*, June 2005, questions 25, 26, www.washingtonpost.com.

30. Ibid., question 5.

31. Ibid., questions 26a-d.

32. Pew/CFR, "America's Place," questions 21, 38eF2.

33. GMF, "Worldviews 2002," question 14j; combined poll of Great Britain, France, Germany, the Netherlands, Italy, and Poland.

34. PGAP, "America's Image," questions 4a-b.

35. PGAP, "American Character," questions 31, 32.

36. GMF, "Trends 2004," question 20.

37. PGAP, "American Character," question 33.

38. PIPA/Chicago Council on Foreign Relations (hereafter, CCFR), "Americans on Promoting Democracy," September 21, 2005, questions 1, 7, http://www.pipa.org/archives.

39. Ibid., questions 11, 12.

40. Ibid., questions 16, 17.

41. Ibid., question 27.

42. Ibid., question 37.

43. Ibid., question 45.

44. GMF, "Trends 2005," question 15. Although differences in question wording preclude a straight comparison with the PIPA/CCFR survey results above, these same questions were also asked of Americans and the results are given for comparison.

45. Herbert Asher, *Polling and the Public: What Every Citizen Should Know* (Washington, DC: CQ Press, 1998); Steven Kull and I. M. Destler, *Misreading the Public: The Myth of a New Isolationism* (Washington, DC: Brookings Institution Press, 1999); Andrew Kohut and Bruce Stokes, *America Against the World* (New York: Times Books, 2006); John Mueller, *Policy and Opinion in the Gulf War* (Chicago: University of Chicago Press, 1994), esp. chapter 1; Eric Shiraev and Richard Sobel, *People and Their Opinions* (New York: Pearson, 2006), esp. chapters 1-3.

46. Nicholas Lemann, "The Next World Order: The Bush Administration May Have a Brand-New Doctrine of Power," *The New Yorker* (April 1, 2002): 42; Bob Woodward, *Bush at War* (New York: Simon & Schuster, 2002), 282; Bob Woodward, *Plan of Attack*, (New York: Simon & Schuster, 2004), 131.

47. National Opinion Research Center (hereafter, NORC), January 1950, USNORC.500273, R19, Public Opinion Online, The Roper Center Archive at University of Connecticut, accessed through Lexis-Nexis Academic; NORC, June 1951, USNORC.510303, R04, Public Opinion Online.

48. George H. Gallup, ed., *The Gallup International Public Opinion Polls: France 1939, 1944-1967*, vol. 1 (New York: Random House, 1976), 94-95; George H. Gallup, ed., *The Gallup International Public Opinion Polls: Great Britain 1937-1975*, vol. 1 (New York: Random House, 1976), 179.

49. H. Schuyler Foster, *Activism Replaces Isolationism: U.S. Public Attitudes 1940-1975* (Washington, DC: Foxhall Press, 1983), 43; NORC, March 1947, USNORC.47T49, R11, Public Opinion Online.

50. Gaddis, *Strategies*, 115-124.

51. H. W. Baldwin, "A World Balance Sheet: Two Years After the Attack in Korea," *New York Times*, June 22, 1952, E5; Richard W. Stevenson, "Staying the Course in Iraq: Acknowledging Difficulties, Insisting on a Fight to the Finish," *New York Times*, June 29, 2005, A12.

52. Richard M. Nixon, *RN: The Memoirs of Richard Nixon* (New York: Simon & Schuster, 1990), 110.

53. Barton J. Bernstein, "Election of 1952," in *History of American Presidential Elections 1789-1968*, vol. 4, ed. Arthur M. Schlesinger Jr. (New York: Chelsea House, 1971), 3215-3266.

54. Gaddis, *Strategies*, 159.

55. Robert R. Bowie and Richard H. Immerman, *Waging Peace: How Eisenhower Shaped an Enduring Cold War Strategy* (New York: Oxford University Press, 1998), esp. 245-259.

56. Gallup, *Polls: France*, 83-84; Gallup, *Polls: Great Britain*, 241-242, 269.

57. Richard C. Eichenberg, *Public Opinion and National Security in Western Europe* (Ithaca, NY: Cornell University Press, 1989), 198-215.

58. TFT, "Major Change"; TFT, "Dramatic Change of Public Opinion in the Muslim World," November 2005, http://www.terrorfreetomorrow.org/articlenav.php?id=71.

59. Walt, *Taming American Power*.

60. T. Y. Wang, "U.S. Foreign Aid and U.N. Voting: An Analysis of Important Issues," *International Studies Quarterly* 43 (1999): 199-210.

4

The New Psychology of Alliances

PETER SUEDFELD, PHILIP E. TETLOCK, AND RAJIV JHANGIANI

This chapter concentrates on one of the five aspects that this volume has defined as the core of the Bush Doctrine: equivocal (and some unequivocal) alliances and enmities. It is clear, however, that none of the five aspects stands alone. In this case, the state of bilateral relations between the United States and another country plays an important role in deciding to what extent "assertive realism" will govern America's dealings with that nation, whether the nation will be included in or excluded from selectively multilateral policies, its place in the list of priorities for democratic transformation, and whether it is viewed as a danger to American preeminence.

In this chapter, we look at alliances and other forms of relationship from the perspective of the prime mover of the Bush Doctrine, President George W. Bush himself, and during a particularly important and difficult time, the period leading up to the American-led attack on Iraq. What can we infer about the President's orientation to other countries during this crucial time from nonobvious aspects of his public communications?

Eponymous Doctrines: The Interplay between Idealism and Realpolitik

The Bush Doctrine has become a conceptual battleground for the perpetuation and renewed intensity of the argument between the proponents of *Realpolitik* and the supporters of ideologically based policy making. Debates rage around the world in the halls of governments, in the media, and in faculty clubs (all too often, in descending order of sophistication). Is it sufficient for the United States to deter, disable, or destroy nations that threaten it and its allies (ignoring for the moment the question of how imminent that threat should be to justify such a reaction); or should it also try to export individual freedoms, democracy, and capitalism to nations that so far have maintained despotic governance by not introducing those characteristics? President Bush himself, who was initially dismissive of nation building, has now committed his country to exactly that enterprise in Afghanistan and Iraq, with others possibly to follow.

It can be argued that in many respects, the Bush Doctrine does not represent a sharp departure from the major eponymous doctrines of previous

American presidents.[1] The Monroe Doctrine (1823) extended a shield to prevent expelled European colonialists from attempting to reimpose their rule over the "the free and independent condition which they ["the American continents"] have assumed and maintain"; the Roosevelt Corollary (1904—Theodore, not Franklin) to that doctrine asserted that the U.S. might be forced to protect those independent nations from falling into political or economic chaos if their government exhibited "[c]hronic wrongdoing, or an impotence which results in a general loosening of the ties of civilized society." In other words, the United States sided with the independent nations of the Americas both against the European powers and against internal chaos.

Next, the Wilson Doctrine (the Fourteen Points, 1918) spelled out the right to "justice to all peoples and nationalities, and their right to live on equal terms of liberty and safety with one another." The next expansion of the circle was the Truman Doctrine (1947), which promised to "support free peoples who are resisting attempted subjugation by armed minorities or by outside pressures" and affirmed the right of "free peoples to work out their own destinies in their own way." The two major twentieth century doctrines thus extended the protective shield of the U.S. to cover nations outside the Americas.

Each of these promises expressed idealistic but unrealistic goals. It was highly unlikely that the United States of 1823, with a tiny navy and a small army trying to guard its frontier against Indians, could have done much if a major European power had tried to reconquer lost colonies in the Americas, or attempted to gain new ones. Given the endemic nature of civil war, revolution, coup d'etat, and general unrest in many Latin American countries, even Teddy's big stick was not big enough to reach them all—in fact, American intervention during the twentieth century was highly selective. Wilson's hopes were dashed in the face of American isolationism, French vengefulness, and the imperialism of several European allies; and, in fact, the attempt to turn the Fourteen Points into reality was confined to breaking up the Austro-Hungarian, German, and Ottoman empires at home and abroad.

Truman's immediate goal was to help Greece and Turkey from going Communist, and his doctrine experienced an unexpected growth spurt when North Korea invaded South Korea; but helping "free peoples to work out their own destinies in their own way" did not include actually freeing those who were not free already. There was no forceful American intervention against Communist takeovers in China or Eastern Europe in the immediate postwar period; nor did subsequent U.S. administrations step in when the Red Army suppressed revolutions in Hungary, Poland, East Germany, and Czechoslovakia.

Aside from the difference between the doctrines as stated and their implementation, we should also consider whether they were as idealistic as they seemed. All of them were certainly compatible with considerations of *Realpolitik*, from the desire to keep European powers out of the United States' sphere of influence (including a possible attempt by the Russian Empire to appropriate the Northwest coast of North America), to protecting American citizens and investments in Latin America, to dismantling the bellicose Teutonic empires in Central Europe and their colonies elsewhere (a goal even more cherished by America's World War I allies than by the U.S. itself), and to limiting the expansion of the inimical Soviet and Chinese Communist empires. Although we see no compelling historical reason to deny that the successive doctrine-announcing presidents were reasonably sincere in their desire to preserve or enlarge spheres of independent, secure, and free nations, these moves also advanced the national interests of the United States.

This brings us to the first explicitly psychological argument of our chapter. When it comes to debates over the "true motives" driving foreign policy, perhaps especially American foreign policy, there is virtually always plenty of "attributional ambiguity." The awkward phrase, widely used by social psychologists,[2] refers to any situation in which reasonable observers working from the same data can draw very different conclusions about the true causes of behavior—conclusions that usually vary dramatically in how flattering or unflattering they are to those responsible for the behavior. When there is attributional ambiguity, we can count on political partisans, with almost clock-like reliability, to favor those causal explanations that put the most positive possible spin on their side's policies and the most negative possible spin on the other side's.[3] And we can count on social scientists and mass media conspiracy theorists to engage in what C. Wright Mills once aptly called "motive mongering"[4]—the relentless quest for the deeper causal forces, economic or psychodynamic or cultural, pulling the marionette strings that in turn purportedly move individual decision makers.

It is easy to see this process at work with respect to the Bush Doctrine. Its tenets—forceful action against terrorists and the nations that shelter them, preventive war when it is deemed necessary, alliances with free and democratic governments, and fostering the existence of such governments as opposed to tyranny—are all ideologically compatible with the fundamental principles of the United States. However, *Realismus*[5] still affects how one pursues one's high goals: the Bush Doctrine does not threaten the People's Republic of China, the largest tyranny in the world and one that oppresses Tibet, threatens the democratic Taiwanese government, and supports murderous dictatorships in Asia and Africa. Nor does it confront the autocracies of the Arab Middle East, even though Saudi Arabia has been a generous sponsor of clerics and propaganda that promote jihadist values around the world.

These inconsistencies in the application of the Doctrine, coupled with political partisanship, general cynicism, and political paranoia, have led to an intensely polarized debate about the "true motives" of the Bush administration in any one action. With regard to the invasion of Iraq, for example, attributions range from the argument that the administration, along with most major intelligence agencies and possibly Saddam Hussein himself, really believed that Iraqi WMDs posed a potential threat to the United States, either directly or through their possible transfer to terrorist groups, through a variety of mixed-motive explanations, all the way to "it's really all about oil."

The Bush Doctrine and International Relations

Although international alliances have always been largely based on a *realistisch* perception of mutual interests, their relational underpinnings vary widely. The rest of this chapter will consider psychological factors in President Bush's approach to other nations with which the United States is in one or another of the following relationships.

The major axes of the taxonomy are *Realismus*, the perception that cooperation will facilitate reaching an important goal, and affinity, the perception that the two nations share important basic values and compatible political/social/economic systems. The two axes are essentially orthogonal; within the 2x2 space that they define, other variables may place the relationship in a specific time- and context-defined category.

In many cases, expected *realistisch* benefits coexist with a basic affinity in history, political systems, economic symbiosis, ethnic ties, and so on. The friendly relationship between the United States and the United Kingdom, which has endured through more than a century, including collaboration in two world wars and a host of comparatively minor skirmishes from Korea to Iraq, is one such example. Interestingly, this particular relationship developed after a history of ongoing hostility between the two nations, starting in colonial times and persisting through the American Revolution, the War of 1812, and a series of American attempts to eliminate British colonization in North America by either "liberating" or incorporating Canada through direct military action or through Irish nationalist proxies.

In more psychological language, one could argue that the "special relationship" between London and Washington does indeed have a familial, communal-sharing flavor. This does not, of course, imply that there are never conflicts of interest or that one party puts the interests of the other at parity with its own. But it does imply that, all other things being equal, one or both of two conditions are satisfied:

1. There is a non-negligible increment in utility from taking positions that support those of the other nation and a non-negligible decrement in utility from taking positions that undercut those of the other nation. We are not dealing with the ideal theoretical situation in microeconomics, in which each party is utterly indifferent to the well-being of the other or cares about that well-being only insofar as it has some direct or indirect impact on one's own. And we are definitely not dealing with the ideal theoretical situation in neorealism in which,

except for temporary alliances, each side prefers the other side to be weaker than itself; and/or,

2. There is a non-negligible increase in the likelihood of reaching similar interpretations about threats to the world order, as well as about the best ways of coping with those threats.

Other alliances seem to reflect peaceful, but not friendly, relationships aimed at mutual benefit without necessarily any affective component. An example is the alliance between France and the British Empire in both world wars. These, too, followed centuries of episodic warfare and economic rivalry between the two nations, the former of which ended only with the final defeat of Napoleon.

Goodwill that builds up in such relationships is often grounded, very clearly, in calculations of reciprocity and exchange: What have you done for me very recently, or what can you do for me in the near future? One difference between this and the U.S.–U.K. type of relationship is that in the latter, longer deviations from strict reciprocity can occur without impairing the alliance.

Another relevant category is where nations need to support each other despite major disapproval and hostility toward each other's form of government, society, and perhaps even people—negative affects that, however, must be denied or ignored in order to cooperate for a superordinate goal. Perhaps the most obvious recent example is the World War II alliance between the Western democracies on the one hand and the Soviet Union on the other. Churchill put it in a nutshell: "If Hitler invaded hell I would make at least a favorable reference to the devil in the House of Commons."[6] Statesmen leading the U.S. and Britain felt threatened by the USSR's potential for disrupting their societies through Communists and their collaborators in the Western nations, and by what they perceived as Stalin's expansionistic ambitions; Stalin, in turn, thought that the capitalist countries were continuing their efforts to undermine socialism and its historic universal mission. He considered Nazism the lesser of the immediate evils; only after Operation Barbarossa unfolded did he come to believe otherwise. Nevertheless, while fighting the common enemy, neither side of the alliance fully trusted or approved of the other.

Such alliances require the active management of cognitive dissonance—value conflict exists, but the need for cooperation is so great that there is a strong norm to suppress the psychological conflict until the external struggle is over. This relationship involves the reconciliation of incompatible factors: cooperative acts, frequently requiring a façade of friendliness or even admiration (at least in public), coexisting with strong negative underlying affect. It is quite likely that, once the immediate danger is past and the superordinate shared goal has been reached, the incompatibility of basic values will come to trump the need for cooperation (for instance, compare the relations between the USSR and the Western Allies prior to and as soon as Germany's defeat was assured).

The last situation to be considered is one where there is cooperation on some issues but not on equally important others, with the affect underlying the alliance being variable, ambivalent, or concealed. Most recently, the relationship between America and its European continental "allies" demonstrates these qualities. Despite close ties in many areas, some of the latter were engaged in sabotaging American efforts to isolate and bring down Saddam Hussein's regime peacefully, by engaging in illegal trade (violating UN sanctions, while professing to obey them). Souring the relationship further, they tried and succeeded in warding off UN support for a military alternative, afterward criticizing the U.S. for moving ahead without such support. Others, while not actively opposing the U.S., declined to support it and decided to stand aloof. Here, the same nations were simultaneously advancing some of America's goals and thwarting others.

A Taxonomy of Bilateral Relations in the Bush Doctrine Era

Based on some of the factors discussed above, for purposes of this chapter we look at major types of relationships between the United States and a series of other countries in the time of the Bush Doctrine and the attack on Iraq. These other countries may be characterized as the following:

Enemies (the "Axis of Evil," and others): Nations that fund, support, shelter, and arm anti-American (and anti-Western) terrorists and/or whose development and possession of weapons of mass destruction is a threat to the United States and its allies. Examples: Iran, Syria, North Korea, prewar Iraq.

Affinity Allies: Nations that actively support the U.S. action, and that, by and large, also share the values espoused by the United States: human rights, individual freedoms (including freedom of, and from, religion), democracy, and an economy based primarily on private enterprise and property. Examples: Great Britain, Australia, Portugal, Poland, Italy (under Berlusconi), and Spain prior to the Madrid attacks and the subsequent election. Because of the close relationship between the U.S. and the post-Taliban Afghan government, we include it in this category despite the great current differences between the two cultures in religious and social worldviews. Israel is in this category, but was not included in the data analysis because of its special circumstances (e.g., being excluded from the wars against both the Taliban and Saddam Hussein regardless of its own wishes).

Strategic Allies: Nations that side with the United States in the fight against the Saddam Hussein regime and the postwar chaos, terrorism, and "insurgency," but do not necessarily share the fundamental values listed above, or at least not all of them. Example: Pakistan.

Obstructionist Allies (the "Axis of Weasels"): Nations that because of similar values, past history, cultural roots, and other interests would be expected to support the U.S. effort in Iraq, but that for some considerations (*realistisch*, economic, or perhaps just anti-American) not only fail to do so but even hamper that effort in the UN or other fora. Examples: France, Russia, Germany (under Schröder).

Strategic Ambivalents: Nations that could be either significantly useful or seriously troublesome, characterized by pressures in both directions, and either veering from one to the other or exhibiting both at the same time. They may be ideologically distant from the U.S. and the West, but have pragmatic reasons for not wanting to oppose the U.S. openly (e.g., most Muslim countries other than those that are either Enemies or Strategic Allies).

Affinity Ambivalents: Nations that take no part in the American war on terrorism, tyranny, and Saddam Hussein. They are usually in the grip of conflicting values: for example, they may share American and Western ideals but be reluctant to engage in warfare, or may fear adverse domestic political reactions. In other circumstances they might have become Affinity Allies. Examples: Spain (since the 2004 elections) and Canada (before the 2005 election).

A Psychological Approach to the Study of Alliances

The different kinds of relationships can be characterized in terms of several psychological theories. The most obvious, perhaps, is cognitive dissonance theory[7]—in fact, at an earlier stage of development, "dissonant alliances" was in the title of this chapter. Cognitive dissonance occurs when two mutually exclusive, or at least inconsistent, cognitions nevertheless coexist. The classic example is standing outside in the rain, without any rain gear or shelter, yet not getting wet; a more relevant example is having a close friend and supporter suddenly and vehemently attack your most cherished beliefs. The result is psychological discomfort and the arousal of a need to eliminate the dissonance, for instance, by abjuring the friendship, trying to understand and deal with the criticism, or changing your beliefs.

This chapter reports the results of an unobtrusive examination of President Bush's psychological orientation to some of the countries that have played a significant role in the controversy over policy toward Iraq. The examination was conducted through the application of thematic content analysis (TCA).[8] Unlike most content analytic techniques, TCA draws its raw material from qualitative materials but derives quantitatively measured variables from those sources. The materials scored can include almost any kind of connected verbal passage: books, articles, letters, diaries, memoranda, oral histories, interviews in print or electronic media, speeches, debates, etc.

Scoring is performed according to a detailed scoring manual and usually requires fairly extensive training. Depending on the specific manual, passages are randomly selected from the total material available. Each passage is analyzed according to the scoring manual for evidence related to the particular variable of interest, and this evidence is recorded in quantitative form. As far as possible, scorers are kept ignorant of the identity of the speaker or writer, as well as other external factors relevant to the passage. Scores are analyzable by both descriptive (means, graphs) and inferential (statistical significance, power calculation) statistics. Furthermore, the same passages can be scored by other trained personnel to indicate the reliability of the original scores. Thus, these methods combine the advantages of qualitative approaches (e.g., the ability to use a wide range of materials and subjects, high external validity, unobtrusive and nonintrusive procedures) with much of the rigor of quantitative ones (randomization, reliability checks, statistical analyses).

Psychological Correlates of Alliance Category

We expect that the different categories of alliances, and of bilateral relations in general, will engage psychological processes in different ways. To test that hypothesis, we applied TCA techniques in three major psychological areas (cognition, emotion, and motivation) to speeches made by President Bush in which he alluded to nations in the various categories. The variables measured were:

Integrative complexity, a measure of cognitive information processing that assesses perceptions of legitimate disagreements and alternative interpretations, as well as the degree to which these are reconciled.

Immediacy/Nonimmediacy, an unobtrusive measure of positive or negative emotions toward another person or entity. The scoring system can identify such emotions even when attempts are being made to conceal or camouflage them.

Motive imagery, which makes it possible to identify the relative strengths of three important motives: *power*, the desire to influence or control another entity while avoiding being controlled by it; *affiliation*, the motive to establish close and friendly relations with another entity; and *achievement*, the striving for excellence, superiority, or victory or to reach an important goal.

Speeches made by Bush, and presidential interviews and press conferences whose full texts were available in the print media and/or the Internet, served as the data sources. Previous research had found that TCA scores did not differ significantly between official statements that were definitely the product of a particular high-level policy maker (e.g., the original holograph manuscript still existed) and those prepared partly or completely by aides or speech writers. Most such assistants are selected because their writing is compatible with how their employer thinks and speaks, and they generally try to approximate that style. In important speeches or writings, the actual leader frequently engages in considerable guiding, editing, and rewriting of the assistant's draft, up to and including throwing it out and demanding a totally new version.[9] Thus, although some particularly memorable or colorful expression (e.g., "the Axis of Evil") may be attributable to a ghostwriter, this issue is not a significant problem in TCA scoring.

Some nations that fit into one of the alliance categories outlined previously were not mentioned in the President's speeches, and therefore do not appear in the data tables. Others may have been mentioned in only one speech or scoring unit; this can usually be identified by a standard deviation of zero.

Scoring Systems

Integrative Complexity

The scoring of integrative complexity[10] uses the paragraph or equivalent (a topic sentence followed by relevant comments) as the basic unit. The scorer goes through randomly selected units, with identifying material removed as fully as possible, assessing the presence of differentiation (evidence that the source recognizes more than one dimension or legitimate viewpoint) and integration (evidence of the recognition that the differentiated components are interrelated). Obviously, differentiation is a prerequisite for integration. Details of the scoring system are described in Appendix A.

Integrative complexity has been very widely applied in both archival and experimental studies. These have included research on negotiations, military and political leadership, scientific eminence, the outbreak or avoidance of war, newspaper and magazine treatments of important topics, the priority hierarchies of politicians and of groups involved in environmental controversy, etc. Integrative complexity levels have been shown to fluctuate in response to a number of variables, some external (e.g., danger, information underload or overload, urgency, the importance of the problem) and some internal (such as fatigue, theoretical orientation, approaching death, political ideology).[11]

Hypotheses and Theoretical Bases. One internal factor relevant to complexity is value conflict or value pluralism, whose role was first described by Philip Tetlock.[12] According to value conflict theory, integrative complexity is affected by the degree to which the source experiences two important values as mutually exclusive or at least in a trade-off relationship. For example, a politician to whom both freedom of expression and social equality are high in the value hierarchy will experience conflict when deciding how to vote on a "hate speech" bill, whereas neither a First Amendment absolutist nor a typical ethnic minority "spokesperson" will have that problem. Value conflict can be viewed as a special case of cognitive dissonance.

According to Tetlock, reconciling two important but mutually contradictory values requires high integrative complexity, which is not necessary when one value far outweighs the other in the individual's ideological structure. This is why, for example, the point of maximum integrative complexity tends to shift systematically as a function of both the ideological viewpoint of the decision maker and the topic under consideration. For instance, in deliberating on domestic surveillance of suspected spies (or terrorists), integrative complexity peaks among those who place high value on both civil liberties and national security; or, in deliberations of mining and drilling in public parks, complexity peaks among those who place high value on both economic growth and environmental protection. For those who place importance on only one of the two (or more) contending values, such issues are "easy calls."

Another relevant proposition is the cognitive manager model,[13] which suggests that thinking in an integratively complex way requires the expenditure of more psychological as well as material resources (energy, effort, time, information search, etc.) than less complex cognitions. Accordingly, resources for complex approaches are allocated to problems depending on their importance and difficulty within the context of all problems being confronted at the same time.

For the current study, both the value conflict hypothesis and the cognitive manager model predict that President Bush will evidence higher complexity when addressing issues related to nations whose relationship with the U.S. is internally dissonant (Strategic Allies, Obstructionist Allies, Strategic Ambivalents) than those whose relationship is more straightforward, regardless of its positive or negative valence (Affinity Allies, Enemies).

From the value conflict point of view, dissonant relationships generate pressure for greater integrative complexity because the other nation is simultaneously advancing certain American goals and thwarting others, requiring a net assessment that incorporates both characteristics.

An American president will therefore experience more value conflict in dealing with nations whose strategic and ideological relationship with the U.S. are inconsistent, and also because relations with such countries are more difficult to work out to a satisfactory resolution (i.e., trying to gain their support or at least to avert their active opposition). It should be noted that the value conflict and cognitive manager explanations are not alternatives; rather, they supplement each other (conflicted values require more effort to resolve).

Immediacy/Nonimmediacy

Unlike integrative complexity, immediacy (and its opposite, nonimmediacy) is an affective variable that is presumably less influenced by *Realismus* and more by perceptions of affinity. Scores on immediacy reflect the affective relationship between the source and the subject of the communication (the "referent").[14] Scoring is based on connotative rather than literal or denotative meaning; thus, for example, the question, "Do you like John?" may elicit answers such as "I like him very much" or "I think he is an interesting person." The first answer would be scored as indicating higher immediacy or positive psychological closeness than the second: the latter separates out one aspect of John, rather than considering him as a whole individual, introduces an element of uncertainty in the evaluation, and changes the topic of the evaluation from an affective variable (being liked) to a cognitive one (being interesting). It therefore implies nonimmediacy, psychological distance, and negative affect. Appendix B lists some of the scoring categories for immediacy/nonimmediacy.

Like integrative complexity, immediacy scoring was originally applied to material produced under specific circumstances. Early research in both cases has used semistructured sentence/paragraph completion tests and other essay-like writing tasks as databases. As far as we know, immediacy—unlike complexity—has not been widely used to analyze high-level political utterances, with one published exception.[15]

We predict that immediacy will be higher (i.e., nonimmediacy will be lower) in the President's references to Affinity nations than to Strategic or Enemy nations, regardless of the specific position of the other country on the war against Saddam Hussein's regime.[16]

Motive Imagery

The scoring of motive imagery in archival materials has concentrated on three primary motives: power, affiliation, and achievement.[17] This trio is thought to exert a major influence on the goals for which people strive and on how they strive for them. The scoring systems cover overt actions as well as covert psychological processes such as wishes or desires.

The power motive subsumes the wish to influence the behavior, attitudes, and emotions of others, and to fend off reciprocal attempts toward oneself. Some examples are the attempts to control others by exerting authority, giving unsolicited advice, and presenting persuasive arguments. Affiliation includes a concern about affectively positive relations with other people, including being sociable, cooperating, avoiding disagreement or conflict, and trying to please. Achievement implies a desire to do well at some task, to succeed at reaching a goal, to meet standards of excellence, to outdo one's own past performance or that of others. An integrated scoring system exists for the measurement of all three motives together, which adjusts the score for the length of the passages that are being scored.[18]

Our hypothesis concerning motive imagery is that the President will exhibit higher power motivation and lower affiliation motivation when dealing with enemies, ideologically incompatible (Strategic) allies, and Ambivalents, with the opposite relative standing of the two motives when referring to ideologically and strategically harmonious nations (Affinity Allies), even those who stood aside from or disagreed with his actions vis-à-vis Iraq. Achievement motivation is not predicted to vary systematically with the bilateral relationship factor.

It is expected that the results will shed light on the psychological processes (cognitive, emotional, and motivational) that underlie each form of alliance—forms that on the world scene may have similar surface appearances and even outcomes, at least in the short term. The analysis may point the way to a better understanding of the development and nature of each type of alliance.

Method and Results

Database

The TCA data reported below are based on the scoring of paragraphs or equivalent units drawn randomly from speeches and press conferences by President Bush. We restricted the sampling to communications dating between February 15 and March 17, 2003, while the U.S. was seeking UN support for a military intervention in Iraq. This appears to be an appropriate time period for identifying the bilateral relationship in the early life of the Bush Doctrine, the run-up to preemptive (or preventive) war. Various locations were involved, including the White House, a summit meeting in the Azores, several trips to Great Britain, campuses in the U.S., and so on.

Integrative Complexity

The reliability between the main and secondary complexity scorers was r = 0.94. Table 4.1 shows complexity scores by relationship category, indicating the nations in each.

To summarize these results in terms of our predictions, the President's mean integrative complexity when referring to Low-Value Conflict nations was 1.51 (SD = 0.90), and for High-Value Conflict nations it was 2.00 (SD = 0.78). This difference is significant, both statistically [$t(53) = 1.81$, $p = .04$ one-tailed)] and in real-world terms. This sizeable difference confirms the hypothesis based on both value conflict theory and the cognitive manager model.

On the other hand, the fact that Obstructionist Allies were treated at approximately the same level of complexity as Enemies was unexpected, and may reflect the President's view of that group as either straightforward defectors or "free riders," rather than as friends who disagreed on this one issue, thus raising the level of value conflict. This interpretation appears compatible with the findings on immediacy.

Incidentally, the absolute levels of integrative complexity shown by Bush were low, in the range of implicit differentiation. This may reflect his "friend

Table 4.1 Mean (SD) Integrative Complexity (Pre-Invasion)

Category	Countries	M (SD) Cxy
Low Value Conflict		
Enemies	North Korea, Iraq	1.69 (1.01)
Affinity Allies	UK, Spain, Portugal, Afghanistan	1.20 (0.56)
High Value Conflict		
Strategic Allies	Pakistan	2.00 (0)
Obstructionist Allies	France, Germany, Russia	1.60 (0.55)
Strategic Ambivalents	Middle East other than above	2.33 (0.82)

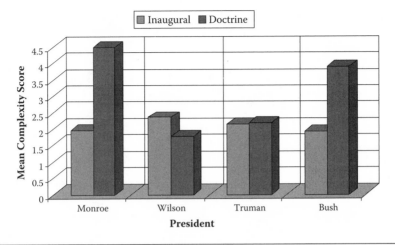

Figure 4.1 Integrative complexity in inaugural addresses and eponymous doctrines.

or foe" stance vis-à-vis other nations in the period before the war, but it is not incompatible with the levels of other statesmen in similar crises, for example UN speeches prior to outbreaks of major wars between Israel and the Arab states, and communications of several national leaders prior to the First Gulf War.[19] As a check on his baseline level of complexity, Figure 4.1 shows the score for his most recent inaugural address and the speeches and documents in which he outlined his Doctrine, compared with the counterpart utterances of the presidents who originated the other eponymous doctrines. President Bush is well within that range.

Immediacy/Nonimmediacy

Immediacy was scored from the same set of speeches and press conferences by Bush as was used in the scoring of integrative complexity. The excerpted passages referred to one or more of the nations that played a potential role in the decision during the period when the President was negotiating to obtain UN sanction for a military solution to the problems posed by Saddam Hussein. Table 4.2 shows the mean *non*immediacy scores by category (the reader should recall that higher scores mean lower immediacy).

In Table 4.2, the bilateral relations between the U.S. and the other countries are divided into three major categories: Enemies, Friends (Affinity Allies), and Ambivalents. The mean nonimmediacy scores by category were, respectively, 1.35 (SD = 0.46), 0.68 (0.42), and 1.14 (0.44). It is clear that, as predicted, the level of nonimmediacy in the President's references to friends was considerably lower than to the other two groups, while his references to enemies showed the highest level. Ambivalents were intermediate. Analysis of variance showed a highly significant main effect for category, $F(2,55) = 10.82, p < .0001$. Post hoc multiple comparisons indicated that the score for Friends (Affinity

Table 4.2 Relationship Category, Country, and Mean Nonimmediacy (Pre-Invasion)

Nation(s)	Mean (SD) Nonimmediacy
Enemies	
Iraq	1.42 (0.45)
North Korea	1.26 (0.50)
Friends (Affinity Allies)	
Spain	0.46 (0.35)
UK	0.63 (0)
UK and Italy	1.00 (0)
UK, Spain, Portugal	0.76 (0.56)
Afghanistan	1.01 (0.32)
Ambivalent (Mixed)	
"Friends and Allies"*	1.52 (0.21)
France and Germany	1.41 (0.03)
France	1.71 (0)
Russia	0.78 (0.19)
Middle East	1.06 (0.47)
Pakistan	1.00 (0)
UN	1.50 (0)

*This reference was in President Bush's answer to a question about the opposition of
France, Russia, and China in the Security Council.*

Allies) was significantly lower by Tukey's test (mean $p < .05$) than for the other two categories, which did not differ significantly from each other.

In summary, the immediacy results support our hypothesis that Bush did in fact feel positive affect toward America's "Affinity Allies"—i.e., nations, or at least governments, that shared both its fundamental values and supported its willingness to act forcefully against Saddam Hussein—as measured by a subtle and nonobtrusive metric. It is highly unlikely that the immediacy scores reflect manipulation for purposes of impression management: the relationship between affect and the verbal indices of immediacy is not at all obvious. By the same token, the President's affect toward mixed-status nations was clearly less positive, and was least so toward outright enemies.

Motive Imagery

The three major motives were scored from the same set of materials as the other two dependent variables. Each extracted passage was scored for each of the three motives; the scores shown in Figures 4.2a, 4.2b, and 4.2c are based on the ratio between the number of times the given motive was mentioned and the number of words in that passage.

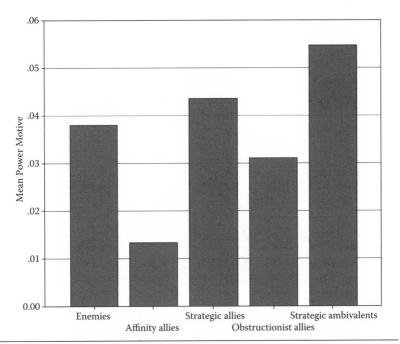

Figure 4.2a Mean scores for power imagery.

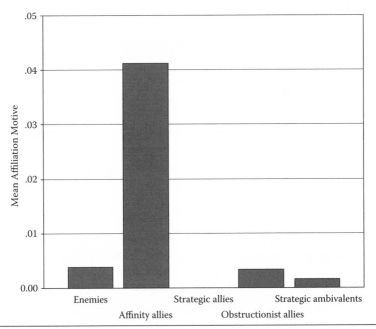

Figure 4.2b Mean scores for affiliation imagery.

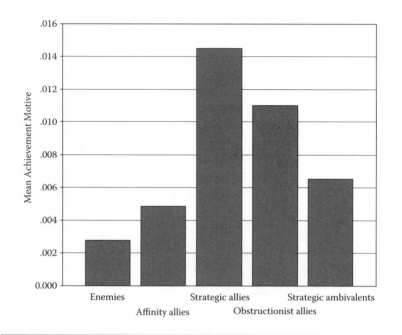

Figure 4.2c Mean scores for achievement imagery.

The statistical analysis of *power* imagery revealed a significant main effect, $F(2,51) = 7.58$, $p = .001$. Pairwise comparisons (Tukey's test) indicated that there was significantly less ($p < .05$) Power imagery in references to Affinity Allies (Friends) than either of the other two groups (Enemies and Ambivalents); the latter did not differ significantly from each other.

There was a significant main effect in *affiliation* imagery, $F(2, 51) = 22.37$, $p < .001$. Because the assumption of homogeneity of variances was violated, the data were also assessed using Welch's test. The statistical outcome was still supported, $F''(2, 28.54$ corrected$) = 11.11$, $p < .001$. As in the case of *power*, Tukey tests show that the Affinity Allies were significantly different ($p < .05$) from both other groups (Enemies and Ambivalents), but that the latter two categories were not significantly different from each other.

The differences among the mean *achievement* imagery scores of the three categories of nations did not reach statistical significance, $F(2, 51) = 2.63$, $p = .08$, although there was a trend for nations in the Ambivalent (Mixed) group to evoke higher *achievement* scores than either the Enemies or Affinity Allies.

There was a positive relationship between *power* imagery and integrative complexity, $r(53) = 0.41$, $p = .002$, and a negative relationship between *power* and *affiliation* imagery, $r(54) = -0.45$, $p < .001$. The number of words in a passage was not significantly related to any of the dependent variables.

The tables show a pattern of motive imagery that is quite reasonable given the relative positions of the U.S. and the other countries. *Power* imagery was lowest in references to nations that did not need to be brought on side: they already shared both America's basic ideology and the Bush Doctrine's view on terrorism and Saddam Hussein. Enemies and Ambivalents did not differ significantly, although one may speculate that different kinds of power or influence may have been paramount: force in the case of enemies, persuasion or future benefits in the case of the Ambivalents. President Bush's score on *affiliation* was by far the highest when he spoke about Affinity Allies, and was considerably lower for all other categories, a pattern that makes complete sense and also echoes the findings for Immediacy.

The intercategory differences in *achievement* imagery were not statistically reliable. However, it is interesting that *achievement* showed a peak when the President referred to nations that either aided in the war against terrorism without sharing American values (i.e., the Strategic Ally, Pakistan) or shared values but tried to thwart the application of the Bush Doctrine to Iraq (the Obstructionist Allies). The other Mixed group, Strategic Ambivalents, was third. Extrapolating from this trend, it appears that ambivalent bilateral relationships raised the President's motive to succeed and excel, independently of his motive to persuade or coerce.

The correlations between dependent variables are also logical. Integrative complexity and *power* imagery are both highest in the context of addressing the ambivalent nations that the President is attempting to persuade: persuasion is by definition a power-based activity, and in these cases required the allocation of significant cognitive resources. Contrarily, in relation to Affinity Allies, the feeling of affiliation is natural and there is no need to exert power, thus resulting in the negative correlation between the two imagery measures.

Discussion

From the point of view of a psychological study, this was a rewarding effort. We found that in a highly important, difficult, international problem situation the nonobtrusive TCA methodology accurately predicted the pattern of cognitive, affective, and motivational processes of the President. Among the three types of variables, the relationship was remarkably consistent and mutually confirmatory. The probability that these results were produced by artifacts such as the work of speech writers, or by a desire to present some kind of façade or public image, is remote: none of the measures is dependent upon obviously and easily manipulated phraseology.

The taxonomy of bilateral relationships also opens the door to interesting research possibilities in applying thematic content analysis to the international system. For example, we referred earlier to the emergence of basic values as more important than strategic cooperation once the need for such cooperation to solve a shared important problem is gone. Such a change would presumably allow the subsidence of value conflict that had been needed during the emergency, and thus lead to a decrease in integrative complexity. One might also look at sources other than a president: Would there be higher immediacy in domestic propaganda toward a Strategic Ally during the common effort, only to be replaced by nonimmediacy afterward ("Uncle Joe" Stalin versus the bloody-handed oppressor of Eastern Europe)? And how would such a shift be reflected in official communications?

More relevant to this book is the next question. What is the value of the study for understanding President Bush and his Doctrine at the critical time shortly before the invasion of Iraq? We think that, contrary to accusations of willful unilateralism, the data indicate that he believed in the importance of his attempt to forge a coalition that would depose Saddam Hussein; that his decision-making processes and his emotions were consistent in his approach to nations that variously helped, hindered, or were potential targets of his vision of America's task in overthrowing dangerous regimes and spreading democracy. Integrative complexity and motive imagery scoring have previously shown themselves to be powerful predictors of peaceful versus military solutions to confrontation; in this case, a more disaggregated analysis showed specific patterns toward countries whose positions ranged from fighting allies to possible armed enemies.

Immediacy, which reveals emotional responses that the individual may wish to conceal, showed no dissembling in this case: friends were liked and held psychologically close, with little desire to manipulate them (perhaps because there was little need to do so). Enemies—contrary to the strategic advice to hold them close—were held at a distance, with negative affect and little desire for affiliation. The President's orientation toward those who could or should have been friends, but chose otherwise, reflected his often-quoted opinion that in the fight against terrorism, those who are not with the United States are against it.

The fact that cognitive, affective, and motivational measures point consistently in the same direction has some interesting implications. Obviously, this pattern avoids internally generated cognitive dissonance on the President's part. It may thus allow him to act with more determination and perseverance, with less self-doubt and second-guessing, than would be expected from a more fragmented psychological orientation. This characteristic also helps him to avoid being perceived as indecisive and vacillating, as individuals operating at higher level of complexity sometimes are.[20]

The President's tendency to see at least the post-9/11 world in stark Manichean terms, and both to act on that basis and to say so bluntly is consistent with his low integrative complexity and the pattern of his immediacy and motive imagery. On the other hand, it may contribute to his low esteem among academics, the media, and the people who pay attention to them; the disdain in which he is held abroad is documented in this volume, and even as we write (April 2006), his domestic approval rating is reported at a near-record low, between 32% and 36%.

As we have discussed elsewhere, social scientists and academics in general tend to have a positive bias toward high complexity.[21] As for a leader being straightforward and blunt, this may be honored more in principle than in reality. Machiavelli would have been pleased by a previous study. Using ratings by 97 academic specialists, it found that the three Canadian Prime Ministers who were judged as having been the least honest with the public were also among the four identified as the most prestigious and as having accomplished the most while in office.[22] We will not speculate as to what this implies for President Bush's long-term position in history, nor as to what strategic, *realistisch* advice he might receive from Niccoló Machiavelli about raising his retrospective ratings.

Other Places, Other Players, Other Times

How relevant is our approach to other sets of bilateral or even multilateral relationships among national and substate entities? Regrettably, we are not able to perform the same kind of content analysis in other interesting cases, even in the context of the Bush Doctrine and much less so in the wide range of other possibilities. As far as our taxonomy of relationships goes, parallels are easily found in other eras. Not to go too far back, we see the strategic alliance between the young American antimonarchical republic and the absolute monarchy of Louis XVI's France against Great Britain; and more recently, the alliance of all three of those now democratic governments with the Soviet Union against the Third Reich. Among other sets of nations around the world, we could study the now developing affinity alliances among old and new leftist governments in South America.

Even more interesting are the mixed and changing cases. When there is affinity along some dimensions but hostility among others, or when affinity and *Realismus* conflict, which will dictate policy? It might be useful to look at mixtures of religious affinity and nationalist hostility between, e.g., Shi'a Muslims in Iraq and Iran, the apparent enmity but more probable strategic alliance between Fatah and Hamas, and the effects of regime change in democratic as well as totalitarian countries. Analyses of the communications of leaders and leadership groups may contribute to a better understanding of their psychological processes, and perhaps to more accurate predictions of their future behavior.

We have already referred to the fact that the Bush Doctrine's dedication to worldwide democracy is expressed much more hesitantly when a nuclear-armed country such as North Korea is posing problems—and, a fortiori, when the other nation is very large, very populous, militarily very strong as well as nuclear, and a major economic powerhouse, such as the People's Republic of China. The fact that China's economic strategy now includes relatively free enterprise may introduce some dissonance and value conflict into American views, although continuing human rights abuses, saber-rattling over Taiwan and foot-dragging about North Korea certainly limit the extent of that change.

Another very interesting changing *and* mixed case is Russia, which was fairly high on both the affinity and strategic dimensions when it joined the anti-terrorist movement during a period of its own democratization and victimization by Muslim Chechen terrorists. It became an Obstructionist Ally during the UN Security Council's dithering over Iraq, and has continued further in that direction vis-à-vis Hamas and Iran. At the same time, Vladimir Putin's government has retreated from capitalism and individual rights until at this point it appears to be an ally in neither sense. It remains to be seen whether in looming international problems the President's approach to Russia and China will reflect high or low value conflict; and if the latter, in which direction.

This brings up another issue: the internal consistency among cognition, affect, and motivation evidenced by Bush may be unusually high, with the results we have already discussed. But his determination and relative single-mindedness will not direct American strategy past 2008, the end of his term in office. Will his successor be of the same sort, or will he (or she) have greater tolerance for internal dissonance? How will the answer to that question affect policy decisions, underlying feelings, and the selection of goals? Would the Bush Doctrine still steer America's relations with the world, would it undergo more or less serious modification, or might it be abandoned in part or in whole? Among the great array of factors that determine the future course of the United States, the psychological characteristics of its Chief Executive are by no means the least important.

Notes

1. Peter Suedfeld, "Liberating Doctrines: A View from the Data Bank," presented at the meeting of the International Society of Political Psychology, Toronto, July 2005.
2. David Schneider, *The Psychology of Stereotypes* (New York: Guilford, 2005).
3. Philip E. Tetlock, *Expert Political Judgment: How Good Is It? How Can We Know?* (Princeton, NJ: Princeton University Press, 2005), chap. 5.
4. Charles W. Mills, "Situated Action and Vocabularies of Motives," *American Sociological Review* 5 (1940): 904-913.
5. In this chapter, we use the German noun (*Realismus*) and adjective (*realistisch*) to indicate derivation from and connection with the concept of *Realpolitik*, and to differentiate the usage from "realism" or "realistic" in the common English meaning of those words.
6. Winston Churchill Quotes, http://www.brainyquote.com/quotes/quotes/w/winstonchu111298.html.
7. Leon Festinger, *A Theory of Cognitive Dissonance* (Stanford, CA: Stanford University Press, 1957).
8. Charles P. Smith, ed., *Personality and Motivation: Handbook of Thematic Content Analysis* (New York: Cambridge University Press, 1992).

9. For example, David Frum, *The Right Man: The Surprise Presidency of George W. Bush* (New York: Random House, 2003).

10. Gloria Baker-Brown, Elizabeth J. Ballard, Susan Bluck, et al., "The Conceptual/Integrative Complexity Scoring Manual," in Smith, op. cit., 401-418.

11. For example, Peter Suedfeld, Philip E. Tetlock, and Siegfried Streufert, "Conceptual/Integrative Complexity," in Smith, op. cit., 393-400; Peter Suedfeld, Karen Guttieri, and Philip E. Tetlock, "Assessing Integrative Complexity at a Distance: Archival Analyses of Thinking and Decision Making," in *The Psychological Assessment of Political Leaders: With Profiles of Saddam Hussein and Bill Clinton*, ed, Jerrold M. Post (Ann Arbor: University of Michigan Press, 2003), 246-270; Peter Suedfeld, Dana C. Leighton, and L. Gideon Conway, III, "Integrative Complexity and Decision-Making in International Confrontations," in *The Psychology of Resolving Global Conflicts: From War to Peace. Volume 1, Nature vs. Nurture*, eds., Mari Fitzduff and Chris.E. Stout (New York: Praeger, 2005), 211-237.

12. Philip E. Tetlock, "A Value Pluralism Model of Ideological Reasoning," *Journal of Personality and Social Psychology* 50 (1986): 819-827; Philip E. Tetlock, David Armor, and Randall S. Peterson, "The Slavery Debate in Antebellum America," *Journal of Personality and Social Psychology* 66 (1994): 115-126; Philip E. Tetlock, Randall Peterson, and Jennifer Lerner, "Revising the Value Pluralism Model: Incorporating Social Content and Context Postulates," in *Ontario Symposium on Social and Personality Psychology: Values*, eds. Clive Seligman, James Olson, and Mark Zanna (Hillsdale, NJ: Erlbaum, 1996).

13. Peter Suedfeld, "Cognitive Managers and Their Critics," *Political Psychology* 13 (1992): 435-453.

14. Morton Wiener and Albert Mehrabian, *Language within Language: Immediacy, a Channel in Verbal Communication* (New York: Appleton-Century-Crofts, 1968).

15. Carmen E. Ramirez and Peter Suedfeld, "Nonimmediacy Scoring of Archival Materials: The Relationship between Fidel Castro and "Che" Guevara," *Political Psychology* 9 (1988): 155-164.

16. One *caveat*: of the collaborators who worked on this project, only the first author of the chapter had experience in scoring immediacy, thus no reliability check on his scoring was possible.

17. Smith, *Personality and Motivation, op. cit.*

18. David Winter, "Measuring Personality at a Distance: Development of an Integrated System for Scoring Motives in Verbal Running Text," in *Perspectives in Personality: Approaches to Understanding Lives*, eds. Abigail J. Stewart, Joseph M. Healy, Jr., and Daniel J. Ozer (London: Kingsly, 1991), 59-89.

19. Peter Suedfeld, Philip E. Tetlock, and Carmen E. Ramirez, "War, Peace, and Integrative Complexity," *Journal of Conflict Resolution* 21 (1977): 427-442; Michael D. Wallace, Peter Suedfeld, and Kimberly L. Thachuk, "Political Rhetoric of Leaders Under Stress in the Gulf Crisis," *Journal of Conflict Resolution* 37 (1993): 94-107; Peter Suedfeld, Michael D. Wallace, and Kimberly L. Thachuk, "Changes in Integrative Complexity among Middle East Leaders during the Persian Gulf Crisis," *Journal of Social Issues* 49 (1993): 183-199.

20. Philip E. Tetlock, Randall Peterson, and Jane Berry, "Flattering and Unflattering Personality Portraits of Integratively Simple and Complex Managers," *Journal of Personality and Social Psychology* 64 (1993): 500-511.

21. Peter Suedfeld and Philip E. Tetlock, "Psychological Advice about Political Decision Making: Heuristics, Biases, and Cognitive Defects," in *Psychology and Social Policy*, eds, Peter Suedfeld and Philip E. Tetlock (New York: Hemisphere, 1990), 51-70.
22. Elizabeth J. Ballard and Peter Suedfeld, "Performance Ratings of Canadian Prime Ministers: Individual and Situational Factors," *Political Psychology* 9 (1988), 291-302.

Appendix A.
The Scoring of Integrative Complexity

With some exceptions (e.g., pure description, sarcasm, clichés), most connected verbal passages can be scored for integrative complexity. Scorers undergo a training seminar (in person or online), and must reach a reliability level of $r = 0.85$ or higher to qualify as fully trained. In research, a proportion (usually 20%–30%) of scored units is independently scored by another qualified person to ensure a high level of reliability. Scoring is on a 1 to 7 scale.

Score	Description
1	Undifferentiated: One dimension or perspective; inclusion-exclusion
3	Differentiated: Several dimensions or perspectives recognized
5	Integrated: Relationships among differentiated units recognized
7	Hierarchically integrated: Hierarchical integration into overarching cognitive schemata

Even numbers, not shown in the table, indicate that there is some, but not sufficient, indication of the next higher criterion.

Appendix B. The Scoring of Immediacy/Nonimmediacy

The number of times that any of the categories listed below is found in a communication is recorded, and the sum (or mean number per scoring unit, when comparing communications that differ in length) of these occurrences is the nonimmediacy score. The scoring unit is somewhat variable, but basically it is either a sentence or an independent clause.

Scoring Categories

Categories	Ex.: Answers to question, "Do you like John?"
Spatio-Temporal Categories	
Spatial distance	*I like that guy.*
Temporal distance	*I used to like him.*
Denotative Specificity	
Part category	*He has very good manners.*
Class category	*Everybody likes him.*
Implicit category	*John is a good guy.*
Agent-Action-Object Categories	
Unilaterality category	*I try to spend time with him.*
Passivity category	*I have to like him, he's a teammate.*
Modified category	*Sometimes I think I like him.*

It should be noted that the categories and examples are actually examples of nonimmediacy, i.e., low immediacy. Therefore, high scores imply high psychological distance from, or negative affect toward, the object of the communication, be it a person, idea, nation, event, etc.

5

Illusionary Promises and Strategic Reality

Rethinking the Implications of Strategic Deterrence in a Post-9/11 World

WILLIE CURTIS

During the Cold War, Americans faced the prospects of instantaneous annihilation at the hands of the Soviet Union. While Russia and perhaps one or two countries will retain into the next century the ability to devastate the United States, Moscow's behavior will be conditioned by the same cold calculus of deterrence that kept the peace during the years of East-West confrontation.[1]

The calculus of deterrence that emerged from the Cold War decades reflected conceptual narrowness because "strategic deterrence was conceived and evolved in a bipolar international environment dominated by two disparate ideologically-oriented superpowers."[2] Indeed, "their condition resembled that of two scorpions in a bottle, each poised to strike, yet prevented from doing so by the knowledge that if either struck first, the other would respond and the demise of both was assured."[3] A major question confronting U.S. policy makers in the first decade of the twenty-first century is whether policies based on bottled scorpions will suffice for confronting the dangers posed by regional powers and nonstate actors armed with nuclear and other weapons of mass destruction (WMDs) in a world of growing strategic multipolarity.

In his speech at West Point on June 1, 2002, President George W. Bush articulated his assessment of the changing strategic landscape and the dangers inherent for the security of the United States since the devastating terrorist attacks on September 11, 2001. That speech was a prelude to the new National Security Strategy (NSS), released September 17, 2002. This document described the new threats and asserted that they had undermined the very principles and foundation of the deterrence and containment strategy that had been the cornerstone of United States policy throughout the decades of the Cold War.

President Bush made it clear in his March 8, 2003 radio address: "September 11th 2001 showed what the enemies of America did with four airplanes. We will not wait to see what terrorists or terrorist states could do with weapons of mass destruction."[4] Having made the association between terrorists and terrorist states, the President further emphasized the threat from rogue states seeking nuclear weapons in his 2002 West Point address:

> Today, our enemies see weapons of mass destruction as weapons of choice. For rogue states these weapons are tools of intimidation and military aggression against their neighbors. These weapons may also allow these states to attempt to blackmail the U.S. and our allies to prevent us from deterring or repelling the aggressive behavior of rogue states. Such states also see these weapons as their best means of overcoming the conventional superiority of the U.S.[5]

The NSS reflected the President's view regarding the utility of deterrence in the post-9/11 environment and suggested that deterrence in the form of massive retaliation against nation-states, so effective during the Cold War era, was of no utility in the new strategic landscape consisting of rogue states and global terrorist organizations armed with WMDs. The document integrated these ideas into a formal presidential doctrine, "The Bush Doctrine," which states. "today, our enemies will use weapons of mass destruction as weapons of choice…we cannot let our enemies strike first,"[6] thus justifying the need for a policy of preemption based on the concept of self-protection. The National Security Strategy also asserted the right of preventive war: "The greater the threat, the greater the risk of inaction—and the more compelling the case for taking anticipatory action to defend ourselves, even if uncertainty remains as to the time and place of the enemy's attack."[7]

Clearly, one implication of the NSS was that for the foreseeable future, the challenges for deterrence would not arise from other great powers, but rather from smaller regional powers and global terrorist organizations. Given that deterrence can fail and does not work against (catastrophic) terrorism, what are the implications for the fate of deterrence in the post-9/11 security environment?

The terrorist attacks of 9/11 provided the administration with the political opportunity and strategic necessity to shift its national security doctrine away from what some critics had long argued emphasized the defensive nature of the Cold War era containment and deterrence strategy toward a more offensive warfare against so-called rogues and the growing threat of global terrorism. In a world as defined by the Bush administration, the attacks of 9/11 allowed the administration to expand the role of the military to include terrorists and state sponsors of terrorism.

A 1998 RAND study suggested that "the emerging and more immediate threat is not one of societal destruction but of smaller, damaging attacks, some of which could originate from states or groups less susceptible to the logical cost-benefit accounting of rational deterrence theory."[8] In a world of strategic multipolarity the two large scorpions have been reduced to one, but it has been joined by several smaller, yet just as deadly scorpions.[9]

Proceeding from the premise that proliferation of nuclear weapons is inevitable and in a world of strategic multipolarity, several regional powers, some with interests and goals hostile to U.S. interests, will become part of the strategic landscape, an examination of the assumptions regarding nuclear deterrence and the capabilities of the United States to provide deterrence in this new post-9/11 threat environment is essential.

The potential for conflicts in the twenty-first century is not limited to conventional wars. With the proliferation of WMDs, the probability that some regional power armed with them might seek to achieve national objectives inimical to U.S. interests could well increase. A policy for responding to the new threats from regional nuclear powers and nonstate actors possessing WMDs is still evolving; what is clear, however, is that the bipolar international system produced an aversion to risk-taking on the part of the superpowers, and in the United States, as a result, a deterrence strategy based on an Assured Vulnerability Paradigm evolved.

It is not hard to imagine that the anticipated proliferation of WMDs will now spread to smaller regional powers and potentially to nonstate actors, thus creating an international system with even more "pole." Indeed, one might characterize it as in a state of "strategic multipolarity," a term that refers to an international system in which an increasing number of regional powers and nonstate actors acquire WMDs sufficient to challenge the major powers.

Strategic multipolarity does not reflect the conventional perception of a multipolar international system based on classical great power criteria. Strategic multipolarity, however, is a fact and the acquisition of nuclear weapons can bestow influence and status all out of proportion to the economic and political capabilities of actors at both the regional and global levels. Even in a "unipolar" system, powers much smaller than the "hegemon" can count; hence, if North Korea has obtained nuclear weapons and Iran acquires them, the United States is no doubt constrained in the options available to its decision makers.

From Bipolarity to Strategic Multipolarity: Deterrence in a New Strategic Environment

September 11, 2001 signaled the end of the brief interwar period lasting from the demise of the Soviet Union until the attacks on the World Trade Center and the Pentagon, a short 10 years in which conflicts were mostly intrastate affairs rather than by-products of superpower competition. In addition, September 11 also shook the Cold War inheritance of the strategy of deterrence. In the bipolar world of the Cold War decades, the aversion to risk-taking on the part of the two superpowers adapted well to a strategy of mutual assured destruction (MAD). For analysts in the first decade of the twenty-first century, the question became one of adapting a strategy of deterrence to the new threats emerging from a world of strategic multipolarity. During this period of bipolarity a sort of nuclear-induced stability existed between the United States and the Soviet Union, an era when only the two nuclear armed super-powers possessed sufficient capability to destroy the planet. While questions existed regarding the details of specific approaches and strategic force struc-tures required to assure mutual destruction, the basic principles of deterrence always remained as elaborated by Princeton University Professor William F. Kaufmann in his 1956 book *Military Policy and National Security*.

Essentially, deterrence means preventing certain contingencies from aris-ing. To achieve this objective, it becomes necessary to communicate in some way to a prospective antagonist what is likely to happen to him, should he create the situation in question. The expectation is that confronted with this prospect, he will be deterred from taking the action that is regarded as inimi-cal—at least so long as other less intolerable alternatives are open to him.[10]

Subsequently, in 1968, Secretary of Defense Robert S. McNamara elaborated the same goals and criteria for United States deterrence policy. In *Essence of Security*, McNamara wrote, "The cornerstone of our strategic policy continues to be to deter deliberate nuclear attacks upon the United States or its allies."[11] He identified capability and credibility under all circumstances, particularly surprise attacks, as keystones of the strategy: "We do this by maintaining a highly reliable ability to inflict unacceptable damage upon any single aggres-sor or combination of aggressors at anytime during the course of a strategic nuclear surprise first-strike. This can be defined as our assured destruction capability."[12]

Thus, McNamara made crystal clear that "it is important to understand that assured destruction is the very essence of the whole deterrence concept. We must possess an actual assured destruction capability and that capability must be credible."[13] Indeed, McNamara's criteria meant that capability and credibility would be the central elements of an effective deterrence strategy. But it was a long process to achieve consensus on the essentialness of cred-ibility and capability, a process passing through three historical periods in the development of a deterrent doctrine and capabilities.

Initially, in the period from 1945 to the early 1950s, the United States pos-sessed strategic impenetrability vis-à-vis the Soviet Union, for the Soviet capac-ity to put the United States homeland at risk was nonexistent—and they did not have the bomb. As successors to World War II "blockbusters," atomic bombs were still thought to have military utility as the ultimate warfighting munitions. However, after the Soviet development of atomic bombs followed by hydrogen bombs, nuclear utilitarian strategists found their position untenable.

Deterrence and what made it work became a central concern of defense analysts and their defense academic colleagues. They were hastened as the Soviet Union gradually developed a strategic force structure based on ballistic missiles and the turboprop Bear bomber. Corollary to this was a realization in the United States that its own forces were vulnerable to preemptive attacks.

As the Soviets approach strategic parity, notions of credibility and capability had been well explored, and developed into an emerging field of deterrence theory.

Richard Rosecrance, a noted theorist of the era, suggests "by 1967 at the latest the Soviet Union had attained a reliable 'assured destruction' capability against the United States. This meant that even after absorbing a surprise first-strike, the Soviet Union could reliably and massively retaliate upon the United States."[14] In fact, by the 1980s many analysts were arguing that the Soviet Union had acquired a position of strategic superiority, making significant elements (intercontinental ballistic missiles [ICBMs] and bombers) of the United States strategic force triad vulnerable to a Soviet first-strike, and thereby denying the United States a secure second-strike capability. Although historians may debate the validity of these assertions, it remains a fact that deterrence rested on shared perceptions of MAD.

What, then, were the major assumptions underpinning this strategic policy? We find clues in a conceptual framework described by Keith Payne as the Assured Vulnerability Paradigm. Payne uses the term Assured Vulnerability Paradigm, while other scholars describe the existing condition between the two superpowers as mutual assured destruction. Payne noted, "The superpowers, calculating rationally and sensibly, would refrain from extreme provocation because of the ultimate possibility of nuclear retaliation. The widespread acceptance of this general deterrence framework set the stage for the prevailing sense that deterrence could be well understood and manipulated reliably by adjusting U.S. and Soviet nuclear arsenals."[15]

Thus, the central assumptions of the deterrence policy during the decades of the Cold War called for: (1) possession of second-strike capabilities to inflict unacceptable levels of destruction on the Soviet Union and its Warsaw Pact allies; and (2) a belief that the Soviet leaders were rational decision makers willing to make policy choices using dispassionate, rational, cost-benefit calculations.[16]

From the early 1960s, when the Soviet Union acquired a strategic balance with the United States, the relationship between the powers was characterized by a condition of MAD. The absence of nuclear war between the two lends credibility to this viewpoint, hence strategic analysts and policy makers became convinced that the reliability and predictability of the MAD paradigm was sufficient to deter the so-called rogue states seeking to acquire nuclear capabilities. This one generic model of deterrence was postulated as sufficient for the interwar period and Cold War era deterrence policy was simply slotted into a world of admittedly novel elements. Thus, we find our bottled scorpions being joined by colleagues of varying sizes, interests, and temperaments.

Twenty-First Century Deterrence

Factors and assumptions governing the strategic relationship between the two superpowers during the decades of the Cold War may no longer provide effective broad-spectrum deterrence from minimal to maximum levels at the global or regional levels.

Further complicating the equation in the twenty-first century is the growing number of nonstate actors that are acquiring the means to develop and deliver devastating attacks with no apparent connection to nation-states. Part of the complexity of the evolving postcontainment international order has been captured by Thomas L. Friedman. Friedman argues that the new globalization system is based on three balancing forces: the balance of power; the balance between nation-states and global markets; and finally, the balance between nation-states and individuals.[17] The balance between the nation-state and the individual is unique, for "it gives more power to individuals to influence both markets and nation-states than at any time in history.... Individuals can increasingly act on the world stage directly, unmediated by states."[18]

Friedman writes that "many of these super-empowered angry people hail from failing states in the Muslim and Third world. They do not share our values; they resent America's influence over their lives, politics, and children, not to mention our support of Israel; and they often blame America for the failure of their societies to master modernity."[19] How does one account for the devastating attacks of September 11 by 19 individuals bent on self-destruction? Friedman provides some insight into this complex situation:

> What makes them super-empowered, though, is their genius at using the networked world, the Internet and the very high technology they hate, to attack us. Think about it: they turned our most advanced planes into human directed, precision-guided cruise missile—a diabolical melding of their fanaticism and our technology. Jihad Online. And think of what they hit: the World Trade Center, the beacon of American-led capitalism that both tempts and repels them, and the Pentagon, the embodiment of American military superiority.[20]

Similarly, Friedman writes, "after he [bin Laden] organized the bombing of the two American embassies in Africa, the U.S. Air Force retaliated with a cruise missile attack on his bases in Afghanistan.... The United States fired 75 cruise missiles, at $1 million apiece at a person! That was the first battle in history between a superpower and a super-empowered angry man."[21] It was quite apparent that both the Clinton and Bush administrations' security planning neglected to consider factors raised by Friedman's assessment of the destructive potential of hostile super-empowered individuals.

Thus, the assumption that the Cold War would provide a generic deterrence model during the interwar period led policy makers to believe that deterring emerging nuclear states such as North Korea and Iran was automatically covered by a deterrence policy deemed to have been successful during the Cold War. This assumption held until the promulgation of the Bush Doctrine after the terrorist attacks of 9/11. How, then did the Bush Doctrine seek to deal with the new threats in the new strategic landscape of the post-9/11 environment?

Illusionary Promises or Strategic Reality: The Fate of Deterrence in the Post-9/11 Strategic Environment

The policy dilemma facing U.S. decision makers in the post-September 11, 2001, international order is whether a strategy based on MAD can provide a credible deterrence in the emerging world of strategic multipolarity of the twenty-first century? In a world of strategic multipolarity, deterrence requires a three-tiered approach. Tier-one threats emanating from great powers such as the Russian Republic or the People's Republic of China are manageable within the MAD paradigm and the current strategic triad (ICBMs, strategic bombers, and strategic nuclear submarines) has sufficient deterrence capability and credibility even within a strategic multipolar environment. Indeed, the United States strategic triad has been modernized while the Russian strategic arsenal has eroded.[22]

Keir A. Lieber and Daryl G. Press suggest that "[t]he age of MAD, however, is waning. Today the United States stands on the verge of attaining nuclear primacy vis-à-vis its plausible great power adversaries. For the first time in decades, it could conceivably disarm the long-range nuclear arsenals of Russia or China with a nuclear first strike."[23] Indeed, they note that the strategic weapon systems of the United States are superior to those of both Russia and China. They noted the following:

- U.S. Ohio-class SSBMs [strategic submarine ballistic missiles] are very accurate; fast to target
- Minuteman III ICBMs are very accurate; 30-minute flight to target
- B-2 Bombers are stealthy aircraft which might reach the targets undetected
- B-52 Bombers carry stealthy and nonstealth cruise missiles[24]

By way of comparison, Lieber and Press suggest that the nuclear balance has shifted during the period 1990–2004: "the best unclassified analysis of the nuclear balance in the 1980s predicted that a surprise U.S. disarming strike would leave the Soviets with more than 800 surviving warheads—more than enough to inflict a "disaster beyond history" upon the United States."[25]

Recent analyses of Russian and Chinese strategic nuclear forces capabilities and trends suggest that while Russian strategic forces are eroding, the U.S. is modernizing its strategic forces and will greatly increase the lethality of its arsenal. For example, Lieber and Press suggest that "[m]ore than 80 percent of Russia's silo-based ICBMs have exceeded their original service lives; failed tests and low rates of production have stymied plans to replace them with new missiles."[26]

According to Lieber and Press, "China's ability to redress the nuclear imbalance is even more suspect.... China has only 18 ICBMs, a number that has remained essentially unchanged for more than a decade. In addition, these missiles are kept unfueled, and their warheads are stored separately."[27] Even a cursory examination of the key characteristics of U.S. strategic weapons systems consisting of 3,246 available warheads with a total yield in kilotons of 2,310, and accuracies ranging from 30 meters for the B-52 bomber to 90 meters for the D-5 submarine launched missile[28] suggest that the U.S. has less to fear from its potential great power adversaries at the nuclear level. Thus, deterrence of tier-one threats is manageable.

Robert Jervis has suggested that "war among the leading great powers—the most developed states of the United States, Western Europe, and Japan—will not occur in the future, and indeed is no longer a source of concern for them."[29] However, the fact that the United States is not menaced by any competing great power obviously does not mean that it faces no threat at all. Free from the threats of great power conflicts, the Bush administration has adopted a grand strategy that is intent on pursuing policies that prevent the rise of competing "peer competitors." This has led to the perception that in this new threat environment the only way to ensure American security is to maximize the United States' freedom to respond to threats without the constraints of allies.

Given the administration's initial response to multilateral approaches to global agreements and its relations with its European allies, did the Bush administration develop a Gulliver complex after the terrorist's attacks of 9/11? One has only to recall the title of Stanley Hoffmann's 1968 classic study, *Gulliver's Troubles or the Setting of American Foreign Policy,* during the height of the Cold War. The title of that study uses the analogy of the literary character Gulliver to highlight the troubled relations between the United States and its European allies in confronting the Soviet Union. After 9/11 the growing perception among U.S. policy makers was that, unlike Gulliver, the United States cannot allow itself to be tied down by a group of lesser powers (Lilliputians) with different perspectives on how the administration should protect the American people in the new threat environment. Thus, the Bush administration would not allow itself to be bound by multilateral constraints, treaties, international legal regimes, and norms that are not deemed effective in providing security for the American people.

Deterrence of second-tier threats from rogues or regional armed nuclear powers, however, is more problematic, and deterrence would seem to have even less utility in deterrence of third-tier nonstate actors such as global terrorist organizations. Credible deterrence within a regional context may well differ from Cold War models. Classic East-West ideological issues no longer dominate the international agenda, for the seeds of conflicts rest in other areas, every thing from irredentism, to fear of losing status, coupled with a penchant for taking higher risk particularly if "status is already marginal."[30]

United States policy makers obliviously worry about foreign leaders who want to acquire WMDs. In this context questions of "rationality" inevitably pop up. Kenneth Watman and Dean Wilkening suggest "few states or leaders appear to be truly 'crazy' or 'undeterrable' and argue that...a more useful characterization of the motivation of potential adversaries is based not on 'craziness' but rather on the critical distinction between adversaries motivated to gain and adversaries motivated to avert loss (where loss or gain is determined from the adversary's perspective)."[31]

A critical factor in developing deterrence policies to dissuade potential regional adversaries from using WMDs is to understand that Western perceptions and criteria for rational action may not apply to these adversaries. Incongruent socialization processes along with other factors characteristic of Western societies may appear quite irrational in other regions.

Michael O. Wheeler sums up the complex demands of rational decision making and exposes possible flaws in assuming that mutual assured destruction applies to a world of strategic multipolarity as much as it did in a bipolar one. He argues that "traditional deterrence theory assumes a human actor who can reason, communicate, anticipate and assess consequences, weigh them against interests and values, form intentions, assess risks, balancing gains and losses, and act accordingly—an actor who knows his own mind, keeps emotions out of his decisions."[32]

The logic of rational decision-making by the two superpowers appears to have been valid in a bipolar world in which the Soviet Union and the United States arrived at similar views through negotiation, confrontation, hotline exchanges, surrogate warfare, nuclear testing, and mutual knowledge of the destructive potential of nuclear weapons.

Indeed, one might argue that they evolved toward similar "Western" perspectives on the use of force in the nuclear-induced stability of the Cold War decades. However, can we infer that similar evolving perspectives will exist in a world of strategic multipolarity with nuclear powers of different cultural and decision-making processes?

Wheeler caution that "when one moves from one culture to another, symbols can change. Behavior based on the symbolic meanings internal to a culture may affect what counts as 'rational' behavior in ways that policymakers can anticipate and adjust for in their deterrent policies."[33] According to this view, an essential task is to be aware of the impact of culture on perceptions of rationality. While this element of policy awareness was of diminishing concern in deterrence calculations between the two superpowers in the Cold War decades, it is essential in a world of multicultural actors. Therefore, "instead of thinking in terms of general deterrence theory," Wheeler argues that "we need to develop culture and society specific theories of deterrence."[34]

While this chapter does not propose to examine this issue in minute detail, it does suggest that further research should be conducted and resources allocated for an in-depth analysis of the impact of cultural norms on perceptions of rational decision making and risk taking. Despite the importance of this research, one should be aware of the complexity and pitfalls associated with the problem for, as Wheeler suggests, "one must rely heavily on area experts to help sort out the subtle influences on communications, reasoning, and decision-making which arise in difficult cultural settings. As opposed to a general deterrence theory, it is more appropriate to seek culturally-specific theories."[35]

Wheeler also caution that "[a]t the same time don't assume that there lies at the end of the path of greater knowledge about a particular rogue actor some consensus of area experts that allow perfect prediction of his behavior… experts can be (often are) wrong. It is worth recalling that Saddam Hussein's closest and most culturally similar neighbors didn't believe until the last minute that he was serious in the gulf crisis of 1990."[36]

Wheeler further reminds us that "what is 'rational' behavior may be quite complicated to figure out, even within one's own culture much less across cultures."[37] As Keith Payne argues, "assuming a generically sensible foe will present considerable risk. In contrast to past practice, deterrence goals of the second nuclear age will require devoting at least as much attention to the question 'How much do you know?' of the opponent as to the traditional question 'How much is enough?' "[38]

An important element in devising an effective deterrence approach for regional nuclear states in the emerging world of strategic multipolarity is to develop an understanding of the impact of culture on the risk-taking propensities of regional leaders possessing WMDs. Yaacov Y. I. Vertzberger explains, "culture represents a unified ensemble of ideas that are shared by the members of society," and "culture-based attitudes are more pertinent than other attitudes in unfamiliar, ill-defined, and ambiguous situations."[39]

What then is the impact of culture on the propensity of a regional leader with WMDs to take risks? Vertzberger notes that "[c]ulture plays a role in molding perceptions of risks as acceptable or not. Culture would seem to be the coding principle by which hazards are recognized."[40] He elaborates on the influence of culture in shaping leaders' perceptions of risk by explaining that "by providing filters through which people look at the world, culture may affect the assessment of all three components of risk."[41] He cites as an example "the value of human life varies across culture. In cultures that put a high premium on life, decisions involving risk to lives produce a risk-averse propensity, whereas in cultures that put a low premium on life, similar decisions do not preclude a risk acceptant propensity."[42]

Vertzberger concludes that "not only is risk assessment culture-bound, but the preferred strategy of coping with risk sometimes depends on attitudes nested in cultural norms about the desirability of risk acceptance and risk aversion."[43] What then does this mean for the deterrence of regional second-tier threats? First, it is clear that regional leaders' propensities for risk taking are linked to culture and United States strategic analysts must carefully assess cultural factors relevant to threat-specific responses.

Second, Vertzberger offers three caveats:

> Culture explanations cannot account for or predict by themselves, or even be the main explanatory variable for, risk-acceptance or risk-averse preferences in specific instances.

> [A]n exclusively culture explanation would have to be based on the assumption that individuals with identical culture biases would have similar risk propensities, meaning that individuals from the same culture would respond identically to similar risk, an inference that is not empirically justified.

> Finally, cultural values and customs can affect the criteria by which the validity of outcome-probability and outcome-value assessments are evaluated. In other words, the criteria for judging what is valid vary across cultures.[44]

One has only to consider the current situation with the issue of Iran's attempted acquisition of nuclear weapons. A recent *U.S. News & World Report* article points to the complex nature of Iran's current president, Mahmoud Ahmadinejad. When religion, mixed with a complicated governmental structure and a risk-acceptance personality, it is difficult to predict what will deter a leader driven by a strong messianic desire to acquire nuclear weapons for both domestic and regional purposes. For example, Jay Tolson explains in his article, *"Aiming for Apocalypse,"* that "[c]lues to this seemingly humorless technocrat lie, not surprisingly, in the branch of the Islamic sect to which he and most Shi'as subscribe—the 12th Imam, who is also called the Mahdi, shall return in the Last Days to reign over a just world in which Islam is universally embraced."[45] Consider the problems facing U.S. decision makers in seeking to determine how to deter Iran's leaders, when as Tolson suggest, there appears to be no consensus among the believers themselves.

Tolson writes, "But here arises a point on which Twelvers differ: Will the Mahdi come back only after chaos has erupted and the apocalypse has begun, intervening just in time to save righteous believers from total destruction? Or will his followers have to pave the way for the Mahdi's return by building a just order themselves, thereby enticing him to come out of hiding?"[46] Bernard Lewis, a noted Middle Eastern scholar, argues that "Ahmadinejad and his circle are in an apocalyptic mood.... The use of a nuclear weapon wouldn't bother them in the least."[47]

Consequently, further research is necessary to develop databases that, along with other information, will provide a basis for understanding the many factors that influence regional leaders' risk-taking propensities and preferences for challenging United States interests. While the MAD strategy may have been useful in the past, it has been argued that it is not in U.S. interests to formulate policies based on MAD to influence regional nuclear powers. It is essential that the United States develop strategies and force structures that maintain capabilities to deal with any regional or combination of regional nuclear adversaries.

The security dilemma may motivate second-tier state leaders to obtain nuclear weapons for the primary reason of national security, but the security environment becomes more fragile after nuclear acquisition. For example, India acquired nuclear weapons because of primary concern raised by a nuclear-armed China. Pakistan responded as a secondary consequence to India's acquisition by developing its own nuclear weapons. Given the topography, demography, and weather patterns of the region, one finds MAD with a vengeance and in the extreme. There is probably no other example of two regional scorpions guaranteeing mutual destruction under all circumstances of use. Still, for the leaders of India and Pakistan, nuclear weapons make sense. As George H. Quester suggested, "With regard to a South Asian confrontation, it is easy to find strategic analysts in both countries who (sounding totally in agreement with each other) argue that mutual deterrence will work to keep nuclear weapons from being used, even if the countries go to conventional war, just as mutual deterrence worked between Moscow and Washington during the Cold War."[48]

Paradoxically, American power makes the decision to seek nuclear status appear "rational." The North Korean decision to acquire nuclear weapons may appear irrational to many Americans, given North Korea's dire economic status and inability to feed its citizens, yet, because the acquisition of nuclear weapons provides a sense of international status as a player and provides bargaining power, all out of proportion to its size and status, North Korea's nuclear program has a clear-headed logic. In sum, the motivations and objectives of regional leaders must be viewed as central in the development of effective second-tier level deterrence strategies.

This is not a simple task, for regional leaders have at least three major motives for acquiring WMDs. In their 1994 RAND study, analysts Kenneth Watman and Dean Wilkening noted:

> The first, and perhaps most obvious, objective an opponent might have for threatening nuclear first use is to deter the United States from intervening in regional conflicts.

> A second objective for threatening nuclear first use is to intimidate U.S. allies.

> A third objective regional powers may seek with nuclear threats is regime protection should war occur.[49]

The first motive for acquiring nuclear weapons by a regional power may be found in the advice General K. Sundarj of the Indian Army gave when he said that one of the lessons of the Gulf War (1991) was that states should acquire nuclear weapons before engaging the United States in a regional conflict. North Korea's possession of nuclear weapons and their large conventional capability clearly constrain the United States policy options in its attempts to restrict North Korea's development of its nuclear arsenal. The very hint of possession of nuclear weapons by regional second-tier states serves to effectively create a moment of pause for decision makers contemplating action, further complicating the strategic chessboards of Asia and the Middle East.

The second motive may be illustrated by regional states threatening to use nuclear weapons to coerce allies of the United States into denying over-flight rights or basing rights to U.S. forces. The objective is to create fissures within alliances or coalitions arrayed against the regional state or, ultimately, to split allies or coalition partners away from the United States in an unfolding regional crisis.[50]

Indeed, this tactic has worked in the past with an economic instrument of statecraft, during the U.S. air attacks on Tripoli, Libya, during the Reagan administration. Admiral William J. Crowe Jr., former Chairman of the Joint Chiefs of Staff, provided an earlier example of using threats to pressure U.S. allies in denying over-flight rights to the U.S. in his book *The Line of Fire: From Washington to the Gulf: The Politics and Battles of the New Military*. Admiral Crowe writes:

> Regarding the use of FB-111.... At the same time requests were made to allow us to overfly France and Spain, but those governments kept us hanging by our teeth. We especially wanted to go across France, which would have shortened the flight by two or three hours. Without French permission we were looking at the F-111s spending seven hours in the air and refueling five times on the way down.[51]

Iraq's use of Scud missile attacks on Israel during the 1991 Gulf War was also an attempt to attain this second objective. It is logical to predict that regional nuclear-armed states in a strategic multipolar environment will also seek to accomplish similar objectives.

The crisis in North Korea provides an excellent case study of the third objective. The case of North Korean quest for nuclear weapons is instructive for "a stronger case, based on recent events and statements of U.S. officials, could be made to support the argument that North Korean leaders increasingly face a U.S. led attack, thus, Pyongyang's foremost goal of reunification [has been supplemented] with a concern with regime survival."[52]

Further evidence of the concerns of North Korea is explained by Victor D. Cha and David C. Kang in *Nuclear North Korea: A Debate on Engagement Strategies*. Cha suggest that "with the recently announced National Security

Strategy that moves the U.S. toward a stated policy of preemptive strikes, the North is worried that if it agrees to disarm and abandon its deterrence posture, the United States will move to destroy it."[53] Cha argues that "[i]n a nutshell, the problem is this: the United States refuses to give security guarantees to North Korea until it proves it has dismantled its weapons program. The North refuses to disarm until it has security guarantees from the United States."[54]

Referring to the North Korean decision to develop weapons-grade plutonium, George J. Tenet, former Director of the Central Intelligence Agency, informed the Senate Intelligence Committee that "the example of new states that seem to be able to deter threats from the more powerful states, simply by brandishing nuclear weaponry, will resonate deeply among other countries that want to enter the nuclear weapons club."[55]

As Jack Snyder writes in his article "Imperial Temptations," "It is difficult to imagine North Korea using nuclear weapons or mounting a conventional artillery barrage on the South Korean capital of Seoul for the purpose of conquest, but it is much easier to envision such desperate measures in response to preventive U.S. attacks on the core power resources of the regime."[56] In short, we see the third objective of regime survival becoming more salient since the removal of Saddam Hussein's regime in Iraq, for as Shaharan Chubin suggests, "States that feel threatened by U.S. claimed right to resort to preventive war and preemptive attacks, not as a last resort but now elevated to the level of doctrine, are liable to resort to extreme measures."[57]

It would be naïve of our decision makers to ignore the perceptions of regional leaders and nonstate actors in the emerging strategic multipolar international order. However, despite the complexity of providing second-tier deterrence, this writer would suggest that there is some historical evidence that the perceptions of the rationality of the once rogue leaders are viewed quite differently by American decision makers after the so-called rogue states had acquired nuclear weapons. That is, once regional leaders acquire nuclear status, they would also acquire a rational approach within the Western context of the word, to foreign and security decision making. This suggests a condition of nuclear-induced rationality and this assumption is given historical support by the relatively peaceful end to the Cold War between the two superpowers.

Indeed, with respect to China's acquisition of nuclear weapons and the reactions of the United States, the change in perception regarding the rationality of the leadership should be noted. Beijing once fit the description of a "rogue state"; some of Mao's most provocative statements regarding the effects of a nuclear exchange between the United States and China seem to have been forgotten and the leadership suddenly became rational actors.[58] This is not to suggest that further proliferation of nuclear weapons will usher in a period of nuclear-induced rationality on the part of regional leaders; it does suggest that historically, both the United States and the Soviet Union have adjusted to the addition of new nuclear states.

An important pillar of the Bush Doctrine addressing the issue of threats from rogue states seeking nuclear weapons is that these states represent grave threats to United States' security and to international stability. Yet, rogue state leaders are characterized as terrorist and given their propensity for risk-taking, United States policy must be based on deterrence by denial instead of deterrence by punishment. Therefore, policies based on international agreements for denying items that are critical to the development of WMDs should be emphasized. Clearly, any "strategy requires a multifaceted approach, including enhanced international cooperation in intelligence sharing, greater efforts to secure the still dangerous WMD inheritance of the former Soviet Union."[59] Because deterrence may not always be possible against rogue states seeking nuclear weapons, the United States must be ready to engage in preemption and wage preventive wars even acting against emerging threats before they are fully developed.

The outcome of events in Iraq, however, will shape the success of this policy and even a Gulliver free of the constraints of its Lilliputian allies may find that the task is greater than even the world's only superpower can accomplish. Indeed, coping with tier-three threats will demand that the United States abandon its Gulliver complex and work more closely with the Lilliputians in the post-9/11 world order.

The Illusion of Deterrence Sufficiency Tier-Three Threats to Deterrence Effectiveness

In the first decade of the twenty-first century, "The relatively orderly super-power-dominated world of the last half of the twentieth century is giving way to a disorderly and increasingly 'polyarchic' world in which the hegemonic power of the United States is being challenged by numerous actors, both state and nonstate."[60] For that reason, MAD as a deterrence policy is not sufficient to deter at all levels of threats to the United States. The view that it can be is an illusory promise because new threats from tier-three actors have emerged.

The deterrence of tier-three threats from nonstate actors, such as global terrorist organizations, is especially complex. The prospect of deterring what Friedman calls super-empowered individuals is highly problematical. To use the term "strategic multipolarity" when including individuals or collections of terrorists may indeed be misplaced, for the classical view of multipolarity only applies to relations between nation-states.

In confronting tier-three (nonstate actors) threats it would be irrational to suggest that deterrence through the threat of devastating retaliation as promised by the generic model of strategic deterrence will be useful or effective. The assumption that international terrorist organizations can be deterred from acquiring and using nuclear weapons can lead to unwise decision making. This unique challenge to deterrence theory leaves a gap that is yet to be fully explored.

One of the most complex challenges for strategic deterrence is posed by the potential of nuclear-armed terrorist groups. Recent research has offered a rather pessimistic assessment of the potential threats from nuclear-armed global terrorist groups, specifically, al-Qaeda. A 2005 RAND Corporation study caution that "[t]he historical record of terrorists pursuing nuclear and radiological capabilities is small in size, complicated by significant information gaps, and not well understood."[61] The study admits that "the size of the dataset and the considerable unknowns about cases where groups have sought these capabilities make it difficult to assess the nature of the danger and to anticipate new developments in the nature of the threats."[62]

The study emphasized that developing an effective and comprehensive strategy to prevent terrorist acquisition of nuclear and radiological weapons capabilities must begin with a through understanding of the historical record of terrorist efforts and opportunities to acquire these capabilities."[63] In their case study of alleged al-Qaeda attempts to acquire nuclear capabilities, the study sought to explain why al-Qaeda has failed in its efforts to acquire nuclear weapons. The analysts cite the following:

- Nuclear weapons may in fact be more secure than Western analysts have thought.
- The price demanded may simply have been too high for al-Qaeda to accept.
- Al-Qaeda members are still climbing the learning curve—developing the expertise, skills, and experience necessary to execute a nuclear weapons design.
- Al-Qaeda failed to attract the right experts.
- The nuclear weapons and materials market is a difficult and dangerous place to negotiate.[64]

Regarding al-Qaeda's prospects for the future, the study concluded, "There is no solid evidence that al Qaeda, or indeed any terrorist group, has acquired nuclear weapons although the desire clearly is there…[we] don't have any evidence to support concerns over lost, stolen or misappropriated nuclear devices."[65] Despite this rather positive conclusion, the study warns, "while the likelihood might be low, the consequences of the terrorist use of nuclear weapons are likely to be high. In 2002, an al Qaeda spokesman declared the organization's intention to kill four million Americans, albeit with chemical or biological rather than nuclear weapons."[66]

Regarding the issue of chemical and biological weapons use by tier-three actors it is reported that President Clinton predicted "that there is a 100 percent likelihood of a biological or chemical terrorist attack on U.S. soil in the next 10 years."[67] Nuclear weapons, however, are in a class by themselves for their destructive potential, far exceeding those of chemical or biological weapons for immediate effects. Regarding chemical and biological weapons use by second-tier states, "the focus should be on the nonproliferation efforts aimed at acquisition of such weapons and the deterrence efforts focused on their use."[68] Tier-three threats from nonstate actors such as global terrorist groups represent a most difficult problem for deterrence and defy the ability of deterrence theory to offer new strategies for policy makers.

The September 11, 2001, terrorist attacks and the October 2001 anthrax attacks increased public demands for governmental actions to deter potential terrorist use of chemical and biological attacks. In the study, *Deadly Arsenals: Tracking Weapons of Mass Destruction,* Joseph Cirincione suggests that "recent technological developments have contributed to the threat posed by chemical and biological weapons. The spread of dual-use chemical technologies has facilitated the surreptitious acquisition of indigenous chemical weapons programs by potential proliferators, while advances in biotechnology could expand the availability and lethality of common biological weapons agents."[69]

The news is both positive and negative for "the level of technical expertise for acquiring a biological warfare capability remains unclear. Several key traits make pathogens or toxins suitable for use as biological weapons: availability or ease of production; lethality; particle size and weight; ease of dissemination; and stability. To maximize their efficacy, biological agents must be delivered over a widespread area in appropriate doses and under conditions that ensure agent survival."[70] The potential positive news is that:

> Some experts argue that while agent production is not technically difficult, combining a stable biological agent with an effective dissemination device requires sophisticated technology and expertise. Agent survival is a prerequisite for infection, and biological warfare agents are vulnerable to environmental conditions, including desiccation, humidity, and oxidation. Many agents, particularly live organisms, die when exposed to light or oxygen. Other agents require moisture to survive. Most cannot withstand heat or explosive force.[71]

The negative news, however, is that the study found that "developing a crude biological weapons requires only a modest level of expertise. Recent advances in the biological sciences, or the "biotechnology revolution," have increased the availability of dual-use equipment and the number of individuals with the knowledge necessary for biological weapons production."[72]

It is not my intention to assess the chemical and biological threats as a part of the logic of deterrence strategies in the post-9/11 environment. Suffice it to conclude that a strategy for preventing chemical, biological, and radiological terrorist attacks would have to be multifaceted and would have to address the full spectrum of activities, from prevention to retribution and prosecution to domestic preparedness. The Bush Doctrine's response to tier-three threats is based on the assumption that terrorists are fanatics, and are quite risk-acceptant. Thus, preemption and preventive actions are necessary. However, can decision makers rely on the assumption that all terrorists have this flaw? Are we to assume that Osama bin Laden and al-Qaeda are unaware that Muslims around the world also could be awed by bin Laden's capability to inflict such destruction? But nuclear use does have the potential of provoking revulsion among the very communities that bin Laden is seeking to rally to his restored Muslim Caliphate. Thus, this very different element of al-Qaeda's targeting code—its emphasis on the impact of attacks on the broader Islamic audience—could raise questions about the desirability of mass killing on the nuclear level. Put most starkly, use of even nuclear weapons could be regarded as fully permissible in principle but in practice not seen at a particular time to be a necessary or helpful means to pursue al-Qaeda's goals.[73]

While bin Laden has emphasized the duty to acquire nuclear weapons, it remains to be seen what purpose al-Qaeda would use them. If bin Laden and al-Qaeda's objective is to reestablish the Islamic Caliphate, then the use of nuclear weapons in the region would undermine that goal.[74] Given the potential for nuclear use, the Bush Doctrine's focus on a strategy of preemption and preventive war is logical. As Dunn argues, "Prudence demands that U.S. policy and posture be based on the assumption that Osama bin Laden and al Qaeda would be fully prepared to use nuclear, biological, chemical, or radiological weapons."[75]

The Bush Doctrine and the Fate of Deterrence in the Post-9/11 World

The American people should be aware that the Truman administration's response to the Soviet threat evolved over a period of years and that the containment strategy was modified with each successive administration. It required the development of a new worldview, an adequate assessment of the threat and that worldview becoming policy. George F. Kennan's 1946 "Long Telegram," the Truman Doctrine, Marshall Plan, and NSC-68 (National Security Council, 1950) were responses to the perceived threat resulting in the containment policy that guided the United States' foreign and security policies for at least four decades.

The Bush Doctrine is not a complete and therefore unchangeable strategy for providing security in the post-9/11 world order. Just as the containment policy evolved over time in response to the threat, so will the Bush Doctrine in its attempt to cope with the post-9/11 threats.

Developing effective deterrence policies for the post-9/11 international order will require encompassing an interdisciplinary approach and the allocation of human and material resources that were not critical factors during the bipolar world of the Cold War decades. Clearly the challenges are more complex, and it is now necessary for decision makers to include experts not considered important during the Cold War era. Perhaps, as Michael O. Wheeler suggests, "instead of thinking in terms of a general theory of deterrence, we need to develop culture and society specific theories of deterrence."[76]

Reflecting on the past and now the future, it is difficult to conceive of an all-encompassing general deterrence approach that will act as a credible deterrent to the numerous and culturally diverse mini-scorpions. Whereas the threat-specific nuclear strategy that had evolved during the Cold War was perceived to be credible within an overall grand strategy of containing communist expansion, it is highly questionable that such a holistic strategy would obtain in the post-9/11 order.

Given the diverse regional nuclear powers and potential nuclear armed nonstate actors that make up the strategic landscape in the twenty-first century, the task for decision makers will be to enhance the ability of the United States to (1) assess character and motivation of regional powers and nonstate actors, (2) develop multilateral allies in countering proliferation struggle and global terrorism, (3) develop ways of making deterrence credible, and (4) acquire the diverse capabilities tailored to credibly implement denial, dissuasion, and punishment strategies.

Developing an effective deterrence strategy for the post-9/11 world order should be based on a three-tiered approach. A deterrence approach based on MAD will have continued utility for deterring the first-tier threat (i.e., Russia or China). However, the task will be more difficult for second- and third-tier threats. Deterrence in the post-9/11 world order will present United States decision makers and strategic planners with the highly complex tasks of developing broad-spectrum deterrence strategies in a world of disparate political entities. The very diversity of potential nuclear states and nonstate actors, with their unique cultures, religions, regime stability or instability, and diverse risk-taking propensities might well doom forever notions of general deterrence.

One approach is to adopt an Adaptive Strategic Option. This approach would not depend on a "generically rational opponent" model for planning and would allow for a more flexible response based on the development of a capacity to analyze cultural factors that will shape the potentially hostile leader's decision-making process and, of key importance, predict the leader's risk-taking propensities. The development of a database that contains these factors will enhance the development of targeting plans for deterring second-tier regional nuclear states.[77]

The third-tier threats presents the most difficult, complex, and hence troublesome challenge due to the relatively diverse and complex views, religious motivations, and the levels of the stakes involved. Therefore, acquiring maximum knowledge of the interests, culture, decision-making processes, and leaders' risk-taking proclivities must be considered only as a beginning of the list of actions to be accomplished. It may well be threats from nuclear-armed states and nonstate actors will require tailor-made strategies and force mixes. One of the most compelling strategic options in the Adaptive Strategic

Options approach is for the United States and its allies to assist in reforming Islamic views of the West.

In the final analysis, every student of strategic nuclear deterrence is familiar with Bernard Brodie's advice regarding the use of nuclear weapons: "thus far the chief purpose of our military establishment has been to win wars. From now on, the chief purpose must be to avert them."[78] This is true of deterrence even in the post-9/11 environment of the twenty-first century.

Notes

1. Zalmay Khalizard and Ian O. Lesser, *Sources of Conflict in the 21st Century: Regional Futures and U.S. Strategy* (Santa Monica: Arroyo Center, RAND, 1998), 18.
2. Willie Curtis, "The Assured Vulnerability Paradigm: Can It Provide a Useful Basis for Deterrence in a World of Strategic Miltipolarity?" in *Searching for National Security in an NBC World*, ed. James M. Smith (Colorado: USAF, Institute for National Security Studies, July 2000), 16.
3. Ibid.
4. George W. Bush, President's Radio Address, "War on Terror," White House press release, March 8, 2003.
5. See White House, "National Strategy to Combat Weapons of Mass Destruction," December 2003, 1.
6. The National Security Strategy of the United States, September 17, 2002, 4, http://www.whitehouse.gov/nsc/nss.pdf; hereafter, 2002 NSS.
7. Ibid.
8. Khalizard and Lesser, *Sources of Conflict in the 21st Century*, 18-19.
9. Ibid.
10. Christoph Bertram, *Strategic Deterrence in a Changing Environment*, Adelphia Library 6, The International Institute for Strategic Studies (Montclair, NJ: Allanheld, Osmun, 1981), 7.
11. Ibid.
12. Ibid.
13. Ibid.
14. Ibid., 7-8.
15. Keith B. Payne, *Deterrence in the Second Nuclear Age* (Lexington: The University Press of Kentucky, 1996), 61.
16. Ibid. 61-62.
17. Thomas L. Friedman, *Longitudes & Attitudes: Exploring the World After September 11* (New York: Farrar, Straus and Giroux, 2002), 4-5. Friedman writes that several features of the new globalization system are quite relevant if we are to understand the events of 9/11.

    Whether by enabling people to use the Internet to communicate instantly... or enabling them to use the Web to transfer money or obtain weapons designs that normally would have been controlled by states, or by enabling them to go into a hardware store now and buy a five-hundred-dollar global positioning device connected to a satellite, that can direct a hijacked airplane—globalization can be an incredible force-multiplier for individuals. As you have today not only superpower, not only supermarkets, but also what I call "super-empowered individuals." Some of these super-empowered individuals are quite angry, some of them quite wonderful—but all of them are now able to act much directly and much more powerfully on the world stage. (5-6)

18. Ibid.
19. Ibid, 46-47.
20. Ibid., 46.
21. Ibid., 6.
22. Keir A. Lieber and Daryl G. Press, "The End of MAD? The Nuclear Dimension of U.S. Primacy," *International Security* 30 (Spring 2006): 13.
23. Ibid., 7-8.
24. Ibid.
25. Ibid., 11-12.
26. Ibid., 26.
27. Ibid., 27.
28. Keir A. Lieber and Daryl G. Press, "The End of MAD? The Nuclear Dimension of U.S. Primacy," *International Security* 30 (Spring 2006): 18.
29. Robert Jervis, *American Foreign Policy in a New Era* (New York: Routledge), 12.
30. Kenneth Watman, Dean Wilkening with John Arquilla, Brian Nichiporuk, *U.S. Regional Deterrence Strategy* (Santa Monica, CA: RAND, 1995), xi.
31. Ibid.
32. Michael O. Wheeler, "Weapons of Mass Destruction in Regional Equation: The New Deterrence Equation," White Paper on Deterrence (Washington, DC: SAIC, January 1995), 18-19.
33. Ibid., 19.
34. Ibid., 37.
35. Ibid., 21.
36. Ibid.
37. Ibid.
38. Keith B. Payne, *Deterrence in the Second Nuclear Age* (Lexington: The University Press of Kentucky, 1996), 157.
39. Yaacov Y. I. Vertzberger, *Risk Taking and Decisionmaking: Foreign Military Intervention Decisions* (Stanford: Stanford University Press, 1998), 60.
40. Ibid., 61.
41. Ibid.
42. Ibid.
43. Ibid., 62.
44. Ibid., 61.
45. Jay Tolson, "Aiming for Apocalypse," *U.S. News & World Report*, May 22, 2006, 34.
46. Ibid.
47. Ibid., 35.

48. George H. Quester, *Nuclear First Strike: Consequences of Broken Taboo* (Baltimore: The Johns Hopkins University Press, 2006), 129. Quester also writes, "Deterrence can indeed work between Pakistan and India, or between any two countries that might face each other with nuclear arsenals in the future, just as it worked between the nuclear superpowers during the Cold War. However, in the midst of that Cold War period, we were never certain that nuclear deterrence would work, and there were constant risks that it might fail" 130.

49. Kenneth Watman and Dean Wilkening, *U.S. Regional Deterrence Strategies* (Santa Monica, CA: RAND, Arrovo Centre, 1994), 32.

50. Ibid.

51. William J. Crowe, Jr., *The Line of Fire: From Washington to the Gulf, and Politics and Battles of the New Military* (New York: Simon & Schuster, 1993) 137.

52. Homer T. Hodge, "North Korea's Military Strategy," *Parameter* (Spring 2003): 70. Also see Quester's analysis of the situation in *Nuclear First Strike*:

    When a country like Israel or North Korea today moves to acquire nuclear weapons and in the process reinsures its own continued existence, despite the hostility and disapproval of its neighbors, one could read even this as the world's giving in to the fear of nuclear destruction. But, as long as such basic deterrence works without the weapon's actually having to be detonated, we do not have the violation of the nuclear taboo…we instead have only a continuation of the nuclear deterrence by threat that has been the pattern for all the years since Nagasaki, as has been so aptly analyzed by Pierre Gallois, Kenneth Waltz, and many others. (45)

53. Victor D. Cha and David C. Kang, *Nuclear North Korea: A Debate on Engagement Strategies* (New York: Columbia University Press, 2003), 43.

54. Ibid.

55. Walter Pincus, "CIA Head Predicts Nuclear Races," *Washington Post*, February 12, 2003, A1.

56. Jack Snyder, "Imperial Temptation," *The National Interest* 71 (Spring 2003): 31.

57. Shahram Chubin, "Evil Axis": One Year On," Geneva Centre for Security Policy, http://www.gcsp.ch/E/publications/Security_Challenges/OpEd_NewsArticles/Chubin_Jan03.htm.

58. In George H. Quester, *Nuclear First Strike*:

    The earliest 1960 speculation about nuclear weapons being acquired by Communist China voiced the kinds of concerns we feel today about irresponsible behavior by a "rogue state." Beijing was then seen as being much more revolutionary and anti-Western than Moscow, and as perhaps ready to use nuclear weapons even when the Soviet leadership would have been deterred. Mao issued some statements (when the Chinese as yet did not have any such weapons) indicating that China would welcome nuclear war, because it had such a large reserve of population. The fanatical Chinese Communists were thus seen as much more likely than any other state to initiate the use of nuclear weapons, or at least to push crises to the brink of such use. (46-47)

59. Aspen Strategy Group, *In Search of an American Grand Strategy for the Middle East* (Washington, DC: The Aspen Institute, 2004), 9.

60. Seyom Brown, *The Illusion of Control: Force and Foreign Policy in the 21st Century* (Washington, DC: Brookings Institution Press, 2003), 2. Brown defines polyarchy as a "Pattern of international relations featuring many different kinds of actors—government and nongovernmental—characterized by diverse alignments and adversary relationships subject to change issue by issue and lacking a dominant axis of cooperation and conflict."

61. Sara Daly, John Parachini, and William Rosenau, *Lessons from Aum Shinrikyo, Al Qaeda, and the Kinshasa Reactor: Implications of the Three Case Studies for Combating Terrorism* (Santa Monica: RAND, 2005), iii.

62. Ibid.

63. Ibid.

64. Ibid., 49-50.

65. Ibid., 52.

66. Ibid.

67. Richard Clarke, National Coordinator for Security, Counterterrorism, and Infrastructure Protection, *60 Minutes*, October 22, 2000, transcript.

68. Ibid., 22.

69. Joseph Cirincione, *Deadly Arsenals: Tracking Weapons of Mass Destruction,* (Washington, DC: Carnegie Endowment for International Peace, 2002), 45.

70. Ibid., 46.

71. Ibid., 47.

72. Ibid. The study also suggest that "[t]he acquisition of a BW capability requires advanced expertise in various disciplines, including microbiology and aerobiology. Once obtained, however, biological weapons are extremely suitable for covert delivery. As a result, their use by terrorists has been identified as a growing threat to international security. Terrorist intentions involving biological weapons were exposed publicly by the repeated attempts of the Aum Shinrikyo cult to produce and distribute two lethal biological agents in Japan in 1994 and 1995."

73. Lewis A. Dunn, "Can al Qaeda Be Deterred from Using Nuclear Weapons?," Occasional Paper 3 (Washington, DC: Center for the Study of Weapons of Mass Destruction, July 2005), 11.

74. Ibid., 19.

75. Ibid., 22.

76. Wheeler, "Weapons of Mass Destruction in Regional Equation."

77. Willie Curtis, "The Assured Vulnerability Paradigm: Can It Provide a Useful Basis for Deterrence in a World of Strategic Multipolarity" in *Searching for National Security in an NBC World*, ed. James M. Smith (Colorado: USAF Institute for National Security Studies, 2000), 46-48.

78. Bernard Brodie, ed., *The Absolute Weapon: Atomic Power and World Order* (New York: Harcourt, Brace, 1946), 76.

6

Deterrence in an Age of Asymmetric Rivals

Rogue Leaders and Terrorists

JERROLD M. POST

The security doctrine of the George W. Bush presidency has been materially shaped by post-Cold War actors. The transnational terrorist threat of al-Qaeda under the leadership of Osama bin Laden, signaled by the coordinated attacks of 9/11, ushered in the "war on terrorism," with the initial attack on the Taliban regime in Afghanistan. The perceived threat to Middle East stability and the imminent threat of a nuclear capability, coupled with the stated association with the al-Qaeda terrorist threat posed by Saddam Hussein of Iraq was the stated justification for the March 2003 Second Gulf War with Iraq.

In this chapter, I will provide summaries of actor-specific behavior models for the psychology and political behavior of two rogue national leaders, Saddam Hussein of Iraq and Kim Jong-il of North Korea, as well as the social psychology of nonstate terrorist actors, and discuss in a post-Cold War framework the implications of these understandings for policies designed to inhibit and counter the policies and goals of these adversaries. Note: Inhibit and counter, *not* deter. This will be both broader and less specific than that of the doctrine of deterrence theory in the Cold War era.

Indeed, this is the principal argument of this chapter, that we must not uncritically apply doctrine developed during the Cold War for deterring our superpower rival in the new post-Cold War security environment, where the nature of our adversaries, especially since 9/11, is so different. As Alexander George has emphasized, it is critical to have actor-specific behavioral models of our adversaries, to understand their political psychologies, and to craft policies that are informed by those psychological understandings. For the two rogue leaders selected to illustrate this point, Saddam Hussein and Kim Jong-il, actors in leader-dominant societies, this requires nuanced political personality profiles that are accurately located in their political and cultural contexts. With Saddam, on trial for war crimes at this writing, I will focus on several key junctures. With Kim Jong-il, whose regime poses a continuing major threat, I will, after presenting a summary political personality profile, suggest an approach predicated on those psychological understandings. And with the transnational terrorist threat, after presenting a social psychological analysis, I will suggest a long-range program that, in my judgment, is necessary to put into place.

Saddam Hussein

An examination of the record of Saddam Hussein's leadership of Iraq for the past 34 years revealed a judicious political calculator, who however often miscalculated, and was by no means irrational, but was dangerous to the extreme. Drawing on a clear pattern of being able to reverse himself when a policy direction was proved to be counterproductive, I testified to Congress in December 1990 that he had explained that all actions of the revolution were justified by the "exceptionalism of revolutionary needs." In fact, an examination of Saddam Hussein's life and career reveals this was but the ideological rationalization for a lifelong pattern in which all actions were justified if they were in the service of furthering his needs and messianic ambitions. Accordingly, he could—note could, not would—reverse himself and withdraw from Kuwait *if*, and only *if*, he could do so and preserve face and preserve his power base, a double contingency.

To understand why he did not withdraw in the face of an overwhelming military force, it is necessary to describe the dynamic that unfolded between Hussein and the U.S. under the leadership of President George H. W. Bush and the impact on Hussein of the international reaction to the invasion of Kuwait.

In trying to understand Hussein's complex psychology, it is useful to consider the three principal layers of Hussein's psychology, layers for which the architecture of his three principal residences provides an apt metaphor. At the core of his personality is profound insecurity, a "wounded self," symbolized by the mud hut. His compensatory grandiose self, his dreams of glory, is represented by the magnificent palaces with which he dotted the landscape of Iraq. And under the palaces were underground bunkers, representing the default position in his political psychology, the defiant siege state, ready to be attacked, ready to defend.

The failure of Hussein's mother to nurture and bond with her infant son and the subsequent abuse at the hands of his stepfather would have profoundly wounded his emerging self-esteem, impairing his capacity for empathy with others. Such profound trauma in the first years of life would produce what has been called "the wounded self," a metaphor for which is the mud hut, representing the emotional impoverishment of his early years. One course in the face of such traumatizing experiences is to sink into despair, passivity, and hopelessness. But another is to etch a psychological template of compensatory grandiosity, as if to vow, "Never again, never again shall I submit to superior force." This was the developmental psychological path Hussein followed. His political mentor, his uncle Khairallah Talfah, inspired Hussein with dreams of glory, predicting that one day he would follow in the path of his relatives and of two historical heroes of the Arab world, Nebuchadnezzar and Saladin, who liberated Jerusalem from the Crusaders.

Fulfilling His Dreams of Glory

Throughout his career, Hussein craved the heroic recognition his uncle had prophesied. He believed he should be ranked with history's great socialist leaders—Mao Zedong, Ho Chi Minh, Tito, and Fidel Castro. He created a cult of personality within Iraq, with statues and murals of him throughout Baghdad and in other cities and towns of Iraq.

But the international community never gave Hussein the recognition as a world-class leader that he so craved—that is, until the summer 1990 invasion of Kuwait, which was a transformational event. He gave a guttural grunt, and oil barrel prices jumped $20 a barrel, the Dow Jones stock average fell 200 points. He had the world by the throat. More importantly, radical Arabs were cheering for him, Palestinians saw him as the leader who would regain Jerusalem for them. It was a fulfillment of his uncle's prophecy. It was a fulfillment of his dreams of glory.

So this was a transformational moment for Hussein. With the Gulf crisis, for the first time in his entire career, Saddam was exactly where he believed he was destined to be—a world-class political actor on center stage, commanding world events, and he could not easily retreat from the pinnacle of glory. Nevertheless, as I had observed in my Congressional testimony, should circumstances demonstrate that he had miscalculated, he was capable of reversing his course. In these circumstances, he did not acknowledge he had erred, but rather that he was adapting to a dynamic situation. Why, then, faced with superior military force, did he not withdraw?

While Hussein appreciated the danger of the Gulf crisis, it did provide the opportunity to defy the hated outsiders, a strong value in his Ba'ath ideology. He continued to cast the conflict as a struggle between Iraq and the United States, and even more personally as a struggle between the gladiators: Saddam Hussein versus George Bush. When the struggle became thus personalized, it enhanced Saddam's reputation as a courageous strongman willing to defy the imperialist United States.

When President Bush depicted the conflict as the unified civilized world against Saddam Hussein, however, it hit a tender nerve for Hussein. Hussein had his eye on his role in history and placed great stock in world opinion. If he were to conclude that his status as a world leader was threatened, it would have important constraining effects on him. Thus, the prospect of being expelled from the United Nations and of Iraq being castigated as a rogue nation outside the community of nations would have been very threatening to Hussein. That the overwhelming majority supported the UN Security Council resolution at the time of the conflict must have confronted Hussein with the damage he was inflicting on his stature as a leader, despite his defiant rhetoric dismissing the resolutions of the United Nations as reflecting the United States' control of the international organization.

But now that he was at the very center of international attention, his appetite for glory was stimulated all the more. The glory-seeking Hussein would not easily yield the spotlight of international attention. He wanted to remain on center stage, but not at the expense of his power and his prestige. In my testimony before the House, I observed that Hussein had a long-standing pattern of reversing counterproductive policies, and could withdraw from Kuwait, but that Hussein would only withdraw *if* he calculated that he could do so with his power *and* his honor intact, and that the drama in which he was starring would continue, a double contingency. Thus it would be important not to insist on total capitulation and humiliation, for this could drive Hussein into a corner and make it impossible for him to reverse his course.

How can it be, then, that this self-described revolutionary pragmatist, faced by an overwhelming array of military power that would surely deal a mortal blow to his regime, entered into and persisted in a violent confrontational course? Cultural factors probably contributed to his calculation and miscalculation. Hussein may well have heard Bush's Western words of intent through a Middle Eastern filter and calculated that he was bluffing. Even though he expected a massive air strike, he undoubtedly was surprised by the magnitude of the destruction wrought on his forces.

But more important, the dynamic of the crisis affected Hussein. What began as an act of naked aggression toward Kuwait was transformed into the culminating act of the drama of his life. Although he had previously shown little concern for the Palestinian people, the shrewdly manipulative Hussein had wrapped himself and his invasion of Kuwait in the Palestinian flag. The response of the Palestinians was overwhelming. They saw Hussein as their hope and their salvation, standing up defiantly and courageously to the United States to force a just settlement of their cause. This caught the imagination of the masses throughout the Arab world and their shouts of approval fed his already swollen ego as he went on a defiant roll.

Intoxicated by the elixir of power and the acclaim of the Palestinians and the radical Arab masses, Hussein may well have been on a euphoric high and optimistically overestimated his chances for success, for his heroic self-image was engaged as never before. He was fulfilling the messianic goal that had obsessed him—and eluded him throughout his life. He was actualizing his self-concept as leader of all the Arab peoples, the legitimate heir of Nebuchadnezzar, Saladin, and especially Egyptian President Nasser.

His psychology and his policy options became captives of his rhetoric. He became so absolutist in his commitment to the Palestinian cause and to not yielding Kuwait until there was justice for the Palestinian people and UN Resolutions 242 and 338 had been complied with, that it would have been extremely difficult for him to reverse himself without being dishonored. To lose face in the Arab world is to be without authority. Unlike past reversals, these absolutist pronouncements were in the full spotlight of international attention. Hussein had, in effect, painted himself into a corner. The Bush administration's insistence on "no face-saving" only intensified this dilemma.

Not only, then, had Hussein concluded that to reverse himself would be to lose his honor, but he also probably doubted that his power base would be preserved if he left Kuwait. Hussein doubted that the aggressive intention of the United States would stop at the border of Iraq. For years he had been convinced that a U.S.-Iran-Israeli conspiracy was in place to destroy Iraq and remove him from power.

By late December 1990 the semblance of diplomatic flexibility had disappeared, and Hussein seemed intent on challenging the coalition's ultimatum. It is likely that he had concluded that he could not reverse himself and withdraw without being dishonored and needed to enter the conflict to demonstrate his courage and to affirm his claim to pan-Arab leadership.

Hussein hoped to consolidate his place in Arab history as Nasser's heir by bravely confronting the U.S.-led coalition. On the third day of the air campaign, his minister of information, Latif Jassim, declared victory. To the astounded press he explained that the coalition expected Iraq to crumble in two days. Having already survived the massive air strikes for three days, the Iraqis were accordingly victorious, and each further day would only magnify the scope of their victory.

Weapons of Mass Destruction

To Hussein, nuclear weapons, and weapons of mass destruction (WMDs) in general, were important, indeed critical. After all, world-class leaders have world-class weapons. Especially because the military was grievously wounded by the 1991 conflict, with a marked reduction in conventional strength, unconventional weapons had become all the more important. Moreover, defying the international community on this matter was a regular reminder to the military of his courage in defying the superior adversary and that he had not and would not capitulate. Aided by the divisions within the UN that Hussein helped promote, Iraq succeeded in winning important concessions on the sanctions front relating to weapons inspections. This was crucial in continuing to build Hussein's support among the Iraqi people—it was seen as a victory. The embargo was dissipating slowly, and yet Hussein did not have to give up his WMDs. His power elite felt more empowered, resulting in solidifying Hussein's position in Iraq. Those who might have challenged a leader perceived to be a loser did not dare challenge a leader who had successfully challenged the United Nations and the United States. The nuclear threat, of course, was the primary stated reason for the 2003 invasion of Iraq.

While there was no reason to believe Hussein would proactively employ weapons of mass destruction against the U.S. or Israel, nor that he would yield control over such weapons and give them to a terrorist group, the persistent calls for regime change may well have moved him into that dangerous "back against the wall" posture. The setting afire of the Kuwaiti oil fields as he retreated in 1991 was an example that might well be repeated with his own Iraqi oil fields, as if to say, "If I can't have them, no one will." Moreover, with his back to the wall it is probable that he would, if he had such weapons within his armory, attempt to use chemical/biological weapons against Israel and against U.S. armed forces in the region. The question then would be the degree to which he could continue to sustain the loyalty of his senior military commanders or whether they could be induced to disobey Hussein in extremis in order to safeguard their own futures.

In any event, after the conflict, no weapons of mass destruction were found. The most likely explanation had to do internal insecurity. A principle of Hussein's leadership that has always been true—ensuring his domestic stability and eliminating internal threats to his regime—intensified in the postwar period, and was Hussein's central concern. The three greatest threats to Hussein's domestic stability after the 1991 conflict came from a dramatically weakened military, fractures in tribal loyalties, and fault lines in the family. Thus Hussein's leadership position was quite fragile after the 1991 conflict, especially with a major weakening of his conventional military apparatus. To sustain military support he needed to be able plausibly to convey that Iraq maintained a WMD capability, even though it meant sustaining large financial losses.

Hussein: Lessons for the New Deterrence

Perhaps the most important lesson is the absolute requirement in the post-Cold War environment for accurate nuanced political personality profiles of our adversaries. One cannot deter an adversary one does not understand. It may well be that a flawed image of Hussein by U.S. leadership contributed to some of the judgments leading to the conflict—two of the images in particular, that of the relationship between Saddam Hussein and Osama bin Laden, and that which supported the notion that he was a threat to distribute WMDs to terrorist groups out of his control. While often misguided, Hussein was prudent, and this notion was inconsistent with his leadership style.

How does one deter a leader who gains strength from defiance, whose stature is magnified by courageously confronting the superior adversary, who cannot back down without being seen as capitulating and accordingly in threat of losing his power? After the 1991 conflict, those who had too rapidly shown their enthusiasm for Hussein's overthrow were ruthlessly hunted down, and they and their families were arrested, tortured, and executed. This was at the foundation of the reluctance in the 2003 conflict of Hussein's followers to defect until it was a certainty that Hussein could not return to power.

But with the understanding that loyalty to Hussein came out of the barrel of a gun, there were lessons to be learned that could be, indeed were, employed to undermine Hussein's power and control over the security apparatus. In the fall before the conflict, Secretary of Defense Donald Rumsfeld in a public address asserted that the generals had an important role to play in the reconstruction of Iraq, but of course if they became involved in weapons of mass destruction, all bets were off. Two weeks later, President Bush stated that Saddam Hussein might well order his military commanders to use weapons of mass destruction. If he did, he went on to say, they would be well advised to disobey those orders. This was a clear example of public information operations, rhetoric in support of undermining Hussein's support, of breaking the connection between the leader and his followers. The battlefield was then leafleted with messages that any military commander using weapons of mass destruction could not use the excuse that he was following orders but would be found liable under war crimes acts. Was this conventional deterrence? No. Was it designed, employing a nuanced understanding of the power dynamics in Iraq, to undermine Hussein's authority and inhibit the potential for the user of weapons of mass destruction? Absolutely. And we believe the new deterrence must encompass such techniques.

In the Shadow of His Father: Kim Jong-il of North Korea[1]

It is always a daunting psychological challenge to succeed an important father and create one's own distinctive identity. But being the son of God is quite another matter, quite dangerous as religious history records. And that was the challenge facing Kim Jong-il, stepping into the giant shoes of his father, the God-like charismatic leader Kim Il-sung, who founded the nation.

One cannot understand the political psychology of the son without placing it in the context of the life and charismatic leadership of his father, Kim Il-sung, North Korea's first leader. One of the difficulties in assessing the personality and political behavior of Kim Il-sung has always been discerning the man behind the myth. The gap between the facts that scholars have been able to piece together and the hagiographic portrait presented to the people of North Korea is staggering. This extends to the gap between the facts of the life of Kim Jong-il and the mythic public presentation. Examining this gap is instructive, as it may reflect areas of sensitivity, the ideal versus the real.

Throughout the course of his life, Kim worked tirelessly to create a cult of personality that sustained him not only in life, but has continued to persist after his death. The Korean Workers Party (KWP) Department of Propaganda and Agitation has been devoted since its inception to furthering the image of Kim Il-sung and his family as loyal and fiercely patriotic Koreans through recreating the family history of Kim Il-sung and his family. Known as The Great Leader, the near divine image of Kim Il-sung continues to influence North Korean policy from the grave, and to materially influence the leadership decisions of his son. Indeed, Kim Il-sung was named Eternal President in the 1972 revision of the constitution, and the slogan "The Great Leader Will Always Be With Us" is in bold, yellow letters across the bottom of the Democratic People's Republic of Korea (DPRK) Web site.

It is important to emphasize that the architect of the cult of personality surrounding Kim Il-sung was his son, Kim Jong-il, who at age 30 was appointed director of the Department of Propaganda and Agitation, with a principal responsibility of enshrining his father's God-like image. He knew the gap between the man and the myth. Moreover, the subsequent campaign to identify the son with the father was also Kim Jong-il's creation.

Kim Jong-il used his position in the Department of Propaganda and Agitation to deepen and influence ideological indoctrination throughout North Korea, enforcing political conformity and continuing to build the myth of the Kim family. It became clear in the early 1970s that his father had designated Kim Jong-il as the heir to the North Korean power seat. By grooming his son to succeed him, Kim hoped to avoid in North Korea what happened in the aftermath of Stalin's death in the Soviet Union and of Mao's demise in the People's Republic of China. Kim Il-sung hoped to provide a basis not only for stability but also for perpetuation of the unique aspects of the DPRK's system. This became clearer as Kim Jong-il became a KWP secretary in September 1973 and a full member of the Politburo in 1974 at the tender age of 30.

It was during the 1970s that Kim Jong-il consolidated his position of power within the North Korean political system. Not tolerant of dissent during the 1970s, Kim "replaced thousands of officials at all levels of the party with younger members who would be personally loyal to him in gratitude for their promotion." Kim has worked assiduously to incorporate or eliminate peers of his father depending on their support for him. It is rumored that in 1973 he orchestrated the death of Nam Il, a partisan of Kim Il-sung, who died in a mysterious car accident shortly after expressing his reservations concerning Kim Jong-il's growing power.

In April 1974 Kim Jong-il announced the "Ten Principles" which, at their core, were designed to require absolute loyalty and obedience to Kim Il-sung. Not only did this move reinforce the centrality of Kim Il-sung to the North Korean people, but it also very cleverly reinforced the image of Kim Jong-il as fully aligned with his father and representative of his father's goals. Although Kim Il-sung remained as The Great Leader and the symbol of North Korea, by the end of the 1970s it was clear that Kim Jong-il had assumed day-to-day control over much of North Korea's government, party, and military affairs.

It was not until the early 1990s that Kim Jong-il began to take on official government positions, as opposed to party positions. In 1990 he was named the first deputy chairman of the National Defense Commission and, in 1991, Supreme Commander of the Korean People's Army, despite having no military background himself. The issue of his lack of military experience was of concern and thus the Department of Propaganda and Agitation, where the younger Kim began his party career, began to fabricate a suitable résumé for him. In addition to fabricating a military background for the younger Kim, the Department of Propaganda and Agitation aimed to further enhance Kim Jong-il's image as not only the rightful leader of North Korea, but to portray him as an extension of his father.

It was his ascension to the rank of Marshall in 1992 that signaled his move into the political spotlight. With his acceptance of the Chairmanship of the National Defense Commission in 1993, Kim Jong-il's hold on power in North Korea was cemented. Although Kim Il-sung died in 1994, it was not until 1997 that Kim Jong-il took over as general secretary of the KWP. Nor did he assume the Presidency of North Korea until the 10th anniversary of his father's death, but rather maintained his control and power through chairing the National Defense Commission. Indeed, he designated his father, the charismatic founder of the nation, as in effect President for Eternity. This on the one hand was characterized as an adroit political move, sparing him the ultimate responsibility for policies that misfired, but it may also suggest apprehension concerning fully stepping into the giant shoes of his father.

Kim Jong-il the Man

Descriptions of Kim Jong-il range from shy and uncomfortable among strangers to humorous, affable, and engaging, from reclusive to bold and sophisticated. Because of the veil of secrecy surrounding North Korea, and more specifically the Dear Leader, what we know of Kim is compiled from reports of defectors, which have often been filtered through South Korean intelligence services. The few rare visitors who have had the opportunity to meet with him, and the South Korean actress Choe Un-hui and her husband, who spent eight years as "guests" of the North Korean leader, are among the few sources on the personality idiosyncrasies of Kim. It is important to note that information about Kim's personality, personal habits, and interpersonal relations is based on very little directly observable behavior, but rather on second-hand reports that are often provided by people with political agendas.

Insecure about Personal Appearance and Stature   Kim Jong-il, reportedly taking after his mother, is described as a short, overweight man who is very self-conscious about his appearance. Standing roughly 5 feet 2 inches tall, Kim reportedly has platform shoes custom built for him to reach his height of 5 feet 6 inches, and weighs in around 175 pounds. Clearly, his short stature is a long-standing issue for him. Kang Myong-to, a son-in-law of (former) Premier Kang Song-san, in a book he wrote after defecting to South Korea, recalled: "The elders of the village [Ch'ilgol, the hometown of Kim Jong-il's mother] called Kim Jong-il 'Shorty.'" Upon first meeting the South Korean actress Choe Un-hui, Kim reportedly asked, "Well, Madame Choe, what do you think of my physique? Small as a midget's droppings, aren't I?" His hair is worn in a flamboyant style adding additional height. He wears only custom-tailored clothing made in North Korea, and is rarely seen without his dark glasses. He is traditionally seen in custom-made gray or tan factory foreman's slacks and a short jacket, and for formal occasions, he most often is seen wearing a gray "Mao-style" jacket. The reason that Kim Jong-il never appears wearing a military uniform in public places is thought to be because he has a complex about never having served in the military.

Considered Eccentric and Self-Indulgent   Kim Jong-il is considered eccentric and self-indulgent by many and has a known penchant for French cognac, Western movies, and beautiful women. Hennessy, the maker of Paradis cognac, has confirmed that Kim is the biggest buyer of the cognac, with Kim maintaining an estimated annual account of $650,000 to $800,000 since 1992. The Dear Leader annually spends 770 times the income of the average North Korean citizen ($1,038) on cognac alone! It is estimated that thousands of bottles of Paradis are shipped to North Korea annually. One of the world's oldest commercially available cognacs, Paradis, sells for $630 a bottle in Seoul.

Hedonistic Lifestyle—A Vivid Contrast with the Suffering of His Own Population   A great deal of care goes into the preparation of Kim's meals. The KWP Finance and Accounting Department has under it an office called the "Kim Jong-il Longevity Institute." This institute is in complete charge of the health management of Kim and decides on his meal menus. In preparing Kim's meals, cooks use rice grown at special farms in Mundok-kun, South Pyongyang Province. Female workers check each and every grain of rice, and remove grains that are chipped or look damaged in other ways. Cooks have to cook his rice by the traditional way of using firewood, and they have to use wood chopped at Mt. Paektu. Kim Jong-il was treated specially from earliest years, befitting the son of Kim Il-sung, shaping his narcissistic personality. Defectors have characterized Kim Jong-il as self-centered and lacking empathy. Reflecting a fundamental narcissism, he tends to view nearly everything and everyone from the stance of self-interest. Both Kim's lack of empathy and sense of entitlement are revealed in his indulgent lifestyle, which contrasts with the struggle of most North Koreans simply to feed themselves. Kim lives in a lavish seven-story pleasure palace in Pyongyang and defector reports indicates that Kim maintains lavish villas in each of North Korea's provinces and has them furnished with imported luxury goods. He is reported to have secreted upwards of $10 billion in Swiss bank accounts.

Entertains Guests with His "Joy Brigades" and Luxury Goods   Kim Jong-il apparently likes to entertain and party. He is reported to host lavish parties where he drinks heavily and expects those around him to do so as well. According to the memoirs of the South Korean actress Choe Un-hui, and several other sources, Kim is a heavy drinker. At these parties, according to the bodyguard, Kim and his associates regularly drank to excess while female entertainers wore "micro-minis and tank tops" but were directed not to drink too much. These parties reportedly included entertainment provided by strippers and his "Joy Brigades." The Joy Brigades are composed of beautiful young women trained to entertain him and his cronies. Members, who reportedly are recruited from junior high schools every July, must be virgins and have pale, unblemished skin.

While he enjoys these parties with his cronies, he prefers to stay out of the public eye. In contrast to his father who seemed at ease with large crowds and comfortable with people, Kim has been likened to the Wizard of Oz, "remaining out of sight, pulling levers from behind a screen." He has rarely spoken in public; in fact, his "Glory to the heroic Korean People's Army" spoken at the end of a two-hour military display in 1992 was the first time that Kim is known to have spoken in public. Even his speeches on TV and radio are read by narrators.

When in a benevolent mood, Kim Jong-il is known to lavish his guests and friends with expensive gifts ranging from TVs and stereos, to bananas, pineapples, and mandarin oranges, all rare luxuries in North Korea. Kim appears to maintain power both through such special perquisites, as just noted, as well as through domination and fear. Defectors report Kim's manipulative style includes combinations of providing special privileges with humiliation and threat of punishment, including execution. They report that stories abound concerning executions ordered by Kim, although there is no direct evidence. There are even stories he himself has carried out some of these executions; again, whether true or not, the persistence of these stories circulating in his leadership circle serves to further his image. Regardless of the accuracy of these reports the simple fact that they are so widespread adds to the cult of personality surrounding Kim, reinforcing his image as a strongman.

According to some reports, Kim likes to stage fights between soldiers or security agents alá the gladiators of the Roman Empire, and creates strange contests for his entertainment. In one such contest participants were reportedly required to change back and forth between army and navy uniforms with the losers ordered to shave their heads or go home naked. On one occasion, he reportedly ordered a senior officer who had annoyed him to strip at a public function and sent him home naked. Putting down his subordinates through public humiliation seems to be a consistent theme in Kim's interpersonal relations, perhaps reassuring himself that he is in control as he puts others down.

Lack of Empathy for North Korean People   Recent events also testify to his comfort with tolerating high levels of deaths at home. In confronting North Korea's famine, saving lives has not been a top priority. Early in the famine cycle Kim cut off nearly all food supplies to the four eastern provinces and denied these provinces access to international aid. Large numbers of deaths also occurred when, between 1997 and 1999 on Kim's orders, several hundred thousand people displaced by the famine were herded into camps where conditions allowed few to survive. Moreover, according to the testimony of eyewitnesses, Kim has ordered the systematic killing of babies born in North Korea's camps for political prisoners. This lack of concern for the Korean people is in contrast to the image of his father, Kim Il-sung. Kim Jong-il reportedly acknowledges only one occasion where he disobeyed The Great Leader:

> Only once have I disobeyed President Kim Il-sung. The President said, "can you shave off some defense spending and divert it for the people's livelihoods?" I responded, "I am afraid not. Given the military pressure from the U.S., the Korean people must bear the hardship a little longer." How much pain I felt at my failure to live up to the expectations of the President who is concerned about raising the living standards of the people!

Gap between Mythic Image and Self-Indulgent Reality   The gap between the self-indulgent hedonistic lifestyle of Kim and his inner circle in Pyongyang and the privation of his people, and, for that matter, that of the lower level military, is extreme. Kim regularly calls for sacrifice from the North Korean people in pursuit of the mission of reunification. But the lack of sacrifice in the life of Dear Leader and his inner circle is striking. Information is tightly controlled. Penetrating those information barriers and describing the lavish self-indulgent lifestyle of the Dear Leader and his inner circle could significantly undermine the legitimacy of his leadership and his capacity to sustain the public psychology.

Creative Self-Image—Kim Jong-il as Producer of the DPRK Survival Show   Kim thinks of himself as a highly creative and artistic individual. Kim has a movie collection rumored to be between 10,000 and 20,000 tapes. A personal favorite is reported to be *The Godfather* (which is reportedly also the favorite movie of Saddam Hussein). As a result of his fondness for movies, a pet project of Kim's has been the development of a North Korean movie industry. Being a man of action, he took a direct route to acquiring expertise. In 1978 Kim reportedly orchestrated the kidnapping of Choe Un-hui, his favorite South Korean actress, and her husband, a noted film director-producer. They were taken to North Korea where they were held in house arrest for eight years. At times it appears that Kim's conception of the leader's role is influenced by the Western movies to which he is addicted. The manner in which he employs the nuclear cudgel to extort economic support from the West suggests a strategy deriving from the 1959 political farce, *The Mouse that Roared*. And his confrontational style at times is reminiscent of the heroic role of the lawman

Wyatt Earp played by Burt Lancaster in *Gunfight in the O.K. Corral*. Yet he must not be mistaken for a posturing clown. For he has been shrewdly effective in maintaining a firm control on North Korea's leadership, while keeping international adversaries off balance.

Emotional Volatility   Kim Jong-il is rumored to be extremely emotional, volatile, and unpredictable in his behavior. Impulsive, he expects to be obeyed immediately. He is said to yell at subordinates and order the execution of officials who displease him. This creates a sycophantic leadership circle with his subordinates often lying to him about the deteriorating economic and social conditions. He is apparently very concerned with appearances, although prefers to stay out of the public eye as much as possible, sometimes even described as a recluse. Kim has been officially described as extremely intelligent, creative, and artistic; it's claimed that he is responsible for much of the architectural design of Pyongyang, and that he plays the piano and violin as well as conducts the chamber orchestra that plays at his parties. Truly a Renaissance man! Despite his lack of public speaking, North Korean sources portray him as articulate and quick-witted. Such contradictions are not unique, for it is extremely difficult to separate Kim Jong-il the man from Kim Jong-il the myth created by North Korean propaganda.

Decision-Making Style   Reports about Kim Jong-il's work and management style vary greatly, although observers uniformly describe him as a micromanager who gets involved in the minute details of an issue. Kim's decision-making style can be likened to a starburst, with him at the center and a series of lines to his principal analytic and policy groups—U.S. analysis and policy, South Korea, Japan, China, Russia, others, with the U.S. being the most prestigious, but with no systematic process for coordinating among them. Moreover, after receiving analysis and recommendations, Kim announces his decision with no apparent opportunity for internal debate. So when Assistant Secretary James Kelly's confrontation concerning the DPRK's violation of the Agreed Framework occurred in 2002, it was treated by Kim as a bilateral matter, with no apparent consideration given to the impact on Japan of his defiant acknowledgment of North Korea's nuclear capability. This decision-making style has the potential for major miscalculation.

The Man Behind the Mask

Being the son and designated successor of a major political leader is a daunting task. Being the son and successor of a charismatic leader and nation founder of almost God-like stature, as noted earlier, is overwhelming. Unlike his father, Kim Jong-il grew up in luxurious surroundings, pampered, raised to be special. This is the formative recipe for a narcissistic personality, with a grandiose self-concept and difficulties with empathy. Insofar as Kim Jong-il was in charge of the propaganda machine, and directed the cult of personality around his father as well as stressed the continuity between his father and him, he must be particularly conscious of the magnitude of the myths that he has played a central role in creating, particularly his identity with his father, painfully aware of the man that he is not. Unlike his father, Kim Jong-il did *not* persist in the long struggle, did *not* found a nation, and did *not* shape its governing philosophy based on experiences as a guerilla leader. Kim Jong-il must have stood in awe of his father, and while the prodigious propaganda machine he directed has stressed the seamless continuity from father to son, under his arrogant facade, there assuredly is profound self-doubt and insecurity. This would suggest that his narcissism is by no means a relatively healthy narcissism, but a fragile narcissism, quite primitive in nature. Indeed the characteristics he displays indicate that he has the core characteristics of the most dangerous personality disorder, malignant narcissism, which is characterized by:

- Such extreme grandiosity and self-absorption, there is no capacity to empathize with others. This is reflected in his lack of empathy with his own people, as well his difficulties in understanding his principal adversaries, the United States, South Korea, and Japan; and can be associated with major political/military miscalculation.
- There is no constraint of conscience. Kim's only loyalty is to himself and his own survival. But he also recognizes the need to sustain his inner circle's perquisites and indulgent lifestyle, for he requires their support. He combines lavish indulgence of his leadership circle with humiliation to maintain his control over them.
- Paranoid orientation. Not paranoid in the sense of psychotic, out of touch with reality, but always on guard, ready to be betrayed, seeing himself surrounded by enemies.
- Unconstrained aggression. Will use whatever aggression is necessary, without qualm of conscience, be it to eliminate an individual or to strike out at a particular group.

There is no good information on the workings of his inner circle, regarding whether there is a free give and take, whether he can reveal uncertainty and ask for advice, and whether he is open to constructive criticism. While fragile egos rarely are open to admitting uncertainty and ignorance, and are not usually open to criticism, in the service of providing intelligence shrewd advisers can often help shape the decision making of the narcissistic leader.

While reportedly a micromanager in most aspects of his leadership, Kim makes an interesting exception in terms of economic development, and devotes little or no time in his weekly schedule to economic matters. He has said:

The Leader, while alive, told me that I must never get involved in economic issues. If I get involved in the economic issues, I can never take part in the party's activities or military activities. He said this to me over and over so that I do not forget the advice. [passage omitted in original] He told me I must let party officials and the administration's economic officials take charge of economic issues.

This quote, from a secret speech he gave to senior officials following an inspection tour of Kim Il-sung University in December 1996, can be taken as reflecting an artful shifting of responsibility for economic problems to his subordinates.

What is not entirely clear is the degree to which he is aware of the magnitude of his country's economic difficulties. Is he aware that less than 10% of the plants in North Korea are currently running? He is assuredly well aware that South Korea is above North Korea in all aspects except in military capabilities, although he criticized South Korea, saying all that South Korea industry is doing is assembling products, using parts imported from other countries. But, on the other hand, he frankly admitted that 60% of North Korean factories were not operating. It was on August 4, 1984 that Kim Jong-il made his statement that only 40% of plants in North Korea were in operation.

No Core Organizing Ideas or Principles   Given that his position flows from his identification with and succession to his father, he cannot appear to abandon founding principles of the republic, both *juche*[2] and the ultimate goal of reunification of the Korean peninsula. But if we accept the premise that his basic loyalty is to himself (and by necessity his inner circle) and that their survival with the perquisites of power are the number one priority, how he lives up to his father's core principles is subject to interpretation. One can pay lip service to these principles while modifying them significantly from their initial intent, and not being bound by them in a doctrinaire fashion. After all, the self-reliance of *juche* is not consistent with a program of actively seeking foreign assistance. Like relationships, ideas are instrumental for the consummate narcissist, and if they are no longer useful can be radically modified or discarded. Yet, while Kim Jong-il does not possess core organizing ideas or principles, he is in many ways a captive of his oft-declared public policy, for he employs the twin doctrines of *juche* and reunification to call for sacrifice on the part of the North Korean people.

Inherited Charisma: Kim Jong-il Is Not His Father—And He Knows It   Charisma is not a quality of an individual but is a property of a relationship; in this case, between a leader and his wounded followers. The charismatic leader-follower relationship between Kim Il-sung and his followers was extremely powerful. Kim Il-sung worked at shaping the cult of personality surrounding him, and his followers identified with his career-long dedication to this nation. Kim Jong-il in his role as director in effect of the propaganda ministry continued to foster the myth of Kim Il-sung and of his own identification with his father. But charisma is not automatically inheritable. And despite the adroit management of internal communication, Kim Jong-il is not identical to his father. The gap between the myth and the man, between the kleptocratic self-indulgent leadership and the starving masses, remains a major vulnerability, a vulnerability that should be at the heart of tailored deterrence.

Policy Implications

Because of Kim's self-oriented focus and lack of constraint of conscience, the only diplomatic stance that will deter Kim is one based on self-interest. He will regularly be calculating "What's in it for me and my senior leaders? What can we get away with? What are negative consequences for us?" Clarity of positive and negative consequences, and a consistency in implementing them, is key to effective coercive diplomacy. There must be clearly defined limits and consequences. This is crucial in dealing with Kim Jong-il and his regime, both in restraining any impulses toward aggressive action and to deter his aggressive military stance, with particular reference to his WMD program. And tailoring a package of coercive diplomacy and information operations to Kim's idiosyncratic leadership is an exemplar of the new deterrence that is tailored to the specific nature of the adversary, especially in a personality-dominant leadership.

In particular, that which threatens Pyongyang and the hedonistic lifestyle of Kim and his cronies will be particularly threatening. And here, too, there is an important role for an information/education program designed to call the attention of the general population and low-level military personnel to the gap between his hedonistic lifestyle and the sacrifices he regularly calls for from his impoverished nation. Such a program could assist in undermining his support in the tightly controlled information space of North Korea.

The Psychological and Behavioral Bases of Terrorism: Implications for Counterterrorism[3]

Waging the continuing "war on terrorism" has been the dominant theme of the Bush presidency. If one accepts the premise that terrorism is a vicious species of psychological warfare, waged through the media, one doesn't counter psychological warfare with smart bombs and missiles—one counters it with psychological warfare. And that in turn requires a nuanced understanding of the psychologies—plural—of the spectrum of terrorisms—plural. For terrorism is a very diverse phenomenon, thus there is not a one-size-fits-all explanation; and the nature of the followership, different group and organizational dynamics and decision patterns, will differ from group to group. While psychology plays a crucial role in understanding this complex phenomenon, to fully understand it requires an interdisciplinary approach, incorporating knowledge from political, historical, cultural, economic, ideological, and religious perspectives. It is important to consider each terrorism in its own political, historical, and cultural contexts. Terrorism is a product of its own place and time. It is an attractive strategy to a diverse array of groups that have little else in common.

Explanations of terrorism at the level of individual psychology are insufficient in trying to understand why people become involved in terrorism. Indeed, it is not going too far to assert that terrorists are psychologically "normal" in the sense of not being clinically psychotic. They are neither depressed, severely emotionally disturbed, nor are they crazed fanatics. Indeed, terrorist groups and organizations attempt to screen out emotionally unstable individuals. They represent a security risk. There is a multiplicity of individual motivations. For some it is to give a sense of power to the powerless; for others, revenge is a primary motivation; for still others, it is to gain a sense of significance. Rather it is group, organizational and social psychology, with a particular emphasis on "collective identity," that provides the most powerful lens to understand terrorist psychology and behavior. For some groups, especially nationalist-terrorist groups, this collective identity is established extremely early, so that "hatred is bred in the bone." The importance of collective identity and the processes of forming and transforming collective identities cannot be overemphasized. This in turn emphasizes the sociocultural context, which determines the balance between collective identity and individual identity. Terrorists have subordinated their individual identity to the collective identity, so that what serves the group, organization, or network is of primary importance.

It is important to distinguish leaders from followers. The role of the leader is crucial in drawing together alienated, frustrated individuals into a coherent organization. The leader provides a "sense-making" unifying message that conveys a religious, political, or ideological goal to the disparate followers. The crucial role of the leader is identifying the external enemy as the source of their problems, as well as drawing together into a collective identity otherwise disparate individuals who may be discontented and aggrieved, but who, without the powerful presence of the leader, will remain isolated and individually aggrieved. The political entrepreneur or hate-mongering leader plays a crucial organizing role. Osama bin Laden has become a positive identification object for thousands of young Arab and Muslim youths, a major recruitment incentive. For them, he serves as the heroic avenger, with the courage to stand up against the superpower. And in following his lead, the individual follower can be seen as unselfish, altruistic, and heroic to the point of self-sacrifice.

Suicide terrorism is a group rather than an individual endeavor. Almost all terrorist suicide attacks have been carried out by groups, rarely by independent individuals. Mohammed Hafez has identified three conditions for a suicide terrorism campaign: a culture of martyrdom, an organizational decision to employ this strategy, and a willing supply of recruits.[4] Willingness to be recruited for a suicide mission is greatly influenced by public support for such missions in the suicides community. The number of individuals drawn to "martyrdom operations" is much larger in situations where a large segment of the community perceives the situation as an existential struggle (e.g., Palestinians, Tamils, Chechens). Social psychological forces play a crucial role in ensuring that the suicide candidate sticks to the mission. Commitment to the group and the mission is achieved by creating a "social contract" that one cannot break without losing self-esteem and the respect of peers.

The terrorist lifecycle is important to understand. The process of becoming a terrorist involves a cumulative, incrementally sustained, and focused commitment to the group. It is useful to unpack the life course of terrorists to consider the psychological process they are undergoing at different phases of the terrorist lifecycle. Given that the attraction to and entrance into the terrorist path is a gradual process, which for some groups begins in early childhood, where "hatred is bred in the bone," changing the influences on this pathway will necessarily occur over an extended time frame, for generational change will be necessary, and this will require a sustained program over decades. For the majority of contemporary terrorists, there is an early entrance onto the pathway into terrorism, whether religious or secular, with many way stations along the way and continuing reinforcement by manipulative leaders, consolidating the collective identity, externalizing, justifying, and requiring violence against the enemy. This implies that early intervention is required; for once a youth is embedded within the group, his extremist psychology will be continually reinforced, and doubt diminished. The power of group dynamics, especially for the closed group, is intense; and once an individual is in the group, it is very difficult to penetrate his psychology and extricate him.

Groups may adhere to the same underlying ideology but differ remarkably in organizational structure. Thus both Hamas and Islamic Jihad and al-Qaeda find justification in the Koran, but the organizational form of Hamas and Islamic Jihad is traditionally more hierarchical and authoritarian, with followers in action cells being directed from higher organizational levels to carry out an action, a decision that cannot be questioned, and having only limited say in the conduct of operations. On the other hand, al-Qaeda has a much looser organizational form with distributed decision making, reflecting the leadership style of bin Laden. This is particularly reflected after the effective destruction of al-Qaeda command and control in Afghanistan in 2001, so that what has been termed the "new al-Qaeda" or "al-Qaeda 2.0" is considered by many to be more an ideology than an organization. Al-Qaeda in its original form is deemed by some to be functionally dead as an operational organization. The successor global Salafi Jihad network is widely distributed and semiautonomous, operating more out of hubs than nodes, with wide latitude to plan and execute operations. The 3/11 Madrid commuter train bombing is a reflection of this emerging network. The diaspora has been identified as particularly important for the global Salafi Jihad, with a large percentage (80%) of recruits joining and becoming radicalized in the diaspora.

Policy Implications

Can terrorists be deterred? Not in the conventional sense. Conventional deterrence theory is clearly inapplicable to these nonstate actors with no fixed address. Indeed, many actions designed to counter terrorism have counterproductive effects. The "war on terrorism" is a war unlike other wars, and will require concerted efforts over decades to counter. Especially considering the early entrance into the path of terrorism, systematic programs that are sustained over time to inhibit the terrorist production line are required. As the "collective identity" has been shaped gradually over many years, so too the attitudes that have been formed and hardened that are at the foundation of terrorism will not easily be altered. When "hatred is bred in the bone," when socialization to hatred and violence begins early and is reinforced and consolidated into a major theme of the collective identity, this implies that there is no short-term solution, and that interventions designed to break this cycle must begin early before that identity is consolidated.

Particularly important is reducing the attractiveness of the path of terrorism. In other words:

a. Inhibit potential terrorists from joining the group in the first place. The impact of the new media environment, especially the 24/7 cable news environment and the Internet, on the shaping of the terrorist identity and broad support for the activities is a serious dilemma for counterterrorism. The new media, particularly the Internet, probably plays an important role in establishing a sense of community among otherwise widely dispersed alienated youth. Identifying the impact of the new media and grappling with the approaches to countering these influences is a serious challenge. Countering the influence of radical madrasahs and radical mosques in the socialization of Muslim youth that early set them on the path of militant Islamism will also be an important challenge. The growing population of alienated Muslim youth in European societies represents a growing internal threat. Western governments should directly support the development and implementation of community-based interventions aimed at promoting community- and individual-level changes that would support greater incorporation and integration of immigrants and diaspora youth into the political culture of Western liberal democracies. Once in the group, though, the power of group dynamics is immense, continually confirming the power of the group's organizing ideology and reinforcing the member's dedication to the cause. Nevertheless, it will be important to:

    b. Produce dissension in the group.

    c. Facilitate exit from the group. It is important to stimulate and encourage defection from the group. A number of nations with significant terrorism problems—Italy, Spain in the Basque region, and Great Britain in Northern Ireland, in particular—have creatively employed amnesty programs to facilitate terrorists leaving the group.[7]

    d. Reduce support for the group and its leader. If for every terrorist killed or captured there are 10 more waiting in line, it is critical to marginalize the group, and to de-romanticize and delegitimate the leader. This, in the case of radical Islamist terrorism, can only be done from within Islam. The goal here is to alienate the terrorist organization from its constituency, which is required to provide a reservoir of new recruits for the organization. This in turn will facilitate the goal of inhibiting potential terrorists from joining the group or organization in the first place.

These points all represent components of public diplomacy and strategic communication programs, an area insufficiently addressed by the West in its attempts to counter terrorism. It will require decades to change the culture of hatred and violence. It is important in this struggle to maintain the moral high ground, in strengthening the rule of law and exemplifying good governance and social justice; for to depart from these standards is to lower ourselves to the level of the terrorists. This emphasizes that the struggle against terrorism is by no means solely a military and security responsibility, but one that involves the entirety of society.

The Psychology of Weapons of Mass Destruction Terrorism: Psychological Incentives and Constraints[5]

It is a broad consensus among scholars of terrorism that for most terrorist groups WMD (or CBRN [chemical, biological, radiological, and nuclear]) terrorism would be counterproductive; most terrorist groups seek to influence the West or establishment and call attention to their cause, and mass casualty terrorism would be counterproductive for their cause. It is necessary to discriminate between discriminate and indiscriminate terrorism, for some terrorist groups would entertain the use of such weapons on a limited tactical basis if they would not injure their own constituents. Exceptions in terms of motivation are religious fundamentalist Islamist terrorists, especially the Salafi jihadists, who often seek revenge against Western society that they believe has humiliated Islam, and are not interested in influencing the West, but in expelling the West with its corrupt modernizing values. The Salafi jihadists who are not embedded in a particular nation are without constraint and are particularly dangerous, in contrast, for example, to the Egyptian Islamic Jihad which is more constrained in its actions. For both radical Islamist extremists and right-wing extremists (such as Oklahoma City bomber Timothy McVeigh), in addition to motivations and psychology, resource and expertise are required, and many would opine that the assistance of states would be necessary in terms of weaponization, especially of nuclear terrorism. Without the assistance of states, biological terrorism is the most threatening WMD terrorism in which substate groups might become engaged.

Conclusions

Alexander George, in his foreword to my 2004 book, *Leaders and their Followers in a Dangerous World,* observes that for "US leaders to deal effectively with other actors in the international area, they need images of their adversaries," and cites historical examples of foreign policy disasters predicated upon faulty images. Emphasizing the requirement for actor-specific behavioral modeling, George observes the damaging consequences of the assumption in interstate conflicts that the adversary is a rational, unitary actor. Such assumptions "seriously oversimplify the task of understanding and influencing adversaries." Referring to terrorists, he observes that this is particularly problematic in dealing with nonstate actors, who "may lack identifiable or valuable assets that can be targeted in efforts to coerce them." Moreover, "the mindsets, goals, motivations and behavioral patterns of non-state actors may be very difficult to ascertain…. When reliable information on terrorist motivations is lacking, the coercing power may develop simplified stereotypes that emphasize fanaticism and irrationality, particularly when their acts of terrorism are highly destructive." In his important 2001 book, *The Fallacies of Cold War Deterrence: A New Direction,* Keith Payne, president of the National Institute for Public Policy, critically examines the premises of deterrence theory conceptualized during the Cold War, and the requirement in the post-Cold War era to modify and adapt deterrence theory to fit the contemporary security environment. Payne, who later served as Deputy Assistant Secretary of Defense for Strategy, was in a position to incorporate his concepts into the Bush Doctrine.

The three examples summarized in this chapter of actor-specific behavioral models—Saddam Hussein of Iraq, Kim Jong-il of North Korea, and a summary review of terrorist psychologies—emphasize that traditional deterrence theory based on Cold War doctrine cannot be uncritically applied to the problems of the post-Cold War era. Rather, understanding each actor, be it rogue national leader or terrorist organization, must be understood in his or its unique political, cultural, historical contexts. Policies designed to deter, dissuade, and influence that actor must be crafted with reference to that particular psychology. Deterrence after all depends on the targeted deteree, and what deters one actor may stimulate another. There is no one size fits all. This in turn emphasizes the requirement to develop nuanced profiles of our adversaries' leader personalities and strategic cultures in order to develop optimal policies for dealing with them in the current unstable international climate.

Endnotes

1. This summary profile is drawn from Jerrold Post, "Kim Jong-il of North Korea: In the Shadow of His Father" in *Leaders and Their Followers in a Dangerous World* (Ithaca, NY: Cornell University Press, 2004), chapter 12. References for the evidence underlying this summary profile will be found in this published profile.

2. *Juche*, a word of Kim Il-sung's own construction, is a combination of two Korean words. The first *chu* means lord, master; the second, *ch'e*, means the body, the whole. The concept *chuch'e* or *juche* signifies an intense need for independence and a desire to make one's own decisions. It often appears with the suffix *song*, forming the word *chuch'esong*, meaning to act in accord with one's own judgment. *Juche* was the most important political idea with which Kim Il-sung ruled his people. It pertains both to domestic and to international policy. Internationally, it signified the end of political dependence and subservience to the Soviet Union, and represented the elevation of Kim as a leader and political philosopher to the nonaligned world. (Dae-Sook Suh, *Kim Il-sung: The North Korean Leader* [New York: Columbia University Press, 1988], 301). While it grew out of Kim Il-sung's personal experience, Korea as a nation had long struggled to establish its identity and independence from its surrounding great powers: Japan, China, and the Soviet Union. Internally, it meant to Kim forwarding the revolution on the basis of his own ideas, without slavishly following the precepts of Marxism. As Suh (302) notes, *juche* became the ideological system for North Korea, encompassing the idea of *chaju* (independence) in political work, *charip* (self-sustenance) in economic endeavors, and *chawi* (self-defense) in military affairs.

3. This section on the psychological roots of terrorism is drawn from a summary essay prepared for the Madrid Summit on Terrorism and Democracy in March 2005 by the committee on the psychological roots of terrorism which I chaired. It is published in Volume 1 of the Club de Madrid Series on Democracy and Terrorism, *Addressing the Causes of Terrorism* (Madrid: Club de Madrid, 2005), 7-12.

4. Mohammad Hafez, *Manufacturing Human Bombs: Strategy, Culture and Conflict in the Making of Palestinian Suicide Bombers,* Vol. II, Peaceworks Series (Washington, DC:United States Institute of Peace Press, 2005).

5. This summary is drawn from testimony provided by the author to the United Nations International Atomic Energy Agency in the fall of 2001 at a special session on nuclear terrorism.

7

Preventive War and the Bush Doctrine
Theoretical Logic and Historical Roots

JACK S. LEVY

Prior to the enunciation of the Bush Doctrine and the 2003 Iraq War, scholars commonly argued that democracies do not fight "preventive wars" against rising adversaries.[1] Scholars now debate whether the George W. Bush administration's doctrine of "preemption," which is actually based on the logic of prevention, constitutes a new departure in American foreign policy, or whether it has deeper historical roots.[2] Either argument, but especially the latter, contradicts the earlier conventional wisdom that democracies do not fight preventive wars.[3] These debates raise a number of questions. What is preventive war? How does it differ from preemption? How influential was preventive or preemptive logic in the American initiation of the 2003 Iraq War? Does preventive logic have deep roots in American foreign policy? Is it true, more generally, that democracies never, or perhaps only rarely, fight preventive wars? If so, how can we explain that pattern? Under what conditions is preventive war morally justifiable?

My aim here is to answer some but not all of these questions. Given the amount of conceptual confusion that still persists about the meaning of preventive war and how it differs from preemption, among scholars as well as policy makers, I begin by clarifying the meaning of these concepts. I then turn to the question of the role of prevention and preemption in American foreign policy, and engage the debate about whether the Bush Doctrine represents a significant new development in American foreign policy or whether earlier American leaders resorted to preventive military action. In doing so, I am interested as much in the terms of the debate as in any substantive conclusion. Given the amount of attention to the role of prevention in the 2003 American war in Iraq, in this volume and elsewhere, I devote only limited attention to that case. I also leave aside important questions about the conditions, if any, under which preventive war might be morally justifiable. That is a different question and one that has increasingly attracted the attention of philosophers as well as political scientists.[4]

The Concept of "Preventive War"[5]

The conceptual question is fundamental, because until we define what a preventive war is we cannot begin to answer the questions of whether the Bush Doctrine is based on preemption or prevention, whether that policy is new or old, whether preventive war is a common tool of statecraft, for states in general and for democracies in particular, and whether preventive military action is morally defensible under certain conditions. Despite the importance of the conceptual question, scholars continue to confuse preemption and prevention and to define prevention in ways that limit the concept's utility for theoretical and empirical analysis.

Preventive war is commonly defined as a war fought to forestall an adverse shift in the balance of power between two states.[6] The focus is on military capabilities, and the strategic logic is "better now than later." When confronted with a rising adversary, the argument goes, under some conditions it might be better to fight now rather than risk war under less favorable circumstances later. The concept is familiar. As Paul W. Schroeder argues, "preventive wars, even risky preventive wars, are not extreme anomalies in politics.... They are a normal, even common, tool of statecraft." Wars commonly attributed to preventive logic include, among others, Prussia in the Seven Years War (1756–63), Japan in the Russo-Japanese War (1904–05), Germany in World War I (1914–18), Japan in the Pacific War (1941–45), and Israel in the Sinai War (1956). The paradigmatic example of a preventive strike is the Israeli attack on the Iraq nuclear reactor in 1981.[7]

The historical frequency of preventive war—or the preventive use of force short of war—depends on exactly how the concept is operationally defined. Definitions vary, and a given definition can be interpreted in different ways. Some scholars define preventive war so broadly as to encompass nearly all wars. A. J. P. Taylor, for example, claims that "[e]very war between Great Powers [in the 1848–1918 period] started as a preventive war, not a war of conquest." Dale Copeland argues that decline and prevention account for most of the major wars during the past two centuries of history, and Michael Howard argues even more broadly that wars originate in "perceptions by statesmen of the growth of hostile power and the fears for the restriction, if not the extinction, of their own."[8]

These are strong claims, and they need to be tested, as do assertions that the Bush Doctrine's emphasis on "preemption" does or does not represent a significant departure in over two centuries of American foreign policy. Hypotheses like these can be validated only if the theoretical concepts used to structure empirical inquiry are defined precisely and used consistently. Otherwise, there is a danger that arguments regarding the history of prevention are shaped more by definition than by history. If prevention is defined broadly, then we will find numerous examples of prevention in the history of American foreign policy, or in diplomacy more generally. If prevention is defined narrowly, then we will find few such examples.[9] These dangers are particularly worrisome given the political passions surrounding evaluations of the Bush Doctrine, even if many analysts are unaware of the impact of their definitions on their conclusions.

Perhaps the major source of a broad conception of prevention is the tendency to confound prevention with other sources of better-now-than-later logic. It is particularly common to see prevention confounded with preemption, despite the fact that scholars have emphasized the analytic distinction for at least two decades.[10] Whereas prevention involves fighting now in order to avoid the risk of war under less favorable circumstances later, preemption involves the initiation of military action because decision makers believe that an adversary's attack is imminent and that there are advantages in striking first, or at least in preventing the adversary from doing so. Preemption is a response to the threat of an imminent attack. Prevention is a response to the more distant threat deriving from a negative shift in relative military capabilities.

It is important to emphasize, since this point is often neglected in the literature, that the threat leading to prevention goes beyond the risk of a future war, and an increasingly costly war, with an ever-stronger adversary. A negative shift in power leads to a decline in a state's bargaining leverage and influence on a wide range of issues. As a result, the declining state will be forced to make greater and greater concessions in order to satisfy its adversary and avoid a possible war. Thus the anticipated threat includes a state's loss of political influence as well as risk of war.

These considerations make it clear that the Bush administration's emphasis on "preemption," in its National Security Strategy of 2002 and again in 2006, and in the intervening Iraq War, is based more on prevention than on preemption. The administration did not anticipate, and its rhetoric did not emphasize, an imminent threat from Iraq, but instead the consequences—for the United States, for its allies, and for the stability of the region—of a sudden increase in Iraqi relative power that would follow from the its development of weapons of mass destruction (WMDs), particularly nuclear weapons.[11]

The 2006 National Security Strategy, for example, states that the fight in the "War on Terror…involves using military force and other instruments of national power to kill or capture terrorists, deny them safe haven or control of any nation; prevent them from gaining access to WMD; and cut of their sources of support." Several pages later it argues that "[t]o forestall or prevent such hostile acts by our adversaries, the United States will, if necessary, act preemptively in exercising our inherent right of self-defense."[12] The emphasis is on denying perceived adversaries the military capabilities to inflict damage on the United States. The military elements of the American strategy designed to accomplish this objective fit the category of prevention. The National Security Strategy document goes on to say, however, that "In the long run, winning the war on terror means winning the battle of ideas." Winning the battle of ideas aims primarily to influence the intentions of potential adversaries, not their military capabilities, and that goal requires a different set of influence strategies, not prevention.

The blurring of the distinction between prevention and preemption is not unique to the Bush administration. Numerous scholars have either unknowingly conflated the concepts or deliberately used them interchangeably, as if the differences were negligible. But the differences are in fact quite substantial. While prevention is relatively common, preemption is relatively rare.[13] The circumstances that lead states to consider undertaking preventive action are quite different from those that lead them to consider preemption. The primary driver of prevention is the changing dyadic balance of power (more accurately, the perception of an adverse power shift), whereas preemption can occur quite independently of changing power differentials between states.

Preemption usually emerges from international crises, when one state comes to believe, correctly or incorrectly, that an adversary is about to attack. Prevention can occur during a crisis, as political leaders seize the opportunity provided by the crisis to deal with deteriorating structural conditions, or perhaps as a result of leaders deliberately creating a crisis for the purposes of rationalizing preventive action they want for other reasons.[14] Prevention can also occur outside of a crisis period, in part because political leaders hope to forestall the shift in power that might give the adversary the bargaining leverage to make demands that might lead to a crisis in the first place.

A related difference between prevention and preemption concerns the initiation of war. With preemption, a state has incentives to initiate war and secure first-mover advantages; with prevention, a state wants war, but may not necessarily want to initiate it. Under some conditions, a state may prefer that its adversary initiate war. Its aim is to shift the blame for the war and reap the diplomatic and domestic political advantages of being seen as the victim, or at least to avoid the costs of being perceived as the aggressor.[15] This assumes that the stronger state is the one doing the preventing, which is true most of the time. It is conceivable, however, that a weaker actor that perceives that its position will worsen even more over time might conclude that a risky military action might be a reasonable gamble.[16] The difference between preemption and prevention is also important for policy. As Richard K. Betts argues, "Countermobilization is the best way to deter an enemy contemplating preventive attack and the worst way to deter one considering preemption."[17]

The difference between prevention and preemption is also important on normative and legal grounds. Preemption has traditionally been regarded as easier to justify than is prevention, in both just war theory and in international law.[18] Michael Walzer, for example, argues for "the moral necessity of rejecting any attack that is merely preventive in character, that does not wait upon and respond to the willful acts of an adversary." Walzer goes on to argue that provocations and even imminent threats are not sufficient conditions for a just war. He argues that "[t]he line between legitimate and illegitimate first strikes is not going to be drawn at the point of imminent attack but at the point of sufficient threat," which he defines in terms of three criteria: "a manifest intent to injure, a degree of active preparation that makes that intent a positive danger, and a general situation in which waiting, or doing anything other than fighting, greatly magnifies the risk." Walzer argues that preemption by Israel in 1967 fits these criteria.[19]

These normative and legal considerations might explain why the Bush administration cloaked its essentially preventive logic in the language of preemption—to enhance the perceived legitimacy of its actions, although I have yet to see evidence that might confirm or disconfirm this interpretation.

There is a growing debate, among scholars as well as policymakers, as to whether traditional conceptions of self-defense in theories of just war and international law are adequate in the contemporary era, given changing technological and political realities of contemporary warfare. The assumption has always been that for a state faced with a rising and hostile adversary, the costs of waiting were tolerable and the state had time to adopt alternative strategies to provide for its security. It could find allies to help deter an attack, or at least repulse the attack if deterrence failed. Or it could try to appease its adversary.

In the contemporary world, however, it is highly problematic whether traditional strategies of deterrence or appeasement are feasible responses to terrorist groups with access to nuclear weapons and with radical ideologies calling for a fundamental structuring of the international system, or whether a strategy of fighting back when attacked is a viable response to the threat of catastrophic terrorism. In fact, Walzer's above-mentioned criteria for a legitimate first strike—a sufficient threat defined in terms of a manifest intent to injure, active preparation, and a situation in which the failure to act greatly magnifies the risk—would appear to provide a justification for preventive action against al-Qaeda and some other global terrorist groups, at least under certain conditions. It is a complicated issue, however, and philosophers and international legal theorists are currently in the process of rethinking the morality and legality of prevention, preemption, and other aspects of self-defense in the contemporary era.[20]

While the confounding of prevention with preemption is problematic on descriptive, theoretical, and normative grounds, the argument that most wars are preventive owes more to a broader form of better-now-than-later reasoning, one that subsumes both prevention and preemption and includes other motivations as well. This is the argument that all wars are motivated by the aim of heading off some future threat, or by the aim of preventing something worse from happening. Instead of restricting the concept of prevention to attempts by states to forestall an adverse shift in the dyadic balance of power, some analysts broaden it to include state strategies aimed to avoid any development that might leave the state worse off in the future.

Some scholars are quite explicit about this. Jonathan Renshon, while recognizing the dangers of an excessively broad definition, rejects the standard practice of restricting the concept of preventive war to efforts to avoid a change in the balance of power as too narrow. For Renshon, "a preventive action is one fought to forestall a grave national security threat."[21] This more expansive definition can include fears of the loss of status or prestige as well as a decline in relative military power. This view is the basis for Renshon's argument that the Suez War of 1956 was a preventive war for Britain, not because British leaders feared a decline in relative power, but rather because they feared the loss of Britain's great power status. I do not challenge Renshon's interpretation of British motives in the crisis, only his decision to label them as preventive.[22]

John Gaddis also uses a broad conception of the term when he argues that "preemption" is an "old tradition" in American foreign policy, with roots in the policies of John Quincy Adams and those of several subsequent presidents. Adams, as Secretary of State in the administration of James Monroe, defended a military response to cross-border incursions from Spanish Florida on grounds that if Spain could not control the armed infiltration, the United States had the right to do so. Adams argued that "the marauding parties...ought to be broken up immediately." Gaddis argues that Adams' reasoning was based on "preemptive" logic, as was Andrew Jackson's policy of using military force on the vulnerable western frontier before specific threats materialized.[23]

The Polk administration also used preemptive logic, Gaddis argues, to justify its annexation of Texas in 1845, which precipitated (some would say deliberately provoked) the war with Mexico. Similar logic led to the view that the incorporation of California required the extension of American sovereignty over all the territory between California and Texas. The argument in each case was that the territory was vulnerable to threats from and incorporation by other great powers, and that the United States needed to act to forestall those possible threats from materializing. Decades later, fears that political instability in Central and South America led Theodore Roosevelt, William Howard Taft, and Woodrow Wilson to use similar arguments to justify what Gaddis calls a "succession of preemptive interventions" in Venezuela, the Dominican Republic, Haiti, Nicaragua, and Mexico. Gaddis concludes that "[t]he doctrine of preemption also came, in time, to justify expansion at the expense of states that *might* fail," that "even the prospect of power vacuums invited preemption," and that "concerns about 'failed' or 'derelict' states, then, are nothing new in the history of United States foreign relations, nor are strategies of preemption in dealing with them."[24]

Gaddis makes a strong argument that territorial annexations and military actions motivated by existing or potential security threats from weak or unstable states or territories that are vulnerable to influence or penetration by other great powers have been a common theme in American foreign policy for nearly two centuries. This argument is reminiscent of John S. Galbraith's "turbulent frontier" explanation of nineteenth century British colonial expansion—the idea that each new territory needed to be defended, generating further expansion, which in turn created new threats and additional motivations for expansion, in an unending process.[25] Both Gaddis and Galbraith emphasize a defensively motivated expansion driven by the security dilemma and a worst-case analysis of potential threats.[26] This argument serves as a useful counter to interpretations that emphasize a more offensively oriented expansionism, one driven by the goal of overturning the existing status quo. My question here is whether it is useful to describe such actions as preventive, or whether the concept of prevention should be limited to military action motivated primarily by the anticipation of a decline in relative military power and potential and by fear of the consequences of that decline.[27]

The analytical problem with such a broad conception of prevention or preemption—and even more so with Renshon's definition of prevention as an attempt to forestall a grave national security threat—is that it incorporates too many different things under a single category. It is important to understand—for theory, for history, for policy, and for questions of just war—whether a military action is motivated by fear of imminent attack, fear of a rising and hostile adversary that might leave one vulnerable to direct military attack in a few years, fear that a region external to a state's territory is either politically unstable or otherwise vulnerable to exploitation or possible annexation by a rival state, or fear of a loss of prestige or status in the international system.

These are all potentially serious threats, of course; actions to avoid them are all motivated by better-now-than-later logic; and it is useful to differentiate this behavior from actions driven by current issues and interests. We gain additional analytic leverage, however, by preserving the ability to differentiate among these threats. If prevention, whether by war or the more limited use of military force, is defined in terms of avoiding any future threat, even those perceived as grave, then we would end up identifying a significant number of wars as preventive. Such a broad definition of prevention leads to the classification of military action driven by the fear of the loss of credibility or of instability on the "turbulent frontier," or by the security dilemma more generally, into the same category as behavior driven by an adverse shift in the balance of power. More specifically, we would classify American interventions in Central America and elsewhere in the same category as the Israeli attack against the Iraqi nuclear reactor, or as the contemplated U.S. strike against North Korean nuclear facilities in 1994. This expansive conception of the preventive motivation for war is not very useful. It is much preferable to define preventive war as a military response to the anticipation of a negative shift in the dyadic balance of military power, the fear of its consequences, and the hope of blocking or delaying that shift.

This is not to say that a decline in relative military power is necessarily more important than other kinds of future threats or generates different policy responses, only that it is analytically distinct.[28] It is important to know whether one type of threat is more serious than another, whether it occurs more often, or whether it is more likely to lead to a military response; but this is possible only if we first analytically distinguish among these threats and then investigate them empirically. To incorporate various types of future threats under the same conceptual umbrella is a classic form of "conceptual stretching," and only distracts from rigorous theoretical and historical analysis.[29]

To summarize, my definition of prevention focuses on a particular state strategy in response to a particular kind of future threat—a military response to the perception of an adverse power shift and the fear of its consequences. Those consequences include not only the risk of war under less favorable conditions in the future, but also the continued deterioration of the status quo and the erosion of one's bargaining leverage and influence over a variety of issues. Prevention differs from preemption, which is a military response to the anticipation of an imminent attack. Prevention also differs from other sources of better-now-than-later logic driven by other kinds of future threats. Thus, motivations for war based on the fear of a decline in reputation, political instability, change in the adversary's regime or ideology, and similar factors would not be included in the category of prevention. I say this without passing judgment on the causal importance of these other factors relative to prevention.

It is also useful to separate the motives for a policy and the means used to implement it. One might identify several alternative strategies for the goal of blocking or retarding the rise of the adversary's military power, ranging from bribery to diplomacy to containment to a military attack. I restrict the concept of preventive war, or the logic of prevention, to the use of military force. Thus I exclude policies of deterrence and containment.[30] I also exclude Gaddis' category of peaceful territorial annexations. Similarly, preventive war should not be confused with "preventive diplomacy," which generally refers to strategies of conflict prevention adopted by the United Nations and other international organizations.[31]

So far I have adopted the standard usage and referred to the concept of "a preventive war." This is in fact quite problematic, because it implies that preventive war is a type of war. Such an approach essentially defines a war in terms of its cause, which confounds cause and effect in a single concept. This practice raises the question of how to classify wars in which the preventive motivation is just one of several contributing causes.[32] This is a critical problem, since most wars have multiple causes, and so-called preventive wars are no exception.

Although preventive war is defined in terms of a military response to the anticipation of an adverse power shift, not all power shifts lead to war, as illustrated by the power transition involving Britain and the United States at the end of the nineteenth century.[33] In addition, not all power shifts that lead to war necessarily involve the preventive motivation. It is conceivable that the rising state might initiate the war. Power transition theorists, for example, have long emphasized the central importance of power transitions in the processes leading to war, but they have consistently dismissed the argument that the preventive motivation plays a significant role. They argue that it is the rising (and dissatisfied) challenger who initiates the war in order to speed up the transition of power, gain a dominant position, and use its power to create a new set of international political, economic, and legal arrangements that will bring the benefits it derives from the system into line with its newly acquired military power.[34]

Rather than focus on "preventive war" as a type of war, it is analytically preferable to focus on the preventive motivation for war, or preventive logic, as a causal variable. It is an intervening variable, one possible causal mechanism linking power shifts and war. This approach allows us to assess the causal weight of the preventive motivation relative to that of other variables in the processes leading to war.[35]

Although preventive (not preemptive) logic played a role in the processes leading to the 2003 Iraq War, I do not find it useful to characterize that war as a preventive war. Some key actors in the Bush administration may have been driven primarily by the preventive motivation of destroying Iraq's nuclear weapons program, whatever its stage of development and however much they may have exaggerated it. Other key actors may have been driven more by the goals of overthrowing a brutal dictator, bringing democracy to Iraq and perhaps the Middle East as a whole, securing access to oil, demonstrating the effectiveness of U.S. power projection capabilities and sending a signal to other potential adversaries, or by other motives. The decision-making process was conducted within a domestic political context shaped by the September 11 attacks. It is important to assess the relative causal impact of these different policy preferences and domestic constraints and opportunities, and this task is not advanced by using the label of "preventive war" to describe the entire enterprise.

Having said that, I recognize that "preventive war" is a widely used linguistic shorthand, and I occasionally use it to refer to a war driven primarily by the goal of forestalling an adverse power shift. The meaning of the term, however, should be clear from the preceding discussion.

The preventive motivation for war is driven by the anticipation of an adverse shift in the dyadic balance of power and by perceived incentives to use military force to block or retard the adversary's further growth while the opportunity is still available. I have distinguished this factor from other sources of better-now-than-later logic, but it would still be useful to highlight certain aspects of this definition. Let me preface this discussion by reminding the reader that the perceived threat is not only the risk of war against a stronger adversary in the future, but also the erosion of the declining state's bargaining power, resulting in an increase in the concessions made by the potential preventer to its rising adversary.

It is important to note, first of all, that my definition does not limit the preventive motivation for war to situations involving power transitions. Even a limited increase in the adversary's relative military capabilities, one that falls short of a complete power transition, can generate incentives for war by eroding the leading state's bargaining power, reducing the probability of victory in any war that might occur, and increasing the costs associated with that war, even if victory were still the most likely outcome.[36] Complete power transitions are presumably more likely to lead to war than are more limited power shifts, but the latter can still be perceived as threatening.

Limited power shifts can be particularly threatening if they involve step-level changes in relative military power. Most of the theoretical literature on preventive war, at least prior to the Bush Doctrine, assumed a gradual rise in one state's military power relative to another, and most systematic empirical investigations of power shifts have focused on aggregate levels of military capabilities and economic foundations of military potential. One can find little if any theoretical discussion of step-level power shifts resulting from technological breakthroughs, arms imports, or other processes. Historically, however, some of the most famous cases described as preventive wars involved step-level changes in power, or at least the anticipation of such. Germany's fear of the completion of Russian railroad system and army reforms by 1917 was a major incentive for war in 1914. Israel's fear that the 1955 Czech/Russian arms sales would give Egypt a quantitative and qualitative military advantage over Israel was a major factor in, and perhaps a necessary condition for, Israel's Sinai campaign against Egypt in 1956.[37]

Step-level changes in military power short of power transitions are particularly threatening if they are expected to cross a critical threshold of military power. The nuclear threshold is the obvious example here. Israeli fear that Iraq was about to acquire nuclear weapons was necessary and nearly sufficient for the Israeli strike against the Osiraq reactor, and the threat of "rogue states" and terrorist organizations acquiring nuclear weapons was the primary force behind the emphasis on "preemption" by the second Bush administration.

The preventive motivation for war applies to limited military strikes as well as to all-out wars, as illustrated by the Israeli strike against the Iraqi nuclear reactor in 1981 and by U.S. deliberations about a possible preventive strike against North Korea in 1994. It is important to note, however, that whether a strike stays limited or escalates to a full-scale war depends not only on the actions of the preventer, but also on the actions of the target. Moreover, the preventer's anticipation of the target's response can be an important consideration in the preventer's decision calculus. We speak of Israel's preventive strike, rather than a preventive war, in 1981 because Iraq did not retaliate, and Israel's anticipation of that nonresponse influenced its decision to strike in the first place. By contrast, the United States anticipated that a limited strike against North Korean nuclear facilities in 1994 would probably lead to a North Korean invasion of South Korea and consequently an all-out war on the Korean peninsula, and those perceptions were critical in deterring an American strike.[38]

Although most discussions of preventive war focus on the dyadic power relationship between two states, third parties can also play important roles. The rising challenger may be a greater threat if it has allies and a lesser threat if the declining leader has allies. Germany's fear in 1914 was not that it would be unable to defeat Russia in bilateral war in 1917, but rather that it would not be able to defeat a Franco-Russian alliance. In addition, allies may be an important source of armaments and economic aid, which can compensate for an adverse dyadic power shift. Russian arms sales to Egypt through Czechoslovakia in 1955 generated Israel's preventive motivation for war, and Israel's failure to secure armaments from France or the United States eliminated an alternative to a military solution for Israel and made a decision for war much more likely.[39]

Having defined the preventive motivation for war and distinguished it from preemption and from other sources of better-now-than-later logic, let us now turn to its role in American foreign policy. I focus on the period after World War II, where a dominant United States was confronted with the rising power first of the Soviet Union and then of China, and then with the possibility that North Korea, Iraq, and now Iran might acquire nuclear weapons and pose a potential threat to the United States, its allies, and its interests.[40]

Preventive Logic in American Foreign Policy since 1945

In the early years of the Cold War, American political leaders recognized that the U.S. atomic monopoly would be temporary and that the Soviet Union would soon develop the atomic bomb. They feared an adverse shift in the balance of power, believed that the Soviets were an implacably hostile and immoral adversary that was bent on world domination, and expected that the Soviets would probably go to war once they had the capability to do so. There was some talk about the strategy of prevention among U.S. decision makers and their advisors in the late 1940s, but uncertainty about whether the United States could actually win a war against the Soviet Union, combined with the belief that a preventive attack was inconsistent with American values and politically impractical, quickly silenced such talk. Instead of preventive war, the U.S. preferred a policy of massive rearmament, incorporated such a policy into NSC-68 (National Security Council, 1950), and adopted it once the Korean War created the political conditions that made it feasible to formally adopt that policy.[41]

American leaders gave more serious thought to the feasibility and desirability of a strategy of prevention in the 1950s, but they came nowhere close to adopting one.[42] President Dwight D. Eisenhower, in a note to Secretary of State John Foster Dulles, asked whether "our duty to future generations did not require us to *initiate* war at the most propitious moment," and raised the issue several times at meetings of the National Security Council in the 1952–54 period.[43]

In emphasizing that preventive logic was one of several factors leading the United States to take a tough line against the Soviet Union, Marc Trachtenberg suggests that a primary American motivation was to test the Soviet Union, to assess what its intentions really were, and to determine whether a war was inevitable. If the Soviet Union responded with a hard line even while they were weak, it would be reasonable to infer that they would be likely to take an even stronger line once the balance of power had shifted and the Soviets were in a stronger position. If that were the case, the U.S. could think more seriously about a strategy of prevention.[44]

This is an interesting argument, one that implicitly adopts a signaling model framework, but it is several steps removed from a strategy of prevention. The validation of that argument would require a lot more evidence that U.S. decision makers were thinking along these lines, that they would have been willing to seriously consider military action in the case that the Soviets had adopted a harder line, and at what point they would have done so. It is easier to speculate about how you might hypothetically act in such a situation than to actually make such consequential and irreversible decisions once you get there.[45]

Discussions about the viability of a strategy of prevention were more prominent in the Kennedy administration. During the Cuban missile crisis, American decision makers seriously considered the possibility of an air strike (surgical or more massive) against Soviet missile sites in Cuba. Although President John F. Kennedy chose the naval blockade strategy over the surgical air strike or alternative strategies during the Cuban missile crisis, his administration conveyed (on October 27) a clear threat of an air strike to Premier Nikita Khrushchev, and there is substantial evidence that Kennedy was planning to authorize an air strike by October 30 if Khrushchev did not remove the missiles.[46]

This raises several questions. One is the counterfactual one of whether Kennedy would have actually authorized air strikes if the Soviets had not complied with American coercive threats. A second question is the interpretive historical one of *why* Kennedy and other American decision makers were considering an air attack or some other hardline strategy. A third question, closely tied to the second and central for our purposes, is whether it is useful to describe Kennedy's thinking as involving preventive logic, and whether we would describe a hypothetical air strike as preventive.

In terms of the definition offered here, the thinking was clearly not preemptive, because no one anticipated an imminent Soviet attack against the

United States. Whether the logic is best described as preventive raises some difficult issues. My definition of prevention emphasizes perceptions and motivations—perceptions of an adverse shift in power and the motivation of blocking or retarding that power shift. If Kennedy and his advisors perceived that the introduction of the Soviet missiles into Cuba constituted a significant increase in Soviet military power against the United States, if they feared the consequences of that adverse shift in power, and if they sought an air strike and possibly an invasion primarily in order to forestall that shift in the dyadic balance of power, then I would describe the thinking and any subsequent air strike as preventive.[47]

If, on the other hand, Kennedy's contemplation of a possible air strike was driven primarily by domestic political considerations, or even by a loss of credibility that might affect others' perceptions of U.S. intentions in future crises, I would not describe his thinking as preventive.[48] Similarly, if it were true, as many argue, that Kennedy and most of his advisors did not see the new Soviet missiles as constituting a significant increase in Soviet military power vis-à-vis the United States, and that Kennedy's policy of demanding their removal—by persuasion if possible and by force if necessary—was driven more by domestic politics or concerns about alliance cohesion or credibility than by a perception of a shift in the strategic balance, then I would dissent from Trachtenberg's argument that Kennedy was driven by preventive thinking in the missile crisis.[49] This discussion makes clear that the labeling of state strategies as preventive can be a highly data-intensive task, one that requires detailed information about decision makers' perceptions and intentions.

The Kennedy administration also worried about China's nuclear weapons program. They believed that a nuclear-armed China would be "intolerable" and hoped that diplomatic efforts associated with the planned nuclear test ban treaty would convince Chinese leaders to abandon their program. At the same time, they considered the possibility of either an American or a Soviet preventive strike if diplomatic efforts failed.[50] Kennedy approached the Soviets in July 1963, in the context of negotiations over the Test Ban Treaty, about their willingness to go along, but the Soviets declined.[51] Trachtenberg raises the question of what Kennedy would have done if he had not been assassinated, or if the Soviet reaction had been more positive. Whether the Kennedy administration's discussions and approach to the Soviets were idle talk, as some have argued, or whether they were much closer to a preventive strike, is something that requires more evidence to resolve.

It is interesting to note that later in the decade, as the Nixon administration was attempting to bring China into the balance against the Soviet Union, the U.S. was not at all receptive to the possibility of a preventive strike against China. During the Sino-Soviet crisis and border skirmishes in 1969, President Richard Nixon warned the Soviet Union that the United States "would not remain indifferent" if the Soviets attacked China. Four years later, when the

Soviets appeared to approach the United States about a possible Soviet preventive attack against China, the United States did not respond.[52]

Another situation in which preventive logic played a role is the 1990/91 Persian Gulf War. One factor contributing to the first Bush administration's decision to intervene in the war was its fear that the completion of the Iraqi nuclear weapons program would catapult Iraq beyond a critical threshold of military capabilities, upset the balance of power in the Middle East, threaten U.S. regional interests and allies (Israel in particular), and undermine the deterrent threat of American intervention. The Iraqi invasion of Kuwait provided the opportunity to destroy Iraqi nuclear facilities while driving Iraqi forces out of Kuwait, and in this sense the preventive motivation was one of several factors leading to the American decision for war in January 1991.

The relative causal weight of preventive logic compared to that of other factors is difficult to assess, though it was probably not the primary consideration. We can say, however, that fears of an Iraqi nuclear program turned out to be the primary means by which the first Bush administration was able to mobilize public support for operation Desert Storm. After eliciting relatively little public response to arguments that war might be necessary to protect oil supplies, to reverse an immoral action by an immoral regime, to protect the American way of life, and to protect American jobs, the administration shifted (in late November 1990) its emphasis to the risks posed by the Iraqi nuclear program, which finally struck a chord with the public.[53] Thus preventive logic contributed to the American decision for war in January 1991 in two ways. It was one of several factors that directly influenced President George H. W. Bush and his advisors. Perhaps more significantly, it was the critical factor in the mobilization of public support for the war, which was itself an important causal path leading to war.

The 1994 North Korean nuclear crisis provides a much clearer case in which American anticipation of a step-level shift in an adversary's military capabilities and the fear of its consequences led to the serious consideration of a preventive attack to forestall an adverse shift in military power, namely North Korea's acquisition of a nuclear weapons capability.[54] American intelligence had suspicions about the North Korean nuclear program since the early 1980s. The International Atomic Energy Administration initiated inspections of the North Korean nuclear complex at Yongbyon in January 1992 and demanded more intrusive inspections. North Korea rebuffed these demands and in March 1993 withdrew from the Treaty on the Non-Proliferation of Nuclear Weapons. By fall 1993, the Clinton administration believed that North Korea might already have enough plutonium to make two nuclear bombs, enough fuel rods to make five or six more, the capability of making ten or twelve nuclear bombs a year once its reactor moved into full-scale operation, and the ability to multiply that several times once its larger reactors were completed. The risks were seen to be "intolerable."[55]

After a series of diplomatic efforts failed, and it was clear that North Korea was intent on proceeding with its nuclear program, the Clinton administration developed plans both for a preventive strike against the North Korean military facility at Yongbyon, and for a defense against a North Korean invasion of the South. With support from Japan and South Korea, it publicly demanded that North Korea either stop its nuclear program or face economic sanctions. North Korea responded by threatening "to turn Seoul into a sea of flames" and warning that sanctions would constitute an "act of war."[56]

Secretary of Defense William Perry later said that the Clinton administration was faced with the choice between an "unpalatable" option and a "disastrous" one. They believed that a nuclear North Korea would be a nightmare, but that a preventive strike was "very likely to incite" North Korea to attack the South, and even building up American military forces in the South to defend against a possible North Korean attack risked a preemptive attack by North Korea.[57] Domestically, Republicans in Congress and conservative commentators were demanding a hard line against North Korea, and opinion polls showed substantial support for military action to keep North Korea from acquiring nuclear weapons, even at the risk of a broader war.[58]

As Trachtenberg notes, "the smell of war was in the air." Perry later said that he was aware at the time that "we were poised on the brink of a war that might involve weapons of mass destruction." Don Oberdorfer reports that the top U.S. Air Force general in Korea said that "although neither he nor other commanders said so out loud, not even in private conversations with one another, 'inside we all thought we were going to war'."[59]

In the end, however, the Clinton administration settled for a compromise with North Korea, one that the U.S. had rejected earlier in the crisis. The primary factors working against military action were the perceived likelihood and costs of a major war,[60] the absence of diplomatic support from China and Japan,[61] and the unwanted and unexpected mission of former President Jimmy Carter to North Korea in the middle of the crisis. President Bill Clinton was "within minutes" of adopting one of three options to increase U.S. troop deployments in South Korea, which he recognized would have increased the risk of a general war on the peninsula and possibly lead to a preemptive attack by North Korea, when word of a provisional agreement negotiated by Carter arrived. Thus the U.S. came very close to war with North Korea in 1994, and the process was driven primarily by the anticipation of a step-level increase in North Korean military capabilities and by the U.S. willingness to run a high-risk war to forestall that development.[62]

Just as we can be confident that preventive war logic was more important as a rationale for the American war against Iraq in 1991 than as a leading cause of that war, we can also be fairly confident that preventive logic was more important as a means of gaining domestic support for the 2003 Iraq War than as a leading cause of that war.[63] There is little doubt that the fear that Iraq was close to developing a nuclear capability, along with (secondarily) the virtual certainty that Saddam Hussein had chemical weapons and that he had used them, was the primary means by which the George W. Bush administration mobilized public support for its war in Iraq, at least in its early stages.[64]

The actual decision for war was more complicated.[65] Although many have argued each side of the issue with great confidence, this is in fact a difficult conceptual and methodological question. Conceptually, the decision for war, like many decisions for war, was quite complex. The President and his advisors had multiple and sometimes conflicting motivations: they could agree on war but not on why it was desirable or necessary; the mix of factors may have varied for different individuals at different stages of the decision-making process; and the September 11 terrorist attacks created a permissive domestic political context for war. How to aggregate all these factors, and to assess the relative weight of preventive logic, is a difficult question. This analytic problem is compounded by the methodological problem of lack of access to all of the data necessary to resolve the factual question, and by the fact that actors have incentives to conceal not only their primary motivations but also what information they had and when they had it. Given that the causes were complex and that the evidence is incomplete, I believe that too many observers have expressed too much confidence in emphasizing the dominant role of one particular factor in the outbreak of the war, whether it be preventive logic, a Wilsonian liberal agenda, the domestic political agenda of the Bush administration, or the religious views or personal agenda of the President. Thus, in my view, a definitive assessment of the causal role of the preventive motivation in the processes leading to war would be premature at this time.

Conclusion

I have defined prevention, distinguished it from preemption and from other sources of better-now-than-later logic, and briefly examined the role of preventive logic in American foreign policy since the end of World War II. This survey suggests that there are a number of interesting historical and theoretical questions that have yet to be fully answered and that require a great deal more research. These questions include the extent of official thinking about a possible preventive strike against the Soviet Union and then China; how to explain the Clinton administration's decision to pull back from a preventive strike against North Korea in 1994; the causal role of preventive logic in the U.S. decision to go to war against Iraq in 1991 and again in 2003; and the conditions, if any, under which the United States would be most likely to initiate, alone or in conjunction with other states, preventive strikes against North Korea, Iran, or other potential adversaries in the future.

My survey of the historical influence of preventive logic has generated one finding that might be surprising to some but that draws considerable support from the historical record. That is the finding that the American public appears to be quite open to preventive logic as a justification for military action. This, combined with evidence from the Israeli public's reaction to the preventively motivated Sinai campaign against Egypt in 1956 and attack against the Iraqi nuclear reactor in 1981,[66] runs contrary to the argument, quite common before the 2003 Iraq War, that democracies do not fight preventive wars.[67] An important causal mechanism underlying this hypothesis is the notion that democratic publics will not tolerate preventive wars on moral grounds. Hans J. Morgenthau argued that preventive war is "abhorrent to democratic public opinion" because of the moral condemnation of war in the West, and Bernard Brodie argued that "there now exists a powerful and rigid barrier, largely on moral grounds, to American planning of preventive war."[68]

The two U.S.-Iraqi cases are particularly clear. The fear of the development of an Iraqi nuclear capability under Saddam Hussein was the primary means by which each of the Bush administrations mobilized public support for a war against Iraq, first in January 1991 and then in March 2003. In the latter case, the Iraqi nuclear program was one of the factors explicitly cited in the October 2002 Congressional Resolution authorizing the President to use military force against Iraq. After it became clear that the war would be much more costly and less successful than the Bush administration had predicted, many Democratic political leaders stated that they never would have supported the war had they known at the time that Iraq did not pose a nuclear threat. Their statements, combined with their support of the Congressional Resolution authorizing war, suggest that they believed that a strategy of military prevention was justified, or at least good policy.

The North Korean crisis provides supportive but not conclusive evidence on behalf of the hypothesis that the American public is willing to support preventively motivated military action. Approximately half of the American public reported that they would support military action to prevent North Korea from acquiring nuclear weapons, despite the risks of a wider war. True, the Clinton administration's decision against a preventive strike was motivated in part by the anticipation of the enormous casualties that they expected would follow from the likely result of a general war on the peninsula, but to the extent that domestic considerations were important, Clinton was probably more concerned about charges that he was too soft in reaction to a serious foreign threat.[69]

Thus we must reject any unconditional statements that public opposition and moral considerations prevent the United States from initiating preventive military action. An interesting question to explore, however, is what impact the Iraq War will have on public attitudes toward possible preventive strikes against future adversaries. Will preventive logic continue to appeal to the American public? Or will frustration over the Iraq War and the grounds on which it was initiated lead to skepticism both about a future government's claims about an adversary's nuclear weapons capabilities and about the utility of a military solution to the threats said to be confronting the United States?

Notes

I thank the editors of this volume for their comments and suggestions.

Endnotes

1. Randall L. Schweller, "Domestic Structure and Preventive War: Are Democracies More Pacific?" *World Politics* 44 (January 1992): 235-269. This argument is distinct from the widely supported finding that democracies rarely if ever go to war against each other.

2. This debate, not surprisingly, is clouded by politics. It is not a coincidence that many critics of the Bush administration argue that the Bush Doctrine and its preventive logic marks a sharp break in American foreign policy, while supporters often emphasize continuity with the past. Demetrios James Caraley, in his edited volume, *American Hegemony: Preventive War, Iraq, and Imposing Democracy* (New York: Academy of Political Science, 2004), uses the title "Experiences from the First Preventive War" for the second section of the book. Arthur M. Schlesinger, Jr., in *War and the American Presidency* (New York: Norton, 2004), argues that the Bush administration's policy of prevention is a revolutionary break from a tradition of American security policy based on deterrence and containment: "Mr. Bush replaced a policy aimed at peace through the prevention of war by a policy aimed at peace through preventive war" (21). For scholarly treatments of the deeper roots of preventive thinking in American foreign policy, see John Lewis Gaddis, *Surprise, Security, and the American Experience* (Cambridge, MA: Harvard University Press, 2004); Marc Trachtenberg, "Preventive War and U.S. Foreign Policy," unpublished manuscript, 2006.

3. This contradiction is reminiscent of the contrast between the argument during the Cold War that the bipolar U.S.-Soviet rivalry was likely to persist for many years, and arguments in the 1990s and after that the collapse of the Soviet Union and end of the Cold War were overdetermined.

4. See the special issue of *Ethics and International Affairs*, 17/1 (Spring 2003); Charles W. Kegley, Jr. and Gregory A. Raymond, "Preventive War and Permissive Normative Order," *International Studies Perspectives* 4 (2003): 385-94; David Luban, "Preventive War," *Philosophy & Public Affairs* 32 (July 2004): 207-248; Jeff McMahan, "Preventive War and the Killing of the Innocent," in David Rodin and Richard Sorabji, eds., *The Ethics of War: Shared Problems in Different Traditions* (Aldershot, UK: Ashgate Publishing, 2005): 169-90; David Rodin, "The Ethics of Preventive War," paper presented at the 2006 annual meeting of the International Studies Association, San Diego, CA.

5. This section builds on Jack S. Levy, "Declining Power and the Preventive Motivation for War," *World Politics* 40 (October 1987): 82-107; Jack S. Levy and Joseph R. Gochal, "Democracy and Preventive War: Israel and the 1956 Sinai Campaign," *Security Studies* 11 (Winter 2001/02): 1-49.

6. Huntington, for example, defines preventive war as "[a] military action initiated by one state against another for the purpose of forestalling a subsequent change in the balance of power between the two states which would seriously reduce the military security of the first state." Walzer says that "[a] preventive war is a war fought to maintain the balance, to stop what is thought to be an even distribution of power from shifting into a relation of dominance and inferiority." Betts argues that "[p]reventive war is waged in anticipation of eventual vulnerability, not against immediate threats, and is designed to engage an enemy before he has improved his capabilities." Samuel P. Huntington, "To Choose Peace or War: Is There a Place for Preventive War in American Policy?" *United States Naval Institute Proceedings* 83 (April 1957): 360, cited in Jonathan B. Renshon, *Why Leaders Choose War: The Psychology of Prevention* (Westport, CT: Praeger, 2006), chap. 1; Michael Walzer, *Just and Unjust Wars* (New York: Basic Books, 1977), 76; Richard K. Betts, *Surprise Attack* (Washington, DC: Brookings Institution Press, 1982), 145.

7. Paul W. Schroeder, "World War I as Galloping Gertie: A Reply to Joachim Remak," in Paul W. Schroeder, *Systems, Stability, and Statecraft: Essays on the International History of Modern Europe*, ed. David Wetzel, Robert Jervis, and Jack S. Levy (New York: Palgrave, 2004), 139; Alfred Vagts, *Defense and Diplomacy* (New York: King's Crown, 1956); Levy, "Declining Power and the Preventive Motivation for War"; Stephen Van Evera, *Causes of War: Power and the Roots of Conflict* (Ithaca, NY: Cornell University Press, 1999), chap. 4; Dale C. Copeland, *Origins of Major War* (Ithaca, NY: Cornell University Press, 2000); Shlomo Nakdimon, *First Strike*, trans. Peretz Kidron (New York: Summit Books, 1987).

8. A. J. P. Taylor, *The Struggle for Mastery in Europe, 1848-1918* (New York: Oxford University Press, 1954), 166; Copeland, *Origins of Major War*; Michael Howard, *The Causes of War* (New York: Cambridge University Press, 1983), 18.

9. Arnold Wolfers, *Discord and Collaboration* (Baltimore: Johns Hopkins University Press, 1962), 153. I suspect that Wolfers' statement that "there seems to be no case in history in which a country started a preventive war on the grounds of security" derives from his narrow (but unstated) definition.

10. Walzer, *Just and Unjust Wars*, chap. 5; Levy, "Declining Power and the Preventive Motivation for War," 90-93; Betts, *Surprise Attack*, 145; Van Evera, *Causes of War*, chaps. 3-4. Some suggest that the distinction between prevention and preemption is not as clear in other languages as it is in English. Gareth Evans, "When Is It Right to Fight?" *Survival* 46/3 (Summer 2004), 65. Cited in Alan M. Dershowitz, *Preemption* (New York: Norton, 2006), 59-60.

11. The National Security Strategy of the United States, September 17, 2002, 4, http://www.whitehouse.gov/nsc/nss.pdf; The National Security Strategy of the United States, March 16, 2006, http://www.whitehouse.gov/nsc/nss/2006/nss2006.pdf; hereafter, 2006 NSS. Other scholars emphasizing the preventive motivations underlying the Bush administration's policies include Lawrence Freedman, "Prevention, Not Preemption," in *Reshaping Rogue States*, eds. Alexander T. J. Lennon and Camille Eiss (Cambridge, MA: MIT Press, 2004), 37-49; Robert Jervis, *American Foreign Policy in a New Era* (New York: Routledge, 2005), 84-86.

12. 2006 NSS, 9, 18.

13. Dan Reiter, "Exploding the Powder Keg Myth: Preemptive Wars Almost Never Happen," *International Security* 20 (Fall 1995): 5-34. The classic case of preemption is Israel's strike against Egyptian airfields to initiate the 1967 Arab-Israeli War. Michael B. Oren, *Six Days of War: June 1967 and the Making of the Modern Middle East* (New York: Oxford University Press, 2002). Another might be Germany's decision for war after the Russian mobilization in 1914 (which involved a combination of prevention and preemption). Jack S. Levy, "Preferences, Constraints, and Choices in July 1914," *International Security*, 15 (Winter 1990-91): 151-186. While preemption is rare, Betts argues correctly that during the Cold War it was a more likely path to nuclear war than was prevention. Richard K. Betts, "Surprise Attack and Preemption," in *Hawks, Doves, and Owls*, eds. Graham T. Allison, Albert Carnesale, and Joseph S. Nye, Jr. (New York: Norton, 1985), 56-58.

14. See Richard Ned Lebow's discussion of "justification of hostility crises" in his *Between Peace and War* (Baltimore: Johns Hopkins University Press, 1981).

15. For an argument that Germany wanted a preventive war in 1914 but wanted Russia to initiate military action, see Fritz Fischer, *Germany's Aims in the First World War* (New York: Norton, 1967).

16. This is a possible explanation for the Japanese attack on the United States in 1941. Akira Iriye, *The Origins of the Second World War* (New York: Longman, 1987); Jeffrey W. Taliaferro, *Balancing Risks: Great Power Intervention in the Periphery* (Ithaca, NY: Cornell University Press, 2004).

17. Betts, *Surprise Attack*, 144-145.

18. On the right of self-defense in international law, as it has developed over time, see Stephen C. Neff, *War and the Law of Nations: A General History* (New York: Cambridge University Press, 2005); Mary Ellen O'Connell, *International Law and the Use of Force: Cases and Materials* (New York: Foundation Press, 2005); Anthony Clark Arend, "International Law and the Preemptive Use of Military Force," in *Reshaping Rogue States*, eds. Lennon and Eiss, 19-36. The right to use military force in self-defense is quite restricted in the United Nations Charter. The sole exception is Chapter VII, Article 51, which allows for "individual and collective self-defense if an armed attack occurs." This is generally interpreted as prohibiting the use of force except in response to actual or imminent violations of territory boundaries. For a philosophical treatment see David Rodin, *War and Self-Defense* (Oxford: Oxford University Press, 2002).

19. Walzer, *Just and Unjust Wars*, 80-85. Note that Walzer's concept of "manifest intent to injure" implies that preemption requires that the adversary actually intends to initiate an attack. This is too strong. I require only that the target perceives that an imminent attack is virtually certain.

20. See note 4.

21. Renshon, *Why Leaders Choose War*, chap. 1. See also J. Renshon's chapter in this volume.

22. Renshon, *Why Leaders Choose War*, chap. 2. It is true that concerns about status or credibility are often closely linked to concerns about relative power, and this raises questions about the utility of separating them. One difference is that my narrow definition of prevention focuses on one's future capabilities relative to an adversary, whereas the incorporation of status or credibility bears on future intentions as well as capabilities. International relations theorists have

long distinguished capabilities from intentions or reputation. This distinction is reinforced by evidence suggesting that leaders' expectations regarding the likely impact of their state's reputation on its future influence may be misplaced. Adversaries' perceptions of a state's resolve in a crisis are influenced far more by their assessments of their opponent's military power and interests at stake than by their assessments of its reputation deriving from past behavior. Daryl Press, *Calculating Credibility: How Leaders Assess Military Threats* (Ithaca, NY: Cornell University Press, 2005). This may or may not be correct, but we cannot assess their relative weight empirically unless we first distinguish them analytically.

23. Gaddis, *Surprise, Security, and the American Experience*, 16-22 (quote on pp. 17-18).

24. Ibid., 18-21.

25. John S. Galbraith, "The 'Turbulent Frontier' as a Factor in British Expansion," *Comparative Studies in Society and History* 2 (January 1960): 34-48.

26. The argument assumes that the expansionist behavior is driven more by fear than by ambition, more by a concern to avoid losses than to maximize gains. The "loss aversion" hypothesis draws support, on the individual level, from prospect theory. For a summary and applications to international relations, see Jack S. Levy, "The Implications of Framing and Loss Aversion for International Conflict," in *Handbook of War Studies II*, ed. Manus I. Midlarsky (Ann Arbor: University of Michigan Press, 2000), 193-221.

27. None of the instances described above, with the possible exception of the incursions from Spanish Florida leading to an American military response, involved an imminent threat of external attack, so that none of these qualifies as preemption.

28. Perhaps an example will illustrate the issues involved. Renshon (*Why Leaders Choose War*, chap. 2) makes a strong argument that the primary factor leading British political leaders to intervene with military force in the 1956 Suez crisis was their concerns about Britain's declining status and prestige in the global system. Given his definition of prevention, he classifies British behavior as preventive war. I agree with Renshon's analysis of British motivations but prefer not to use the concept of preventive war to describe it. It would be useful to compare British perceptions and motivations with those of Israel in the same war. Britain anticipated a continuing decline in its status, but no future threat of a military attack by any particular adversary. Israel anticipated that the Czech/Russian arms sales to Egypt and the incorporation of the new weapons into the Egyptian arsenal would lead to a shift in the qualitative and quantitative dyadic balance of power in Egypt's favor, and that in the context of ongoing hostilities and Egypt President Nasser's bellicose rhetoric there was a high probability that Egypt would initiate a war within two or three years. Levy and Gochal, "Democracy and Preventive War." The expectations and motivations underlying British and Israeli behavior are sufficiently different that we should use different concepts to describe them. The question is not which view is correct or incorrect, but rather which is most useful for various theoretical purposes.

29. On the dangers of "conceptual stretching" see Giovanni Sartori, "Concept Misinformation in Comparative Politics," *American Political Science Review* 64 (December 1970): 1033-1053; David Collier and James Mahon, "Conceptual Stretching Revisited: Adapting Categories in Comparative Analysis," *American Political Science Review* 87 (December 1993): 845-855.

30. While Copeland (*Origins of Major War*, chap. 6) includes the "preventive containment" of the Soviet Union by the United States in the early Cold War period as a case of prevention in response to anticipated decline, I do not include that in a category of the preventive use of force.

31. In his *An Agenda for Peace: Preventive Diplomacy, Peacemaking, and Peacekeeping*, former UN Secretary-General Boutros Boutros-Ghali defined preventive diplomacy as "action to prevent disputes from arising between the parties, to prevent existing disputes from escalating into conflicts and to limit the spread of the latter when they occur." Cited in Fen Osler Hampson, "Preventive Diplomacy at the United Nations and Beyond," in *From Reaction to Conflict Prevention: Opportunities for the UN System*, eds. Fen Osler Hampson and David M. Malone (Boulder, CO: Lynne Rienner, 2002), 139-157.

32. For similar reasons, we have to be careful in referring to a state strategy of preventive war, because a state strategy may be the product of a collective decision by actors who support the strategy for different reasons. The U.S. decision to invade Iraq in 2003, rationalized under the rubric of "preemption," may be an example.

33. The probability that a power shift leads to war depends on the magnitude and the speed of the shift, images of the adversary's current hostility and future intentions, the expected costs of an immediate war, the availability of alternative strategies (including alliances) for dealing with the threat, and a state's risk orientation and time horizons. See Copeland, *Origins of Major War*; Van Evera, *Causes of War*; Norrin M. Ripsman and Jack S. Levy, "The Preventive War that Never Happened: Britain, France, and the Rise of Germany in the 1930s," *Security Studies*, forthcoming.

34. Ronald L. Tammen, et al., *Power Transitions: Strategies for the 21st Century* (New York: Chatham House, 2000). See also A. F. K. Organski and Jacek Kugler, *The War Ledger* (Chicago: University of Chicago Press, 1980). Similarly, long-cycle theorists, who argue that global wars coincide with power transitions between the leading actors in the system, make no claim that the war is triggered by a direct attack by the declining state against a rising challenger in an attempt to forestall the power shift. Karen A. Rasler and William R. Thompson, *The Great Powers and Global Struggle, 1490-1990* (Lexington: The University Press of Kentucky, 1994).

35. Levy, "Declining Power and the Preventive Motivation for War." The one situation in which the concept of preventive war is not analytically problematic is one in which the preventive motivation is both a necessary and a sufficient condition for war, but I can think of no clear historical example. The Israeli strike against the Iraqi nuclear reactor in 1981 comes close, but if Peres rather than Begin had been prime minister—a reasonable counterfactual to invoke since for a time Peres was ahead in the polls at the time—the war would probably not have occurred. Jack S. Levy and Joseph R. Gochal, "When Do Democracies Fight Preventive Wars?"; Renshon, *Why Leaders Choose War*, chap. 3.

36. On "rapid approaches" that fall short of complete power transitions, see Frank Whelon Wayman, "Power Shifts and the Onset of War," in *Parity and War*, ed. Jacek Kugler and Douglas Lemke (Ann Arbor: University of Michigan Press, 1996), 145-162.

37. Fischer, *Germany's Aims in the First World War*; Levy and Gochal, "Democracy and Preventive War."

38. Leon V. Sigal, *Disarming Strangers: Nuclear Diplomacy With North Korea* (Princeton, NJ: Princeton University Press, 1997); Joel S. Wit, Daniel Poneman, Robert L. Gallucci, *Going Critical: The First North Korean Nuclear Crisis* (Washington DC: Brookings Institution Press, 2004); Levy and Gochal, "When Do Democracies Fight Preventive Wars?"

39. Levy and Gochal, "Democracy and Preventive War."

40. Trachtenberg ("Preventive War") interprets American entry into World War II as preventive, motivated by the fear of Germany's growing power in Europe, the recognition that American public opinion would not support American intervention, and by the belief that the only way to bring the United States into the war against Germany was to provoke a war against Japan. This is based on a very broad conception of prevention.

41. Marc Trachtenberg, *History & Strategy* (Princeton, NJ: Princeton University Press, 1991), 110-11. Trachtenberg, "Preventive War"; John Lewis Gaddis, *We Now Know: Rethinking Cold War History* (Oxford, UK: Clarendon Press, 1997).

42. Trachtenberg argues that the evidence, while not conclusive, suggests that the North Atlantic Treaty Organization had a policy of preemption against the Soviet Union (until Kennedy rejected it in 1963), in the sense that NATO planned to respond to a Soviet conventional invasion of Europe, or even to evidence that war was unavoidable, with a massive nuclear attack against the Soviet Union. That, of course, is distinct from a policy of prevention in response to a negative shift in the balance of power. Marc Trachtenberg, *A Constructed Peace: The Making of the European Settlement, 1945-1963* (Princeton, NJ: Princeton University Press, 1999), 158-164, 182-183.

43. Eisenhower to Dulles, September 8, 1953, *Foreign Relations of the United States 1952-54*, 2, 461 [emphasis in original]. Cited in Trachtenberg, "Preventive War." See also Russell D. Buhite and William C. Hamel, "War for Peace: The Question of an American Preventive War against the Soviet Union, 1945-1955," *Diplomatic History*, 29 (September 2005): 367-384.

44. Trachtenberg, "Preventive War."

45. Any supporting evidence would have to reflect a systematic pattern of thinking and be tested against alternative explanations. The fact that a political leader mentioned a particular policy option once or twice is far from evidence that he or she supported it. They might have suggested an option, thus leaving it in the historical record, only to quickly abandon it if they became convinced that it was intellectually flawed or politically impossible. They might also have deliberately played the devil's advocate role in raising certain possibilities.

46. In an October 29 cabinet meeting, President Kennedy stated, "We had decided Saturday night to begin this air strike on Tuesday [October 30]." Ernest R. May and Philip D. Zelikow, eds., *The Kennedy Tapes: Inside the White House During the Cuban Missile Crisis* (Cambridge, MA: Harvard University/Belknap Press, 1997), 656. The air strike might very well have been massive and followed by an invasion. See Sheldon M. Stern, *Averting 'The Final Failure': John F. Kennedy and the Secret Cuban Missile Crisis Meetings* (Stanford, CA: Stanford University Press, 2003). I thank Lori Gronich for her suggestions regarding recent research on the missile crisis.

47. Trachtenberg ("Preventive War") argues that the Kennedy administration's relatively hard line in Cuba was driven by the fear of what the Soviets might do in the near future in Berlin, and concludes that the underlying logic was basically "preemptive."

48. To illustrate a point I emphasized earlier, whether the contemplated U.S. air strike option was driven more by the goal of forestalling an adverse shift in the strategic balance of power or by the goal of forestalling a decline in U.S. image and credibility is an important question. Describing both as preventive would not facilitate an assessment of their relative causal impact.

49. President Kennedy repeatedly said in meetings with the ExComm that the Soviet missiles in Cuba did not substantially increase the Soviet nuclear threat to the U.S. The president's brother, Robert Kennedy, was particularly sensitive to the possible domestic implications of the crisis. Secretary of Defense Robert McNamara, in arguing for an all-out air and land attack on Cuba (after initially rejecting such options), stated that "it's not a *military* problem that we are facing; it's a *political* problem; it's a problem of holding the alliance together; it's a problem of...conditioning Khrushchev for our future moves." It was a "problem of dealing with our domestic public," rather than a change in the military balance of power that he said justified an invasion of Cuba [emphasis in original]. In Stern, *Averting 'The Final Failure'*, 98-100, 127. While some members of the ExComm, including the Joint Chiefs of Staff, believed that the missiles constituted a military problem, no one dissented from the view that it was a major political problem. As Roger Hilsman (a Kennedy advisor, but not a member of the ExComm, said, "The United States might not be in mortal danger, but...the administration most certainly was." Roger Hilsman, *To Move a Nation: The Politics of Foreign Policy in the Administration of John F. Kennedy* (Garden City, NY: Doubleday, 1967), 197. The stakes were all the higher because Kennedy had publicly warned Khrushchev that he would not tolerate Soviet missiles in Cuba, and thus staked his reputation on the issue. Lebow and others conclude that the continuing presence if Soviet missiles in Cuba would have crippled Kennedy's presidency and possibly led to a Republican control of Congress in November. Richard Ned Lebow, "The Traditional and Revisionist Interpretations Reevaluated: Why Was Cuba a Crisis?" in *The Cuban Missile Crisis Revisited*, ed. James A. Nathan (New York: St. Martins, 1992), 173. See also, Barton J. Bernstein, "Reconsidering the Cuban Missile Crisis: Dealing with the Problem of the American Jupiters in Turkey," in *The Cuban Missile Crisis Revisited*, ed. Nathan, 68-69.

50. A Soviet strike would be accompanied by American efforts to ensure that West Germany would not acquire nuclear weapons, which was a major Soviet concern.

51. William Burr and Jeffrey Richelson, "Whether to 'Strangle the Baby in the Cradle': The United States and the Chinese Nuclear Program, 1960-64," *International Security*, 25 (Winter 2000/2001): 67; Trachtenberg, "Preventive War."

52. Henry Kissinger, *Diplomacy* (New York: Simon & Schuster, 1994), 723. In a 1973 conversation with Brezhnev about China, Kissinger came away with the impression that "Brezhnev was clearly fishing for some hint of American acquiescence in a Soviet preemptive attack." Henry Kissinger, *Years of Upheaval* (Boston: Little Brown, 1982), 233.

53. Levy and Gochal, "When Do Democracies Fight Preventive Wars?"; Lawrence Freedman and Efraim Karsh, *The Gulf Conflict, 1990-1991: Diplomacy and War in the New World Order* (Princeton, NJ: Princeton University Press, 1993); Stanley A. Renshon ed., *The Political Psychology of the Gulf War* (Pittsburgh: University of Pittsburgh Press, 1993). For polling data see John Mueller, *Policy and Opinion in the Gulf War* (Chicago: University of Chicago Press, 1993).

54. The key sources include Don Oberdorfer, *The Two Koreas: A Contemporary History* (Reading, MA: Addison-Wesley, 1997); Sigal, *Disarming Strangers*; Wit, Poneman, and Gallucci, *Going Critical*.

55. Ashton B. Carter and William J. Perry, *Preventive Defense: A New Security Strategy for America* (Washington, DC: Brookings Institution Press, 1999), 126.

56. Ibid., 129.

57. Ibid., 128-131; Oberdorfer, *The Two Koreas*, 323.

58. A June 1994 poll revealed that nearly half of the public were willing to risk war to prevent North Korea from acquiring nuclear weapons. Oberdofer, *The Two Koreas*, 323; Sigal, *Disarming Strangers*, 302-303.

59. Trachtenberg, "Preventive War"; Oberdorfer, *The Two Koreas*, 306; Ashton B. Carter and William J. Perry, *Preventive Defense: A New Security Strategy for America* (Washington, DC: Brookings Institution Press, 131).

60. There was a wide range of estimates regarding the costs of a general war if it did occur, but all involved casualty rates substantially higher than the 1950–1952 Korean conflict. Perry, Head of JCS General John Shalikashvili, and General Luck told Clinton on May 19 that a war to repulse a North Korean attack before it reached Seoul, followed by a counterattack into North Koran, would result in 52,000 U.S. troops killed or wounded, 490,000 Republic of Korean military casualties, "enormous" number of North Korean and civilian deaths, and a $61 billion cost, mostly to be paid by the U.S. Oberdorfer, *The Two Koreas*, 315; Sigal, *Disarming Strangers*, 211-212.

61. Sigal, *Disarming Strangers*, 9, 118.

62. As we now know, the negotiated settlement did not achieve its objectives.

63. On the causes of the war, see Ivo H. Daalder and James M. Lindsay, *America Unbound: The Bush Revolution in Foreign Policy* (Washington, DC: Brookings Institution Press, 2003); Bob Woodward, *Plan of Attack* (New York: Simon & Schuster, 2004); James Mann, *Rise of the Vulcans: The History of Bush's War Cabinet* (New York: Viking/Penguin, 2004); Michael R. Gordon and General Bernard E. Trainor, *Cobra II: The Inside Story of the Invasion and Occupation of Iraq* (New York: Pantheon Books, 2006), chaps. 1-10; Thomas E. Ricks, Fiasco: The American Military Adventure in Iraq (New York: Penguin, 2006), part I.

64. Chaim Kaufmann, "Threat Inflation and the Failure of the Marketplace of Ideas: The Selling of the Iraq War," *International Security* 29/1 (Summer 2004), 5-48.

65. Also unclear, at least at this point (spring 2006), is exactly which decision makers had what degree of confidence in how close Saddam was to acquiring nuclear weapons, and how those estimates changed over time in response to new information. Intelligence estimates may have been influenced by a variety of psychological mechanisms or political considerations. Policy preferences for war may have led some officials, through a process of "motivated biases" (wishful thinking) to a genuine belief that Saddam was getting close to acquiring nuclear weapons. Others may have realized that an Iraqi nuclear capability was a more distant prospect, but consciously and deliberately distorted intelligence in an attempt to influence others' policy preferences and advance their own policy agendas. Such distortions may have included the restructuring of the intelligence collection apparatus itself to produce the desired intelligence, as illustrated by the creation of the Office of Special Plans in the Pentagon. Finally, some actors may have been driven by unmotivated (purely cognitive) biases, independent of their policy preferences, to the conclusion that the Iraqi nuclear capability was far along. After all, this conclusion appeared to make sense in light of Saddam's refusal to allow inspections and reports that the Iraqi military believed that Iraq had nuclear weapons. Plus, U.S. intelligence had underestimated the extent of the Iraqi nuclear weapons program in 1990, and they did not want to make the same mistake again. On the influence of cognitive biases on perceptions of an Iraqi nuclear capability, see Robert Jervis, "Reports, Politics, and Intelligence Failures: The Case of Iraq." *Journal of Strategic Studies*, 29,1 (February 2006), 3-52.
66. Levy and Gochal, "Democracy and Preventive War"; Levy and Gochal, "When Do Democracies Fight Preventive Wars?"
67. Schweller ("Domestic Structure and Preventive War") qualified this hypothesis by saying that democracies might fight low-cost preventive wars against much weaker opponents, but other scholars subsequently stated the hypothesis in more unconditional terms.
68. Hans J. Morgenthau, *Politics Among Nations* (New York: Alfred A. Knopf, 1967); Bernard Brodie, *Strategy in the Missile Age* (Princeton, NJ: Princeton University Press, 1965), 237. Cited in Levy and Gochal, "Democracy and Preventive War," 13-14.
69. Oberdorfer, *The Two Koreas*; Sigal, *Disarming Strangers*; Wit, Poneman, and Gallucci, *Going Critical*.

8

The Psychological Origins of Preventive War

JONATHAN RENSHON

Introduction

One of the most startling and controversial aspects of the Bush Doctrine is its reliance on preventive action. It is this feature of the Doctrine as much as any other that has elicited fervent opinions on either side of the ideological divide. The stated reason for this policy of prevention was a confluence of threats: catastrophic terrorism, proliferation of weapons of mass destruction (WMDs), and "rogue states." However, not one of these three threats was a new feature of the international system, or a consequence of the terrorist attacks on the United States on September 11, 2001. In fact, these threats very obviously predated President George W. Bush's administration. The core of the issue then is, why this policy, and why now?

The policy of prevention has been traced to 9/11, to President Bush's personality, and even to a supposed obsession with removing Saddam Hussein from power. However, these explanations are simply not convincing. If it were Bush's personality alone, then we could have expected a drastic shift in foreign policy immediately upon his election to the presidency in 2000; if it were only 9/11, then why did the policy take a full one year to emerge after the terrorist attacks; and if it were only a rationalization for removing Hussein from power, then why would the administration have wasted time with a war in Afghanistan, and another full year of diplomacy before the Iraq War?

In fact, the best explanation for President Bush's policy of prevention must encompass both psychological and strategic factors; alone, neither is sufficient. And the best way to understand how these factors led to the policy of prevention is to think about it in context of other similar decisions. While the adoption of prevention as part of a "grand strategy" may be unique in history, preventive action itself is not.

This chapter addresses the issues of preventive war and the Bush Doctrine by focusing on the psychological motivations for preventive action within the context of the strategic circumstances that the United States faced post-9/11. It is important to be clear about the nature and meaning of that policy and to analyze what factors are relevant in decisions to initiate preventive action. This is best accomplished by examining how these factors operated in several cases in recent history. Putting the Bush Doctrine in historical context is inherently important, but it also helps to explain why American foreign policy has changed course so dramatically since the turn of the century.

What Is Preventive War?

Before undertaking an analysis of the motivations behind preventive war, it is imperative to distinguish clearly between preemption and prevention. Consider two countries, Country A and Country B, between which there is an adversarial relationship.[1] Let us imagine that Country B has received intelligence that Country A is preparing to launch a military strike against it. If Country B then takes action to make sure that Country A cannot attack it as planned, then they have preemptively attacked. According to Lawrence Freedman, a preemptive action "takes place at some point between the moment when an enemy decides to attack—or, more precisely, is perceived to be about to attack—and when the attack is actually launched."[2] True preemption can be thought of as defensive in motivation and offensive in effect. However, since it is primarily defensive, it is generally seen as more morally legitimate than prevention.[3]

In another situation, imagine that Country B's capabilities are increasing relative to Country A's; that is, B is still weaker than A, but the power differential between the two countries is shrinking. If Country A acts militarily to prevent Country B from continuing to increase its relative power, then Country A has launched a preventive war. This is a preventive war in the classic sense of the term, a war fought to preserve the status quo balance of power.

Most previous explanations of preventive war have focused on this particular aspect. For example:

> Samuel P. Huntington described preventive war in 1957 as a military action initiated by one state against another for the purpose of forestalling a subsequent change in the balance of power between the two states, which would seriously reduce the military security of the first state.[4]

> Jack Levy argues that the "preventive motivation" for war arises from the "perception that one's military power and potential are declining relative to that of a rising adversary, and from the fear of the consequences of that decline."[5]

> Michael Walzer, coming from a notably different perspective than both Huntington and Levy, also describes preventive war as a war fought to maintain the balance, to stop what is thought to be an even distribution of power from shifting into a relation of dominance and inferiority.[6]

Thus, conventional explanations of preventive war focus on the balance of power, and define preventive war as a war to prevent a change in that balance.[7]

In fact, what these scholars describe is only one possible motivation for a preventive war, not its defining characteristic.[8] In defining preventive war as a war to maintain the balance of power, previous scholars have conflated a motivation for war, with a type of war. Thus, the War of Spanish Succession (one of Walzer's examples) was, in fact, a preventive war. And, a desire to maintain the balance of power, or status quo, did play a part in England's motivation.

However, not all preventive actions are wars to maintain the balance of power (in fact, not all preventive actions are necessarily wars, either). There can be numerous other motivations at work in states' decisions to initiate preventive action. Thus, a more useful and inclusive definition is that a preventive action is one fought to forestall a grave national security threat. True prevention is a response to a serious threat that lies in the future, not an attack that is already under way. "Action" here refers to an array of forceful initiatives, ranging from limited strikes to total war.

There is a tendency to rely on the term "imminence" in definitions of preemptive war. However, there is also a tendency to confuse the true meaning of the word, and equate it with the time period in which a threat resides. Consider the following terms: "imminent," "impending," "looming," and "gathering." All can refer to threats that are days or weeks away. Because of this, defining "imminent" as a threat that is "days or weeks away" can, and often does, lead to considerable confusion. "Imminence" carries with it the implicit assumption that an attack might happen at any second, that events have been set in motion. An imminent threat is one that must be preempted without delay. Conversely, preventive wars are waged when the threat is in the distance, but that is merely a descriptive comment, not a "key" defining characteristic. Threats are always in the distance—where else could they be? What defines a preventive war is not where in time the threat is, but rather the prime motivation of the decision maker in initiating the war.

Just as we must be careful to not be overly restrictive in our definitions, we must also be careful not to define preventive action too broadly. In a recent article, former Deputy National Security Advisor James Steinberg defined four categories of "preventive force": action taken against terrorists; action taken to eliminate a dangerous capability; interventions in the case of state failure; and the preventive use of force to effect regime change.[9]

However, this is an overly expansive definition, and not all of Steinberg's examples qualify as true preventive action. For instance, consider Steinberg's example of the use of preventive force to handle an infectious disease outbreak. In this case, the state that is supposedly utilizing preventive force is merely going about the ordinary business of government, just as it might raise or lower interest rates, build roads or subsidize the construction of a hospital (the interest rate changes to prevent an economic crisis, the roads to prevent accidents and the hospitals to prevent a high mortality rate). However, to include these as examples of preventive action is quite a stretch. Similarly, Steinberg's example of the U.S. invasion of Afghanistan does not stand up to close scrutiny. U.S. action in Afghanistan was punitive and retaliatory, not preventive.

In fact, almost any action a state (or individual) takes can be framed in terms of stopping something from happening. A state might grant an extension on loan payments to another state, in order to make sure they did not default on their obligations. Does this qualify as preventive action? Following from my earlier formulation, the motivation must be primarily defensive in the minds of the leaders waging war and must be aimed at dealing with what is perceived to be a grave threat to national security.

Not all scholars have associated preventive war with aggression. While Levy focuses primarily on the shifting balance of power as a source of motivation for war, by terming it the "preventive motivation" for war (based on a fear of a negative change in the status quo), he clearly separates aggression from the "preventive" motivation for war.[10] Outside observers, or later historians and academics, might debate whether the leader "had no choice" but to launch a preventive war. But what is central to such a debate is whether the decision maker, operating within the constraints imposed by limited information and his or her own psychological biases, had a reasonable belief that it was necessary in order to prevent a later threat to vital national interests.

One other particularly important motivational factor in preventive war is fear. Fear, or suspicion, of others' intentions play an important role in preventive war decisions. The paradox that is at the heart of the "security dilemma" in traditional international relations theory is central to our discussion here.[11] States' fears may lead them to take steps to increase their security as a defensive measure. However, these same steps can increase the insecurity of other states; in the end, increasing one's security too much can have the paradoxical effect of making a state seem more threatening to others, decreasing its security.

This has important implications for preventive war decisions. First, states seeking only to increase their own security may arouse the suspicion or concern of other states, who may initiate preventive action if they feel sufficiently threatened. Second, states that do initiate preventive action for what they feel are primarily defensive motivations may trigger a "balancing" reaction by other states in the system, who now feel threatened by the "aggressive" state that initiated preventive action.

As technology has improved and weapons have become more destructive and easy to conceal, the consequence of making a mistake in underestimating the danger has become an even more powerful factor in leaders' decisions. This poses a critical dilemma for leaders faced with such threats. If they overreact, their decisions can lead directly to an armed conflict that may have been avoidable, but it will at least be on their own terms; if they underreact, they risk destruction. Leaders have always had to make judgments weighing the consequences of a potential action/event against the likeliness of its occurrence. For some issues, there is a willingness to take a slight risk if the reward is thought to be worth it, or if the chance of something bad happening is minimal. However, for issues involving chemical, biological or nuclear weapons, the cost of miscalculation is so high that even a small amount of risk is often considered unacceptable. This is especially true when it is combined with the perception that it is possible to take action to eliminate the threat, thereby reducing the risk to zero.

Preventive War Factors

In a recent work, I developed a theory of the psychological motivations for preventive action that drew on five case studies: British action in the Suez Canal Crisis; Israel's strike on the Osiraq nuclear reactor; American preventive war thinking, 1946–54; Indian preventive war thinking, 1982–2002; and the American preventive war against Iraq that began in 2003.[12] In examining those cases, I found that several variables appear to be associated with decisions concerning preventive war; the declining power motivation, inherent bad faith relationship with an adversary, a belief that war is inevitable, the belief that there is only a short window in which to act, a situation that favors the offensive (or is believed to), and black-and-white thinking.

While all of these factors appear to be influential in preventive war decisions, the leadership and the psychology of the decision maker prove very important in developing a theory of preventive war. The importance of leaders' psychology, motives and choices are elements that not only run through the cases, but help to explain the outcomes as well. Rather than a "factor" that can be categorized as either present or not present, leadership psychology appears to act as a catalyst that can either emphasize or diminish the importance of the other variables.

Leadership Psychology   The importance of individuals runs contrary to many mainstream theories of international relations. Most such theories concentrate on "big picture" factors, such as the structure of the international system or relative national capabilities and the balance of power. To the extent that they refer to motivation at all, it is usually in the form of imperatives such as "human nature" that leave little room for individual psychology, leadership or choice.[13] The case studies I examined make clear that individuals do, in many circumstances, exercise vast influence over the course of events. One basic reason is that individual leaders filter similar information in different ways. Another is that not everybody reacts the same way to similar circumstances or reaches similar judgments about them. President Bush saw Iraq as a serious threat and invaded, while Al Gore says he would not have done so. Or to take another example of the way in which different leadership psychologies lead to potentially different outcomes, it is not at all difficult to believe that Shimon Peres would have acted very differently than Menachem Begin had Peres been Prime Minister in 1981. Thus, central to any analysis of preventive war decision making is a close examination of individual motivation, perception and ultimately, judgment.

Of course, individual decision makers face constraints. They must deal with the realities of their circumstances, whatever their personal inclinations and views. Some options are too absurd or dangerous to even contemplate. It would be difficult to imagine Israel's Menachem Begin ordering a strike against the nuclear capabilities of the United States, or a land invasion and occupation of Iraq; Israel simply does not have the necessary capability, and it would be unlikely that anybody within the Israeli government would consider such foolhardy courses of action. However, most potential choices facing decision makers are not nearly so black-and-white. In many circumstances, there is ample room for discretion and choice.

No theory is able to predict with certainty when or whether preventive or preemptive action will occur. However, I believe that the following factors substantially increase the odds of a state initiating preventive action. They also provide considerable explanatory power after the fact.

Declining Power in Relation to an Adversary   Leadership psychology and leaders' beliefs are instrumental in understanding decisions to initiate preventive war, but they are not the only factors leading to such decisions. Jack Levy noted in his work on the "preventive motivation" for war (see also his Chapter 7 on Iraq as a preventive war) that preventive wars are fought not by rising powers seeking to change the status quo, but by declining powers seeking to preserve it.[14] Thus, a decline in power relative to an adversary might lead a state to initiate preventive war in order to "put down" the challenger. It might also lead the declining power to initiate preventive action in order to forestall the rising power from attaining a particular capability (such as the ability to produce nuclear weapons). In both cases, the declining power seeks to maintain its position relative to an adversary. It should be noted, though, that the status quo does not have any inherent value. Therefore, a change to the status quo, if it did not pose an unacceptable risk to the status quo power, might not compel preventive action. The type and degree of change of the status quo would seem to be at least as important as the fact of the change itself. It is also important to define what, exactly, is meant by "declining power." Is it declining power if the country believes that the rise in power of its adversary will result in rough parity? Or does the situation have to result in a substantial and real material power imbalance? I define "declining power" as a situation in which a state believes that its power is declining relative to another country, and is fearful of the consequences of that decline—without specifying what the consequences must be for the factor to be present.[15] One reason for focusing on relative decline (as opposed to an absolute decline) is that by doing so it is possible to link material realities with the psychology of perception. It is likely that a leader's perception of the end result of the decline, parity or imbalance, will affect his or her behavior.

Inherent Bad Faith Relationship with Adversary   A relationship where both parties believe the other to be an enemy is a pervasive and important factor in preventive war decisions. This factor has two separate but linked facets. A leader might perceive a state to be an enemy, but the leader might also hold the belief that the other state sees them as an enemy. As long as there is the possibility that a conflict might be resolved by peaceful means, war becomes less likely. However, in conflicts that are marked by a history of mutual suspicion and hostility, confidence and trust-building measures may not be very effective, as each side fervently believes the other side will never cooperate. This is a psychological version of the security dilemma, in which even actions taken in good faith are assumed by the adversary to be a trick of some kind. As Robert Jervis has pointed out, certain cognitive beliefs can become reified, even in the face of conflicting information.[16] The inherent bad faith model describes an image of the enemy that has become rooted in moral absolutes, and is closed to conflicting or dissonant information.[17]

The bad-faith image contributes to the desire to initiate preventive action by making war or conflict seem inevitable, and by increasing the chances of escalation (and thus preventive or preemptive war) in even a relatively minor crisis.

Related to this is the image of the enemy. Are they perceived as a relatively minor threat, regardless of their intentions? Or are their capabilities potentially dangerous enough that malicious intentions alone might be enough to compel preventive action? How trustworthy are they? After all, international agreements and treaties are only useful in solving disputes so long as states are trusted to keep their end of the agreement.

Arthur Gladstone outlines the basic framework of the psychological conception of the enemy:

> Each side believes the other to be bent on aggression and conquest, to be capable of great brutality and evil-doing…to be insincere and untrustworthy…. Many actions which are ordinarily considered immoral become highly moral.[18]

Heikki Luostarinen writes that an enemy image is a belief held by a certain group "that its security and basic values are directly and seriously threatened by some other group."[19] An inherent bad faith image is simply a negative "enemy image" extended over time, and hardened in the mind of the decision maker. This is a particularly important factor, as the perception of an enemy's intentions can be much more significant than their material capabilities.[20] Additionally, strong enemy images may also cause a greater polarization of good and evil in the mind of the decision maker.[21] This has particular relevance for decision makers whose worldview is already predisposed toward a black-and-white view of the world.

A Belief that War (or Serious Conflict) Is Inevitable   Strategic advantage, coupled with a belief that conflict is likely or inevitable, dramatically increases the probability of preventive action. In these circumstances, it is in the state's interest to act while it is in an advantageous position. Again, leadership perception is relevant. Who believes war to be inevitable is important. Is it just a single leader? Is that leader in effect the chief or only decision maker? Is it all, or most, of his trusted advisors? Is there a broad consensus that conflict is inevitable? Is the strategic advantage diminishing or increasing? While the specific belief that war is inevitable is very important, the more general manifestation of this is that time is working against a country. This belief, though it can sometimes be no more than a vague notion in the minds of decision makers, is no less powerful for its ambiguity. In fact, this belief appears to correlate closely with decisions to initiate preventive war. This vague sense of foreboding about the future permeates many of the key decision makers' statements in the cases that I examined.

A Belief that There Is Only a Short Window in which to Act   The belief that there is only a short window in which to act increases the time pressure felt by decision makers and can lead them to believe that "something must be done before it is too late." This window is a limited period of time during which one state has a strategic advantage over another. The crisis might not be directly observable to the public at large. It is even possible for things to appear normal on the surface while a crisis mentality begins to form within the leadership. This type of window-thinking usually prescribes some positive action to either reverse or forestall the trend toward a period of danger in the future. It might be thought of as a "slow-motion crisis."

The idea of "windows of opportunity" has been thoroughly documented, though scholars give different accounts of its importance.[22] However, I present evidence that the concept of perceived windows of opportunity can be an important factor in decisions to initiate preventive action.

A Situation that Favors the Offensive (or Is Believed To)   A situation that is believed to favor the offensive is a contributing factor toward preventive war because it leads decision makers to believe that the most likely way to win a war is to strike the first blow.[23] If the threat of war is great enough, striking the first blow (although it changes war from a possibility to a certainty) might be seen as the only, or best, option. This type of thinking is exacerbated by the highly destructive nature of nuclear weapons, which precludes any state willingly waiting to be struck first.

Black-and-White Thinking   The last important factor in preventive war decision making is the individual leader's worldview and its permeability, or openness, to change. A worldview/belief system is, in essence, a leader's assumptions about the nature of the world, which operate as a cognitive filter. As Alexander George put it, it is a set of general beliefs about the fundamental issues of history and central questions of politics.[24] The specific content of a leader's worldview matters, but so do some of its structural aspects. How open is that view to new or conflicting information? How nuanced or complex is it?[25] Consider Betty Glad's work on black-and-white thinking. She describes the structure of such a worldview as one that sees the "world as divided into two camps, with all morality on one side, all evil on the other, with two possible outcomes—to win or to lose. There is no political middle ground." Glad notes that this type of Manichean view of the world is also linked to certitude that this is the "correct" view.[26] Glad presents this as a criticism however; it is also the case that this self-confidence allows leaders to make difficult decisions that are sure to provoke heavy criticism such as undertaking a preventive war.

The black-and-white worldview also has implications for the inherent bad faith image, with which it interacts and can reinforce. Additionally, both the black-and-white worldview and the inherent bad faith image are connected to a leader's propensity to see the world in moral dichotomies: good and evil, right and wrong.

It is important, however, to distinguish between two types of black-and-white thinking. First, there is the idea of black-and-white thinking as essentially a simplistic way of processing information. In this view, people take in new information that is immediately categorized internally into one of two possible categories. This, I think, is the sense in which the term is often used, and carries with it the implicit assumption that this is a poor way to process information.

The second type of black-and-white thinking is more complex. In this case, leaders are able to process information in a much more complex and nuanced manner before deciding which of the two categories its fits in to. This is an important distinction to make, as it carries with it significant implications about the type of leader we are dealing with. In the first type, there is little room for complexity or nuanced understanding; while in the second there is, but the end result is "boiled down" so that the decision maker is not lost in endless shades of grey.

It is important not to assume a direct link between either a leader's worldview or its structure and the output, the foreign policy action that results in the end. There are numerous sources of "slippage" between decisions and implementation.[27] However, to the extent that individual leaders and advisors are important in preventive war decisions, their individual worldviews are critical to the decision-making process. All of the factors mentioned above interact with the fundamental beliefs of the individual leader. A leader's world view has important implications for what types of action he believes to be the most effective (i.e., diplomatic, military, economic), the prospects for peaceful resolution (whether conflict is inevitable), and the nature of their perception of political opponents (how fixed, or rigid, his "enemy image" is).

Preventive War in Historical Perspective

There is no doubt that President Bush's enunciation of a doctrine which is, at its core, predicated on preventive action is unique in American history. However, preventive action itself is less unusual than is commonly thought, and a short survey of other cases in which preventive action was either taken, or seriously considered, can provide important context for understanding this aspect of the Bush Doctrine.

This section will describe two cases of preventive war planning in which a state eventually initiated preventive action. Each of these two mini-cases contains elements that will help to shed light on the U.S. adoption of the Bush Doctrine and the Iraq War.

Israel's Preventive Strike

On June 7, 1981, six Israeli F-15 and eight F-16 fighter jets dropped their payload of 2,000-pound bombs on the Osiraq nuclear reactor in Tuwaitha, outside Baghdad.[28] The bombs were dropped in a single pass, and in just over two minutes, Iraq's nuclear ambitions suffered what would turn out to be a devastating setback. The significance of this action has become even more clear in the ensuing years. Israel's strike on the Osiraq reactor was the first preventive strike on a nuclear facility in history, and the first example of "the forceful nonproliferation" policy that the United States would follow over two decades later. But just as important as the fact of the action itself was its outcome: it was successful. Israel suffered no casualties and effectively ended one of its most serious security threats, one that had preoccupied Israeli leaders for over a decade.

This case also very clearly illustrates the inherent bad faith image of an enemy, and black-and-white thinking. Israel's estimate of Iraqi capabilities (or potential capabilities) played an important role in the process, but as with all decisions of war and peace, the crux of the matter is capabilities *plus intent*. It was Menachem Begin's perception of Saddam Hussein's intentions, based on a combination of Saddam's stated goals and Begin's personal frame of reference, that led to the decision to destroy the Osiraq reactor.

Iraq's nuclear program was begun with assistance from the Soviet Union in 1963.[29] However, because of the low capacity of the reactor and the Soviet Union's historic caution with nuclear technology, it did not seem to arouse much outcry in the international community, including Israel.[30] The Director of Israeli Military Intelligence in 1974, Shlomo Gazit, recalled later that Israel "knew the Soviet Union would not permit its [the reactor's] exploitation for the production of nuclear arms."[31]

However, the 1963 project had the benefit of training Iraqi scientists in nuclear technology. Under Saddam Hussein's leadership, Iraq pursued an aggressive modernization program. During the 1970s, Iraq had the sixth largest oil reserves in the world and Iraqi leaders counted on this natural asset to provide them leverage in acquiring more advanced nuclear technology.[32]

During the 1970s, French dependence on Iraq was on the rise. In 1973, France's imports of Iraqi oil came to 357,000 tons and 15% of all French oil. By 1979, those numbers had risen to 489,000 tons and 21%.[33] In December 1974, newly elected French Prime Minister Jacques Chirac traveled to Iraq. During his visit Chirac signed a general "nuclear cooperation agreement" with Iraq.[34]

In 1976, the budget for Iraq's Atomic Energy Commission jumped from $5 million to $70 million a year. But it was not just Iraqi expenditures that had begun to concern Israeli leaders. The rhetoric of Iraqi leaders had also become increasingly belligerent. In 1973, Iraqi Oil Minister al-Baqi al-Haditi told a Greek journalist that "Israel must be eliminated...by armed struggle and threats against the imperialist powers that protect Israel."[35]

In 1975, France signed a deal with Iraq to provide it with a 70 MW Osiristype reactor, and a smaller 800 kW Isis-type reactor, as well as over 70 kg of uranium enriched to over 92%.[36] The Osiris reactor was worrisome on multiple accounts. It required enriched uranium which might be diverted by the Iraqis to manufacture weapons; the reactors had the capability to produce significant amounts of plutonium as a side-reaction; and finally its size seemed to indicate that Iraq's intentions might not be only in the realm of peaceful nuclear energy. Additionally, although Iraq had claimed to be interested in a civilian power-generating program, the natural choice for such a program would be a much different reactor. However, civilian-power reactors are not useful for the production of excess plutonium, nor do they use enriched uranium. The Iraqis chose a reactor that was completely unsuited to their stated needs, but well suited to a clandestine nuclear weapons program.[37] Iraq also successfully lobbied to buy 93% enriched uranium instead of a new type of fuel dubbed "Caramel," which was enriched to only 6-10% and would have been much less useful in producing nuclear weapons.[38]

All of these developments played a significant role in the Israeli decision to launch a preventive strike against Iraq. But the linchpin of this decision was the psychology of Prime Minister Menachem Begin and his fervent belief that a nuclear Iraq represented a dire threat to the existence of Israel.

By 1980, Begin and other Israeli leaders had focused on the Iraqi program as one of the top of threats of Israeli security. A campaign of diplomacy had borne little fruit. Even strong U.S. pressure could not dissuade France from providing enriched uranium to Iraq and the International Atomic Energy Agency's complete inaction when Iran's Revolutionary Council banned IAEA inspectors provided Israel even less reason to put their faith (and their security) in the hands of international diplomacy.[39]

In the summer of 1980, the Israeli General Staff Senior Officer Forum met to discuss the growing threat of Iraq's nuclear program. We have evidence that the issue was discussed at length, and a variety of opinions were put forward. Those who opposed the attack on Osiraq did so on the grounds that it would not destroy the 12 kg of enriched uranium the French had already supplied to Iraq, nor any other small stockpile it had acquired from other sources.[40] Those who supported the raid argued that if Iraq were able to activate the reactor, it would continue to acquire up to 37 kg of enriched uranium a year indefinitely, and eventually produce enough plutonium to construct two to three bombs per year. They also argued that a strike now might induce Italy and France to reconsider their assistance to the Iraqi regime, and perhaps add stricter controls.[41]

Labour Party leader (and Begin's main opponent in the coming elections) Shimon Peres expressed his concerns to Begin in a top-secret note in May, 1981. Peres was convinced that the French President-elect Mitterand, a socialist and a personal friend, would provide a solution to the Iraq problem.[42] He declared in his note to Begin that should Israel continue on this course of action, it would be "like a tree in the desert" in the international community.[43]

In response to the idea that Mitterand's election might solve the problem, Begin declared in a cabinet meeting that such an event would only delay Israeli action, not change the actual situation. "It was not a French reactor," he said, but an Iraqi reactor. And "the problem was not France, but the existence of the state of Israel."[44]

Biographer Amos Perlmutter wrote that, for Begin, it was an "ideological decision," a question of averting another Holocaust.[45] Begin refused to listen to expert advice when, as he saw it, the very existence of the state of Israel was at stake.

However, his certainty in his own decisions did not mean that he was oblivious to the potential consequences of the attack.[46] In an article published after the attack, William Claiborne reported that Begin was warned that the strike could result in the suspension of U.S. arms shipments to Israel.[47] What is relevant here is that Begin—with a full understanding of the potential consequences—still chose to initiate preventive action. The decision to initiate an operation that carried such risks for Israeli citizens, the security of Israel, and even his own political career, is a testament to the strength and rigidity of his image of the enemy that Begin held.

Britain and Suez

On October 29, 1956, Israel invaded the Sinai. This action followed months of negotiations between Egypt, France, Britain, and the United States regarding Egyptian President Gamal Abdel Nasser's nationalization of the Suez Canal. It is now known that Britain secretly colluded with France and Israel to wage a preventive war against Egypt. The plan called for Israel to launch an attack on Egypt at a prescribed time, and Britain and France to send troops to Egypt in the guise of "peace keepers" in order to reestablish control over the canal. However, economic pressure by the United States soon forced Britain and France out of Egypt in a humiliating fashion.

British action in this case was not intended to crush a rising power, though the end goal of the military action would certainly have accomplished that. Nor was it intended to prevent Egypt from acquiring a particular capability; Egypt had already drastically altered the balance of power by seizing the canal. British action was intended to prevent the utilization of Egypt's newly acquired power. In this case, Egypt's seizure of the canal had given it the ability to exert influence over the British Empire through control of British oil shipping routes. The possibility of blackmail by Egypt was exacerbated by British perceptions of Nasser as a "mortal enemy" and Prime Minister Anthony Eden's belief that a showdown was inevitable.

The Suez Crisis originated with the building of another major project in Egypt, the Aswan High Dam. On December 14, 1955, Great Britain and the United States made a formal offer to finance the Aswan Dam. Part of the impetus for this came from British Prime Minister Anthony Eden, who became even more agitated after the Soviet Union (through the Czech government) sold Egypt a large shipment of MiG fighters, tanks, and other heavy equipment.[48] Yet, far from placating Nasser and drawing him closer to the West, funding for the dam seems to have spurred him to further antagonize the West without fear of reprisal.

However, the United States soon reversed course and backed out of the Aswan Dam loan, with Eden and the British government following suit. The French Ambassador to Washington, Maurice Couve de Murville, accurately predicted of Egypt: "They will do something about Suez. That's the only way they can touch the Western countries."[49]

On July 26, 1956, Nasser announced the nationalization of the Suez Canal in a public speech in Alexandria.[50] However, though Britain was understandably shocked by the move, it was difficult to make the case to the international community that it was an illegal seizure. The Suez Company was registered as an Egyptian company, and Nasser had indicated that he intended to compensate its shareholders. Though Britain condemned the act as a "high-handed act of seizure against an international company," it was clear even to British leaders that they did not have a compelling legal argument.[51]

Anthony Nutting, a Deputy Foreign Minister, wrote:

> In fact, as frequently happens in international disputes, both arguments could be supported on legal grounds, which made it all the more necessary that the issue should be resolved by political and diplomatic negotiation and agreement.[52]

In addition, British leaders recognized early that economic pressure was not feasible. In the first cabinet meeting after the nationalization, the possibility of using economic pressure was discussed and quickly abandoned.[53]

Thus, only one day after the nationalization of the Canal, both economic and legal pressure had been ruled out as effective means to resolve the dispute. The only options still available were (1) do nothing, and let Nasser's action stand; (2) the use of political pressure and diplomacy; or (3) the use of military force to take back control of the canal.

Contributing to the developing crisis was the changing perception of Nasser by British leaders. In 1952, Selwyn Lloyd (then Minister of State for Foreign Affairs) reported being "favorably impressed" with Nasser during their first meeting.[54] And, as late as March 1954, Evelyn Shockburgh reported that Eden had "come to the conclusion that Nasser is the man for us."[55]

However, between 1954 and the 1956 Suez Crisis, the British perspective on Nasser had changed dramatically. By March of 1956, Eden had already taken to comparing Nasser to Mussolini.[56] In fact, Eden compared Nasser to Hitler so often that Winston Churchill once remarked, after a conversation with Eden, that he "never knew before that Munich was situated on the Nile."[57] In March 1956, Nutting wrote a memo to Lloyd asserting that "appeasement of Nasser" would not work, and that Nasser would likely break any deal that he made. Lloyd reports that this memo confirmed his own intuition.[58]

The allusion to "appeasement" and fascist dictators by British leaders is telling in what it reveals about the historical analogies that resonated with them. World War II was obviously fresh in the minds of British leaders; but it was the year 1936 that was probably in the back of the minds of Eden, Lloyd, and Nutting. 1956 was the 20th anniversary of the 1936 remilitarization and reoccupation of the Rhineland by Hitler. It was also the 20th anniversary of Western Europe doing nothing to oppose Hitler, a decision that had been widely condemned in the intervening years. Harold Macmillan (then a backbencher MP) had gone against the tide in advising forceful action in March 1936. Eden, however, had not; claiming that public opinion in Europe would not support action against Germany for "returning to their own backyard."[59] However, he had a falling out with Prime Minister Neville Chamberlain in 1938 after the Munich conference, from which we can infer that the "lesson of appeasement" had been quickly learned.[60]

For instance, one letter written by Eden to President Dwight D. Eisenhower read:

> In the nineteen-thirties Hitler established his position by a series of carefully planned movements.... It was argued either that Hitler had committed no act of aggression against anyone, or that he was entitled to do what he liked in his own territory, or that it was impossible to prove that he had any ulterior designs.... Similarly, the seizure of the

Suez Canal is, we are convinced, the opening gambit in a planned campaign designed by Nasser to expel all Western influence and interests from Arab countries.... You may feel that even if we are right it would be better to wait until Nasser has unmistakably unveiled his intentions. But this was the argument which prevailed in 1936 and which we both rejected in 1938. Admittedly there are risks in the use of force against Egypt now. It is, however, clear that military intervention designed to reverse Nasser's revolutions in the whole continent would be a much more costly and difficult undertaking.[61]

This letter clearly indicates that importance of this historical analogy for Eden. This "lesson" was most likely learned by most people of his generation. However, Eden's experience was somewhat unusual. In 1936, as British Foreign Secretary, he personally had a hand in appeasing Hitler. Then, in 1938, after learning his lesson, he was unable to exert influence over Chamberlain. In 1956, confronted again by aggression, he was in the position to act. Eden made a public comparison of Nasser to fascist dictators:

Why not trust him? The answer is simple. Look at his record.... Instead of meeting us with friendship Colonel Nasser conducted a vicious propaganda campaign against this country. He has shown that he is not a man who can be trusted to keep an agreement.... The pattern is familiar to many of us.... We all know this is how fascist governments behave, as we all remember, only too well, what the cost can be in giving in to Fascism.[62]

On Sunday, October 14, Nutting and Eden met with French representatives. Albert Gazier, the French Minister of Labour, cautiously asked Eden what Britain's response would be if Israel were to attack Egypt. Eden replied that Britain "had no obligation...to stop the Israelis attacking the Egyptians."[63] Eden then asked his secretary to stop recording the minutes of the meeting and asked General Challe, a French representative, to speak openly. The plan was that Israel would be invited to attack across the Sinai Peninsula. Upon being "informed" of the attacks, Britain and France would simultaneously make appeals to the Israeli and Egyptian governments to halt the fighting after which Britain and France would order both sides to withdraw from the Suez Canal, at which point the canal would be under de facto Anglo-French control.[64]

On October 21, Eden decided that Selwyn Lloyd should travel incognito to Paris the next day to meet French and Israeli leaders.[65] Finally, upon Israeli urging, a document containing the details of the aforementioned plan, which later became known as the "Sevres Protocol," was signed.

British initiation of a preventive war in this case hinged on the belief that conflict with Egypt, with Nasser, was inevitable. In Eden's mind, the ambition and intentions of Nasser were destined to be in fundamental opposition to the interests of the British Empire. The constant use of World War II-era analogies by Eden and other British leaders prescribed a specific solution: aggression must be met with force. But more than prescribing a solution to a problem, the analogies give us insight into how the leaders framed their relationship with Nasser. After all, the fundamental lesson of the "Munich analogy" is not just that you cannot appease dictators (although that follows from the real lesson), it is the *reason* you cannot appease them: leaders such as Adolf Hitler are, at their core, expansionist, and there is no way to avoid an eventual showdown with them. The best that you can hope for is to confront the threat before it is fully formed (e.g., during the Rhineland phase, or at Munich).

The Transformation of the United States Security Strategy

Security Strategy

Some of the preventive war factors that were exhibited in these case studies are also very clearly exhibited in the Bush Doctrine. However, of the factors delineated earlier in the chapter, not all are evident in the Bush Doctrine nor in the more general transformation of U.S. national security strategy. Window thinking, for example, does not seem to be evident in the Bush Doctrine. There is an important distinction to be made here, between the Doctrine itself and certain actions (such as the Iraq War) that followed from it. A case can certainly be made that there was a closing window of opportunity before the Iraq War (i.e., before Iraq's nuclear program produced an arsenal of WMDs). However, the Iraq War was not itself part of the Bush Doctrine, but rather a logical extension of it. There is no evidence of window thinking in the Doctrine itself.

The declining power motivation for preventive war is not present in the Bush Doctrine either. Quite the contrary, in fact, the Bush Doctrine is an attempt to grapple not only with new threats, but also with the changed reality of American power in the twenty-first century. The last grand strategy of the U.S. was in response to the Cold War, and was premised on a bipolar system, with the U.S. and the Soviet Union balancing each other. Rather than being in response to declining American power, the Bush Doctrine is a response to American hegemony in the post-Cold War international system.[66] Thus, the aspects of the Doctrine that are related to a strategy of prevention have nothing to do with declining power, but rather a change in the nature of the threats facing the U.S.

Inherent Bad Faith Image of the Enemy

One important aspect of the Bush Doctrine (discussed in greater depth in Post, Chapter 6) is its stance on deterrence. In fact, this is intrinsically related to one of the most important psychological factors related to preventive war thinking: the inherent bad faith image. How a leader perceives his adversary has a direct correlation to how much faith he places in his ability to deter that adversary.

Here one can see the importance of global norms of accepted behavior. Describing the superpower relationship during the Cold War, Thomas Schelling wrote, "Khrushchev [and the Soviets] understood the politics of deterrence."[67] Successful deterrence is based on mutual understanding, and some base level of agreement on what constitutes an unacceptable loss. Therein lies the problem: it takes some type of mutual understanding for deterrence to work. The assumption of mutually assured destruction (MAD) provided a measure of safety because both the U.S. and the Soviets believed it to be true. The basis of deterrence was that although neither side would be able to prevent an attack, either side would be able to retaliate and inflict disastrous harm on the perpetrator, thus deterring potential aggressors by the threat of harsh retaliation.

Part of the bad faith image that is illustrated by the Doctrine is the view, declared in the National Security Strategy (NSS), that the enemies of the U.S. are undeterrable. There are two important components of Bush's bad faith image of these enemies. The first is the view that conventional strategies of deterrence will not work against terrorists and rogue regimes because they play by a fundamentally different set of rules (or norms).

The 2002 NSS recognizes that there can be no mutual understanding between the U.S. and terrorists. How does one deter suicide bombers whose goal is to die? Does the logic of deterrence work on extraterritorial groups such as loosely linked terrorist networks? Robert Jervis writes of terrorists that "[they] cannot be contained by deterrence. Terrorists are fanatics, and there is nothing that they value that we can hold at risk."[68] John Lewis Gaddis, a historian of the Cold War, agrees, asking, "How does one negotiate with a shadow?.... How does one deter somebody who's prepared to commit suicide?"[69] This was certainly the conclusion of President Bush in the aftermath of 9/11.[70]

The other aspect of the bad faith image of the adversary is that the United States cannot trust either terrorists or rogue states to stand by any agreement that is made. This belief, especially with regard to Iraq, is made clear by the many statements by Bush stating that Saddam Hussein cannot be trusted to keep his word on any inspection agreements.[71]

In his West Point address, Bush foreshadowed the conflict with Iraq by declaring: "We cannot defend America and our friends by hoping for the best. We cannot put our faith in the word of tyrants, who solemnly sign non-proliferation treaties, and then systemically break them."[72]

This image of the adversary—as one with whom no agreements can be made and who does not conform to the norms of international conduct—will be explored in further depth shortly, but at this point, it is striking how clearly this imagery is enshrined in America's National Security Strategy.

The NSS states that the there can be no mutual understanding between the U.S. and terrorists. Because of this belief, as well as the realization that successful deterrence is more difficult to achieve with shadowy terrorist groups than with traditional nation-states, the NSS proposes that the U.S. no longer rely exclusively on deterrence, and instead meet threats before they have fully materialized: a doctrine of prevention, not preemption.

Offensive Thinking

One factor that is clearly evident in the Bush Doctrine is the lure of the offensive in strategic calculations. The "ideology of the offensive" is a well-documented phenomenon, but in this case it comes with something of a twist. The reason for the offensive emphasis, in this case, is not the result of a military culture biased toward offensive action, or even the development of a new technology that renders existing military planning obsolete. Instead, strategic evaluation of the nature of the threat led to the prominence of the offensive in the Bush Doctrine.

Bush's comment that "the only path to peace and security is the path of action" makes clear the importance (in the minds of the administration) of taking the initiative.[73] In fact, it is not just that the situation favors the offensive, but rather that it requires the offensive. The implication of this argument for Iraq is clearly spelled out in the NSS: the scale of destruction made possible by rogue states (and terrorists) equipped with WMDs makes preventive action necessary. The risk is too great to wait on events.

The NSS groups terrorists and certain "rogue states" (Iraq, Iran, and North Korea) together in declaring that the nature of these new threats means that the U.S. "can no longer rely on a reactive posture." Terrorism and these "rogue states" are inextricably linked in that there is always the possibility that rogue states that have or are pursuing WMDs might give these weapons to terrorists and attack Western countries by proxy. In fact, this possibility was mentioned specifically in Bush's commencement address at West Point, where he declared: "Containment is not possible when unbalanced dictators with weapons of mass destruction can deliver those weapons on missiles or secretly provide them to terrorist allies."[74] Bush's use of the term "unbalanced" indicates his perception that there is something intrinsic to the psychology of leaders like Saddam Hussein that makes any kind of mutual understanding very difficult, and makes deterrence impossible to achieve.

A Belief that War Is Inevitable

The last factor that is illustrated by the NSS is the view that war, or serious conflict, is inevitable. In a striking parallel to similar declarations by leaders in the two case studies reviewed above, the NSS is clear in enunciating that not only is war inevitable, but it has already begun. However, this "war" is different in nature from previous wars. Unlike wars of the past, the war described in the NSS is not against a single adversary, country, group, or individual. Instead, this broad-based war is a "War on Terror."[75]

It is clear from Bush's actions and words that this was not just a clever turn of phrase meant to make a rhetorical point. Rather, Bush seems to feel that the U.S. really is in a state of war, whether or not others agree with him. Moreover, it is not just the words that count, but also the actions behind them. For President Bush, the "war on terrorism" is not just a rhetorical device. War is not meant in the figurative sense utilized by so many past presidents. Instead, it is meant in the very real sense that any U.S. action is a response to a war that is already under way.

The implication of this is that it is not business as usual; the rules and even laws that govern peacetime do not necessarily apply anymore. Whether or not one agrees with the policies they embody, the passage of the Patriot Act in 2001, the controversy over the status of detainees and their treatment, the semantic wrangling over the issue of torture, and the status of "enemy combatants" indicate clearly that Bush perceives the United States to be in a time of extraordinary circumstances that require something above and beyond the usual methods.

While America's war on terror might have started out as essentially a metaphorical concept, it has come to take on greater significance. Gilles Andreani, Head of Policy Planning in the French Foreign Ministry, wrote that "in the case of 11 September, the use of the word 'war' has gone far beyond metaphor to acquire a strategic reality."[76] Andreani lists the reasons why the war on terror has taken root in American consciousness, the most important of which was that, having suffered an "unprovoked and unjustifiable attack…psychologically, America found itself at war."[77] It is exactly this sensibility that informed the Bush Doctrine's assumption that America is already at war.

Worldview

At least as important as any of the other factors mentioned in this chapter is President Bush's worldview. In fact, Bush's worldview—both its content and its relative rigidity—has acted as a catalyzing factor, magnifying the importance of the other psychological factors.

Bush took office viewing the world as a dangerous place, a world in which America is threatened by powerful and dangerous enemies. 9/11 dramatically confirmed that view. He also sees America's enemies as implacable and evil, and therefore sees force as the appropriate means to combat them. The morality of the conflict flows easily from this view: they are evil, the U.S. is simply protecting itself, and thus has right on its side. Also relevant is Bush's perception of the "War on Terror" as part of a historical trend of good versus evil, and the stark morality implied by such a conflict.

In an address to Congress nine days after the terrorist attacks, Bush described al-Qaeda, and other terrorist organizations, as heirs to the "murderous ideologies of the 20th century," such as fascism, totalitarianism, and Nazism.[78] Thus, in a manner similar to the fight against Nazism in World War II, the fight against extremist and terrorist ideologies was a fight for the future of civilization.

Only days after the terrorist attacks, Bush spoke at the National Cathedral, and declared: "Just three days removed from these events, Americans do not yet have the distance of history, but our responsibility to history is already clear; to answer these attacks and rid the world of evil."[79] This remark clearly illustrates Bush's view of America's war on terrorism as a struggle of good versus evil. However, it also shows that Bush feels the responsibility to history, the sense that the U.S. stands at a pivotal moment in history, and must act not just for the present, but also for the future.

The events of 9/11 confirmed Bush's view that the world is a dangerous place, but they did more than that. They made the world seem much more dangerous than it had been before. Whereas before Saddam Hussein might have been contained, in the light of 9/11 his actions and intentions looked much more menacing. In an interview two years after 9/11, Bush spoke of the effect of the terrorist attacks: "Saddam Hussein's capacity to create harm…all his terrible features became much more threatening. Keeping Saddam in a box looked less and less feasible to me."[80]

The second aspect of Bush's worldview that is significant for his Iraq decision is his stark sense of morality. This is the "with us or against us" mentality that has been so often criticized. Bush has taken the rhetorical stance that there is no neutrality in the war against terror, no shades or degrees of cooperation. He takes the position that any "shades of grey" are simply ways of obfuscating what is readily apparent to him: there is good and there is evil, and all of the degrees in between just confuse the issue. It follows from this that there could be no conceptual distinction between the actual terrorists and countries that harbor terrorists, although in practice (Saudi Arabia and Pakistan being two obvious examples) there is obviously a difference between statements and policy.[81]

This has particular bearing on preventive war decisions. A stark, black-and-white sense of morality does two things. It tends to throw into sharp relief the dangers and risks of a given threat once a leader such as Bush decides that such a threat exists. The lack of degrees, in essence a lack of gradation or subtlety in viewing adversaries, also exacerbates the effects of the inherent bad faith image of one's adversary. Evil is evil, and one simply cannot negotiate with evil, especially if its goal is your destruction. By invoking the specter of Nazism in his speeches, Bush consciously or unconsciously implied the natural course of action when dealing with such a serious threat. The use of the Nazi/Fascism analogy holds important implications for action: the type of threat is dire, negotiation is not possible, and the conflict will end only when one side has been decisively defeated.[82]

The second effect of this worldview is the implication for Bush's view of the United States in this matter. If terrorism—embodied in the threat of Osama bin Laden and al-Qaeda—is evil, then it follows that the United States is on the other side, the side of good. This imbues the actions of the United States with an inherently virtuous quality, and in Bush's eyes, legitimacy. Obviously, many people domestically and abroad do not see things this way (see Foyle, Chapter 3, on domestic and world opinion). However, this sense that America is on the right side of history does contribute to Bush's resilience to criticism, discussed earlier. For Bush, believing that he is on the right side, fighting evil, makes him more resilient to outside critics, who simply don't see the threat in the same way as he does.

The Future of Preventive War

The Bush Doctrine, and the subsequent war against Iraq, brought preventive war to the forefront of the world's attention. However, like many important events in history, the aftereffects for the future of preventive war are not yet apparent, and will not be for some time. Will the Iraq War be viewed as successful by later generations? Will world and American public reluctance to support such ventures prove insurmountable in the future? Does a successful campaign of preventive war lessen the need for such strategies in the future, or does it guarantee future conflict? Certainly, the lethal mix of WMDs, rogue regimes, and catastrophic terrorism will remain a dire threat. But will preventive war continue to be utilized as a strategy?

Preventive Wars and Deterrence

One of the most important questions raised by the Iraq War is what effect it will have on the stability of deterrence in the future. Deterrence theory is inextricably linked to questions of preventive war, since it is a failure of deterrence that leads to strategies of prevention. More specifically, it is the perception that a specific threat cannot be deterred that leads decision makers to consider (and sometimes take) preventive action. A strategy of preventive war is the result of the perception that deterrence is likely to fail. Note that it need not have failed already, but there must be the perception that it is likely to fail, combined with the belief that the consequences of such a failure would be unacceptable. Here is the sliding scale of decision making: the potential consequences of an event balanced against the likelihood of that event occurring.

Preventive war is linked to deterrence in another critical way as well. Preventive war may help to strengthen a state's deterrent ability for the future, especially in cases where states had previously been thought of as weak, or unwilling to suffer casualties. Recall that Osama bin Laden specifically called attention to the weak American response in Lebanon, Vietnam, and Somalia as evidence that the U.S. was, if not a "paper tiger," then at least a timid one. A determined and clear-cut willingness to go to war and stay there, despite intense difficulties and international pressure, is one method of revitalizing one's credibility, and with it the viability of future deterrence.

More generally, preventive war may affect deterrence in any of three ways: it may damage it, strengthen it, or not have any effect at all. Historical example suggests that there is no one answer to the difficult question of which is most likely. Different circumstances will bring different outcomes. The Israeli attack on the Osiraq reactor is generally deemed a successful preventive strike, and it is true that the strike brought a level of relief to Israeli leaders and citizens. Yet, Israel was and still is under the shadow of Iraqi SCUD missiles. In the aftermath of World War II, the U.S. chose not to initiate preventive action against the Soviet Union, and yet a relatively stable deterrence evolved. Anthony Eden's preventive war against Egypt likely destroyed any moral credibility that Britain had left after the decline of its empire, and its forced departure from Suez at the insistence of the United States did nothing to burnish its credentials as a power to be reckoned with. In a similar vein, the U.S. action in Iraq might have increased the credibility of American will and resolve, but the perception that the U.S. is bogged down in Iraq and weakened by an overstretched military might negate any potential gains from the war in terms of benefits to future deterrence, surely a paradoxical effect.

It seems likely that if preventive war does have a positive effect on deterrence, its benefits would primarily be in the short term. Certainly, demonstrating commitment and resolve ("will") is one likely consequence of preventive action. But what is the shelf life of resolve? Is one precision strike enough? Is one major war enough? Do preventive actions (whether strikes or wars) have to be followed up by other actions to sustain credibility? Do these follow-up actions risk labeling the actor as a bully, or worse, an aggressor? In short, how much "maintenance" does deterrence require?

There is another shelf life question: Do the deterrent effects of a preventive war outlive an administration? Assume that President Bush has demonstrated his resolve to potential adversaries. Will his successor need to do so as well? There is reason to suppose that this credibility is "nontransferable." President Eisenhower demonstrated his resolve by threatening to bomb the North Koreans, breaking the stalemate in talks about ending the Korean War. Yet, when Kennedy succeeded to the presidency, he was immediately tested by the Soviet Union's Nikita Khrushchev. Eisenhower's "will" did not carry over to the next administration, and there is no good reason why it should in other circumstances. The nature of democratic government means that the credibility of any one administration is destined to be short lived. Authoritarian governments do not suffer from this same problem, and it is conceivable that their deterrent capability might improve and last for quite a while. As long as a dictator remains in power, there is no reason to believe that their deterrent capability would diminish without some precipitating event, such as failing health.

Still another issue is whether credibility gained by preventive war (and the benefit to a state's deterrent ability) is transferable over geographical and political circumstances. Some have argued that Syria's withdrawal from Lebanon was a short-term result that followed from the change in risk calculations brought on by Bush and his policies. On the other hand, so far the preventive war against Iraq does not seem to have had much of an effect on North Korea's behavior. In retrospect, it seems mistaken to assume that preventive war will compel changes in behavior in all circumstances; but there is, as yet, no delineation of those circumstances that favor it and those that do not. Consider the situation of North Korea. President Bush has repeatedly stated that he favors a diplomatic solution. Why? Is it that North Korea is thought to already have multiple nuclear weapons? That it has large numbers of soldiers stationed a few miles from the capital of South Korea? That its leader, Kim Jong-il, is considered by many to be wildly unreliable and unpredictable, possibly even unbalanced? (See Post, Chapter 6, on deterring rogue leaders.) What separates situations that are perceived to require or call for preventive action from those that do not?

The Likely, the Unlikely, and the Improbable

In considering the future of preventive war, one point is very clear after September 11: leaders must worry about the unlikely and the improbable, especially if the consequences of inaction are high. Nineteen terrorists hijacking four planes simultaneously and using them as missiles to attack the United States was unlikely, and yet it happened. That they lived for years in the United States undetected by American intelligence services is even more unlikely, yet it, too, happened. In fact, the entire course of events that led to the events of 9/11 might be considered unlikely. And yet, they happened. Catastrophic consequences lower the threshold at which the "unlikely" must be taken seriously by leaders.

There are two types of events that fall into this category of high-impact, relatively low-probability events: the proliferation of nuclear weapons to unstable regimes and potential terrorist attacks. After the end of the Cold War rivalry, it appears that these two threats have emerged as two of the most pressing problems of the early twenty-first century. It is worth exploring why it is precisely these types of threats that seem most appropriate for preventive action.

The Appeal of "Positive" Action: From Deterrence to Prevention

In order for preventive action to be a viable choice, the threat must entail particularly disastrous consequences, such that the decision maker sees guaranteed conflict now, on his own terms (even with the risks it carries), as better than possible conflict later. But it is not enough for the stakes to be high. After all, the stakes were as high as they could go during the Cold War, when the fate of the world rested on the restraint of two opposing superpowers.

In addition to severe consequences, deterrence must not be an option in order for preventive war to appeal to leaders. In the case of terrorism, it is generally accepted that deterrence is not possible against suicide terror attacks. Deterrence is at its heart an understanding between two parties, where one party "deters" the other by threatening retaliation against something of value. To the extent that deterrence worked during the Cold War, it did so because the Soviet Union and the United States shared some core values, an understanding of the "rules of the game" and a secure second-strike capability.

There are numerous reasons for a leader to believe, given some circumstances, that deterrence will not work against another state. A leader might believe that his adversary is irrational and unpredictable, that he is risk-prone in his decision making, that at some basic level there is no agreement on fundamental values (such as the sanctity of human life), or that the adversary will find some indirect way to attack (such as giving WMDs to terrorist groups) that would make retaliation difficult. For any of these reasons, once a leader believes that deterrence is no longer viable, there are few options left. The leader may do nothing, in the hope that an "unlikely" scenario will not become reality, or he may take positive action to either realign the balance of power or capabilities (as in Israel's strike on the Osiraq reactor) or to remove a threat completely (as in the war in Iraq).

The Future of U.S. National Security Strategy

The Iraqi insurgency and the difficulties of nation rebuilding have proved to be much more difficult than the Bush administration anticipated. Saddam Hussein is gone, and a new elected government is in place, but the long-term prospects are hardly a given. Even more than the long-term effects in Iraq, the immense costs of the war (in political capital, relationships with allies, money, and lost lives) for the United States raise the question of whether another American-led preventive war is likely in the future.

The presidency of George W. Bush has been remarkable in the enormous consequences that followed from one initial judgment, and has had important ramifications throughout the world. The recognition that terrorism represents a unique type of threat, wholly different from that faced by the U.S. during the Cold War, was arguably an inevitable conclusion after 9/11. However, the implications drawn from that one conclusion were far-reaching and controversial. That Bush linked terrorism, weapons of mass destruction, and rogue regimes together in the national security strategy was enormously significant for America's post-9/11 stance toward the world. Yet, his decision to use Iraq as a "test case" for preventive action was equally significant. Many policy makers agreed that the United States and its allies must actively prevent acts of terrorism; that deterrence would not suffice to keep the U.S. safe from further attacks. However, it was a huge risk, both for the country and his own political career, for Bush to have initiated a war not because of a direct and immediate terrorist threat, but because of his judgment that Iraq posed a long-term threat to U.S. security.

If the Iraq War was a test case for preventive action, then did it pass the test? Will this preventive war be an isolated incident, an anomaly in the history of modern U.S. foreign policy? Or did Bush's National Security Strategy signal a major and long-lasting change of "grand strategy"? Will the Iraq War mark the beginning of a new era of increased international conflict and suspicion, marked by more and more states acting preventively? Will the policies of Bush outlast his presidency?

How we answer these questions in the future will depend on a great many factors: how well the war in Iraq goes and how deeply democracy takes root there, how successful the U.S. and its allies are in eradicating the most dangerous terrorist cells throughout the world, and how well the U.S. can help other countries deal with some of the root causes that allow terrorists to flourish by earnestly helping countries on the path to economic and political development. What is certain, however, is that in the near future, the United States will face severe threats from a number of quarters that will force dire situations and stark choices upon our leaders. Underestimating the threat might lead to catastrophe. And yet, preventive war is a blunt instrument, not a panacea. If used unwisely, or without thought given to the likely consequences, its effects may be more detrimental than beneficial.

As always, American presidents and allied leaders will be forced to make decisions with profound consequences, and yet they will often be required to do so on the basis of incomplete or imperfect information. This is inevitable. As a result, the security of the United States will ultimately still hinge on the best judgments of leaders and their advisors. These decisions will engage their motives, worldviews, perceptions, and emotions. To the extent that there are answers to the questions posed in this chapter, they will be found in the recesses of the human mind, and not solely in material circumstances. It is critical, therefore, in examining preventive war to focus substantial attention there.

Endnotes

1. An adversarial relationship may result for many different reasons, such as economic competition, territorial disputes, ideological disputes, "sphere of influence" conflicts, ethnic conflict, historical events, access to trade routes or resources, etc.

2. Lawrence Freedman, "Prevention, Not Pre-Emption," *The Washington Quarterly* 26 (Spring 2003): 106.

3. For this line of argument, see Michael Walzer's *Just and Unjust Wars* (New York: Basic Books, 1977), 75-80.

4. Samuel P. Huntington, "To Choose Peace or War: Is There a Place for Preventive War in American Policy?" *United States Naval Institute Proceedings* 83 (April 1957): 360.

5. Jack S. Levy, "Declining Power and the Preventive Motivation for War," *World Politics* 40 (October 1987): 87.

6. Walzer, *Just and Unjust Wars*, 76.

7. Another such explanation can be found in Robert Gilpin's *War and Change in World Politics* (New York: Cambridge University Press, 1981), 191.

8. Interestingly, neither Levy nor Gilpin make a distinction between the "preventive motivation" for war, and "preventive war" as a *type* of war. However, both authors still overemphasize balance of power calculations in their explanations.

9. James Steinberg, "Preventive Force in US National Security Strategy," *Survival* 47 (Winter 2005-06): 59-62.

10. Levy, "The Preventive Motivation for War," 87.

11. Robert Jervis, "Cooperation Under the Security Dilemma," *World Politics* 30 (1978): 167-214.

12. See Jonathan Renshon, *Why Leaders Choose War: The Psychology of Prevention* (Westport, CT: Praeger, 2006).

13. See Hans J. Morgenthau, *Scientific Man vs. Power Politics* (Chicago: University of Chicago Press, 1946), 192, 200

14. Jack S. Levy, "Declining Power and the Preventive Motivation for War," *World Politics* 40 (October 1987): 87.

15. In fact, this is very close to Levy's definition.

16. Robert Jervis, *Perception and Misperception in International Politics* (Princeton, NJ: Princeton University Press, 1976), 288-291.

17. Douglas Stuart and Harvey Starr, "The 'Inherent Bad Faith Model' Reconsidered: Dulles, Kennedy, and Kissinger," *Political Psychology* 3 (Fall/Winter, 1981-82): 1. Much of the work on inherent bad faith relationships and enemy image is derived from the path-breaking work of Ole Holsti, who examined the belief system of John Foster Dulles in a graduate dissertation. Holsti noted that "the more his [Dulles'] image of the Soviet Union was dominated by ethical rather than political criteria, the more likely it would be that the image would resist any change." See Ole Holsti, *The Belief System and National Images: John Foster Dulles and the Soviet Union* (Unpublished doctoral dissertation; Stanford University, 1962, 231-232).

18. Arthur Gladstone, "The Conception of the Enemy," *The Journal of Conflict Resolution* 3 (June,1959): 132.

19. Heikki Luostarinen, "Finnish Russophobia: The Story of an Enemy Image," *Journal of Peace Research* 26 (May 1989): 125.

20. Hermann and Fischerkeller correlate an "enemy" image with the perception that the enemy will be exposed as a "paper tiger" if met with strong opposition. However, the results of the cases in this book indicate that the enemy image is often associated with the opposite belief: that capabilities of an enemy are greater than empirical evidence suggests. See Richard K. Hermann and Michael P. Fischerkeller, "Beyond the Enemy Image and Spiral Model: Cognitive-Strategic Research After the Cold War," *International Organization* 49 (Summer 1995): 428.

21. David J. Finlay, Ole R. Holsti, and Richard R. Fagen, *Enemies in Politics* (Chicago: Rand McNally Press, 1967), 21.

22. For two opposing points of view on this issue, see Stephen Van Evera, *Causes of War* (doctoral dissertation; Berkeley, University of California, 1984), 61-71, 89-95, 330-339, 650-654; and Richard Ned Lebow, "Windows of Opportunity: Do States Jump Through Them?" *International Security* 9 (Summer 1984): 149.

23. This is the theory underlying Jack Snyder's work *The Ideology of the Offensive: Military Decision Making and the Disasters of 1914* (Ithaca, NY: Cornell University Press, 1984). This is also the premise behind Stephen Van Evera's *Causes of War: Power and the Roots of Conflict*, which explores the different reasons for which the offensive comes to be favored by leaders (Ithaca, NY: Cornell University Press, 1999).

24. Alexander George, "The 'Operational Code': A Neglected Approach to the Study of Political Leaders and Decision-Making," *International Studies Quarterly* 13 (June 1969): 191. George reformulated Leites' concept of an operational code into a series of questions, the answers to which formed a leader's operational code. These questions regard different aspects of the decision maker's relevant political beliefs: (1) What is the essential "nature" of political life? Is the political universe essentially one of harmony or conflict? What is the fundamental character of one's political opponent's? (2) What is the utility and role of different means for advancing one's interests?

25. Peter Suedfeld and Philip E. Tetlock, "Integrative Complexity of Communications in International Crises," *Journal of Conflict Resolution* 21 (1977): 169-184.

26. Betty Glad, "Black-and-White Thinking: Ronald Reagan's Approach to Foreign Policy," *Political Psychology* 4 (Spring 1983): 33.

27. Stephen G. Walker, "The Interface between Beliefs and Behavior: Henry Kissinger's Operational Code and the Vietnam War," *Journal of Conflict Resolution* 21 (March 1977): 131.

28. Ian Black and Benny Morris, *Israel's Secret Wars: A History of Israel's Intelligence Services* (New York: Grove Press, 1991), 332.

29. Jed C. Snyder, "The Road to Osiraq: Baghdad's Quest for the Bomb," *Middle East Journal* 37 (Autumn 1983): 565.

30. Ibid., 566.

31. Quoted in Shlomo Nakdimon, *First Strike: The Exclusive Story of How Israel Foiled Iraq's Attempt to Get the Bomb* (New York: Summit Books, 1987), 57.

32. Snyder, "The Road to Osiraq," 566.

33. Nakdimon, *First Strike*, 47.

34. Shai Feldman, "The Bombing of Osiraq-Revisited." *International Security* 7 (Autumn 1982): 115.

35. Quoted in Nakdimon, *First Strike*, 48.

36. Feldman, "The Bombing of Osiraq-Revisited," 116; and Nakdimon, *First Strike*, 62

37. Snyder, "The Road to Osiraq," 569. There were a host of other worrying developments during this time, such as Italy's sale to Iraq of a large-scale plutonium separation facility and a "hot lab," capable of separating plutonium from uranium and other fissile materials. Iraq also purchased (from Brazil, Portugal, and Niger) over 20 tons of uranium. This was particularly suspicious given that Iraq's reactor was not powered by natural uranium. [Perlmutter, Handel, and Bar-Joseph, *Two Minutes Over Baghdad*, 47; and Feldman, "The Bombing of Osiraq-Revisited," 117.]

38. Milton R. Benjamin, "France Plans to Sell Iraq Weapons-Grade Plutonium," *Washington Post*, February 27, 1980, A29.

39. Edward Cody, "Israel Angered as French send Uranium to Iraq," *Washington Post*, July 20, 1985, A15; Amos Perlmutter, Michael I. Handel, and Uri Bar-Joseph, *Two Minutes Over Baghdad* (London: Frank Cass, 2003), 52; Feldman, "The Bombing of Osiraq–Revisited," 121.

40. Amos Perlmutter, *The Life and Times of Menachem Begin* (New York: Doubleday, 1987), 363.

41. Ibid., 363.

42. Perlmutter, Handel, and Bar-Joseph, *Two Minutes Over Baghdad*, 69.

43. Ibid., 69.

44. Nakdimon, *First Strike*, 191.

45. Perlmutter, *The Life and Times of Menachem Begin*, 365.

46. In addition, Yehoshua Saguy, Chief of IDF Intelligence Services, had warned Begin that the strike would lead to the reestablishment of the "anti-Israeli Eastern Front" composed of Syria, Jordan, and Iraq, and might even compel Iran and Iraq to forget their differences and turn their collective wrath toward Israel. (Black and Morris, *Israel's Secret Wars*, 335.)

47. William Claiborne, "Begin's Raid Tied Hands of U.S., Astonished His Own Cabinet." *Washington Post*, June 14, 1981, A29.

48. Selwyn Lloyd, *Suez 1956: A Personal Account* (New York: Mayflower Books, 1978), 28.

49. Henry Kissinger, *Diplomacy* (New York: Simon & Schuster, 1994), 530.

50. Keith Kyle, *Suez: Britain's End of Empire in the Middle East* (London: I.B. Tauris, 2003), 133.

51. Lloyd, *Suez 1956*, 83-85.

52. Ibid., 47.

53. Quoted in Anthony Gorst and Lewis Johnman, *The Suez Crisis* (London: Routledge, 1997), 57 [emphasis added].

54. Lloyd, *Suez*, 15.

55. Shockburgh, *Descent to Suez*, 155.

56. Ibid., 341.

57. Quoted in Ann Lane, "The Past as Matrix: Sir Ivone Kirkpatrick, Permanent Under-Secretary for Foreign Affairs," in *Whitehall and the Suez Crisis*, eds. Saul Kelly and Anthony Gorst (London: Frank Cass, 2000), 206.

58. Lloyd, *Suez, 1956*, 54.

59. Alistair Horne, *Harold Macmillan, Volume I: 1894-1956* (New York: Viking Press, 1988), 112.

60. Kyle, *Suez: Britain's End of Empire in the Middle East*, 11.

61. Anthony Eden, *Full Circle: The Memoirs of Anthony Eden* (Boston: Houghton Mifflin, 1960), 519-521.

62. Quoted in Kyle, *Suez: Britain's End of Empire in the Middle East*, 184.

63. Anthony Nutting, *No End of a Lesson: The Story of Suez* (New York: Clarkson N. Potter, 1967), 92.

64. Ibid., 93.

65. David Carlton, *Britain and the Suez Crisis* (New York: Basil Blackwell, 1989), 63.

66. In fact, some have linked the doctrine of preventive war *directly* to America's hegemonic position. Robert Kagan offered the following parable: "A man armed only with a knife may decide that a bear prowling in the forest is a tolerable danger, inasmuch as the alternative—hunting the bear only with a knife—is actually riskier than lying low and hoping the bear never attacks. The same man armed with a rifle, however, will likely make a different calculation of what constitutes a tolerable risk? Why should he risk being mauled to death if he doesn't have to?" Robert Kagan, *Of Paradise and Power: America and Europe in the New World Order* (New York: Knopf, 2003), 31.

67. Thomas C. Schelling, *Arms and Influence* (New Haven, CT: Yale University Press, 1966), 39.

68. Robert Jervis, "Understanding the Bush Doctrine," *Political Science Quarterly* 118 (Fall 2003): 369.

69. John Lewis Gaddis, *Surprise, Security and the American Experience* (Cambridge, MA: Harvard University Press, 2004), 70-71.

70. Robert Pape has recently argued for the "strategic logic" of suicide terrorism. Pape's conclusions are based on his view that, in the past, terrorism has been moderately successful at achieving political goals. However, while *leaders* of terrorist organizations might be "rational" in the conventional sense of the word, those who carry out suicide attacks do not necessarily share that quality. Moreover, even Pape seems to acknowledge "deterrence" of suicide terrorism is difficult to achieve, and instead suggests that the best course of action is to make suicide terrorist attacks as difficult to carry out as possible, by improving domestic security. Surely this is a reasonable suggestion, but taken alone it is unlikely to appeal to a leader given to forceful, proactive solutions. See Robert Pape, "The Strategic Logic of Suicide Terrorism," *American Political Science Review* 97 (August 2003): 1-19.

71. For instance, see David Stout, "Bush Calls Iraqi Vow a Trick," *The New York Times* (September 18, 2002); Richard Stevenson, "Bush Says Iraq Isn't Complying With Demands to Disarm," *The New York Times* (January 21, 2003).

72. "West Point Commencement Address," June 1, 2002. [http://www.whitehouse. gov] (Accessed February 5, 2005)

73. Ibid.

74. George W. Bush, "President Bush Delivers Graduation Speech at West Point," June 1, 2002, www.whitehouse.gov/news/releases/2002/06/20020601-3.html.

75. The National Security Strategy of the United States, September 17, 2002, 5, http://www.whitehouse.gov/nsc/nss.pdf.

76. Gilles Andreani, "The 'War on Terror': Good Cause, Wrong Concept," *Survival* 46 (Winter, 2004-05): 31.

77. Ibid., 32.

78. George W. Bush, "Address to a Joint Session of Congress and the American People; President Declares 'Freedom at War with Fear'," September 20, 2001, http://www.whitehouse.gov/news/releases/2001/09/20010920-8.html.

79. "President's Remarks: 'We Are in the Middle Hour of Our Grief'," *New York Times*, September 15, 2001, A6.

80. Bob Woodward, *Plan of Attack* (New York: Simon & Schuster, 2004), 27.

81. It should be noted that Bush is very capable of carrying out policy based on a more subtle and nuanced perception of the world. For instance, though Iran, North Korea, and Iraq were all mentioned as the "axis of evil," Bush was clear that there were very important differences between the three countries that necessitated different approaches.
82. For one of many such references by Bush, see David E. Sanger and Julia Preston, "Bush to Warn U.N.: Act on Iraq or U.S. Will," *New York Times*, September 12, 2002.

9

The "Democracy Doctrine" of President George W. Bush

MARVIN ZONIS

Introduction

President George W. Bush has put democracy promotion at the center of his foreign policy, what I call his "Democracy Doctrine." He has articulated that commitment from the beginning of his presidency. But his commitment deepened and became the primary focus of his foreign policy when the initial rationales for the American invasion of Iraq proved to be baseless. No weapons of mass destruction were found at the time of that invasion. Nor were any links between Saddam Hussein and "global terrorism" established. As the rationales disappeared and as the war turned from a campaign against the army of Hussein to a war against an Iraqi insurgency joined by foreign terrorists eager to damage the United States, the President turned to his Democracy Doctrine to justify the entire enterprise. But the promotion of democracy in other countries, especially in the countries of the Islamic world whose people tend to view the United States as the problem and Islam as the solution, will be neither easy nor likely to produce governments friendly to the United States.

The President's Commitment to Advancing Democracy

President Bush has articulated his commitment to advancing democracy from his first Presidential Inaugural Speech:

> Through much of the last century, America's faith in freedom and democracy was a rock in a raging sea. Now it is a seed upon the wind, taking root in many nations.
>
> Our democratic faith is more than the creed of our country, it is the inborn hope of our humanity, an ideal we carry but do not own, a trust we bear and pass along.... But the stakes for America are never small. If our country does not lead the cause of freedom, it will not be led[1]

From that brief comment, really in passing in the context of the President's first address as president, the doctrine developed and took its most articulate form in the National Security Strategy (NSS) of the United States of America of September 2002. The very first sentence of the document is a ringing declaration of the President's views on the world.

> The great struggles of the twentieth century between liberty and totalitarianism ended with a decisive victory for the forces of freedom—and a single sustainable model for national success: freedom, democracy, and free enterprise. In the twenty-first century, only nations that share a commitment to protecting basic human rights and guaranteeing political and economic freedom will be able to unleash the potential of their people and assure their future prosperity.[2]

He then went on to articulate the basic philosophical position that underlies this claim:

> Freedom is the nonnegotiable demand of human dignity; the birthright of every person—in every civilization.[3]

The President returned to his Democracy Doctrine with every major speech he subsequently made.In his 2006 State of the Union speech, the President remained true to his commitment. [4]

> Abroad, our nation is committed to an historic, long-term goal—we seek the end of tyranny in our world. Some dismiss that goal as misguided idealism. In reality, the future security of America depends on it

Most recently, in March 2006, the President has set out his views in the updated NSS document. The theme of democracy promotion is the same, but here with an added rationale.[5]

> America also has an unprecedented opportunity to lay the foundations for future peace. The ideals that have inspired our history—freedom, democracy, and human dignity—are increasingly inspiring individuals and nations throughout the world. And because free nations tend towards peace, the advance of liberty will make America more secure.

These then are the themes on democracy that have marked the Bush presidency. They can be subsumed in the following points:

The "generational challenge" for the United States is to eliminate tyranny and replace it everywhere with liberty.

Liberty is the "God given birthright" of every human being in the world.

States that can be characterized by words such as liberty or freedom or democracy, words that seem to be used interchangeably by the President, do specific things, including governing by the rule of law, limiting the absolute power of the state, ensuring free speech and freedom of worship, administering equal justice and respect for women, offering tolerance to religious and ethnic minorities, and tending toward peace.

A crucial component of liberty is the protection of private property and
the operation of a market economy.

The United States will not impose liberty on the "unwilling" but will aid
all people in achieving that goal according to their own values.

The global triumph of democracy and market economies is inevitable.

The Functions of Democracy Promotion

It is true—for the President—that liberty is the "non-negotiable demand of
human dignity." It is also true—for the President—that the presence of liberty
or democracy produces certain outcomes.

Democratic states fight terrorism.
Dictatorships shelter terrorists, and feed resentment and radicalism,
and seek weapons of mass destruction. Democracies replace resentment
with hope, respect the rights of their citizens and their neighbors, and
join the fight against terror. Every step toward freedom in the world
makes our country safer—so we will act boldly in freedom's cause.[6]

Democracy will "drain the swamp" from which terrorists are recruited.
As long as the Middle East remains a place of tyranny and despair and
anger, it will continue to produce men and movements that threaten the
safety of America and our friends. So America is pursuing a forward
strategy of freedom in the greater Middle East.[7]

Democratic states are stable and peaceful.
Our aim is to build and preserve a community of free and independent
nations, with governments that answer to their citizens, and reflect their
own cultures. And because democracies respect their own people and
their neighbors, the advance of freedom will lead to peace.[8]

Only free countries become prosperous.
In the twenty-first century, only nations that share a commitment to
protecting basic human rights and guaranteeing political and economic
freedom will be able to unleash the potential of their people and assure
their future prosperity.[9]

The Bush Democracy Project in Iraq

The basic rationales for the invasion of Iraq turned out to be mistaken. What
had turned out to be a short-term brilliant military success quickly turned
into a nightmare. The U.S. had no coordinated plan for managing the country
after Saddam's overthrow, committed as it was to the belief that after removing senior Ba'ath officials, the institutions of the state would continue to function. The studies and discussion papers that had been done by the Department

of State were ignored by the Department of Defense, which had been charged by the President with administering the country.

The U.S. was, amazingly, unprepared to deal with the looting of the country that followed. Virtually everything of value was stripped from buildings and electrical towers. Whole military bases and arsenals, libraries, museums, and hospitals were sacked and their contents carted away. (Somehow the U.S. managed to protect only one building in Iraq—the Petroleum Ministry.)

Then the nearly fatal decision was made to disband the Iraqi Army. While the army had begun to melt away as soldiers abandoned their uniforms and headed to their homes, the formal disbanding of the military meant that hundreds of thousands of young men with weapons were suddenly left without their salaries, however meager.[10]

It became clear to Administrator Paul Bremer that more U.S. troops were needed to quell the violence. According to his book on his Iraq service, "I had a private meeting with [Commander of Coalition Forces in Iraq General Ricardo] Sanchez, to discuss the war. 'What would you do if you have two more divisions, Rick?' I asked him.... He answered immediately, 'I'd control Baghdad'.... I could see other uses for 35,000 or 40,000 additional troops. [Elsewhere in the book, Bremer makes clear he meant securing Iraq's borders and protecting critical infrastructure.].... On May 18, I gave [National Security Advisor Condoleezza] Rice a heads-up that I intended to send Rumsfeld a very private message suggesting the Coalition needed more troops.... That afternoon I sent my message to Rumsfeld.... I stressed that while I did not think the mission was on the brink, I felt we were in a dangerous situation. I recommended that he consider whether the Coalition could deploy one or two additional divisions for up to a year. I verified the secretary received my message. I did not hear back from him."[11]

The Secretary of Defense claims he acknowledges having received the message. But he did not accept the request for extra troops.

Even without the extra troops, the U.S. pressed ahead throughout a very challenging 2004 and largely retrieved the initiative against the insurgency. The U.S. found itself fighting three simultaneous wars: a war to oust the U.S. "occupiers" from Iraq, a war fought by Sunnis to preserve the power they had exercised under Hussein, and a war fought by Islamists to establish a radical Islamist state. Nonetheless, the U.S. managed to hold an election for a transitional National Assembly on January 30, 2005 and get an Iraqi transitional government in place on May 3, 2005. A constitution was drafted by the assembly and approved in another national referendum held on October 15, 2005. Then Iraqis turned out in great numbers in a national election for an Iraqi National Assembly on December 15, 2005, from which a legitimate government would be drawn.

A lengthy vote-counting process ensued and the results indicated a stunning victory for three groups. The United Iraqi Alliance, an amalgam of Shi'a parties widely understood to be the choice of Ayatollah Sistani, the leading Shi'a cleric in Iraq, won 41% of the vote and 128 seats. The Democratic Patriotic Alliance of Kurdistan won 22% of the vote and 53 seats. The Iraqi Accord Front, a grouping of Sunni parties, won 15% of the vote and 44 seats. The groupings of parties that represented cross-ethnic or secular interests were effectively shut out.

Horse trading began immediately to parcel out the ministries so that a majority coalition could be created. When it looked as if the Sunnis would be shut out of any coalition and out of the government, the U.S. feared a renewed surge of Sunni-sponsored violence. U.S. Ambassador Zalmay Khalilzad stepped in and pressed for a national unity government. "The United States," he said, "is investing billions of dollars" in Iraq's police and army. "We are not going to invest the resources of the American people to build forces run by people who are sectarian."[12] Khalilzad was referring to the fear that a Shi'a-dominated government would continue the death squads run out of the Shi'a Ministry of Interior that kidnapped, tortured, and killed Sunni Arabs. Appreciating his meaning, the Prime Minister designate, the religiously conservative Shi'a Ibrahim al-Jaafari retorted, "We think that sovereignty means no one interferes in our affairs."[13] In short, the Iraqi people expressed their wishes through the ballot box and had chosen three sectarian coalitions to represent them. Rather than allowing two of these coalitions to form a majority government and exclude the other—most likely the Sunnis would have ended up on the outside—the American government chose to interfere in the democratic process that it did so much to create by insisting on the composition of the future Iraqi government.

The pressure seems to have worked; Jaafari resigned and was replaced by a Shi'a politician more acceptable to the Sunnis, Nouri Kamel al-Maliki. Five months after the elections, a new government was approved by the Iraqi parliament. Initially, missing two key ministers, Interior and Defense, the new government, nonetheless, managed to include Shi'a, Sunni, and Kurds.

Promoting democracy in countries whose political elites have not been socialized into a political culture of compromise may require such intervention in its fledgling stages. But the dilemma such intervention presents is comparable to that faced by overseas aid agencies. To the extent the donor country implements a project, the recipients do not learn how to do so. To the extent the recipients are left with the implementation, it often does not get done, at least in a timely manner.[14] So it is with democracy promotion. It takes a very deft hand to know when to intervene and when to refrain from such intervention.

The President Adjusts His Message

The key to understanding the Bush Democracy Doctrine is to see how the President's project changed in relation to facts on the ground in Iraq. Democracy promotion was clearly a foreign policy priority of the President from his first inaugural address. Then came the terrorist attacks of 9/11. The consequences were a powerful psychological blow to the President. In the words of a White House staffer, "The President has 9/11 tattooed on his brain."[15] After all, as the President himself acknowledges, his most "solemn obligation" is "to protect the security of the American people."[16] In that, he failed. From then on, the President was fixated on dealing a mortal blow to al-Qaeda. He unleashed American forces to overthrow the Taliban, which had provided safe harbor to Osama bin Laden and his terrorist accomplices in return for their protection and funding. The speed and the extraordinary low cost with which the Taliban were dispatched demonstrated the capabilities of lightly armed, mobile small forces.[17]

That victory also, certainly, emboldened the President and his key advisors. Acting with different and complex personal motives, the senior members of the administration—the President, Vice President Dick Cheney, Secretary of Defense Donald Rumsfeld, Deputy Secretary of Defense Paul Wolfowitz, and Undersecretary of Defense for Policy Douglas Feith appear to have been the key decision makers—coalesced around the idea of ousting Saddam Hussein. The speedy and low-cost ouster of the Taliban seemed to indicate what could be expected in Iraq.

Absent as a major motivating factor for Hussein's ouster was the desire to bring democracy to the Iraqi people. But that became an ever more powerful explanation offered by the President as the primary motives proved illusory. He had consistently sought elections in Iraq to generate a legitimate government. But as the earlier explanations for the invasion proved inconsequential, the President focused increasingly on democratization as the purpose for ousting Hussein.

By the end of 2004, the President was offering his Democracy Doctrine as the principal explanation for the entire Iraq project. In the absence of weapons of mass destruction and any links between Hussein and al-Qaeda, the President's already genuine commitment to spreading liberty and democracy was presented as the prime purpose of America's role in Iraq.

The Desirability and Feasibility of the Bush "Democracy Doctrine"

The question of whether or not the Bush Democracy Doctrine provides a legitimate basis for U.S. intervention in Iraq or for "staying the course" need not be answered here. Each reader, each American, each Iraqi needs to answer that question.

What needs to be addressed here is the desirability and feasibility of the Bush Democracy Doctrine serving as a general basis for U.S. foreign policy. Several questions need to be posed:

Is it desirable for the U.S. to adopt a serious effort to promote democracy
    in other countries?
Is it feasible?
Where should it be applied?
How should it be applied?

The United States has stood for democracy and freedom for much of its history. It has done so through example, harkening back to the words of the Governor of the Massachusetts Bay Colony John Winthrop, who insisted, "For we must consider that we shall be as a City upon a hill. The eyes of all people are upon us."[18] Championing democracy by exemplifying its benefits has been a principal preoccupation in this land for nearly four centuries.

President Bush clearly recognizes that traditional American mode of promoting democracy. At the very end of the 2006 NSS, for example, the very last paragraph reads:

> There was a time when two oceans seemed to provide protection from problems in other lands, leaving America to lead by example alone. That time has long since passed. America cannot know peace, security, and prosperity by retreating from the world. America must lead by deed as well as by example. This is how we plan to lead, and this is the legacy we will leave to those who follow.[19]

Of course one of the most interesting questions about American leadership is just what the President means by "leadership." He does not appear to mean that the U.S. will seek to inspire its allies by its words or example, but rather that the U.S. will "take the lead," which means going first with the hope or insistence that others follow. It is well to remember here Paul Wolfowitz's definition of leadership, despite his having left the administration for the World Bank presidency. The former Deputy Secretary of Defense thought that leadership was accomplished when your friends know that they will be taken care of, your enemies that they will be punished, and "that those who refuse to support you will live to regret having done so."[20]

That type of "you are either with us or against us" approach to leadership was much in evidence in the 2002 NSS document, but is considerably toned down in the 2006 version. The newer statement is much more committed to international coordination and cooperation and much less to American unilateralism.

America's championing democracy through its actions and not just through its example is also a traditional component of its foreign policy, especially in the twentieth century. Whether under Woodrow Wilson or Franklin D. Roosevelt or whether under Harry S. Truman or Ronald Reagan, the United States has sought to advance its interests by strengthening the world's democracies and creating new ones. To be true to American values and purposes, and from the point of view of national interest, it is highly desirable that the U.S. support and promote democracy.

But President Bush's making democracy promotion the very centerpiece of U.S. foreign policy is a new twist on an old theme. Grave doubts remain about just what the President means by his Democracy Doctrine. In his most recent State of the Union Address, quoted above, he said, "At the start of 2006, more than half the people of our world live in democratic nations. And we do not forget the other half—in places like Syria and Burma, Zimbabwe, North Korea, and Iran—because the demands of justice, and the peace of this world, require their freedom, as well."[21] By the time the 2006 NSS had been issued, two new countries were added to the list, Cuba and Belarus.[22] To many, this renewed emphasis on a Democracy Doctrine, following the Iraqi hardships of 2005, appears to be just another method for accomplishing the President's original goal of "regime change" for a slightly expanded list of countries in a 2006 version of the original "Axis of Evil."

With the U.S. armed forces stretched beyond their capacity in Iraq, the U.S. is not likely to invade another country any time soon. Instead, it appears that the President means to bring about his cherished "regime change" through fostering democracy where tyranny now exists.

It seems clear that the President lacks public support for his activist, democratizing foreign policy. As of this writing, the President's overall approval rating stands at near 30%, the lowest of his presidency. Only 42% of the people approve of his handling the terrorist threat, also the lowest of his presidency. Most shatteringly, the adjective most frequently used to characterize the President is now "incompetent," whereas until recently, it was "honest."[23] The American people, it seems, do not support the President nor do they support his "activist" foreign policy.[24]

In short, the President's activist conception of democracy promotion is not feasible in the sense that he has failed to convince the American people that it is desirable. Nor, given his low approval ratings, is it likely that the American people can be convinced by him.

Of course, another dimension exists to the feasibility question—the extent to which, even with the most profound domestic support, democracy promotion can "work." Is it possible for one state to implement democracy in another country? A vast literature exists on theories of democracy, prerequisites and requisites of democracy, and democracy promotion (a literature which need not be examined in detail here).[25] But the conclusion that must be drawn from the literature is that democracy is the product of many different political, social, and economic realities and processes; that those cannot be created whole cloth by anyone, much less by a foreign state; and that the realities and processes are mutually reinforcing.

A foreign state can, with the support of a host government, begin to create the conditions on which political democracy depends. But those conditions can neither be created instantaneously nor do they instantaneously lead to democracy. It is, as the President has suggested, a "generational effort." But to create the conditions that might, eventually, result in a functioning democracy in a country whose government resists those conditions, is a certain impossibility.

The U.S. can, and has, forced change on a country over which it had control. Recent examples include Afghanistan and Iraq where the U.S. produced elections. But to argue that, in turn, the elections produced democracy, is fanciful. One American observer who has lived in Kandahar since late 2001 had this to say about the Afghan elections.

"Parliamentary elections last Fall, hailed as free and fair—or at least as free and fair as anyone could expect in a place like Afghanistan—have allowed many Western observers to regard the nation-building process here as a success. In Kandahar, those elections were considered a joke—even by the people who won. Less than a quarter of the population voted, and as most locals predicted, the counting process functioned like a bazaar with plenty of extra zeroes for sale."[26] In short, holding elections is desirable. But elections are not the same as democracy. They may be a step toward democracy if they are followed by other significant changes. But absent constant U.S. pressure, those changes are unlikely to happen in countries like Afghanistan and Iraq.

In short, a functioning democracy must include openly competitive and fair elections, which produces a representative, authoritative, functioning government, which in turn voluntarily surrenders power if it loses the vote as a result of the outcome of the next, regularly scheduled, and openly competitive free and fair election.

Thus, elections are important, especially elections where would-be candidates were free to enter the elections and all adults would be free to vote and all votes would be counted equally. But such elections do not a democracy make. Democracies are bred of the choices of the electorate, but require a set of institutional practices for a government reflecting the will of the voters in order for that government to function effectively and authoritatively. Both Afghanistan and Iraq, then, fail the democracy test. They are not now democracies and it is not likely they will become democracies in the foreseeable future.

Of course that does not mean that the government of President Hamid Karzai, which controls certain parts of Afghanistan, resulting in his being referred to as "the mayor of Kabul," which he does control, is no better than the Taliban because neither were effective democracies.[27] The Taliban were loathsome, oppressive—especially of women—and primitive and corrupt. President Karzai's regime, in comparison, is a model of tolerance and pluralism. Saddam Hussein's regime was truly loathsome, vicious, corrupt, and despicable. Whatever Shi'a-dominated government will yet be formed, it is likely to be a vast improvement over its predecessor.

The conclusion to be drawn from the American experiences in Afghanistan and Iraq and from the literature on democracy is that "effective democracy" cannot be implemented by force. Paul Wolfowitz, in his 2000 *National Interest* article, reminded us that "[w]e must proceed by interaction and indirection, not imposition."[28] In short, it is feasible to promote democratization with the view, in some distant future, of witnessing the creation of an effective democracy. Building a civil society, promoting human rights, working to ensure functioning bureaucracies, diminishing corruption, protecting property rights, spreading education, and, in particular, driving economic development—all can contribute to that end goal. Each requires interaction with local authorities in countries seeking such changes and indirection, focusing on the immediate goal in the short term and letting the democratization take its own sweet time.

One inevitable conclusion of the American experience in Afghanistan and Iraq is that if effective democracies could not be built relatively quickly in the two countries in which the United States was able to apply massive force, they certainly cannot be imposed anywhere else. It is unlikely, therefore, that the withdrawal of American troops will be followed by deeper democracy development in those countries.

The immediate answer to the question of where America's democratization efforts should be applied appears to have been settled. Secretary of State Condoleezza Rice recently appeared before the Senate Foreign Relations Committee to request $85 million from Congress to support political opposition to the clerics of Iran and civil society groups in that country. Call it promoting democracy or, more accurately, promoting regime change. Some "$50 million of the new outlay would allow the United States to broadcast Persian language programs 24 hours a day. Another $15 million would be earmarked for increasing participation in the political process, including measures such as expanded Internet access. The administration hopes to spend $5 million to fund scholarships and fellowships for young Iranians, and the State Department said $5 million 'would go to public diplomacy efforts aimed at Iran, including its Persian-language website.'"

It will be politically risky for groups and individuals within Iran to accept the $15 million funding from the United States Government (if the U.S. Government first changes its own laws forbidding the transfer of funds to Iran). The Iranian secret police frequently discredit their opponents by forcing them, often through torture, to admit they have taken funds from foreign governments—especially from the U.S. It seems unlikely that groups within Iran will be able to accept those funds. More likely, the funds will go to Iranian opposition groups in exile outside Iran which, since the victory of the Islamic revolution, have not been demonstrably effective.

U.S. Ambassador Khalilzad has been authorized by the President to meet with Iranian government officials to discuss Iranian cooperation in pacifying the Iraqi insurgency. He has been given strict instructions that the only subject he is authorized to discuss refers to internal Iraqi matters only—definitely not to Iranian nuclear matters, for which the U.S. is seeking sanctions authorized by the UN Security Council. The Iranians claim to have accepted these ground rules. Recently, representatives of Iranian intelligence have been showing a letter written in Persian and allegedly signed by Ambassador Khalilzad asking them for talks. The response of the U.S. embassy was, "Ambassador Khalilzad has the authority to meet with Iranian officials to discuss issues of mutual concern. But he has not sent a letter in any language to the Iranians."[29]

The Iranian regime would also like nothing better than to show the world a letter from Ambassador Khalilzad to claim that the Americans—"the Center of Global Arrogance" as the U.S. is now called by the Iranian government (no longer "the Great Satan")—had caved in to Iran. But the risk of the Iranians using the talks to "prove" their having outwitted the U.S. is a poor reason for not proceeding.

So it is with the outrageous letter which Iranian President Mahmoud Ahmadinejad recently sent to President Bush. In it, among other things, he sought to teach the U.S. leader the teachings of Jesus Christ and other matters about which the American president has far more knowledge than the Iranian. But the key to dealing with Iran, and for that matter with Hamas and Hezbollah and Syria, is to deal in asymmetric diplomacy just as terrorists deal in asymmetric violence. In short, not to respond to what, for example, the Iranian wrote, but to respond with what we want to say and therefore for us to set the agenda.[30]

A much more powerful reason for the President not to write the letter, in fact, is that the U.S. fears that any talk with the Iranians, whether there are letters shown about or not, will merely strengthen the legitimacy of the clerics and delay their ouster. In Iran, at least, it looks very much as if democracy promotion and regime change are synonymous.

But the case of Islamic Iran is a special case and should not be taken to be representative of Bush democracy promotion. In fact, a host of programs have been established to advance democracy and prosperity. The President proposed the establishment of Millennium Challenge Account in Monterrey, Mexico, in 2002, and pledged a $5 billion per year contribution by 2006. The Account limits grants to countries that are judged to have made significant progress along sixteen dimensions, including six that refer explicitly to "governing justly."[31] The President has managed actually to deliver $3 billion in funds for fiscal year 2006, and a number of countries that meet the criteria are receiving MCA funds.[32]

President Bush also managed to substantially increase total U.S. Overseas Development Assistance from $10,884 billion in 2001 (0.11% of GDP) to $19,705 billion in 2004 (0.17% of GDP).[33] While this small percentage generates large funds, given the size of the GDP, the U.S. still gives the second lowest percentage of its GDP as aid of any aid-giving country (slightly ahead of only

Greece). Moreover, more than $3 billion of U.S. aid goes directly to Israel each year. Israel is hardly a low-income country and hardly needs democracy promotion. Its GDP per capita is higher than Greece or Portugal, and is roughly equal to Spain or South Korea.[33]

The U.S. also supports the National Endowment for Democracy, which "makes hundreds of grants each year to support pro-democracy groups in Africa, Asia, Central and Eastern Europe, Eurasia, Latin America, and the Middle East."[34] The utility of such an approach is indicated in a survey of 67 countries where dictatorships fell since 1972; Freedom House found that "nonviolent 'people power' movements are the strongest force in most successful transitions to democracy."[35] But it seems obvious that the experiences of countries replacing communist dictatorships with more democratic forms of rule are not especially relevant to the experiences of the Islamic world discussed here. For one thing, the populations of those countries were fundamentally eager to adopt the ways of the West, whereas many in the Islamic world tend to see the West as "the problem."

Still other U.S. Government agencies support democracy initiatives around the globe. For example, the Middle East Partnership Initiative of the Department of State has been funded to $300 million by Congress to "fund programs that help put in place the building blocks for democratic change."[36]

In fact, then, the President has implemented new initiatives for democracy promotion. But the level at which these initiatives are funded hardly suggests that he has himself been convinced or has been able to convince Congress that democracy promotion is a "generational challenge" to advance the supreme national interest of the United States. Thus, while the budget of U.S. aid was increased by more than $8 billion from 2001 to 2004, the budget of the U.S. Armed Forces was increased by more than $100 billion in the same period.[37] While planes and tanks and destroyers cost an awful lot more than programs and personnel, the increase for democracy promotion seems relatively paltry and unlikely to represent a major commitment.

Of course, the United States is at war in Iraq. But recall that the first sentence of the 2006 NSS is: "America is at war." That war is the war against global terror of which the Iraqi war is a part, but only a part. The other component of the war is democracy promotion. The document goes on to say, "These inseparable priorities—fighting and winning the war on terror and promoting freedom as the alternative to tyranny and despair—have now guided American policy for more than four years."[38] As an "inseparable priority," the commitment of the President to democracy promotion, as measured in dollars, does not match the rhetoric.

Nor does it seem plausible to imagine that democracy promotion for the 300 million Arabs in the Middle East and the more than 1 billion Muslims in the world, not to mention advancing democracy for the billions of others who live under tyranny,[39] can be meaningfully implemented or advanced by the sums the U.S. is spending. The conclusion must be reached that it is not feasible to implement the President's Democracy Doctrine with the level of American domestic support for him or for his policies. Nor is it feasible to implement his program with the level of funding that he has managed to devote to the program, no matter how successful he has been in increasing that funding. Nor, in the case of Iran at least, remembering Wolfowitz, will democracy implementation be feasible without "interaction."

If the program is not feasible in any meaningful sense, the question of where and how it should be applied becomes moot. But it can be argued, and I would claim, should be argued, that any program for democracy promotion is better than no program for democracy promotion; that we may be on the verge of higher levels of public funding; and that, in any case, as a "generational challenge," this move to democracy need not be completed anytime soon. Moreover, the President's commitment to democracy promotion gives ammunition to those in the U.S. Government who seek to advance democracy elsewhere against other officials who seek to advance competing goals in foreign countries.[40] These assertions, then, return us to the where and how questions.

Clearly, from the point of terrorism, the where question must be answered in terms of the Islamic world, and more precisely and more immediately, the Arab states, Iran, Pakistan, and Afghanistan. The threat of terrorism to the West and the U.S. drives one to that answer. That point is obvious, and is the basis of the President's oft-stated commitment to the goal of democracy promotion.

But the U.S. has another motive for promoting democracy in the Middle East. As the President said recently, "I spend a lot of time worrying about the disruption of energy because of politics or civil strife in other countries—because tyrants control the spigots. And it is in our national interest that we become less dependent on oil."[41] In addition to terrorism, it is also Western and U.S. dependence on Persian/Arabian Gulf oil, where some two-thirds of international oil supplies are said to be located, which drives democracy promotion.[42] Given the urgent need for democracy promotion in the Islamic world, it is disheartening to note that no countries from the Middle East or South Asia have qualified as eligible to apply for funds from the Millennium Challenge Account, indicating their failure to meet the criteria for proper good governance or property protection or civil liberties.

Nonetheless, two key questions remain to be answered: Would more democracy in those countries mean they would be less likely to withhold energy supplies from the West? Would a more democratic Islamic world or Middle East be less likely to produce terrorists?

The question of the stability of oil supplies seems easiest to answer. Greater democracy in the Middle East would seem to do little to guarantee oil exports. In fact, any radical Islamist government produced through free elections might very well fail to supply the West with oil at current export levels. For example, in 1978, under the last full year of rule by the shah, Iran produced

6.2 million barrels of oil per day and exported 5.6 million barrels. The clerics have never managed to produce more than 4 million barrels per day and given Iran's vastly increased population, have supplied world oil markets with far less than 4 million barrels per day.[43]

Before addressing the question of terrorism, it is useful to address an underlying issue: Islam and democracy are not necessarily incompatible.[44] (There is, of course, a deep incompatibility between the wishes of the radical Islamists now everywhere in the ascendancy in the Islamic world and democracy.) Most scholars of Islam and of the Middle East see no basic reason why a state that is Islamic cannot also be democratic. But in the absence of such democratic Islamic states, one most also search for alternative explanations to understand the "democracy deficit" in the Middle East. Mark Tessler, for example, claims there is little evidence, at least at the individual level of analysis, to support the claims of those who assert that Islam and democracy are incompatible. The reasons that democracy has not taken root in the Arab world must therefore lie elsewhere; perhaps in domestic economic structures, perhaps in relations with the international political and economic order, or perhaps in the determination of those in power to resist political change by whatever means are required. But while these and other possible explanations can be debated, what should be clear is that cultural explanations alleging that Islam discourages or even prevents the emergence of support for democracy are misguided, indeed misleading, and thus of little use in efforts to understand the factors shaping attitudes toward democracy in the Arab world.[45]

Islam is as diverse and complex as any of the other monotheistic faiths, and is as susceptible to the most liberal interpretations. Yet the fact is that Islam is everywhere being interpreted in the most retrogressive manner, and it is true that no state with a majority population can be considered a functioning democracy, with the possible exception of Turkey. Turkey is a democracy populated overwhelmingly by Muslims. Yet it does not provide an empirical example of the compatibility of Islam and democracy because it is constitutionally secular.[46] As Islam is now being interpreted—in a retrogressive manner—it may, in fact, be incompatible with democracy. Islam will need to be interpreted in a more liberal fashion to be the system underlying democratic rule. Still, it should not be argued that democracy and Islam are necessarily incompatible, even if they are practically incompatible now.

As Tessler suggests, there really is no satisfying answer to this puzzle. It is a puzzle that the three impressive *Arab Human Development Reports,* sponsored by the United Nations Development Program in 2002, 2003, and 2005, have failed to solve.[47] But suppose we give the benefit of the doubt to those scholars who argue that there is no incompatibility between Islam and democracy, that democracy can be achieved in the Islamic Middle East and South Asia.

Would such democracy in the heart of the Islamic world advance U.S. foreign policy interests? The answer must be a resounding "no," at least in the short term. As we have seen from recent democratic-like experiments in the Middle East, the outcomes invariably advance the power of radical Islamic groups whose hatred for the United States is more burning, even, than their hatred for their own governments. Ahmadinejad, the radical Islamic former mayor of Tehran, won the presidential elections in Iran. Hamas won a majority of seats in the newly elected Palestinian parliament. In an election in Egypt, members of the Muslim Brotherhood increased their representation in parliament by a factor of five. In Jordan, only electoral manipulation kept the Islamic representation as low as it was. In Saudi Arabia, elections for municipal councils produced a smashing Islamist victory.[48]

To the extent that elections in the Middle East are free elections, there is little doubt that the results will sweep radical Islamists to power. And there is no doubt of what their program is. Ahmadinejad advocates a "World Without Zionism" and rapid Iranian mastery of an independent nuclear fuel cycle. Article Seven of the Hamas Charter, recently reaffirmed by both of its leaders, Khaled Mashal in exile in Damascus and Mahmoud Zafar in the Gaza, states:

> The Islamic Resistance Movement is one of the links in the chain of the struggle against the Zionist invaders.... It goes on to reach out and become one with another chain that includes the struggle of the Palestinians and Moslem Brotherhood in the 1948 war and the Jihad operations of the Moslem Brotherhood in 1968 and after....
>
> The Prophet, Allah bless him and grant him salvation has said: "The Day of Judgment will not come about until Moslems fight the Jews (killing the Jews), when the Jew will hide behind stones and trees. The stones and trees will say O Moslems, O Abdullah, there is a Jew behind me, come and kill him."[49]

It is not just that Islamists challenge the State of Israel. They also threaten the United States in Iraq and everywhere else in the world, including within the United States. Any missive from bin Laden or al-Zawahiri makes that clear. So, at least for the foreseeable future, greater democracy in the Middle East would, if anything, produce more and not less terrorism.

But let us take the point on a more general level. Does tyranny contribute to its subjects turning to terrorism? There appears to be no relation between the form of government and recruits for terrorism. Radical Islamist terrorists are drawn from repressive societies, be it Saudi Arabia or Egypt or Jordan. And to the contrary, India is a democracy whose Muslim population numbers some 130 million. Very few Indian Muslim terrorists have been reported. But there are numerous non-Muslim terrorist groups in India. On the other hand, in the more or less democratic Philippines, the Abu Sayyaf Group is a terrorist organization that seeks to build an independent homeland. Other democratic states also produced their own terrorist groups: the Red Brigades, the Baader-

Meinhof Gang, the Japanese Red Army...the list is lengthy. Of course, tyrannical regimes have produced their share as well.[50]

Rather than generated as a response to a tyrannical, nondemocratic government, terrorism seems to arise in response to a sense of personal or group humiliation. A vast array of processes can produce this sense of humiliation. Basically, any imbalance between an individual's expectations and his or her sense of perceived reality can be understood as humiliating to that individual, as an individual or as a member of a group. Humiliation can be produced by an exaggerated sense of entitlement in relation to the realities of the society in which the person lives. Or the humiliation can be produced by repression, poverty, social failure, cultural and intellectual backwardness, or a host of other factors. The three *Arab Human Development Reports*, mentioned above, highlight a variety of truths about the Arab world, each of which would be sufficient to produce a deep sense of humiliation among individual Arabs.

Feeling humiliated does not, of course, lead directly to terrorism. A number of other outcomes are possible, even typical. Depression, addictions, violence against those near-by are common. So is proving that those who are seen to inflict the humiliation are wrong. The Japanese and the Germans took a highly productive route to escaping their humiliations after World War II. So did U.S. industrialists after the "hollowing out" to which they had been subject by the Japanese in the 1980s.

To turn toward terrorism as a response to humiliation requires a powerful ideological explanation for one's humiliation that places responsibility on hateful, more distant figures. They may be local repressive rulers or "Zionist occupiers" or "American imperialists" or infidels or what have you. In addition, the ideology must be accompanied by individual leaders who then use the ideology to exploit the humiliation to bring a recruit to terrorism.[51] But the key to the process is that there is no special role for nondemocratic governments in terrorism, and such governments may or may not be a factor in the generation of terrorists.

It is, then, very hard to argue that more democracy in the Middle East would be better for the West and the United States, at least for as long as one can imagine. (Whether or not it will be good for the peoples of the Middle East is a decision that should be left to them.) So, what then, of U.S. foreign policy? Gregory Gause, who has written perhaps the most trenchant criticism of the Bush Democracy Doctrine, concludes as follows: "The United States must focus on pushing Arab governments to make political space for liberal, secular, leftist, nationalist, and other non-Islamist parties to set down roots and mobilize voters. Washington should support those groups that are more likely to accept U.S. foreign policy and emulate U.S. political values."[52]

In short, instead of pressing for any immediate democracy and free elections, the U.S. should pursue a long-term policy of supporting secular and liberal groups in Islamic countries—the civil society so necessary for democracy.

The more the immediate pressure for free elections in the Middle East, the more likely will the outcomes be inimical to U.S. national interests.

The answer to the how question, agreeing with Gause, is a very long-term U.S. commitment to the very values that significant numbers of Muslims find objectionable, secularism, for one. The result over time of America's pursuing such a policy, for the foreseeable future, is likely to be worse, and not better, relations with the states and peoples of the Middle East.

In short, there is no easy answer to the questions about democracy promotion in the Islamic world. Neither the feasibility, nor the means, nor the outcomes are certain. What seems best to count on is the likelihood that U.S. relations with the Islamic world will remain strained and painful for both the Middle East and the West; that terrorism against American interests will be a thing of the future as well as of the past; that radical Islamists will gain power in states they do not now control; and that President Bush will maintain his single most important foreign policy initiative: the promotion of democracy for everyone, everywhere.

Endnotes

1. All quotes from the President's speeches were accessed from http://www.white-house.gov.
2. The National Security Strategy of the United States, September 17, 2002, Preface, http://www.whitehouse.gov/nsc/nss.pdf; hereafter, 2002 NSS.
3. Ibid.
4. January 28, 2006.
5. The National Security Strategy of the United States, March 16, 2006, http://www.whitehouse.gov/nsc/nss/2006/nss2006-pdf; hereafter, 2006 NSS.
6. Ibid. State of the Union, 2006.
7. George W. Bush, State of the Union Address, January 20, 2004.
8. George W. Bush, State of the Union Address, February 2, 2005.
9. 2002 NSS, Preface.
10. For an interesting if not completely compelling defense of this decision, See L. Paul Bremer, with Malcolm McConnell, *My Year in Iraq: The Struggle to Build a Future of Hope* (New York, Simon & Schuster, 2006).
11. As quoted by Tim Russert, *Meet the Press*, January 15, 2006, http://www.msnbc.msn.com/id/10822231/.
12. "THE WEEK: Iraq at the Precipice," *New York Times*, February 19-25, published February 26, 2006.
13. "Iraqi Leader Scolds U.S. on Politics: Car Bomb Kills 21," *New York Times*, February 22, 2006.
14. See, for example, Francis Fukuyama, *State-Building, Governance and World Order in the 21st Century* (Ithaca, NY: Cornell University Press, 2004).
15. As reported by CNN, February 17, 2006.
16. These quotes are taken form the first paragraph of the President's introduction to the 2006 National Security Strategy.

17. Of course the speed and low cost were only true of the immediate aftermath. Since then the writ of President Karzai has extended little beyond the boundaries of Kabul, while the rest of the country is run by warlords who finance their rule through poppy cultivation and opium processing. Afghanistan is once again the largest exporter of heroin to the West. Worse, testifying to the Senate on February 28, 2006, Lt. Gen. Michael D. Maples, the head of the Defense Intelligence Agency, said, "Despite significant progress on the political front, the Taliban-dominated insurgency remains a capable and resilient threat." Appearing with Director of National Intelligence John D. Negroponte, Maples said attacks within Afghanistan were up 20% between 2004 and 2005, suicide bombings increased "almost fourfold" and use of makeshift bombs, similar to those used in Iraq, had "more than doubled." See Walter Pincus, "Growing Threat Seen in Afghan Insurgency; DIA Chief Cites Surging Violence in Homeland," *Washington Post*, March 1, 2006.

18. It is also the case that he added immediately after these words, "So that if we shall deal falsely with our God in this work we have undertaken, and so cause him to withdraw his present help from us, we shall be made a story and a byword throughout the world." In short, the connection between the U.S. and the Lord, which so many decry in President Bush, has been present from the beginning of the American experiment. John Winthrop, Governor of Massachusetts Bay Colony, "A Model of Christian Charity," discourse written aboard the *Arbella* during the voyage to Massachusetts, 1630; Robert C. Winthrop, *Life and Letters of John Winthrop* (1867), p. 19.

19. 2006 NSS, 49.

20. Paul Wolfowitz, *The National Interest* (Spring 2000).

21. George W. Bush, State of the Union Address, January 31, 2006. The President selected an interesting group of tyrannical regimes for inclusion in this speech. Conspicuously absent was China. In fact, the September 2002 National Strategy document had a lengthy section on China and mentioned, "We welcome the emergence of a strong, peaceful, and prosperous China. The democratic development of China is crucial to that future. Yet, a quarter century after beginning the process of shedding the worst features of the Communist legacy, China's leaders have not yet made the next series of fundamental choices about the character of their state" (27). Yet since that reference, as China has become evermore significant as a trading partner, as a recipient of the foreign direct investment of U.S. companies, and as a financier of the U.S. Current Account Deficit, China has largely disappeared as a focus of the Bush "Democracy Doctrine."

22. 2006 NSS, 3.

23. The second and third words most often used to characterize the President are "idiot" and "liar." The Pew Research Center for the People and the Press, "Bush Approval Falls to 33%, Congress Earns Rare Praise," March 15, 2006, http://people-press.org/reports/display.php3?ReportID=271.

24. See, for example, James M. Lindsay and Lee Feinstein, "U.S. Should Mind Its Own Business," Op-Ed, *Baltimore Sun*, November 27, 2005. Of course these public opinion poll results must be accepted with considerable caution. It is not at all clear what the respondents understand by the question they think they are answering. It is also well established that different phrasings of the same question can produce widely different answers in public opinion polls.

25. For a useful review article of democratic theories with abundant bibliographic references, see Mostafa Rejai, "The Metamorphosis of Democratic Theory," *Ethics* (1967): 202-208.

26. Sarah Chayes, "The Night Fairies," *Bulletin of the Atomic Scientists* (March/April 2006): 17.

27. The term "effective democracy" is taken from the 2006 NSS, especially 4-5. The term is not defined but is described in ways all students of democracy would understand.

28. Wolfowitz, *The National Interest*.

29. See Lindsey Hilsum, "Iran Claims US Has Offered Peace Talks," *Sunday Times*, March 12, 2006, http://www.timesonline.co.uk/article/0,,2089-2081493_1,00.html.

30. This point is brilliantly made by Jim Hoagland, "Thinking Outside the Iran Box," *Washington Post*, May 14, 2006.

31. See Millennium Challenge Corporation at http://www.mca.gov/.

32. U.S. AID has declared 23 countries eligible to apply for MCA funds for fiscal year 2006. "The selected countries from the 'low income' category for FY 2006 are Armenia, Benin, Bolivia, Burkina Faso, East Timor, The Gambia, Georgia, Ghana, Honduras, Lesotho, Madagascar, Mali, Mongolia, Morocco, Mozambique, Nicaragua, Senegal, Sri Lanka, Tanzania and Vanuatu…. Of these 20 eligible low income countries, 16 have been selected as MCA-eligible in prior years. Burkina Faso, East Timor, The Gambia, and Tanzania are MCA-eligible for the first time…. The MCC [Millennium Challenge Corporation] Board also selected three countries from the 'lower middle income' category—a new category in FY 2006 that includes countries with a per capita income between $1,576 and $3,255. The selected lower middle income countries for FY 2006 include two new countries, El Salvador and Namibia. The third country, Cape Verde, was previously selected as MCA-eligible in the low income category and is currently implementing a Compact with MCC."

33. Figures from the Organisation for Economic Co-operation and Development available at http://www.oecd.org/countrylist/0,2578,en_2649_34485_1783495_1_1_1_1,00.html. Inasmuch as some nontrivial amount of this U.S. aid went to Iraq ($2.286 billion in 2004), the increase has not been quite as dramatic as the numbers suggest.

34. National Endowment for Democracy, http://www.ned.org/.

35. See *Adrian Karatnycky and Peter Ackerman,* "How Freedom Is Won: From Civic Struggle to Durable Democracy," Freedom House, http://65.110.85.181/uploads/special_report/29.pdf. They add, "Among the 35 post-transition Free countries, 24 (69 percent) had strong nonviolent civic coalitions, 8 (23 percent) had moderately strong civic coalitions, and only 3 (8 percent) had movements that were weak or absent in the two-year period leading up to the opening for the transition. By contrast, among countries that are Partly Free now, 8 (35 percent) had 'strong' civic coalitions, 7 (30 percent) were 'moderate,' and 8 (35 percent) were 'weak or absent.' Among countries that are now Not Free, the distribution was zero 'strong,' (33 percent) 'moderate,' and 6 (67 percent) 'weak or absent.'"

36. Middle East Partnership Initiative, http://mepi.state.gov/.

37. Department of Defense, National Defense Budget Estimates for FY 2001, March 2000, http://www.dod.mil/comptroller/defbudget/fy2001/fy2001_greenbook.pdf; and Department of Defense, National Defense Budget Estimates for FY 2004, March 2003, http://www.dod.mil/comptroller/defbudget/fy2004/fy2004_greenbook.pdf.

38. 200X NSS, Introduction.

39. For this and other useful information of the state of democracy and liberty in the world, see Freedom House, http://www.freedomhouse.org/template.cfm?page=1.

40. This point is made by Peter Baker, "The Realities of Exporting Democracy: A Year After Bush Recast Foreign Policy, Progress Remains Mixed," *Washington Post*, January 25, 2006, A01, http://www.washingtonpost.com/wp-dyn/content/article/2006/01/24/AR2006012401901.html.

41. George W. Bush on February 27, 2006 as reported in the *Financial Times*, March 1, 2006, 1.

42. Recently, doubters have arisen, suggesting that recoverable oil reserves in the Persian Gulf are far less than claimed by the region's governments. For the most profound of these doubters, see Matthew R. Simmons, *Twilight in the Desert: The Coming Oil Shock and the World Economy* (Hoboken, NJ: Wiley, 2005).

43. U.S. Department of Energy, "Persian Gulf Oil and Gas Exports Fact Sheet," September 2004, http://www.eia.doe.gov/emeu/cabs/pgulf.html.

44. For a powerful statement of this view, see John L. Esposito and John O. Voll, *Islam and Democracy* (New York: Oxford University Press, 1996). Many scholars attempt to explain the "deficit" and offer other explanations. Lisa Anderson, for example, suggests that "Arabs have failed to develop democracy because of soft budget constraints: oil revenues, foreign aid, foreign borrowings and the support of western states for them because of the need for oil, support for the west against the USSR" in Lisa Anderson, "Arab Democracy: Dismal Prospects," *World Policy Journal* (Fall 2001): 53-60.

45. See Mark Tessler in *Democratization in the Middle East: Experiences, Struggles, Challenges*, eds. Amin Saikal and Albrecht Schnabel (Tokyo: United Nations University Press, 2003): 79-101.

46. It is possible, albeit difficult, to make the case that Indonesia is a fully functioning Islamic democracy. The same goes for Malaysia and Pakistan. In any case, neither are in the heart of the Middle East.

47. Gulf Research Center, http://www.grc.ae/?sec=Arab+Human+Development+Report.

48. Rami Khouri, a most astute observer of the region, suggests that Islam is only one factor that contributed to these successes. He also points to other factors "captured" by Islamists such as their reputations for being relatively corruption-free, competent administrators, particularly strong on matters of national identity and on resistance to foreign oppression or subjugation. See Rami Khouri, "The Third Wave of Political Islamism," March 15, 2006, distributed by Agence Global, http://www.agenceglobal.com/article.asp?id=842.

49. Translated at MidEast Web Historical Documents, http://www.mideastweb.org/hamas.htm.

50. F. Gregory Gause makes this point most powerfully. See F. Gregory Gause, "Can Democracy Stop Terrorism?," *Foreign Affairs* (September/October 2005), http://fullaccess.foreignaffairs.org/20050901faessay84506/f-gregory-gause-iii/can-democracy-stop-terrorism.html [requires login].

51. For a closer look at this process, see Marvin Zonis, "Self-Objects, Self-Representation, and Sense-Making Crises: Political Instability in the 1980s," *Political Psychology* 5 (1984): 267-85.

52. Gause, "Can Democracy Stop Terrorism?"

10
The Bush Doctrine Abroad

ALEXANDER MOENS

Introduction

In this chapter, I will attempt to explain why many liberal democracies in Europe and Asia rejected George W. Bush's Doctrine of preemptive warfare in the war on terror. Even when governments tried to stay on good terms, such as in Japan and Britain, their own publics grew increasingly critical of Bush. In the first section, I will show that there was a "deep background" to this rejection. Early in the 1999–2000 presidential primary and election campaign, European, Canadian, and Asian leaders and elites formed unusually negative opinions about Bush. These were followed by negative impressions of his platform, the advisors whom he appointed, and his first year of foreign policy, which was seen as unilateralist and obstructionist. The second section of this chapter will examine the rejection of the immediate policy decisions during the post-September 11, 2001 period and how the gap between Bush and most foreign publics and many governments actually deepened, even though there was an initial wave of sympathy for the losses Americans suffered on that fateful day. Still, Bush's "war on terror," his "with us or with the terrorists" language, the argument that terrorists, rogue states, and weapons of mass destruction (WMDs) had blended into a new "nexus" threat leading to his "axis of evil" pre-Doctrine, made most of the other liberal democracies very uncomfortable.

The third section shows how Iraq and the Bush Doctrine became synonymous. A large segment of public opinion was mobilized in support of governments that tried to stop Bush from going to war with Iraq. Millions protested in cities in Europe and Asia in the weeks prior to the war. Whatever slight understanding was left for the idea of preventive action was further eroded by opposition to this particular war and was further aggravated by the acrimonious United Nations process that preceded it. The next section examines how Bush's quest in 2003 to cast his overall policy in terms of bringing freedom and prosperity to the Middle East did not at first bring these countries closer to the American position. Instead, it caused a general outcry against America's new missionary foreign policy or what one newspaper called, "the Bush Doctrine of liberation."[1]

A final section explores the small cracks in the posture of the global community's rejection of Bush's Doctrine that began to emerge in 2003. Despite the clashes over Iraq, cooperation on preventive intelligence and covert war activities against al-Qaeda operatives grew only stronger between the United States and its critics. The European Union announced a new security strategy that closely mirrored Bush's strategy. As the Taliban–al-Qaeda insurgents in Afghanistan began to adopt the same tactics as the insurgents in Iraq, America's NATO allies in Afghanistan found that their military and strategic needs began to mirror those of the United States. In a final irony, as American military resources were taxed in Iraq and the diplomacy of the three big European states vis-à-vis Iran was faltering, some critics of Bush's Doctrine began to wonder if Iran would not indeed fit exactly in Bush's original Doctrine of striking preemptively.

The concluding section of this chapter will address the possibility of the Bush Doctrine gaining more policy respect as the United States becomes more interested in the legitimacy offered by working closer with democratic allies, and they in turn become more interested in effective cooperation with the United States.

For the purpose of this chapter, "Abroad" refers to the democracies in Europe and Asia as well as Canada. Most of the examples will draw on Western Europe and Canada. While most of these governments were skeptical about Bush and his early foreign policy, they began to divide into two groups in the lead up to the war with Iraq. One group opted for a close relationship with the Bush administration though not without hesitations about the President's policies in the Middle East; the other group became publicly critical of Bush. Meanwhile, public opinion abroad turned increasingly against Bush, with the Bush Doctrine as its lightning rod.

The Rejection of Bush and His Unilateralism

The perception abroad of the Bush Doctrine is situated inside a wide political context. This context needs to be understood properly to appreciate how strong the foreign reaction to Bush's policies from the summer of 2002 and onward has been. It contains early negative impressions of Bush as a political leader, fears of a new trend of American isolationism, followed by dismay and anger over Bush's apparent unilateralism.

In 1999 and 2000, the image of George W. Bush in most foreign capitals and among the media as well as political and academic elites was that of a lightweight in foreign policy. This was a result of his short political career as Texas governor, which was focused solely on domestic issues, and a lack of international interest and personal travel. The belief was that he lacked curiosity for things abroad and that he was briefed only on the files that needed immediate action. The press in the United States fed this impression as two lengthy series in *The Washington Post* and *The New York Times* defined Bush's life in terms of a frivolous youth, aimless career, and a late awakening to politics.[2] The early books on Bush were either partisan attack manuals or scorching critiques. They quickly showed up in Europe. Unlike previous presidencies, the early books about Bush were extraordinarily critical about his political skills and political views. Molly Ivins' *Shrub*, Paul Begala's *Is Our Children Learning?*, James Hatfield's *Fortunate Son*, and Mark Crispin Miller's, *The Bush Dyslexicon*, formed the first wave of "Bush knowledge" to the world.[3] In politics, first impressions tend to become standards of measurement. How could anything good come from this spoiled son who loves Texas and seems beholden to the oil industry and the Christian Right?

The primaries and presidential election campaign of 2000 did nothing to dispel this impression abroad. Bush did not show knowledge or gravitas in foreign policy. In one of the now-famous interviews that turned into a pop quiz, Bush showed that he did not know the name of the then Canadian Prime Minister Jean Chrétien. It was the Canadian reporter Rick Mercer, who has a strong nationalist and soft anti-American reputation in Canada that set Bush up for this gaffe. Bush's mispronunciations on international topics, for example calling the Greeks "Grecians," were heralded widely as evidence of a lack of interest and knowledge in foreign policy.

Given his apparent "lack of understanding" of the issues, foreign observers concluded that Bush would rely extensively on his advisors. Later, analysts would use this impression to argue that Bush had been taken hostage by a cabal of neoconservative activists and that American foreign policy had become a venue for the realization of the goals of the *Project for the New American Century* that had been set up by Irving Kristol and Robert Kagan in 1997. This final point forms an important backdrop to how foreign governments and analysts have perceived the Bush Doctrine: a doctrine that emanated from a somewhat uninformed decision maker who is not only prone to rely on his advisors, but likely to be driven by them.[4] From this early view sprang a sensational set of stories about Paul Wolfowitz and other neoconservatives who allegedly had hijacked the Bush administration.[5] The fact that some of these advisors such as Wolfowitz and Richard Perle were Jewish Americans added to the hype about alleged hidden agendas. Others went so far as to call Vice President Dick Cheney the co-president or the prime minister, with Bush only being the titular or ceremonial head of state.

The European political class reacted very negatively to the Florida election fiasco that captivated the political world in December 2000. Most concluded that the American people actually did not want Bush and that the Supreme Court decision was a narrow technical victory for Bush, given to him by a narrow Republican majority on the Supreme Court, which deprived him of a legitimate mandate to govern. Michael Moore, whose commercial film success was built on people's dislike or fear of Bush, argued that Bush had stolen the election, an interpretation that was received in Europe and Canada as a matter of fact.[6]

Most foreign capitals believed that Bush would pursue a minimalist, even a neo-isolationist foreign policy, based on statements by Bush and his National Security Advisor, Condoleezza Rice, saying that the United States would not engage in nation building or use its armed forces in what Europe and Canada had just coined as the new mission—human security operations. Bush emphasized transforming the military and building national missile defenses. He showed a lack of enthusiasm for multilateral initiatives and gave the impression that he might conduct a minimalist foreign policy.

This expectation actually fit the experience in Europe about new American presidents. Not only is Europe generally wary about new presidents—realizing full well how much capacity a new president has to swing American foreign policy in a vastly different direction from his predecessor—but it tends to assess his foreign policy approach as unsatisfactory at the outset. Ronald Reagan was considered insular, overly ideological with a strong cowboy streak, and generally not appreciative enough of the nuances of Cold War policy. Bill Clinton seemed to Europeans preoccupied with economic issues and very slow in engaging in the Balkan conflicts in which many European nations and Canada had UN peacekeepers on the ground. Even George H. W. Bush, whose foreign policy credentials were never in doubt in Europe, was accused of taking too long a pause to find out if genuine political change was taking place in the Soviet Union.

While foreign policy did not dominate his early agenda, the international community soon found out that George W. Bush's foreign policy was not isolationist. The group of foreign policy advisors, called the "Vulcans" and led by Condoleezza Rice, helped Bush form a new type of conservative American internationalism. This group included neoconservatives such as Wolfowitz and Perle, but was not dominated by them. It also contained "traditional conservatives" such as Robert Zoellick and Stephen Hadley who, like Bush's father, were inclined to building international coalitions based on pragmatic compromises. Finally, there were also more "nationalist conservatives" such as Cheney and Donald Rumsfeld, whose prime interest was the advancement of American national interest by using power.[7] Rice herself was more a classic realist and a traditional conservative when she joined the Bush election campaign as his chief tutor and advisor.

While the Vulcans helped Bush form his worldview before he took office, Bush would compose his own blend early and more so than foreign capitals initially realized. Bush's early views were neither isolationist nor imperialist, but harbored an optimistic sense of the amount of room and power the United States possessed in redefining the international agenda. Just as Margaret Thatcher wanted to benefit from the European Union and was neither emotionally nor politically anti-European, so Bush was neither anti-United

Nations nor anti-multilateral. But his new conservative Americanism had an abrasive streak: international agendas and organizational status quos should never be imposed upon American policy. Bush blocked various multilateral conventions such as the Kyoto Protocol and the International Criminal Court, spearheaded by Canadians and Western Europeans. Bush did not want the freedom of American foreign policy curtailed and, at the same time, America's responsibilities increased as a result of other countries' agendas.

Bush wanted to review his options in the Israeli-Palestinian crisis, on the Korean Peninsula, and in the arms control and proliferation arena. As it happened, Bush was ready to say what he did not want months before his team came up with alternatives. This led to the near-global perspective of Bush as having a "Just-say-no" foreign policy.[8] Even sympathetic analysts such as Michael Mazarr argued that Bush was not idealist enough in that he failed to propose better alternatives to such problems as war criminals and nonrenewable energy sources.[9]

It is at this point in mid-2001 that Europe and Canada collided head-on with America. At this juncture the personal and political dislike of the Bush administration morphed into various policy clashes. The disagreement was made even worse by what allies felt was "supercilious treatment."[10] Indeed, brusque diplomacy did not help matters, as when Rumsfeld told his interlocutors in NATO that missile defense would happen whether they liked it or not. John Bolton, in charge of arms control issues at the Department of State, became the new "Prince of Darkness" for Europeans (as Perle had been in the 1980s) as he tore into the consensus on arms control. Bolton stopped any progress on the Biological Weapons Convention and wanted Bush to withdraw from the Comprehensive Nuclear Test Ban Treaty. Bush had already made it clear that the Anti-Ballistic Missile Treaty would have to be revamped or scrapped. All the sacred cows of international arms control were on the block.

There is one more factor that played a role in how Bush's foreign policy prior to September 11 colored the view of allies, friends, and skeptics. It is the factor of political strategy.[11] Bush came to office in early 2001 with a presidential blueprint. First, he would concentrate on several basic values and put his entire domestic and foreign agenda in terms of values. Second, he would work with a mixed group of political and experienced government advisors—Karl Rove and Karen Hughes on the one hand and Andrew Card and Dick Cheney on the other—in a tightly knit, loyalist dynamic. There would be frank and collegial advice on the inside, but no second-guessing or leaks to the outside. Finally, Bush would launch his policies inside a strategic political agenda in which tax cuts and education reform would lead the way. All other policies—including foreign policy—were ranked second or lower. Thus, in the first half of 2001 Bush said and did relatively little in foreign policy. He and his team knew that was their political strategy. However, to many of America's interlocutors worldwide, and especially in Europe, it looked like neglect, arrogance, and ignorance (benevolent or otherwise).[12]

By May 2001, the Bush White House realized it had a public relations crisis with Europe. Bush's two trips to Europe in the summer of 2001 did not produce dialogue or understanding between Washington and its allies. While Bush listened to the fifteen European Union leaders at a special meeting in Göteborg, Sweden, where they expressed their concern about his unwillingness to move the Kyoto Protocol forward, he would not engage them to find a compromise in the framework of that multilateral treaty. However, Bush appeared very willing to invest in a relationship with Russia's Vladimir Putin. There was a sense in Europe that they had fallen off the American radar screen.

If Europe had been part of the American electorate, Rove and his assistants would have crafted a different strategy, though not likely a different agenda. There were belated attempts to influence European public opinion. Senior American officials such as Secretary of State Colin Powell spent a lot of time making the rounds on European TV shows in the fall of 2002 in the run-up to the war in Iraq. However, in terms of winning the hearts and minds of Europeans, it was arguably already too late.

The Rejection of the "War on Terror"

There is absolutely no doubt that the initial shock and pain the American people suffered on 9/11 was shared and felt deeply in Europe and among America's democratic Asian friends. *Le Monde's* editorial headline the next day written by its publisher, "We are all Americans now," was genuine and heartfelt. And so were the European offers of help. NATO invoked its most important collective defense clause, the European Union declared its solidarity, and almost all regional security organizations signaled a willingness to help. Canadian authorities made an extraordinary effort to land hundreds of American flights, ordered to land by the Federal Aviation Administration on September 11. Canadian airport personnel and volunteer groups proceeded to feed and provide shelter to thousands of stranded passengers.

But just below the surface there was a lot of trepidation about what American actions would follow. There was the immediate worry—given the perception of Bush's leadership style and strong-minded agenda—that he would overreact, further erode the traditional multilateral European agenda, and engage in more "unnerving" unilateralism. The French and Dutch Prime Ministers called respectively for a "reasonable" and "dignified" reaction from the United States.[13] These statements betrayed a sense of ignorance of the trauma the American people had just suffered. Another European Union declaration followed that called for the American reaction to be "proportional."[14]

In his Oval Office address on September 11, Bush made it clear that he would treat the attacks as an act of war rather than a terrorist incident. The Germans and the French did not think the attacks were cause for "a war."[15] French President Jacques Chirac during his visit to Ground Zero made it clear that "war" was not the right response. German Chancellor Gerhard Schroeder and Canadian Prime Minister Chrétien made similar points. Even though more than 20 Canadians perished in the attack on the Twin Towers, the Canadian Prime Minister did not visit the site for months, most likely for fear that his visit might look like an endorsement of Bush's war-like response. In return, Bush did not bother to thank the Canadians for helping the stranded passengers on that fateful day in his famous September 20 address to Congress, even though he did cite many other countries for their help and support, in particular Tony Blair, who was present for the occasion.

In the days and weeks after the attacks, Bush would lay out a series of concepts that deepened and widened the gulf between him and many of the leaders in Europe and Canada. But just as significant was the division that was beginning to show among Bush's earlier critics. The reaction to Bush's foreign policy before 9/11 was largely monolithic with the exception of Tony Blair, who had come to Camp David in February 2001 to invest in a close personal relationship with Bush and who conveyed his disagreements in strict confidentiality. But after the attacks, Blair in Britain, Jose Maria Aznar in Spain, and Italy's Silvio Berlusconi began to distance themselves from the emerging critical Franco-German bloc led by Chirac and Schroeder. However, despite the leader's positions, public opinion in these "friendly" states was much closer to the German and French government positions than to their own.

Bush declared war on both terrorists and their sponsors. Moreover, he declared the terrorists "evil," thereby removing any objective short of total victory. Just as Europeans had recoiled against Reagan calling the Soviet Union the "Evil Empire," they now shook their heads when they heard Bush calling Osama bin Laden the "Evildoer." They felt it would lead to simplistic policies. Some Europeans also reacted strongly to Bush's line in his September 20, 2001 Address to Congress: "Every nation now has a decision to make. Either you are with us, or you are with the terrorists." Bush was not pointing so much at traditional allies as he was at ambivalent allies such as Pakistan and Saudi Arabia. But what the Europeans heard was a new form of American bullying. The Canadian historian Robert Bothwell put it this way: "Instead of consensual alliances, there will be the U.S. and a coalition of the bribed and the bullied, and the sullen acquiescent, which will be us."[16] He turned out wrong on the acquiescence part, but nevertheless spoke for a strong majority of Canadians.

As Operation Enduring Freedom in Afghanistan was winding down in late 2001, another disconnect occurred. Most European allies thought that the war on terror had now run its military course and that it would simply continue along the lines of international cooperation in intelligence, financial, and covert operations. While most of Europe had not participated in the removal of the Taliban regime, France, Germany, and Canada now came to help the

British to conduct stability operations. The European allies stepped forward with humanitarian and military aid, and on December 20, 2001, the UN Security Council authorized the International Security Assistance Force for Kabul. The first 1,500 British troops arrived 10 days later. In 2003, NATO took over the command and control of these operations under the ultimate authority of U.S. forces still involved in combat operations in the south and east. Europe and Canada took up the challenge of trying to stabilize and rebuilt the fractious and war-ravaged country. This was a "nation-building" exercise that fit their view of overcoming the long-term threat of terror.

Rather than casting the conflict in classical liberal terms of good versus evil, and a war on terror, many of America's allies tried to redefine the debate in terms of the modern liberal value scheme, which emphasized solutions and remedies rather than guilt and blame. Europeans were ready to address the so-called root causes of terrorism, including poverty, the drug trade, American-Israeli policy on the Palestinian question, and various other causes. The root-causes-versus-war-on-terror worldviews became the fundamental philosophical divide between America and Europe. In many publications and discussions in Europe, one could hear the refrain summed up in *Le Monde Diplomatique*, "It's too bad for the Americans but they had it coming."[17] The Americans, on the other hand, were allergic to the words "root causes." They quite accurately heard in it a European-Canadian argument that American policies were to blame for the attacks of September 11.

Bush saw Afghanistan as only the first phase in the war against terrorism. In his Oval Office address on September 11, Bush had said, "We will make no distinction between the terrorists who committed these acts and those who harbor them." Thus was born the first connection in the new nexus threat between the al-Qaeda network and host or potential host countries. The terrorist threat level continued in the United States in the fall of 2001 spurred on by a series of deadly but unsolved anthrax attacks and several intelligence reports that al-Qaeda was trying to make and detonate a dirty nuclear bomb in the United States. American soldiers found concrete evidence in Afghanistan that such designs for destruction were under way.

The Bush administration connected the three threats (al-Qaeda, rogue sponsor states, and WMDs) and began to argue that the conventional definition of national security needed to be revamped. Rather than containment or deterrence, a proactive stand was needed. Because this was war and not a crime scene, the bar of evidence would be lowered. The administration spoke about "connecting the dots" and not letting "the smoking gun become a mushroom cloud."[18] In his State of the Union Address in early 2002, Bush connected dots that astonished many allies. He put Iraq, Iran, and North Korea into an "Axis of Evil," where the new nexus threat argument would be put to the test.

The Rejection of the Bush Doctrine in Its First Case of Iraq

Following the 2002 State of the Union Address, Bush made a series of speeches that turned his foreign policy in a more ambitious and proactive direction. Bush grouped the threat of the Axis of Evil, the threat of WMDs, and the threat of al-Qaeda attacks into one overarching global threat, requiring a large policy shift comparable to the containment doctrine developed in the early 1950s. Inside the administration, the build-up to the war with Iraq began as early as February 2002, when regime change became the goal. Colin Powell was not in principle against regime change, but remained skeptical about a military operation as the best means. Just after the 9/11 attacks, Powell had warned the President not to confront Iraq, fearing that "our allies will see it as bait and switch."[19] However, given the new threat nexus, Powell's "smart sanctions" approach to Iraq, begun before September 11, seemed no longer adequate.

While Bush tried to describe the new kinds of threats and the actions he was pursuing to eliminate them, most foreign academics and newspapers chose to see new designs of American hegemony. Iraq was immediately associated with oil, and many foreign observers took it as a given truth that the "real" reason for Bush's concern about Iraq was to secure Iraqi oil and eliminate Russian and French competition. Bush never mentioned the oil factor, which was interpreted as a sure sign that this was the real motive. Bush's Texas oil roots and Cheney's stint as CEO of Halliburton were offered as enough proof of the real agenda.

By the time the National Security Strategy (NSS) was released (late September 2002), Bush had already challenged the United Nations to confront the specific threat of Iraq as the lead candidate in the threat nexus. As a result of Bush putting Iraq in the forefront, the context and nuance of the strategy document was lost in the uproar over the explicit mention of preemptive military action. Powell later explained that preemptive war was not really a "strategy," but only "an option" or one tool in a toolbox of diplomatic, intelligence, development, and robust counter-proliferation options.[20]

The international press reaction to Bush's National Security Strategy was generally negative, with one French daily calling Bush's new policy a "first-strike doctrine." Some believed the strategy was simply a new version of the alleged 1992 Wolfowitz plan to dominate the world. The *Hong Kong Economic Times* editorialized that the new Doctrine was "the written presentation of Bush's 'cowboy' foreign policy." The more positive responses had some papers, such as the German *Frankfurter Allgemeine,* calling on European leaders to engage the Americans for the purpose of moderating American policy. Though China is not an Asian democracy, its reaction was quite negative, given the fact that Beijing had shown interest in cooperating with Bush against Islamic terrorists that also posed a threat in some Chinese regions. Beijing accused Bush of wanting to "consolidate a unipolar world."[21]

There was little time to debate the merits of the new strategy on its own terms, as the United Nations was preoccupied with Security Council Resolution 1441. The unanimous support for this resolution soon proved to be built on clay. For those seeking to moderate American policy—France, Germany, Russia, and Canada—the resolution was a firm exercise in coercive diplomacy but not a license to wage war. The combination of serious threats, backed by American military deployments to the region *and* effective inspections, was believed to remove whatever remaining WMD threat there was in Iraq. The idea of forceful regime change was not something these four countries could stomach. "If you start changing regimes," Canadian Prime Minister Chrétien was quoted as saying in the *National Post*, "where do you stop?"[22]

The bitter controversy over whether the inspections were working and whether a second UN resolution was needed before military force would be legal divided NATO and European allies. Bush was blamed for the bitter split within the European Union. Rumsfeld's comment that Europe was now divided between the old and the new (in which the new states from Eastern Europe cooperated better with the United States) caused enormous resentment. European analysts felt that Bush was cherry-picking allies.

The European Union's President, Romano Prodi, accused Bush of a "divide and conquer" strategy.[23] The American government was just as upset with France and Germany. Chancellor Schroeder had run an election in September 2002 on soft anti-Americanism and hardcore pacifism. Schroeder had said that Germany would oppose war even if the United Nations called for it. Germany, France, and Belgium blocked NATO preparations to defend Turkey. The active policy of trying to defeat or limit American action in NATO caused a serious rupture in that partnership not seen since Reagan insisted on modernizing nuclear missiles in the early 1980s.

To the consternation of some of its NATO allies, America was prepared to go to war with Iraq without another UN resolution or even without consensus in the alliance. In 2003, various public opinion surveys showed that popular discontent with Bush, his policies and with the United States in general had reached dramatic proportions (see also Foyle, Chapter 3). Between 1999 and 2003, the American image "plummeted in Europe," from favorable ratings in 1999 in Britain, France, Germany, and Italy of, respectively, 83%, 62%, 78%, and 76% to all-time lows of 48%, 31%, 25%, and 34%.[24] Thus, only one-quarter of Germans and barely one-third of Italians had a positive perception of the United States. These perceptions would linger for a long time, in part as a result of the continuing uncertainty in Iraq.

Even among war allies such as Japan and Australia, "negative views of U.S. influence" were still high in 2004 with Australia, Indonesia, South Korea, and Japan rating, respectively, 52%, 51%, 45%, and 31%.[25] The Marshall Fund's annual survey of transatlantic attitudes found that in 2005, 59% of Europeans "felt that American global leadership was undesirable." The average disapproval rate of Bush's policies among the ten largest European states was 72%, with France, Germany, and Spain leading the charts with ratings in the 80s. Even traditional allies such as Britain, the Netherlands, and Portugal had disapproval rates in the low 60s.[26]

Though vicious critics such as the British poet and playwright Harold Pinter had called the United States the "most dangerous power the world has ever known" even before September 11, the idea of America as the biggest threat to world peace began to seep into European minds.[27] In many countries Bush ranked only slightly below Osama bin Laden in terms of who people believed was the greatest threat in their lives. In neighboring Canada, a July 2003 poll showed that 53% of Canadians held an unfavorable view of Bush.[28] With such powerful public attitudes, it would be very difficult for politicians in Europe (even if they wanted to do so) to restore some level of normal relations with the Bush administration after the United States, Britain, and a few smaller allies toppled the regime of Saddam Hussein in April 2003.

The Rejection of Bush's Grand Strategy for Freedom and Democracy

As early as 2002, Bush's so-called Middle East Partnership Initiative had begun to act upon the soft power aspects of the 2002 NSS. The plan was to fund teacher education programs, strengthen a free media sector, set up regional banks to provide loans for small businessmen, and help local nongovernmental organizations educate the publics on how to organize elections.

At the National Endowment for Democracy in 2003, and again in his Whitehall Palace address in Britain, Bush cast his push against al-Qaeda and rogue sponsors into an ever-wider context. Not only would the United States eliminate the threat nexus, but in its place it would help plant free societies and free markets. From the early days after 9/11, Bush had been adamant about not casting his new war on terror in terms of political scientist Samuel Huntington's darkest scenario of a "clash of civilizations." Bush made it clear that Islam was not the belligerent, but that political radicals with totalitarian objectives had hijacked the Islamic religion for the narrow purposes of gaining state control. From 2003 onward, Bush framed his new policy less in negative terms of dealing with threats, and more in positive terms of creating freedom in the arc of instability that spans from Morocco to Pakistan.

In the Greater Middle East Initiative of 2003, Bush wanted to set aside some $1 billion for civil society, democracy, and economic development projects. The plan was to get the other G-7 partners to add another billion dollars. Egypt and Saudi Arabia reacted negatively to the idea of fermenting democracy inside their own borders. Even though Bush's soft power resembled European and Canadian policies of development and human security, the negative reaction in these big states clipped European enthusiasm. The G-7 scaled the plans down into what is now called the Forum for the Future project. After Bush's election victory in 2004, freedom in the Middle East became the central plank of his second-term foreign policy. By 2005, the administration spent nearly $300 million on civil-society building projects, some with governments, and others with the help of the private sector or nongovernmental organizations.

Bush's attempts to explain his war on terror and his preemptive actions in Iraq as part of a new grand sweep of American policy to bring freedom to the Middle East fell on very skeptical ears abroad. Most Europeans believed it was a cover, if not an attention diversion plot, from the embarrassment of not finding WMDs in Iraq. Bush's expansion of his theme in 2004 and 2005 alarmed most Europeans. If indeed Bush sought to reform the entire region, they feared he would set the Arab world and Islam at war with the West. The conflict that could follow not only risked Europe's own security, given its proximity to the Middle East, but also endangered Europe's domestic stability as it has large, unassimilated Moroccan, Algerian, and Turkish minorities. The bombing attacks in Madrid and London, and the riots in Paris's suburbs, generally deepened this negative perception about stirring up change in the Middle East. Europeans also feared that a civil war in the Arab Middle East along sectarian or ethnic lines would disrupt the oil flow to Europe. They did not share Bush's rabid idealism, and were trying to steer American policy toward a more realist course.

Bush became more explicit in 2004 that his mission was to help the Middle East join the zone of freedom and prosperity, just as Reagan had helped to liberate Russia and Eastern Europe from Communism. Just as surely, most European intellectuals and government officials were convinced that America had once again embarked on one of its unique bouts of missionary zeal in which it would inevitably overreach and be forced into a hasty and embarrassing withdrawal. Their historical analogy was the fight the United States picked with monolithic Communism in the 1950s. As a result, the argument went, the United States got bogged down in a prolonged struggle of Vietnamese national unification, which it could not win. Bush's appeal to make the Middle East safe for democracy reopened an old debate in Europe about the role of American foreign policy.

The Abroad—many of whom consider themselves pragmatic realists— understands but rarely approves when the United States acts out of sheer national interest, as it did in the invasion of Panama in 1989 to secure a stable government for the management of the Panama Canal. American realism is respected but not liked. Instead, the Abroad, especially Western Europe and Canada, has been trying since the end of the Reagan era to get the United States to join its modern dream of liberal multilateralism.

What this Abroad detests is classical American liberalism with its emphasis on unalienable rights, rigid individualism, freedom, a pivotal role for private property, and representative and accountable government. They resent the policy choices that these ideals have produced in American foreign policy, including strong national policies (unilateralism), the use of force, and a tenacious belief that these classical values can change the world. These states prefer the objectives of (post)modern liberalism, which emphasizes multilateral governance, sustainable development, social justice, and stakeholder diplomacy.

America's closest allies have tried to bring the United States into harmony with the values and policy goals of what is also called globalism. George H.W. Bush was at heart an international pragmatist, and often agreed with the allies (though not because he bought into the new ideology). Clinton's third way Democratic foreign policy was very close to the European agenda, although he was generally more interested in enlarging the zone of economic freedom than political freedom. Al Gore and John Kerry's foreign policy positions followed Clinton's basic positions but were even more favorably inclined toward a multilateral process and a globalist agenda.

George W. Bush put America back into its classical liberal fold. Jonathan Monten identifies two variations inside this school of thought: a cautious and more self-centered type which he calls "exemplarism" and a more activist type called "vindicationism."[29] The first type—practiced by Bush prior to the attacks of September 11—corresponds to what Walter Russell Mead has called the Jeffersonian school in American foreign policy.[30] As Walter McDougall explains, this school was dominant in American history until the 1890 war with Spain.[31] In the exemplarist case, the United States shows its unique example and role model to the world by not getting involved with the rivalries of the Old World. Pat Buchanan's *Where the Right Went Wrong* is a recent call for a return to such exemplarism.[32] The vindicationists, however, believe that it is not enough to be passive. Rather, American policy should pursue the whole array of instruments, even force when needed, to promote the ideals of liberty.

More often than not, the exemplarists reign in quiet times, until the vindicationists are aroused by an external threat such as Pearl Harbor or the Soviet quest to dominate the Eurasian landmass. Rather than setting limited goals in response to these threats, the American republic has a tendency not to define its response merely in terms of redressing grievances or gaining back territory or some other specific national interest. Instead, the American character interprets the threat as a challenge to its fundamental freedoms and responds by making the world safe for democracy or by liberating Europeans and Asians from a Communist stranglehold. Extending the sphere of freedom becomes a necessary ingredient of the response.

Bush's foreign policy began as an exemplarist exercise that challenged the modern liberal multilateral order the Abroad had been trying to organize since the early 1990s. Bush's values were classical liberal before and after 9/11. Before the terrorist threat was recognized, Bush's values generally led him to decline participation in various multilateral schemes. John van Oudenaren has called this a type of unilateralism by "omission."[33] Bush felt that most recent multilateral schemes simply did not work for America's classical liberal goals.

After the attacks, the same values caused him to make American foreign policy more assertive and proactive, in an attempt to push back the threat to American liberal democracy from the potential nexus of a new Islamist radical totalitarian ideology aided by friendly rogue states and in search of powerful weapons that pose a clear and present danger to the American public. Again, Bush found not much help in the multilateralist devices set up by European democracies. Instead of relying on that structure, Bush relied on ad hoc coalitions of the willing.

Seen from the vindicationist or crusader context, the Bush Doctrine is much bigger than a single military strategy or foreign policy option. It is essentially the latest articulation of classical American liberalism under attack by a new threat. It "represents the perfect vindicationist storm."[34] It redefines American foreign policy away from narrow realist goals of seeking political stability in the Middle East and a secure source of oil, to the more ambitious goal of liberal economic and political reform. Freedom to Bush is not a form of cultural imperialism, but that is exactly what most academics and opinion leaders in Europe think of American attempts to spread freedom. Like Reagan, Bush believes that the very idea of people preferring dictatorship to democracy is a type of cultural condescension.[35] This is the American version of root causes, though few people in Europe see it that way.

The First Cracks in the Rejection of the Bush Doctrine

The first change in the Abroad's approach to the Bush Doctrine came as a result of two factors. First, the toll in lives and resources in the operation in Iraq put a much greater strain on American foreign policy than the Bush administration had counted on. If there was an abstract strategy of preemptive war, there would be no second fronts, as the American military was stretching its manpower to the limit in Iraq. Alongside this heavy demand on resources, the cost of the Iraqi operations—well over $150 billion per year—became a political brake on preemption. Of course the heavy loss of life dramatically shown on daily newscasts would seriously constrain any future course of action against another belligerent state. Richard Perle's quip that American foreign policy after 9/11 was "You are next" had suddenly lost its meaning.[36] Europeans and others would not call the Axis of Evil strategy bankrupt, but it was clear that there was no appetite left in Washington to pick another fight. Bush's very multilateral and cautious maneuvering with North Korea underscored the point. Secondly, it became increasingly clear for Europe and other allies that American success in Iraq was as much a necessity for them as for Bush. Although this realization only led to moderate financial aid and military aid in the form of NATO-led training of Iraqi police and military forces, it did dampen the criticism in Europe and Canada.

While Europe felt somewhat assured that the United States would not embark on another preemptive attack soon, it began to examine its own strategic posture. The European Union in 2003 devised a strategy document as a response to Bush's NSS document of 2002. Javier Solana, the EU's High Representative for its Common Foreign and Security Policy, presided over the drafting. Surprisingly, Solana's first draft actually mirrored the American threat assessment. It held that international terror, weapons of mass destruction, and failing states posed a unique mix of threats to Europe. The paper called on the Union to develop more economic, diplomatic, and security tools. Solana's first draft also included a more robust military option that would give Europe the military capacity to do combat operations as it was helping a failing state or fighting a terrorist threat.

At the December 2003 European Council meeting, Solana's paper was watered down and the military toolbox scaled back to a more traditional peacekeeping option.[37] Nevertheless, European and American strategic perspectives were beginning to show some common ground. At the same time, Europeans approved in greater numbers of the idea of "democracy promotion," while Americans—due in part to the Iraq stalemate—showed more caution. The Marshall Fund survey found that in 2005, 74% of Europeans agreed that it was the EU's role to "help establish democracy in other countries," while only 51% of Americans agreed.[38] The key issue that divided Americans and Europeans was *how* one establishes democracy abroad. On this point, the Bush administration and European governments continue to disagree.

For Europe, the remedy remains the softer underbelly of terrorism: poverty, human insecurity, drugs, lack of effective development aid, and failing states. For America, the fight is against "a self-appointed vanguard" of the new ideology of "Islamo-fascism," and their "enablers," including state supporters of terrorism such as Syria and Iran.[39] The American fight is top-down, the European fight is bottom-up. The Americans fight back with hard power and ideology (freedom); the Europeans fight with practical aid and post-conflict stabilization.

Critics have said that the war in Iraq undermined cooperation in the war on terror. While the debate about Iraq and freedom in the Middle East continued, the actual cooperation between the United States and the Abroad, including France and Germany, in intelligence, financial measures, and covert operations increased. It even weathered the storms of controversy over American treatment of prisoners at Guantanamo Bay and CIA activities in Europe.

Another crack in the hardline opposition to Bush's approach in the Middle East became visible when the push for freedom showed some results in the region. First of all, Libya abruptly shifted course and declared itself open to inspection for WMDs and interested in normalizing relations with the West. This happened in the wake of a successful operation in which Germany, Britain, and the United States intercepted a ship bound for Libya with contraband materials. Saudi Arabia and Egypt responded to Bush's frequent calls for freedom by allowing a little bit more electoral competition. One Egyptian newspaper carried the headline, "Egypt Begins a New Era on the Path to Freedom."[40] The suspected Syrian involvement in the bombing of a former Prime Minister in Lebanon led to strong Franco-American action that allowed a United Nations team limited access to Syria for a fact-finding mission. Syria's eventual withdrawal from Lebanon removed a huge restraint on that country's democratic development. The German magazine *Der Spiegel* published a provocative article in early 2005 titled, "Could George W. Bush Be Right?"[41]

The final stream of convergence between the Abroad and Bush was evidenced in the case of Iran. As early as 2003, Britain, France, and Germany embarked on a preventive diplomatic course by direct shuttle diplomacy with Tehran, without at first involving the Americans. Despite nearly three years of promises as well as veiled threats by the three European powers, it appears that the regime in Iran is bent on enriching uranium on its own terms without international supervision to assure it is not building nuclear weapons. Just as the commentators had exhausted their arguments why preemptive war was against international law or against the interests of the West, it appeared that preemptive war might be the only option left to deal with Iran. As Paul Schroeder pointed out, "Preventive wars, even risky preventive wars, are not the extreme anomalies of politics, the sign of the bankruptcy of policy, they are a normal even common tool of statecraft."[42]

In a futuristic piece written in early 2006, Niall Ferguson speculates that the West may soon be sorry that it did not decide to use a preemptive attack on Iran's nuclear facilities. Several of the threat conditions for a preemptive strike are in place, including the fanatical new Iranian president Mahmoud Ahmadinejad, Iran's extensive support of terrorist activities, and a hidden nuclear program. As a bonus, U.S. military capabilities are in the region. However, the experience in Iraq, the controversy with Europe whose publics remain opposed to the idea of a preemptive attack, the power Iran would wield over oil prices in the aftermath, and the lack of leadership in Israel after Ariel Sharon's illness, appear to give Bush pause. Ferguson closes his speculative piece with the following paragraph:

> Yet the historian is bound to ask whether or not the true significance of the 2007-2011 war was to vindicate the Bush administration's original principle of pre-emption. For, if that principle had been adhered to in 2006, Iran's nuclear bid might have been thwarted at minimal cost.[43]

Conclusion

The controversy between the Bush administration and many of its friends and allies in Europe and Asia over whether to invade Iraq and how to stabilize the new democratic state afterward was not the first instance of European discontent over the direction and aim of American foreign policy under George W.

Bush. As argued in this chapter, the controversy started before Iraq and even before September 11, 2001. It started with Bush, with who he was and what he stood for.

After the attacks of September 11, 2001, Bush led the United States and Europe into another chapter of the age-old saga between American boldness and European caution. This time, however, there was a bigger gap between the two than when Reagan challenged Europe to help overcome Communism and the Soviet domination of Eastern and Central Europe. First, the United States had even more absolute and relative power vis-à-vis Europe in 2002 than in 1981. Second, after the end of the Cold War, Europe invested in a new multilateral global agenda that deemphasized military force. Bush upset this Europe more than Reagan, for he challenged not only Europe's propensity for maintaining the status quo but also its new ideology. Some European states moved closer to Bush, and in so doing weakened the coherence of the European Union. This helps explain why resentment to Bush's policies goes deeper in "old" Europe than in the newly emerging democracies in Eastern Europe or the democracies in Asia who did not invest in this ideology to the same extent. Third, by 1986, Reagan was willing to deal and compromise. Likely, Bush cannot show this flexibility until victory in Iraq is certain.

Yet, both sides feel political and practical pressures to close the gap. The European Union's Institute for Security Studies based in Paris and invariably critical of Bush's foreign policy issued a surprising new study in early 2006 entitled *Friends Again? EU-US Relations after the Crisis.*[44] There is pressure in the theatre of operation. European and Canadian operations in the south of Afghanistan are beginning to face the same challenge as American operations in Iraq. American and European cooperation was crucial in concluding a cease-fire in the aftermath of Hezbollah's attack on Israel in the summer of 2006. It will also be needed to reduce Hezbollah's influence in the south of Lebanon. Both transatlantic partners require military power and nation-building tools. To do both, America and Europe need to work more closely together. To do that, European states need to feel that American action is legitimate. Given the depth of rejection of nearly all Bush stands for and has done, such legitimacy is going to emerge slowly.

The real clash between Bush and the Abroad has been a clash of worldviews in which Iraq became the epicenter. The key issue was not only whether preventive or preemptive war is legal or wise, but whether democratic reforms could be introduced by means of military force, and whether an entire region and religion can be spurred into political reforms with a mixture of military pressure and economic and political carrots. In his 2006 NSS, Bush stated that democracy-building would be the main goal of American foreign policy, but clarified that while his approach and goals would be "idealistic," the means used to achieve these would be "realistic."[45] The Abroad remains overwhelmingly skeptical about the idealistic goal of democracy-building. Bush ardently believes it and remains committed to it. While Bush and the Abroad may converge on what realistic or practical means to use in areas such as Afghanistan and Iraq, it is likely that the entrenched rejection of Bush and his Doctrine will continue for years even after Bush's departure and even if real change begins to show in the Middle East.

Endnotes

1. Bruce Klinger, "Asia Wary of New Bush Doctrine," *Asia Times*, January 26, 2005.
2. Seven articles by Lois Romano and George Lardner, Jr. for the *Washington Post* in July 1999: "Bush's Life Changing Year (July 25), "A Texas Childhood" (July 26), "Following His Father's Path" (July 27), "At Height of Vietnam, Graduate Picks Guard" (July 28), "A Run for the House; Courting a Wife, Then the Voters" (July 29), "Life of George W. Bush: The Turning Point; After Coming Up Dry" (July 30), "Moving up the Major Leagues" (July 31). A nine-part series by Nicholas D. Kristof for the *New York Times* in 2000: "A Philosophy With Roots in Conservative Texas Soil" (May 21), "Earning A's in People Skills at Andover" (June 10), "Bush's Choice in War: Devoid of Passion or Anxiety" (July 11), "Learning How to Run: A West Texas Stumble" (July 27), "How Bush Came to Tame His Inner Scamp" (July 29), "A Father's Footsteps *Echo* Throughout a Son's Career" (September 11), "Road to Politics Ran Through a Texas Ballpark" (September 24), "A Master of Bipartisanship With No Taste for Details" (October 16), "For Bush, His Toughest Call Was the Choice to Run at All" (October 29).
3. Molly Ivins and Lou Dubose, *Shrub: The Short but Happy Political Life of George W. Bush* (New York: Random House, 2000); Paul Begala, *Is Our Children Learning?: The Case Against George W. Bush* (New York: Simon & Schuster, 2000); James H. Hatfield, *Fortunate Son: George W. Bush and the Making of an American President* (Brooklyn, New York: Soft Skull Press, 2002); Mark Crispin Miller, *The Bush Dyslexicon: Observations of a National Disorder* (New York: Norton, 2001).
4. Michael Meacher, "This War on Terrorism Is Bogus," *Guardian*, September 6, 2003.
5. Seymour Hersh, "The Iraq Hawks," *New Yorker* (December 24 & 31, 2001); Bill Keller, "The Sunshine Warrior," *New York Times Magazine*, September 22, 2002.
6. Michael Moore, *Stupid White Men* (New York: Regan Books, 2001).
7. These labels are used effectively by Sebastian Reyn, *Allies or Aliens: George W. Bush and the Transatlantic Crisis in Historical Perspective* (The Hague: Netherlands Atlantic Association, 2004), 138-144.
8. Ivo H. Daalder and James M. Lindsay, *America Unbound: The Bush Revolution in Foreign Policy* (Washington, DC: Brookings Institution Press, 2003), 66.
9. Michael J. Mazarr, "George W. Bush, Idealist," *International Affairs* 79 (2003): 521.
10. Reyn, *Allies or Aliens*, 143.
11. Alexander Moens, *The Foreign Policy of George W. Bush: Values, Strategy, and Loyalty* (Aldershot, Hampshire: Ashgate, 2004), Introduction.
12. Roger Cohen, "Arrogant or Humble? Bush Encounters European Hostility," *New York Times*, May 8, 2001.
13. John Vinocur, "EU Solidarity Declaration Gives Both Sides a Victory," *International Herald Tribune*, September 24, 2001.

14. *Keesing's Worldwide News Digest*, September 2001, 44335, 44336.
15. U.S. Department of State, "The United States and the Global Coalition Against Terrorism, September 2001–December 2003," Office of the Historian, June 2004, www.state.gov/r/pa/ho/pubs/fs/5889.htm.
16. As quoted in John Gibson, *Hating America* (New York: Regan Books, 2004), 227.
17. As quoted in Gibson, 22.
18. As quoted in Jeffrey Record, "The Bush Doctrine and War with Iraq," *Parameters* (Spring 2003): 4-21.
19. Bob Woodward, *Bush at War* (New York: Simon & Schuster), 2002, 87.
20. In interview with James Kitfield, "We Act with Patience and Deliberation," *National Journal* (February 1, 2003): 373.
21. Quotes in this paragraph are from Global Security Organization, "'Bush Doctrine' Viewed as Fundamental Policy Shift," September 23, 2002, http://www.globalsecurity.org/military/library/news/2002/09/mil-020923-wwwh2923.htm.
22. Stephen Thorne, "No Need for Iraq War," *Canadian Press*, February 13, 2003, http://www.cp.org/english/online/full/media/030309/X030918AU.html.
23. Reyn, *Allies or Aliens*, 194.
24. "Pew Global Attitudes Project," as quoted in Barry Rubin and Judith Colp Rubin, *Hating America: A History* (New York: Oxford University Press, 2004), 188.
25. Klinger, "Asia Wary of New Bush Doctrine."
26. German Marshall Fund (hereafter, GMF), "Transatlantic Trends: Key Findings 2005," 5-6, http://www.transatlantictrends.org.
27. As quoted in Gibson, *Hating America*, 102.
28. Rubin and Rubin, *Hating America*, 215.
29. Jonathan Monten, "The Roots of the Bush Doctrine: Power, Nationalism, and Democracy Promotion in U.S. Strategy," *International Security* 29 (Spring 2005): 113.
30. Walter Russell Mead, *Special Providence: American Foreign Policy and How It Changed the World* (New York: Routledge, 2002).
31. Walter McDougall, *Promised Land, Crusader State: The American Encounter with the World Since 1776*, reprint ed. (New York: Mariner Books, 1998).
32. Patrick J. Buchanan, *Where the Right Went Wrong: How Neoconservatives Subverted the Reagan Revolution and Hijacked the Bush Presidency* (New York: Thomas Dunne Books, 2004).
33. John Van Oudenaren, "Transatlantic Bipolarity and the End of Multilateralism," *Political Science Quarterly* 120 (2005), 24.
34. Monten, "The Roots of the Bush Doctrine," 140.
35. Peggy Noonan, *When Character Was King: A Story of Ronald Reagan* (New York: Viking, 2001), 206.
36. Perle's full sentence is: "We could deliver a short message, a two-word message: You're next. You're next unless you stop the practice of supporting terrorism." Richard Perle, "Next Stop: Iraq," remarks at the Foreign Policy Research Institute Annual Dinner, Philadelphia, November 14, 2001, http://www.fpri.org/transcripts/annualdinner.20011114.perle.nextstopiraq.html.

37. Council of the European Union, European Security Strategy, "A Secure Europe in a Better World," December 12, 2003, http://ue.eu.int/uedocs/cmsUpload/78367.pdf.

38. GMF, "Transatlantic Trends," 11.

39. George W. Bush, "President Discusses War on Terror at National Endowment for Democracy," October 6, 2005, http://www.whitehouse.gov/news/releases/2005/10/20051006-3.html.

40. As quoted in Issandr El Amrani, "Mubarak to Allow First Direct Elections," *The Times* [UK], February 28, 2005, 7.

41. Claus Christian Malzahn, "Could George W. Bush Be Right?" Der Spiegel Online, February 23, 2005, http://www.spiegel.de/international/0,1518,343378,00.html.

42. As quoted in Robert Jervis, *American Foreign Policy in a New Era* (New York: Routledge, 2005), 84-85.

43. Niall Ferguson, "The Origins of the Great War of 2007—and How It Could Have Been Prevented," *The Daily Telegraph*, January 15, 2006.

44. Marcin Zaborowski, ed., *Friends Again? EU-US Relations After the Crisis* (Paris: Institute for Security Studies, 2006).

45. The National Security Strategy of the United States, Introduction, March 16, 2006.

11

Anti-Americanism

Seeing Ourselves in the Mirror of the United States

JANICE GROSS STEIN

Introduction

The proclamation of the Bush Doctrine and the unilateral exercise of force by the United States seem to have unleashed viral anti-Americanism worldwide. Yet anti-Americanism is more difficult to isolate and culture than this popular explanation would suggest.[1] What does it mean to be anti-American? Clearly, to be critical of the United States, its leaders, its policies, its economy, its society, or its culture is not sufficient to capture the taken-for-granted meaning of anti-Americanism. Most citizens and residents of the United States, at one time or another, are critical of one or more of these dimensions of public life, but this kind of criticism is not usually considered anti-American. The few times it has been have been periods of great stress in the American social and political fabric, where the meaning of citizen loyalty has been narrowed to exclude sustained criticism. These periods historically have been the exception rather than the rule.

Anti-Americanism refers to clusters of negative attitudes about the United States, its leaders, its government, its society, its culture, its norms and practices, from those who live outside the United States and are not Americans. In a cultural as well as physical sense, these are "outside" rather than "inside" judgments. This definitional statement clearly raises far more questions than it answers. How sustained over time and how multidimensional must a cluster be? This definition tells us nothing, moreover, about whether these negative attitudes are appropriate or inappropriate, whether they are connected to empirical referents or largely subjective. It simply describes the valence of an attitude, but is silent about appropriateness or bias and pathology. It is silent because judgments about appropriateness are explicitly political rather than analytical judgments.

Anti-Americanism understood as a set of negative attitudes also tells us very little about salience and nothing about the intensity with which these negative attitudes are held. In short, it tells us nothing of analytical interest about the holder of these attitudes or about why these attitudes are held. And if these attitudes are largely subjective, they may tell us very little that is analytically robust about the United States.

What is missing in the first instance is the "who," the "what," and the "why" of anti-Americanism. We need to understand who holds these anti-American attitudes: Are these negative attitudes individual or collective, or both? Most analyses of anti-Americanism rely heavily on public opinion data that speak largely to individual attitudes. Yet, significant differences in attitudes across peoples and cultures suggest that anti-Americanism is not only an individual attribute but also a collective attribute, at times regional and at times national. At the extreme, as I argue later, deeply embedded clusters of negative attitudes toward the United States may be constitutive of collective identities.

We also need to understand the "what" of anti-Americanism. What do individuals, societies, cultures, nations feel negatively about? In this chapter, I briefly categorize the dimensions of anti-Americanism in an effort to order the arguments.[2] I begin with negative attitudes toward the most visible and personal representation of the United States—President George W. Bush—to explore the personalization of negative attitudes. Personalization of negative affect is common because it allows people to make functional divisions between the current president and the deeper political and social structures of the United States. This kind of division makes affective space for strongly negative attitudes about this particular president, while preserving emotional and cognitive space for positive attitudes toward other dimensions of American life. As we shall see, this functional division characterizes the most recent polling data.

Digging one level deeper, I mine the limited data that are available to explore whether the negative affect is associated with what the United States is doing, with its policies. A spike in negative attitudes toward the United States coincided with the Bush Doctrine and the American use of military force to overthrow the regime of Saddam Hussein in Iraq. Their co-occurrence suggests plausibly that it is American policies that are the focus of dislike and hostility. Of course, disentangling negative attitudes toward Bush from the policies of his administration is logically difficult even when available data are very good. It is impossible given currently available data that limit the ability to make inferences about the importance of one or the other factor. It is possible, however, to identify the clustering of these two attitudes among differing populations.

More deeply embedded than the personality of any president or the policies of any particular administration are the social and cultural systems of the United States. In the wake of Hurricane Katrina, for example, commentary around the world focused on the glaring social gaps within the United States, the terrible poverty of those who were in the stadium waiting for evacuation after the hurricane, and the sharp cleavages along racial and social lines. The visual imagery of the aftermath of Katrina provoked scathing criticism of the social deficits of the United States and of the enduring racism of American society. There are comparable attitudes toward American culture, its mass media, and the films and music that it exports around the world. The golden arches of McDonalds have become the objects of cultural resistance in some parts of the world, understood not only as a threat to local agriculture and commerce but also to deeply embedded customs and habits, to families and to social routines. I mine whatever data are available to look for negative attitudes toward the United States that are not targeted to the personalities of its political leaders or to its policies, but reflect on the social and cultural attributes of American society.

A fourth dimension of anti-Americanism may not be a product of the personality characteristics of its leaders, what the United States does or how it behaves, but rather of what it has. The United States is the world's only superpower, with military capabilities that give it reach around the globe. Debates rage among scholars about whether the United States is not only a superpower but also an imperial power with all the attributes of empire other than the formal control of far-flung territories. When an imperial power flexes its muscles, it generates resentment and hostility in the peripheries. Do those who express negative attitudes toward the United States understand it as empire and focus primarily on its use of its overwhelming economic and military power?

To examine these dimensions of anti-Americanism, I draw heavily on data generated by the Pew surveys of global attitudes, a series of global public opinion surveys done from 2002 to 2005.[3] While these data are helpful, they are not sufficient for a robust analysis of the political psychology of anti-Americanism. They tell us nothing about the intensity of negative feelings and not very much about the interrelatedness of negative attitudes to create a deeply embedded cluster of anti-Americanism. As I have argued, I can make no judgments about bias or pathology, since I have no way of establishing appropriate norms. One useful litmus test is to inquire whether the same kinds of arguments are widely made within the United States. To the extent that they are, it is difficult to conclude that they are pathological and far easier to understand them as deeply contested attitudes about who the United States is or what it is doing.

In this analysis, because of the limits of available data, I can say nothing about the dimension of trust or, indeed, other dimensions of the "why" of anti-Americanism. At the most, I make limited inferences from the explicit content to a menu of factors that may be associated with these negative attitudes. To deepen the analysis, I draw where I can on cultural commentary and editorial opinion to reflect on the larger issues that animate and give texture to these negative attitudes toward the United States.

Finally, I pay particular attention to one subspecies of anti-Americanism that generally does not receive much attention in the scholarly or policy literatures. As one among many perspectives, I look at anti-Americanism as a collective rather than individual phenomenon, as a social construct that refracts through attitudes about the United States a picture of the society that is generating these attitudes. In particular, I argue that countries with weak national identities are especially likely to express negative attitudes toward the United States largely independently of what the U.S. is doing at any given time. Rather, increases in anti-Americanism are more likely to be associated with stresses—economic, political, social—that strain the collective fabric. Under these circumstances, it is especially tempting to externalize an identity conflict, to define a strained society not by what it is, but rather by what it is not—the United States. Here, I understand anti-Americanism as reflection; the United States becomes one of the mirrors in which we reconstruct ourselves. Anti-Americanism is, at least in part and at times, embedded in the politics of identity construction.

The Scope of Anti-Americanism

To put it gently, the United States is not well liked today around the globe. America rode a wave of public sympathy and support after the attacks against Washington and New York on September 11, 2001. Indeed, until before the war against Iraq, pluralities of opinion in most countries that were surveyed were favorable to the United States.[4] Two years later, both friends and adversaries report negative attitudes toward the United States and unhappiness with its policies and practices in global politics. Negative attitudes toward the United States surged after the U.S. war against Iraq and decreased only marginally in the subsequent two years.

Data drawn from a survey of global attitudes confirm the breadth and depth of negative attitudes toward the United States.[5] The Pew survey of global attitudes done in the spring of 2005 reveals considerable breadth and depth of anti-Americanism. The U.K. is the closest ally of the U.S., yet fewer people in Great Britain rate the United States favorably than they do Germany, France, Japan, or even China. Forty-five percent of the British public hold negative opinions of the U.S., while only 35% view China negatively. Among the Canadian, British, French, German, Spanish, Dutch, Russian, and Polish publics, only in Poland does a higher proportion of the public regard the United States favorably than they do other nations. In all the other countries, the United States is regarded favorably by the smallest proportion of the public.

Even though the data show a sustained set of negative attitudes toward the United States since 2003, it is important not to treat this short period in isolation from the past. In the last 50 years, the United States was derided in the 1960s as the handmaiden of imperialism by newly independent states emerging from the colonial period. The U.S. provoked waves of anger and hostility during the Vietnam War, and hundreds of thousands of people demonstrated in the streets of Europe in the early years of the Reagan administration to protest the strategic policies of his administration. What the data are telling us is neither novel nor unprecedented.

How can we understand the current depth and breadth of anti-American-ism? Why does anti-Americanism wax and wane? In attempting to unpack the reasons for these negative attitudes toward the United States, analysts parse several explanations. None of these explanations are mutually exclusive and, in all likelihood, several reinforce and strengthen each other. I examine each of these explanations by drawing first on arguments that scholars and policy analysts have put forward, and then by disaggregating anti-Americanism to examine individual attitudes toward the United States in sixteen countries to search for supporting evidence and interconnections among the arguments. Most of these explanations draw clearly on assumptions of instrumental ratio-nality but the last, anti-Americanism as identity politics, locates itself within the tradition of social constructivism.

The "What" and "Why" of Anti-Americanism: The Leadership and Personal Style of George W. Bush

George W. Bush seems to many to be at the eye of the storm. It is not the office of the presidency but the personality and the attributes of this presi-dent that provoke negativity. Bush speaks bluntly, in language that is direct, and to many who listen outside the cultural context from which he comes, in overly simple terms. The black-and-white thinking—"you are either with us or against us," a phrase the president used repeatedly after the attacks of 9/11—is difficult for many outside the United States to understand. His lack of interest in things "foreign," his deep and explicit religious faith, his frequent invoca-tion of the sacred, seem strange to allies in Europe and Canada, whose public discourses and civic cultures are so sharply different. This is, of course, not the case in the Middle East where religious discourse is the norm.

There is some evidence from survey data that the President is an issue for many who hold unfavorable views of the United States. Roughly three-quar-ters of the publics in Germany, Canada, and France say that Bush's reelection has made them feel less favorable to the United States. Particularly in Western Europe, respondents who express negative attitudes toward the United States tend to blame the President, rather than the policies of the U.S. or American society more generally.[6] Among the publics around the world, a poor opinion of President Bush is more heavily correlated with unfavorable attitudes toward the United States than any other opinion.[7] When respondents who expressed negative attitudes toward the United States were asked directly whether the problem was more with President Bush or with America in general, they tended to place responsibility primarily on the President.

Those who explain the surge in negative attitudes toward the United States largely as a function of the personality and style of its current president can be relatively sanguine about the future. Those who dislike Bush, the argument goes, are no different from approximately half the population of the United States. This argument suggests that anti-Americanism is a function of the idiosyncratic personality and cultural style of the President, and that it will abate with the end of this presidency. It is a time-limited problem with no deep structural roots.

The "What" and "Why" of Anti-Americanism: The Policies of the Bush Administration

A second explanation focuses more broadly on the policies of the Bush administration, policies that at times have provoked or alarmed allies as well as adversaries. The core concern is that the United States under President Bush is unilateralist in impulse and pays little attention to the interests of others. Moreover, the attention that is paid is often erratic and highly instrumental.

The adoption of the national security strategy before the war against Iraq played directly to these fears.[8] Although the strategy speaks at length of the need to strengthen alliances to contain regional conflict and global terrorism, of the importance of free markets and free trade, and of the need to build the infrastructure of democracy, analysts focused heavily on two tenets of what has come to be known as the Bush Doctrine. The first, the stated determination to maintain the supremacy of America's military power against all would-be challengers, while perhaps bolder in its language, was hardly novel in American foreign policy.

More unusual was the assertion that the United States should be prepared to preempt an attack by terrorists against the United States. An emphasis on preemption of an imminent attack is hardly controversial, but the context in 2002 was different. It is far more difficult to get reliable advance warning of an attack by individuals preparing to inflict injury on civilian targets than it is when conventional armies are the instrument of attack. It is easier to detect and warn about the movement of conventional armies and arming of weapons. Consequently, the strategy argued, the United States might need to engage in preventive rather than preemptive attacks against those who harbor and support terrorists. It was not difficult to decode the official language: the Bush administration was making an argument about the limits of traditional military deterrence against terrorism and for an offensive military strategy. Moreover, the Bush administration asserted, it may be necessary to use military force unilaterally if international institutions could not behave "responsibly" in the face of the challenge posed by international terrorism.

A firestorm of controversy erupted, both within the United States and among attentive publics around the globe. Critics alleged that the Bush administration was clearly unilateralist in impulse, prepared to use force alone if necessary, and inattentive to the concerns and interests of its allies. Historically, it should be said that many great powers have used force without the approval of their allies and without the sanction of international organizations. Nevertheless, that was then, and this was now, the beginning of the twenty-first century when attentiveness to the rituals of international organizations, if not their substance, is part of the global social fabric.

It was not only the Bush Doctrine that lent credence to these kinds of concerns. The rejection of the Kyoto Protocol, the aggressively strong and consistent opposition to the International Criminal Court, the war against Iraq, the insistent demand for reform of the UN management system, and the willingness to hold other goals hostage to achieve that objective—in short, what seems to be aggressive unilateralism across a range of issues, a flexing of the political as well as military muscles of the United States—has alarmed many of America's traditional friends.[9] The unwillingness of the United States, for example, to abide by the rulings of NAFTA tribunals on softwood lumber has convinced large numbers of Canadians that the United States does not play fairly, even that it is unwilling to abide by the law when the law does not serve its interests.

Survey data confirm the negative view that the U.S. foreign policy currently devotes very little consideration to the interests of others. While 67% of Americans think that their government takes the interests of other countries into account, a decline of 6% since 2003, only 19% of Canadians think the United States considers the interests of others, a decline of 9% in a two-year period. The German public is most positive: 38% feel that the United States does pay attention to the interests of others. Put another way, in none of the fifteen countries surveyed did a majority of the public think that the United States takes serious account of the interests of other countries.[10] It is only after the 2004 tsunami and the visible pattern of U.S. assistance that the proportion of respondents who thought that the U.S. was considerate climbed somewhat in Turkey, Pakistan, Indonesia, and Lebanon.[11]

One consequence of this view of the United States as self-regarding is growing support for greater policy independence from the United States. Most Western Europeans want their governments to develop foreign and defense policies that are more autonomous, and so do Canadians. Among traditional allies of the United States, Canadians' negative feelings toward the United States, its policies, and its people have increased most sharply. Fifty-seven percent of Canadians now want more independent foreign and defense policies, an increase of 13% in the two-year period. Ironically, the American public favors closer relationship with traditional allies of the United States.

Despite the generally negative reaction to the policies of the Bush administration, however, some argue that these policies are self-limiting. The United States throughout its history has displayed both unilateralist and multilateralist tendencies, and it is reasonable for allies to expect that, after eight years of an administration that was clearly unilateralist in its instincts, a new administration might well be much more multilateralist in its impulses. Should a new administration speak with a different voice and a different tone, it is conceivable that negative attitudes toward the United States that are based largely on unilateralist policies will decline somewhat.

If it is the impulse to unilateralism that generates the negativity toward the United States, then it is reasonable to expect a decline in anti-Americanism as the Bush administration enters its final phases. It may be too simple, however, to focus exclusively on the methods that this administration has used and ignore the substance. There are always disconnects between the rhetoric an administration uses and the policies that it pursues to further its interests. The gap between rhetoric and policy was likely as large for the Kennedy administration in the early 1960s as it is for the Bush administration forty years later. American foreign policy, generally framed in eschatological language, evocative of norms and principles, will always fall short as policies are crafted to meet specific challenges under specific conditions. At best, the edge may come off some of the negative attitudes that are largely focused on policies.

The "What" and "Why" of Anti-Americanism: American Society—Values and Identity

A quite different analysis looks more to structural characteristics of American society and finds these characteristics unappealing. In the past, critics of the United States have tended to focus on the president or on his administration's policies but maintain generally positive opinions of the American people and of American society. This classic pattern, a pattern that made space for criticism of the American government while preserving space for positive feelings toward Americans, generally still holds: most of the publics of Western allies still describe the American people as hardworking, inventive, and honest.

Growing numbers of people, however, now consider Americans as greedy and violent. In Canada, the closest neighbor of the United States, where many people have family on the other side of the border and hundreds of thousands of people cross the border daily, the numbers are striking: 62% of Canadians think of Americans as greedy, 64% think Americans are violent, 53% consider Americans rude, and 34% regard Americans as immoral.[12] It is not only the president or the policies of this particular administration that are a source of concern and dislike, but more general characteristics of American society. The American public seems to agree with at least two of these characterizations; 70% of Americans see themselves as greedy and 49% see their society as violent.

The biggest differentiator between the way others in Western societies see Americans and the way Americans see themselves is religion. Majorities in France and the Netherlands and pluralities in Great Britain and Germany think that the United States is too religious. It is plausible that the perception of the United States among Western publics as too religious is connected to a president who openly expresses his religious convictions and supports faith-based initiatives. The divide among Western publics and the American public, nevertheless, is quite sharp, a divide that is reflected in convergence between Americans and publics in Muslim countries as well as India. Fifty-eight percent of Americans say that their country is not religious enough, and here majorities in Turkey, Pakistan, Indonesia, Lebanon, Jordan, and India agree overwhelmingly.[13]

Generally, the attractiveness or the "pull" of American society globally has diminished. Americans see themselves as a beacon and as a haven for those seeking freedom; this self-image grows out of the foundational myth of American society. There is now, however, a disconnect between the way Americans see their own society and the way others see it. When people were asked where they would advise a young person today to move in order to lead a good life, Australia, Canada, Great Britain, and Germany were all recommended more frequently as first choices than was the United States.[14]

Some of this negativity is far from new. Throughout the recent history of the United States, critics from outside have pointed to the gap between the political narratives of Americans and the social and economic characteristics of American society. Race has long been a focus of attention by European commentators; during the Cold War, Russian commentators frequently leveled allegations of institutionalized racism and discrimination against American society as they defended themselves against charges of human rights abuse made by American legislators. In France, a long line of critics exposed the gaping wounds of racism and inequality in American society and wrote with biting sarcasm about the hypocrisy of American society. Europeans generally prefer the redistributive social democracies they have built to the untrammeled competition within American society and its attendant extremes of great wealth and poverty. They write with incomprehension about the existence of capital punishment in a society that champions human rights.

In the midst of all this cacophony, their young people still saw America as attractive, as experimental, as less constrained, as more daring, as innovative, and as fun. The iconic attractiveness of jeans and music from the United States encapsulated a broader and deeper attraction to America that was insensitive to criticism of government policy. Joseph Nye coined the phrase "soft power" to describe this kind of attraction.[15] If the trend that surveys of global opinion have identified continues, then it appears as if America's "soft power" is declining. This decline is unlikely to be easily reversed: negative feelings about the characteristics of American society and about the behavior of Americans are less likely to change when the presidency changes and a new administration takes office.

It is difficult to know how much of a spillover there is from dislike of the President and criticism of this administration's policies to the negative feelings about Americans and about social and cultural practices within the United States. The data do not permit an answer to that kind of question. To put these trend lines in context, it is important to remember both that Americans share some of these criticisms and that this portrait of an "ugly American" has been painted at earlier times in American history. These kinds of negative feelings speak to significant differences, indeed conflicts, about values. These negative attitudes coexist with positive affect and, therefore, may reflect a nuanced rather than absolutist set of attitudes, or conflicted ambivalence. In either case, they speak to deeper issues about the United States that are structural. They also go to the heart of the way America sees itself and, consequently, are likely to be read by Americans as pointed, felt as painful, and evoke strong reactions in turn.

The "What" and "Why" of Anti-Americanism:
The United States as Imperial Power

A fourth strand of anti-Americanism is even more deeply rooted in structure and is framed in absolutist, at times, apocalyptic language. There are political variants of these arguments but they are all rooted in the unchallenged military primacy of the United States, a primacy that is growing rather than diminishing. It is not American military power alone, but the imperial ambitions which that military power enables and makes real that is the subject of intense opposition. These anti-imperialist arguments are an all-encompassing critique of the United States, its economic and social structures and its behavior beyond its borders. What these critiques share in common is a view of the United States as insatiable in its appetites, ruthless in the exercise of its power, domineering in its imposition of its own values on other cultures, and exploitative in its treatment of others.

This kind of all-encompassing negativity toward the United States has come in many iterations. In the last century, Leninist and post-Leninist theories of imperialism, widely accepted in parts of the newly independent south during the Cold War, traced American exploitation to its capitalist economic structures and saw its political leaders as the handmaiden of global finance capitalism. Even here, some small space remained for those Americans who were unconscious of their exploitation by their own state. This critique only lost some of its potency with the disintegration of the Soviet Union and the visible failure of its experiment. The critique was partly rooted in the ideological competition between the two superpowers for global influence, but also responded to the visible growth and exercise of American military power around the world.

When the Cold War ended, the United States became the world's only superpower, unchallenged in its claim to universal values and unrivalled in its military supremacy. The assertive confidence of the United States in the superiority of its own system, at times almost verging on triumphalism—famously described as a "unipolar moment"—provoked a reaction from those who saw more than the overwhelming military power of the United States.[16]

Radical Islamicist thinkers, first given a global platform by Ayatollah Ruhollah Khomeini of Iran, saw the United States as the Great Satan, morally corrupt and sexually depraved, exporting its decadent culture worldwide cloaked in a language of human rights and democracy.[17] Phrased in strongly normative and absolutist language—a struggle of good against evil, purity against depravity, morality against sexual license, integrity against corruption, divine authority against the secular and profane—the current critique of the most radical Islamicists goes beyond negativity to a call for the defeat, even the destruction of the United States.

The Islamicist critique, though unique in its religious language and cultural idioms, nevertheless situates America within the trope of a global struggle against imperialism, albeit of a different kind than the Leninist variety. It calls for a struggle against imperialism by framing that struggle within a religious context. Those who join that struggle are among the forces of righteousness and will be divinely rewarded for the justness of their sacrifice. It is almost superfluous to point to the obvious irony: this latest critique of America framed in strongly religious language resonates eerily within an American society that speaks increasingly loudly in religious and salvationist language.

It is not only Islamicists who speak about the United States as insatiable in its appetites and as deeply evil in its imperial behavior. Harold Pinter, the British playwright, in his address as the Nobel Laureate in Literature in 2005 does not locate America's ambition in the exceptionalism of the Bush administration, but sees American imperialism as a decades-old response to deep impulses within American society.[18] Pinter is not alone among European writers and artists in his critique of the American empire.

Accepting for the moment the controversial and contested argument that the United States is an imperial power, or at least behaves at times as if it were an imperial power, anti-Americanism then becomes much less of a puzzle. It is not this particular president or that set of policies that have provoked the current wave of negativity toward the United States. Rather, anti-Americanism is the anticipated consequence of imperial domination. Imperial powers are famously disliked in history as underlings chafe at their exercise of power, their smug and condescending expressions of cultural superiority, their insensitivity to others' traditions, languages, and practices, and their inattention to the interests of others. In the contemporary era, the influx of American capital, the opening of markets to the global economy, and the export of American cultural product, all create a sense of threat to the identities of the local and particular.

Anti-Americanism becomes the obvious language of those who are struggling to adjust to the terms of the United States. Even if we do not accept the analytic descriptor of the United States as empire, but simply acknowledge its overwhelming and growing military preeminence, anti-Americanism is not surprising. "There is no getting around the fact," writes James Traub in the *New York Times*, "that no nation as dominant as America now is will be accepted as a benevolent actor; indeed, no nation so easily able to advance its own interests will act benevolently most of the time."[19]

Publics around the world are very aware that the United States is the world's sole military superpower and are uncomfortable with U.S. preeminence. Majorities in every country surveyed support the emergence of another country that would challenge or balance America's supremacy.[20] These kinds of attitudes are likely to persist well into the next decade, at least as long as American military dominance continues. Negative attitudes toward the United States find a receptive host in the large and growing gap in military capabilities between the United States and every other major power. Anti-Americanism, in other words, is at least partly structural.

The United States as Refracted Mirror

There is one additional explanation that attributes the increase in negative affect neither to the President's personality nor to his policies, neither to attributes of American society nor to the unchallenged military supremacy and imperial ambition of the United States. Anti-Americanism, I argue, can be constitutive of societies where it flourishes. When collective identities are stressed and strained, anti-Americanism can become the vehicle through which identity conflict is externalized. Anti-Americanism can help societies to make and remake themselves by affirming that they are what the United States is not. Under these conditions, anti-Americanism becomes part of the foundational narrative of identity politics.

Anti-Americanism as constitutive of identity politics is a very different argument from anti-Americanism as a consequence of imperial ambitions and practices. An anti-American response to empire is the response of an identity that is threatened by the foreign and the outside. It presupposes a collective identity that affirms meaning for those within society on its own terms. Collective identities create boundaries between inside and outside, between "we" and "they," and when the "they" threaten to overwhelm the "we," anti-Americanism becomes an expected and adaptive response.[21]

When a collective identity is strained, when the threads of what joins are stretched and societies lose their optimism about themselves and their collective future, political leaders can more easily come together in public space to agree on what they are not than on what they are. Identity is reconstituted in reference to the "outside" rather than by enriching and expanding the content of the inside. Although anti-Americanism may be the response to both kinds of identity challenges, the dynamics of each are very different. The remaking of identity, rather than its defense, may be helpful in understanding the dynamics of anti-Americanism in as disparate environments as Canada and the Muslim world. It may well be that in an era of globalization shaped by overwhelming American preeminence, large parts of the world are now being "Canadianized."

This constitutive process of identity making through anti-Americanism begins earlier and goes deeper in the formation of the collective identity of Canadians, particularly English Canadians, than it does almost anywhere else. Canada was created by the loyalty of United Empire Loyalists to Britain when the thirteen colonies revolted. Canada was, from the beginning, defined by what Canadians did not do—revolt against Britain. What Canadians did not do was redefined as what Canadians were not. Present at the defining moment of creation was the foundational narrative of separation and difference from Americans. This narrative was overlain with the virtues of loyalty, trust, and order, while Americans talked of life, liberty, and the pursuit of happiness. The border was only the physical manifestation of the divergence of the two conversational narratives. Beneath these differences in the content of conversation lay a latent impulse among Canadians to define themselves, again and again, by what they were not—Americans.

In modern times, anti-Americanism became a political and cultural force again forty years ago as tension between Québec and the rest of Canada grew, and as U.S. corporations become multinational and significant amounts of foreign direct investment began to come into the Canadian economy. Canadians began to write and speak about themselves derisively as a "branch-plant economy" at the same time as Québec mounted its most forceful challenge to Canadian identity and an "indépendentiste" movement emerged as a significant political force.

It is difficult to disentangle the strains and stresses of Canadian identity from other factors that stoked an anti-American response. Relations between President Lyndon Johnson and Prime Minister Lester Pearson were badly strained over the war in Vietnam, so presidential personality and administration policies provoked controversy and disagreement. Were these disagreements enough to evoke consistent anti-Americanism? Earlier policy disagreements between presidents and prime ministers over, for example, nuclear arms or Cuba did not provoke the breadth and depth of anti-Americanism that developed a decade later. It was not only the "pull" of U.S. presidents and their policies but also the "push" of domestic stresses and strains within Canadian identity that evoked negative attitudes toward the United States.

Defining a collective identity in English Canada by what Canadians were not became much easier than creating an identity based on what they were. Anti-Americanism became more and more deeply embedded, an almost reflexive response, a unifying thread across some if not all of Canada's regional fissures. As one of Canada's most respected columnists, Jeffrey Simpson, wrote of Canada's national identity: "It's a self-image born of defining self against other, rather than a rooted confidence in self. And this way of defining self can lead to the twin perils of moral superiority or excessive national self-doubt, neither of which is far from the surface of Canadian life."[22]

The same kind of dynamic operates today in Canada. Anti-Americanism has grown proportionately more in Canada than in any of the other traditional allies of the United States. As we have seen, 57% of Canadians now want more independent foreign and defense policies, the highest proportional increase in the desire for autonomy of any ally. Canadians, more so than any other Western nation, find Americans rude and dishonest. The government of the United States now routinely expects that during federal elections, anti-American sentiments will be used to woo marginal voters.

It is difficult to account for the disproportionate increase in anti-Americanism in Canada in comparison to other allies. There certainly are strains in what is an intense bilateral relationship but European governments and peoples are dealing with some of the same policy challenges and administration personnel. The answer, perhaps, lies within Canada.

In the last decade, Canada has been less engaged in the world, and less willing to commit resources to global action than at any time since World War II. Its identity as a "helpful fixer" internationally is receding as it commits fewer of its people and less of its wealth than it has in the past. After the "indépendentiste" movement in Québec almost won a referendum on sovereignty in 1995, uneasy rumblings are coming out of the province once again. When Canadians look at themselves, they see troubling trends: a reemergence of the perennial debate between Québec and the rest of Canada and a national government that cannot seem to find its voice abroad. What more opportune time to once again remake the Canadian national identity by emphasizing what Canadians are not—the United States—rather than by dealing with the more challenging task of affirming what Canadians are. For Canadians to see themselves in the American mirror is a comfort.

It is possible that the same kind of dynamic is partially at play in Europe, even though the particularities will differ. Germany and France, at the heart of Europe, are beset by economic difficulty, with high unemployment, and their cherished social safety nets and entitlements at risk. It was the French, one of the cofounders of the new Europe, who dealt the death blow to the draft European constitution. Critics of the constitution routinely described it as an "Anglo-American project," as if a document drafted by "Anglo-Saxons" was fatally contaminated and inconsistent with European culture and identity. President Jacques Chirac, defending the draft constitution, reversed the argument but did not change the cultural idiom when he claimed that it was in the interests of "the Anglo-Saxon countries and particularly the U.S." to stop the forward movement of Europe.[23] Disdain for Anglo-Saxons provided a useful template for both sides of the debate in France. In this sense, it is difficult to argue that particular policies or political leaders can explain the resort to an almost reflexive condemnation of Americans, a condemnation that holds across political perspectives.[24] These criticisms of the United States are often as much about France as they are about the U.S.

Governments routinely violate the rules of the European Union on deficit regulation while publics complain about the faceless bureaucracy of Brussels. There is discussion in French newspapers about the imperative to adjust to the world economy, to cut agricultural subsidies, to change deeply embedded habits and to cut long-standing entitlements. The vision of a united Europe is slowing and troubled, and Europe is confronted by surging Chinese and Indian economies. Under these conditions, when what it means to be a European is the subject of controversy if not an object of contestation, defining Europe's identity by what it is not—American—is a safe way of cutting across differences to find consensus. As Europe struggles to answer the question: "What will we become?", one answer that most can agree on is: "What the United States is not."[25]

As odd as it may seem at first, this "Canadian" dynamic runs as one of the threads through much of the discourse of militant Islam that defines itself and its program in opposition to the "decadent, immoral, brazen, sexually licentious, godless, and corrupt West." Conventionally, we understand the Islamicist response as a reaction to an American threat to Muslim identity. It is also important to understand that Muslim identities, particularly Arab Muslim identities, have been shaken in the last century, first at the hands of European colonial governments and then by a wave of military defeats by Israel. To remake their identity, Arab Muslims experimented first with a variant of liberalism and then with socialism, only to be disappointed by what Western institutional norms and practices were able to accomplish. The return to Islam was an attempt to rediscover their authentic voice and to recapture the "way" that had been lost during colonial occupations. It was also an attempt to repair a fractured identity and loss of self-esteem as the Arab and the Muslim world, inheritors of proud traditions and cultures, faced a surging West.

Islamic and Arab anti-Americanism is consequently a complex multifaceted phenomenon, best understood as a response in part to fear and in part as a reassertion in the context of an identity that is fragile and insulted. The United States is certainly feared, in large part because the United States has made it clear that it seeks to change fundamental aspects of Arab and Muslim cultures and identity. Nowhere is this conflict more prevalent, for example, than on the issue of women's rights. But, insecurity within the Arab world about Arab identity and Islamic political and social practices bumps up explosively against the global reach of the United States to create deep-rooted anti-Americanism, one that is bound up in complex processes that intermingle feelings of collective humiliation and failure. Not only is there internalization of the American threat to identity, there is simultaneously externalization of identity conflict through anti-Americanism. This kind of dynamic is similar to a double-loop feedback that amplifies and magnifies effects.

This analysis suggests that the United States has become the global equivalent to a Rorschach test, an inkblot into which we read ourselves. Contemporary anti-Americanism is certainly a function in part of this president and his policies but it is also a response to a deeper global angst in the face of rapid change and structural uncertainty. We live in a time of global anxiety—an age of terror, rapid change, strained identities, global markets—and negative attitudes toward the most powerful state may be one of the few global pacifiers available.

Endnotes

1. Tony Judt and Denis Lacorne, *With Us or Against Us: Studies in Global Anti-Americanism* (New York: Palgrave Macmillan, 2005); Paul Hollander, *Understanding Anti-Americanism: Its Origins and Impact at Home and Abroad* (New York: Oxford University Press, 2004); and Andrew Ross and Kristin Ross, eds., *Anti-Americanism* (New York: New York University Press, 2004).

2. Peter J. Katzenstein and Robert O. Keohane, in an important study of anti-Americanism that is forthcoming, categorize types of anti-Americanism somewhat differently than I have done here. They emphasize as well, however, the interactivity among different types of anti-Americanism and their mutually reinforcing character. Peter J. Katzenstein and Robert O. Keohane, "Varieties of Anti-Americanism: A Framework for Analysis," Annual Convention of the American Political Science Association, Washington, DC, 2005.

3. The Pew Global Attitudes Project (hereafter, PGAP) is a series of worldwide public opinion surveys that gauge attitudes in every region toward globalization and trade, and measures attitudes toward the United States. Data accessed at http://pewglobal.org.

4. These data are drawn from the Pew poll, "What the World Thinks in 2002," December 4, 2002.

5. PGAP, "16-nation Pew Global Attitudes Survey," 23 June, 2005.

6. PGAP, 2005, Table: "Tsunami Relief Boosts U.S. Image Unlike Bush's Re-Election," 4.

7. PGAP, 2005, Table: "What's the Problem With the U.S.?" The questionnaire asks the question in a simple binary way: What's the Problem with the U.S.? Respondents could select "Mostly Bush," "America in General," or "Both."

8. The National Security Strategy of the United States, September 17, 2002, http://www.whitehouse.gov/nsc/nss.pdf.

9. James Chace, "Present at the Destruction: The Death of American Internationalism," World Policy Journal 20 (2003): 1-5.

10. PGAP, 2005, Table: "Does U.S. Foreign Policy Consider Others' Interests?," 3.

11. PGAP, 2005, Table: "Tsunami Relief Boosts U.S. Image Unlike Bush's Re-Election," 4.

12. PGAP, 2005, Table: "How Western Publics View Americans," 5.

13. PGAP, 2005, Table: "America's Religiosity," 6.

14. PGAP, 2005, Table: "Where to Go to Lead a Good Life," 19.

15. Joseph S. Nye, Jr., Soft Power: The Means to Success in World Politics (New York: Public Affairs Press, 2004).

16. Unipolarity, hegemony, and imperialism are not equivalent, although they are all premised on preponderant military power. Unipolarity is a descriptor of an international system with a single, preeminent actor. There are multiple versions of hegemonic theory, ranging from a provider of public goods to ensure stability to a Gramscian analysis of consciousness within a hegemonic system. Imperialism has distinctive theoretical and analytic mechanisms which trace the impact on the ground beyond the borders of imperialist states. See John G. Ikenberry, *America Unrivalled: The Future of the Balance of Power* (Ithaca, NY: Cornell Uni-

versity Press, 2002); and Christopher Layne, "The Unipolar Illusion: Why New Great Powers Will Arise," *International Security* 17 (1993): 5-51, for analyses of unipolarity. For an analysis of hegemonic orders, Robert Gilpin, *War and Change in World Politics* (New York: Cambridge University Press, 1981). See D.K. Fieldhouse, *The Colonial Empires: A Comparative Survey from the Eighteenth Century* (New York: Delacorte Press, 1966), for an analysis of classical imperialism; and Alexander Cooley, *Logics of Hierarchy: The Organization of Empires, States, and Nations in Transit* (Ithaca, NY: Cornell University Press, 2005).

17. Iain Buruma and Avishai Margalit label this critique "Occidentalist," a play on the critique by Edward Said of "Orientalism." See Iain Buruma and Avishai Margalit, *Occidentalism: The West in the Eyes of Its Enemies* (New York: Penguin Press, 2004).

18. Cited by James Traub, "Their Highbrow Hatred of Us," *New York Times Magazine*, October 30, 2005, 15.

19. Ibid., 16.

20. Although there is substantial support in most countries for a military rival to challenge the global dominance of the United States, there is concern about China as a rising military power.

21. Henri Tajfel, *Human Groups and Social Categories: Studies in Social Psychology* (New York: Cambridge University Press, 1981); and Marilyn Brewer and Robert J. Brown, "Intergroup Relations," in *Handbook of Social Psychology*, vol. II, 4th ed., eds. Daniel T. Gilbert, Susan T. Fiske, Gardner Lindzey (New York: McGraw-Hill, 1998), 554-594.

22. Jeffrey Simpson, "They Love Us, We Love Us—What's the Problem?," *Globe and Mail*, July 1, 2005.

23. *Financial Times*, April 15, 2005, 8.

24. Phillippe Roger, *The American Enemy: The History of French Anti-Americanism* (Chicago: University of Chicago Press, 2005).

25. Robert Lane Greene, "Identity Crisis," New Republic Online, January 28, 2003.

12
Premature Obituary
The Future of the Bush Doctrine

STANLEY A. RENSHON

In the fall of 2005 at the American Political Science Association meetings, a group of prominent international relations scholars announced at two symposia in no uncertain terms that the Bush Doctrine was dead.[1] One speaker asserted that it was "fading away." Another thought that the threat of terrorism and weapons of mass destruction were "largely overblown" and said he was more worried about global warming. Another declared that he had "zero interest in the Middle East." The one "conservative" speaker invited to take part in one of the two panels was also critical, saying that a "scaling back [of the Bush Doctrine] is inevitable," and "has already started."

Their policy autopsy rested on several grounds. One speaker warned, "We must not disrupt the broad cooperation of the great powers." Presumably, he had in mind (unnamed) great powers that the Bush Doctrine had alienated. He also declared, without qualification, that "containment was better than preventive war."

Another commented that the Bush Doctrine was "self-defeating," while another quoting Bismarck asserted that the United States "was in danger of committing suicide from fear of death." While the speakers lamented the insular unanimity of the Bush administration, every single one of them agreed with each other that the Iraq war was a "disaster," and, as a consequence the Doctrine of preventive war was dead.

The premise of this chapter's analysis is that the demise of the Bush Doctrine, like accounts of Mark Twain's death, are greatly exaggerated. The reason is not that the Bush Doctrine is without difficulty, or that its policies have not been, or won't be, set back. They have and they will.

What makes the Bush Doctrine relevant still, and in the foreseeable future, is that it provides a set of answers, imperfect as they may be, to a series of questions that must be addressed by any post-9/11 administration regarding American national security. Those questions as noted in the book's first chapter are: How can the United States avoid being the victim of anther major terrorist attack, this time with weapons of mass destruction (WMDs)? What roles do the doctrines of prevention, preemption, containment, and deterrence play in the range of threats with which the United States and its allies must contend? How can the United States resolve the dilemma that arises because it needs the cooperation of allies to address the common threats they face, but may also have different priorities and understandings of these very threats that may require the United States to act without allies? How can the United States resolve the dilemma of needing international institutions to further develop a liberal democratic world order and its own legitimacy with the fact that the "international community" is sometimes neither democratic, liberal, nor supportive of basic American national security concerns?

Critics of the Doctrine have not answered these questions except in broad generalities or specific differences with the implementation of these policies. Most critics want more consultation with allies. That would be fine. Consultation, however, still does not address the issue of what to do when a national security issue is central and you and your allies cannot agree. Most critics argue that the United States should renounce preventive force. All right, but what should the United States do the next time a Taliban-like regime allows catastrophic terrorists free reign? Critics want the United States to more fully immerse its power in the constraints of international institutions. Fine, but what should the Unites States do when the country is threatened and these institutions are not capable or willing to take strong action themselves, are themselves unrepresentative or corrupt, or inhibit the United States from taking actions in its own defense?

An important question to ask with regard to assessments of the Bush Doctrine and its future is: Compared to what? The questions posed at the beginning of this chapter will be with us for some time. Critics therefore have an obligation not just to criticize, but also to demonstrate how their preferred policies more adequately address these questions.

There are alternative grand strategies to the Bush Doctrine: "off-shore balancing" or "selective engagement," both of which minimize American military involvement abroad. They will be examined in greater detail later. Yet, one point worth making at the outset is that these alternatives seem more suited to a time when the number one threat facing the United States was not the confluence of catastrophic terrorism and WMD technology. The recently published Department of Defense Quadrennial Review notes that al-Qaeda now operates in eighty countries.[2] The Department of Defense currently has antiterrorist operations in a number of them. While these initiatives may be selective in the sense of having been chosen for an important purpose, they are hardly the lighter American footprint abroad that critics of the Bush Doctrine prefer.

Assessing the Debates on the Bush Doctrine

Answering the questions posed above is not easy. They are permeated with profound theoretical, strategic, and political uncertainties. It is important to keep this basic fact in mind. When it comes to the many issues that the Bush Doctrine raises, reasonable people can and *should* disagree. The questions are too important to be left unexamined or, alternatively, drained of understanding by snappy sound bites.

The Bush Doctrine is, of course, highly contentious. Yet, at least part of the controversy swirling around the Bush Doctrine is attributable to misunderstandings of what the Doctrine actually says. On the other hand, a part of the controversy over the Doctrine stems from understanding exactly what it says and disagreeing with its premises and the policies that flow from it. Still, another part of the controversy is a by-product of the different locations and viewpoints of the actors and critics in the decision process, and the perspectives associated with their different places. With the Bush Doctrine and the national security questions it tries to address, in some respects, where you stand shapes what you see.

Critics' Theories vs. Command Responsibility

One little commented upon, but critical, divide between supporters of the Bush Doctrine and its critics lies in the domain of command responsibility. To put the point in a nutshell: The president takes an oath of office to preserve, protect, and defend the Constitution of the United States. Implicit in this charge is the physical protection of the country, its institutions, and citizens. His critics may have strong views on what the president ought to do, but they offer their advice with the luxury of having no real, let alone ultimate, command responsibility.[3] If they are wrong, their friends will forgive them and most of the country won't notice or remember what they said in the first place. A president's national security decisions, for better or worse can affect every man, woman, and child in the country—and many parts of the world as well.

This chasm leads to an enormous difference of perspective between those who have ultimate responsibility for national life or death decisions and those who do not. Critics and pundits do not have to answer for any of their erroneous risk calculations, to the extent they seriously make them at all. Invade Iraq? Allow Iran to develop nuclear weapons and the missiles to deliver them? Contain or actively destabilize North Korea? In each of these decisions and hundreds more, the president and his advisors must weigh the risks of a variety of possible actions, and do so in a world in which the actual level of risk for particular events remains opaque, at best.

Critics have every right to their views and their criticisms. Certainly, the Bush administration has made many mistakes in its foreign policy, although not always the ones it is accused of making. However, criticizing a policy is not the same as offering effective alternatives. This is an especially important point with regard to the Bush Doctrine.

Consider a typical criticism of the Bush Doctrine in Iraq from Democratic Senator and possible 2008 presidential candidate Joseph Biden. In an OpEd piece entitled, "For Success in Iraq, Change Course,"[4] Biden suggested the cancellation of the referendum on the Iraqi Constitution because it would further embitter the Sunni Muslims. What, then, should the administration do? He argued, "The Bush administration should support postponing the constitutional referendum until after elections for a new National Assembly are held in December, which would allow a new committee with elected Sunni members to reconsider the draft."

However, the successful passing of the constitutional referendum was the agreed upon process that preceded the December elections. Sunnis *might have* appreciated this U.S. imposed reversal, or they might just have demanded further adjustments having succeeded in gaining this one. Nor is it likely that U.S. demands to halt and reverse a constitutional process that it was instrumental in developing would have encouraged either the Shi'a Muslims or the Kurds, important allies in the quest to stabilize the country. Nor would such a heavy-handed move have furthered the development of Iraqi democratic autonomy.

As it happened, Biden's suggestion failed to anticipate that after the referendum was passed, Sunnis would begin mobilizing for the new assembly elections in December 2005. Belatedly, but necessarily, they organized so that they would not be left behind a second time. One could argue that it occurred not in spite of, but because there was a constitution process unfolding—a train leaving the station with or without them. When faced with that choice they at least decided to take a ride.

Biden also suggested, "For this policy to work, the administration must do what it has failed to do thus far: involve the major international powers and Iraq's neighbors in a stabilization strategy." He mentions France, Germany, Russia, Japan, and NATO. This is, and remains, a common citicism, but it raises some obvious questions. Involve them how? Debt relief? Already done. The training of Iraqi forces? Already done, even if it is "out of theatre." Troops? From whom? Germany? No chance. France? No chance. Russia? No chance. Involvement is a nice-sounding word, but it often runs up against unfortunate and difficult realities. The fact that those countries did not contribute troops to overthrow Saddam Hussein makes them unlikely now to place their nationals in the center of a raging and deadly insurgency.

Finally, Biden urged, "The administration must also develop a regional strategy that either forces or induces Iraq's neighbors to act responsibly." This is easier to suggest than accomplish. What would effective "inducements" to Iran involve? That approach is already being attempted, none too successfully at this point, on the issue of Iran's nuclear power ambitions. What policies would "force" Iran to act responsibly? Is Biden promoting more coercive strategies such as economic sanctions, or perhaps even military actions against Iran and Syria? Such moves would be fraught with enormous political and strategic implications, none of which is addressed by the senator's blithe remarks.

During the 2004 presidential campaign, John Kerry proposed a "global test" for American military force decisions; he was roundly criticized by the Bush campaign. However, he also said that even knowing that Saddam Hussein did not appear to have the WMDs that the administration and many others expected to find, he would have still been in favor of removing him. Of course, he had many criticisms of the Bush administration on specific issues, such as its approach to its allies. Yet, he also said there might well be circumstances when the United States might have to go it alone.[5] A close reading of the Kerry position on the Bush Doctrine suggests that their differences on these issues might not be as large as commonly thought. This in turn implies intriguingly that there may be a bipartisan basis for national security policies in the post-9/11 world. We will examine that possibility at the conclusion of this chapter.

The Uncertainty of International Relations Theory vs. Presidential Reality

It would be extremely helpful if presidents could learn what problems they are likely to face in their years in office. It would also be tremendously helpful if presidents could know, with some assurance, what strategies, tactics or policies would bring about specific desired results, and which would not. It would furthermore be enormously helpful if presidents could count on having accurate, reliable information about facts on the ground—say, the actual state of Saddam Hussein's WMD programs, whether the Iranians are really trying to build a nuclear bomb or not, and if so how long it will take. Regrettably, the President cannot count on having any of these aids at his disposal. Alongside the substantial responsibility gap between persons with command responsibility and theorists without it, there is an equally substantial gap between the contributions of professional international theory and research and the necessity of actual judgments under uncertainty.

To state the matter directly, international relations theory is just that—a gaggle of hypotheses. It has one generally validated proposition: mature democracies do not go to war against each other. All else is debatable and debated. Paradoxically, many of the strongest criticisms of the Bush Doctrine come from international relations theorists who consider themselves realists. Robert Jervis has observed that "most students of international relations, including those who see threats and the use of force as central, opposed the war in Iraq and many other aspects of Bush's policy."[6] He includes himself in that group, and is a member of the Coalition for a Realistic Foreign Policy.[7] It boasts some of the best-known names in the international relations field. They have signed petitions published in the *New York Times* and elsewhere criticizing the administration for moving toward empire, occupying Iraq, and failing to end the Palestinian-Israeli stalemate.

At first glance, the views of this dazzling group of specialists might well be considered to carry enormous weight. After all, their field of study is exactly what all the political debate is about. Moreover, they are all self-described realists, members of a school that prides itself on being able to look tough facts in the eye unflinchingly, without sentimentality, and to act accordingly in the service of national interest.

Regretfully for this rosy view of realism, however, its practitioners are no more immune to debates about what they see as facts, how they weight them, and the conclusions they draw than the rest of the world. There are in fact, varieties of "realists." Some see the expansion of state power as a by-product of human nature.[8] "Offensive realists" such as John Mearsheimer argue that "[t]he great powers do not merely strive to be the strongest great power.... Their ultimate aim is to be the hegemon, the only great power in the system."[9] "Defensive realists" consider the expansion of powerful states like the United States as a function of strategic insecurity in a world where power and force still rule (the assumption of "anarchy"). Most recently, "neoclassical realists" believe that states try to maximize their power while viewing their circumstances through the lens of their own cultures, perceptions, and psychology.[10] They argue the nature of the international system is critical, but so are perceptions of it.

Realists of various stripes do not exhaust the kinds of international relations theorists trying to explain how the world operates and with strong views on what security poicy ought to be. Liberal institutionalists and those who share their premises, but not necessarily their whole perspective, contend that in a world of power, collective security institutions will prove to be our salvation from anarchy.[11] The United Nations is the iconic exemplar of this perspective, but it is not the only international institution that liberals put their faith in. Realists, of course, think such faith is a "false promise,"[12] or in the less polite phrasing of real-world circumstances, dangerously naïve. Here, as in other matters, the realists and Bush administration see eye to eye, with the caveat that the Bush administration is trying to make many of these institutions live up to their promise.

Each of these different views of realism carries with it very different implications for how states ought to act. If aggressive power expansion is the best explanation of foreign policy, then states in the real world had better plan accordingly. If states are aggressive because of insecurity, we must lessen that insecurity. But how?

What can the United States do to ensure that our allies, rivals, and enemies do not feel insecure? The usual answer is a therapeutic term: reassurance.[13] Anne-Marie Slaughter writes, "International legitimacy is the currency of reassurance."[14] I would have thought the reverse is closer to the present reality. Yet, the question remains: How does the United States do that?

Slaughter writes that the U.S. should reassure its Asian and European allies that "it would neither dominate nor abandon them by deliberately enmeshing itself in a set of regional and global institutions and that it would accept certain constraints on how it exercised its power."[15] That sounds fine, but what is the United States to do when one of its chief allies, South Korea, longs for reconciliation with North Korea, while the latter is supplying missile and other dangerous technology to America's enemies? What does a president do when his allies' privacy concerns prevent them from sending the names and background information of passengers traveling to the United States so that they can be checked against a terror watch list?

If reassuring allies is no easy matter, reassuring hostile and dangerous regimes is even more difficult. Does the United States reassure brutal regimes that they can do what they want domestically by averting our eyes? That would seem inconsistent with American ideals and leave the U.S. open to charges of hypocrisy. Moreover, delegitimating brutal regimes can lead to salutary changes in the international community. Did not the Helsinki Accords begin to change Soviet behavior? Moreover, the delegitimation of the Soviet Union's expansion after World War II underpinned containment, an iconic policy for realists.

One problem with reassurance is that it is not always reassuring. It can be disbelieved. It can be used as a strategic bargaining chip to gain more concessions by continually asking for more concrete manifestations of sincerity. Reassurance may then degenerate into naiveté, weakness, or both. Paradoxically, calming your allies via self-imposed constraints may ultimately embolden your enemies' risky (to them, you, and your allies) behavior.

This would add enough complexity to any president's search for useful answers to their foreign policy questions, but consider the fact that some prominent international relations theorists simply exclude trying to understand the actual foreign policies of particular states. They do so because such policies do not take place within "autonomous realms," which is to say that the sources of state foreign policies are complex, being influenced by both domestic and external factors.[16]

Thus, many international relations theorists ignore precisely the issues that would be of most use to presidents and policy makers. They do so by making a very large assumption, namely, that states act "rationally." That stance is best summed up by Robert Keohane's proposition that "the link between system structure and actor behavior is forged by the rationality assumption, which enables the theorists to predict that leaders will respond to the incentives and constraints imposed by their environments."[17] Of course leaders respond to their environments, but whether they do so in the way posited by rationality theory is quite another matter.

What is rationality? In its minimalist formulation, it simply requires leaders to see their circumstances clearly, accurately assess their options and the consequences of their choices, and then act accordingly. Unfortunately, this turns out to be the perfect description of what few decision makers do, in large part because they can't.[18] Circumstances are rarely crystal clear, and even if they were, are viewed through the filters of culture, history, and psychology.

These various filters are rarely neutral with regard to how information is seen, what feelings it arouses, and how it is analyzed. Moreover, even if options are clear, their consequences rarely are. Underneath the assumption of rationality is a cultural conceit, namely, that others would and *should* act as I would.

This is not a dilemma whose resolution is best debated in professional journals. The question of what to do about leaders like Saddam Hussein and Kim Jong-il rests on deciphering their worldviews, calculations, and psychology. *If* they are sufficiently "like us" to see their circumstances and ours the way we do, see their options and ours as we do, and act accordingly, the United States and the concepts of deterrence and containment are in good shape. If not, American national security policy had better consider other alternatives, perhaps something like the Bush Doctrine.

In the meantime, what is a president to do? He must act in a world where international relations theorists have not resolved their theoretical, conceptual, and empirical differences. Meanwhile, strategic life goes on and the president must deal with reality as he finds it.

Calculating Risk and the Security Dilemma

States, and the president, are caught in a terrible bind. They might like to live in a world in which threats, power, and force were not ever-present, and in which determined terrorists would not like to maim the United States catastrophically with WMDs; but that unfortunately does not describe the world they inhabit. They might like to live in a world where they receive sound, authoritative advice from academic experts about policies and their consequences. But they can't, because that knowledge doesn't exist. They might wish they could place the fate of their country and its security in the hands of effective, authoritative international institutions, but those do not yet exist either. They might like to be powerful enough so that no state would dare to attack them, yet they really don't know how powerful that is. In the wake of 9/11, it is quite clear that enemy states are not their only worry, and that unprecedented power is no guaranteed defense against catastrophe.

These circumstances give rise to the well-known "security dilemma" in which states acting to increase their security might unintentionally increase their insecurity instead.[19] Why? States bolstering their own security might make other states insecure and precipitate the very conflict they seek to avoid. It is also possible, however, that there are some states and groups that a state might wish to unnerve so that they will seriously contemplate undertaking provocative or hostile acts. A legitimate case can be made that it is highly preferable to have terrorist groups feel insecure about their future. This is, after all, the foundation of deterrence,[20] another iconic realism concept.

Here again we encounter one of those difficult dilemmas that saddle presidents and bypass international relations theory: If the U.S. does not aggressively protect itself against catastrophic terrorism, it risks unthinkable destruction to its people, culture, and way of life. If it does, it risks making our allies or others insecure about its power or intentions. How then should a president weigh the trade-offs?

The United States may opt to take some risks related to "low-probability" events. But as Jervis asks, what could be less likely than terrorists flying airplanes into the World Trade Center and Pentagon? As a result, he concludes that now "worst-case analysis is hard to dismiss."[21] This would seem to be especially true if you are constitutionally charged to "preserve and protect," and if, as Bush does, you have very deep and strong feelings about the country you serve.[22]

On what basis should a president determine that a potential catastrophic harm is a low probability? There is no accepted yardstick. How much and what kind of insecurity should the United States tolerate, and from what sources? International relations theories provide no settled basis upon which to proceed, even though individual theorists often express strong personal views.

Moreover, the security dilemma is not really a theory, but rather a broad statement of possibilities. And here, as elsewhere, one person's excessive response to security concerns is another's prudence. Should the United States build a missile defense system to guard itself and its European and Middle Eastern allies against attack or blackmail from China, Iran, or North Korea? We know that these countries are developing such capacities and that they are meant to change the strategic balance. Should the United States let that pass? Should the United States rely on a pledge by these countries that they won't use them against us or our allies? Should the United States move to protect itself even if our improved security makes others more insecure?

The security dilemma provides no specific guidelines. It offers a set of possibilities of what *might* happen; but if it is fair, it must also include the possibilities that these things will *not* happen. In the post-9/11 environment, the president must take seriously "low probability" but highly consequential events. He must protect against it while considering the ripple effect on others who are not directly or even indirectly the target of any American security measures. I place the phase "low probability" in quotes, because paradoxically, a WMD strike against the United States is minimal only to the extent that United States has and continues to take strong offensive measures.

Predicting the Future vs. Living in It

Presidents must live in an uncertain present and anticipate an unknown future. Regrettably, international relations theory has been of little help in warning them about the dangers they may confront. It is not that international relations theorists haven't tried. Few have listened to Richard Betts' sensible warning that "no forecast should be considered anything else but heuristic [and] [a]ny sensible reader should be aware of articles (like this one), that pretend to say anything about the future, since by definition they cannot really know what they are talking about."[23] Sage advice; nonetheless, the temptations are very great.

Charles Kupchan predicted in 1998, "An era of unprecedented peace seems to be at hand as the 21st Century draws near."[24] James Kurth wrote in 2000, shortly before 9/11, "At the beginning of the twentieth century, two of the major strategic concepts used by Western powers were *balance of power* and *sphere of influence*; at the midpoint of the twentieth century, two of the major strategic concepts were *containment* and *deterrence*. From the perspective of postmodern and postnational American elites, who conceive of international affairs largely in terms of the global economy and the open society, these four strategic concepts are now hopelessly old-fashioned and irrelevant."[25] Regrettably, a number of actual regime leaders such as Kim Jong-il or Iranian President Mahmoud Ahmadinejad do not appear to have either a postmodern or postnational perspective.

Gholz, Press, and Sapaolsky advocated in 1997 a policy of "restraint" through the withdrawal of American forces from Europe, Asia, and much of the Middle East. They further proposed attending to American domestic problems. What strategic developments afford the United States this luxury? Simple: "there are a paucity of international threats." The three authors find more solace because "[t]he good news is that America faces almost no discernable security threats."[26] Even the extremely thoughtful and perceptive Robert Jervis wrote in 1998, "The reason why the United States will not develop a grand strategy is the same reason why one is not necessary: *the current world*, like the one the nation lived in before the invention of heavy bombers, *presents no pressing threats.*"[27]

The point here is not to single out these mistakes or their authors; every active researcher, including me, who has tried to anticipate outcomes, has had similar experiences. The point here is rather different. Even smart, well-grounded, and thoughtful scholars have failed to anticipate major developments that have unexpectedly arisen for our government. Therefore, it follows that no administration can rest in the knowledge that the experts or academics it relies on can provide any clear defense against uncertainty. This straightforward fact should lead to some humility when outsiders judge the attempts of any administration to address national security issues; it should certainly be a factor in their assessment on the profound set of circumstances as the 9/11 attacks and their implications.

Modesty is also in order when addressing the issue of how an administration should manage specific issues. Consider the primacy of the U.S. position in the world. That is for most scholars a fact, but its consequences are a matter of uncertainty and dispute. Here as elsewhere, predictions drawn from international relations theory have not fared particularly well.

Realists like Stephen Walt argue that American hegemonic primacy will lead other states to create alliances to balance against it.[28] Yet, serious efforts at "balancing the United States," even after the invasion of Iraq, have "failed to emerge."[29] As Jervis puts it, because the new world does have a hegemon (the United States) and no balancing of a serious kind is being attempted, "scholars are exploring new concepts of balancing."[30] Quite.

When intellectuals confront the failure of their theories to account for what happens in real life, they develop new theories. A number of writers have gone back to the drawing board. Walt's recent work details the techniques that other powers may use to stymie or influence hegemons without necessarily balancing against them.[31]

Walt now says that balancing may be "oppositional," similar to North Korea's attempt to use its nuclear weapons program as blackmail to extract security and economic pledges from the United States (this used to be called coercive diplomacy). He notes that some strategies are "accommodating." "Bonding," for example, occurs where close friendship is used to gain influence. It can also appear when friendship is generally more strategic, as when you recruit your friend to aid you against your enemies.[32] Strategies like "delegitimation," which challenge the moral standing of the hegemon, seem to blend both. Delegitimation has the paradoxical effect of allowing both friends and enemies to stymie the United States. The former require more partnership, and the latter seek to free themselves from restraints.

All these balancing strategies are chosen at times by players wanting to influence U.S. policy. Even so, national security decisions must be made and action must be taken, or not. Theories of balancing can give decision makers something to consider. Unfortunately, they include no guidelines about how others *will* act as opposed to how they might act. If administration officials consider assertive policies, the warnings derived from academic literature that such policies *will* lead to strategic balancing against the United States have so far failed to materialize. Balancing is, apparently, not a necessary outcome. Furthermore, even if it were more likely, it might well be considered a cost that most be borne in the service of important national security policies.

The Bush Doctrine: Not Just American

One of the paradoxes of the Bush Doctrine is that while it is indelibly associated with American foreign policy in general, and President Bush in particular, its elements are very much in evidence in other countries as well. This makes a great deal of sense because, while the United States is the primary target of catastrophic terrorism and rogue state actors, it is not the only one. As the recent uncovering of a terrorist plot in Canada attests, liberal political policies and disagreements with the Bush administration over Iraq and the war on terror proffer no safe haven.[33]

Other Western democracies appear to be taking in the same lesson.[34] Australian Prime Minister John Howard observed, "It stands to reason that if you believe that somebody was going to launch an attack on your country, either of a conventional kind or a terrorist kind, and you had a capacity to stop it and there was no alternative other than to use that capacity, then of course you would have to use it."[35] The French government document issued in January 2003 for its 2003–2008 military program addressed preemption as well: "We must…be prepared to identify and forestall threats as soon as possible. In this context, the possibility of preemptive action might be considered, from the time that an explicit and confirmed threatening situation is identified."[36] In Japan, which has been reluctant since World War II even to contemplate taking actions except in self-defense, then Japan Defense Agency Director-General Shigeru Ishiba said in January 2003: "If North Korea expresses the intention of turning Tokyo into a sea of fire and if it begins preparations [to attack], for instance by fueling [its missiles], we will consider [North Korea] is initiating [a military attack].… Once North Korea declares it will demolish Tokyo and begins preparing for a missile launch, we will consider it the start of a military attack against Japan."[37] Ishiba later stressed that, even with Japan's Peace Constitution, "Just to be on the receiving end of the attack is not what our constitution had in mind.… Just to wait for another country's attack and lose thousands and tens of thousands of people, that is not what the constitution assumes."[38]

These quotes underscore the point that a number of countries, not just the United States, face similar threats and must answer some of the same questions posed at the outset of this essay. The Bush Doctrine is clearly unique in the scope of the answers it proposes in response to these questions and its ability to carry them out. However, the United States is not alone in having and attempting to answer them.

A Profound and Very Political Debate

The Bush Doctrine has given rise to a very intense and important domestic political debate in the United States. The debate has often been highly partisan and contentious, but any assessment of the future of the Bush Doctrine must address it. After all, national security strategies, the Bush Doctrine included, not only shape public debate but are also shaped by the stances of political parties and the American public. In that bubbling cauldron of risk, high-stakes national consequences, policy differences, partisan advantage, and claims to office and governing lie some of the most contested areas of American political life.

Sometimes a profound public shift takes place while being hidden in plain sight. That may well be what is happening to the larger implications of the Bush Doctrine. Venomous political fights between American's two major political parties have characterized every step of the unfolding of the Bush Doctrine. However, the larger fights between the two parties have partially obscured what may prove to be an equally profound debate *within* them, especially in the Democratic Party.

With the exception of a temporary truce after the national shock of the 9/11 attacks, Democrats and Republicans have battled over almost every aspect of Bush's policies. They have battled over the abandonment of the Anti-Ballistic Missile Treaty and the building of a missile defense system. They have fought over whether 9/11 could have been prevented. They have argued over the pace of progress during the invasion of Afghanistan. They have disagreed over whether Saddam Hussein could have been contained by "smart" sanctions. They have quarreled about whether the administration misled Congress and the American public in the run-up to the war. They have disputed dozens of specific policies having to do with the occupation, and they have bitterly clashed over a timetable for the withdrawal of American troops. Since 9/11 they have repeatedly disagreed over what the U.S. should (and should not) do to protect itself, including over the use of domestic spying on terrorist suspects. This is not a complete list of partisan foreign policy controversies since Bush assumed office. Some Democrats have argued that Bush should be censured,[39] others that he should be impeached.[40]

"Yes, But" vs. "I'm Doing Everything in My Power"

The Bush administration has taken very strong positions with respect to its national security policies, both rhetorically and strategically. Rhetorical tactics, such as forcing countries to be either "with us or against us," are more nuanced when carried out in practice. Even so, they were strong enough to exert pressures on a number of countries to modify their practices. Pakistan was pressured to confront the tribal provinces bordering Afghanistan that were providing sanctuary to the Taliban and al-Qaeda. Saudi Arabia and Yemen were pressured into giving more intelligence help.

In other policy areas, the administration was even more bold and direct. Saddam Hussein? He would fully comply with UN resolutions or be removed. The UN would either stand behind its rhetoric or be bypassed. American citizens fighting for the enemy either at home or abroad were "enemy combatants." Special judicial approvals for domestic wiretaps and information searches were inherent in the President's role as Commander-in-Chief during wartime.

The administration asserts that it is absolutely within its rights to exercise these broad powers. Critics respond that Bush considers himself above the law. What is very clear is that the war on terror has raised a host of new legal and constitutional questions that are slowly winding their way toward resolution.[41]

Newsweek reporters Evans and Klaidman, writing about the debate on wiretaps without warrants, argue, "For all its histrionics, the debate was narrow and somewhat vacuous."[42] Reality, however, is more complicated. The debates may have been "narrow," but the implications were profound. Moreover, however narrow or profound the debates were as a matter of constitutional law, they had enormous *political* implications.

Bush has applied the fullest powers of his position as president while arguing that they comply with legal precedent and the country's present circumstances. He has won in some areas and been setback in others, sometimes by the same appellate courts.[43] Yet, while almost all these stances have been controversial, they have given him a rhetorical platform. His actions all declare loudly and clearly: I am doing everything that I think is legitimately in my power to protect the American people.

Some of these initiatives may ultimately be modified or even vacated by appellate court review. Some may come to be associated with errors that might have been avoided. Yet, taken together they reflect a determination, perhaps to the point of error or excess, but a determination nonetheless to protect the country.

Democrats, when they have not wholly opposed the President, have adapted a "yes, but" position. Many of them now argue that they would not have supported an invasion of Iraq if they knew then what they know now. The Bush administration argues that Congress received the same information that it did. Democrats preface their criticisms of the administration's Iraq policy with the standard disclaimer that they "support our troops," and then go on to call into question the logic and legitimacy of their mission, how the war is being conducted, or how successful it is likely to be.

In the larger war on terror, Democrats support vanquishing our enemies, but criticize the administration for supposedly imperious strategies that place a strain on our traditional allies and diminish our standing in the international community. On the domestic side, Democrats and their allies have consistently raised issues about the civil liberties violations of the Bush administration, the Patriot Act in general, and the recent revelations regarding domestic spying on suspected terrorists.

My argument here is not that individual Democratic criticisms are wrong; some of their concerns are clearly legitimate and important to debate. Whether the administration went into Iraq without a coherent plan to anticipate the probable disorder in the aftermath of the war is clearly a legitimate and important debate. So is the debate about the trade-offs between safety and privacy in searches for domestic terrorists and their supporters.

The problem for the Democrats is that the accumulated effect of raising dozens and dozens of national security issues, often in a very harsh and dramatic way, leads some to conclude that the party is harder on the administration than it is on our enemies. The Bush administration may have relied on information about Iraqi WMD programs that proved wrong. It may have underestimated the number of troops needed in Iraq. And it may be in error in asserting that the President has the constitutional power to undertake warrantless wiretaps on suspected terrorists domestically. But the administration can and has argued that all these efforts are legitimate, legal and are a result of doing everything in its power to protect Americans from another, perhaps even more, devastating terrorist attack. One may disagree with the linkage or the strategy, but "I'm doing everything in my power" appears to be a more potent political message than "yes, but."

National Security: Democrats Tilt Left

The Democratic Party is caught in a political bind. For the past 50 years there have been more self-identified conservatives than liberals among the American public. In 2004 those figures were 34% and 21%, respectively, with the rest self-identifying as moderates. While in 2005 27% of all rank-and-file Democrats were liberal,[44] the activist base of the Democratic Party looked quite different.

An in-depth study of those who supported Howard Dean for president showed that 82% of the activists said they were liberal, 16% were moderate, and just 1% were conservative.[45] Activists, of course, are the core supporters of a political party and accordingly exert disproportionate pull on the party. This tendency becomes quite pronounced when major establishment figures in the party occupy high political office are themselves from the liberal branch of the party. Here one would have to count Dean, elected head of the Democratic National Committee, liberal Senate icons Patrick Leahy and Ted Kennedy, as well as a host of less vocal but nonetheless reliably liberal Democratic Senators, and an extremely liberal House Democratic caucus headed by House Majority Leader Nancy Pelosi.

Survey data underscores the distinction between "left" and "liberal" on national security matters. Eighty-one percent of Dean supporters say preemptive war is rarely or never needed, while only 52% of rank-and-file Democrats chose those options.[46] Asked whether U.S. foreign policy should heed allied interests or be based mostly on U.S. interests, 78% of Dean supporters and only 49% of the rank and file chose allied interests. Asked whether diplomacy or military strength was the best way to ensure peace, 96% of Dean supporters and 76% of all Democrats choose diplomacy.[47]

What seems clear from these data is that liberal Democrats do differ from "all Democrats"; they are clearly more left leaning. Yet, it is also the case that Democrats as a whole (and remember that this sample includes conservative democrats) are decidedly left-center. One gets a stronger sense of this by examining some further data on foreign policy. In August 2004, the Pew Center in collaboration with the Council on Foreign Relations published a comprehensive survey of American foreign policy views.[48]

They found that for Republicans, terrorism is the number one problem; the economy was the number one problem for Democrats (p. 7). Asked in late September 2001 whether U.S. wrongdoing might have motivated the 9/11 attacks, 40% of Democrats said yes. By July 2004 that number had risen to 51% (p. 7). Asked whether the U.S. should either be the single world leader or the most active among nations sharing leadership, only 29% of Democrats chose the single world leader option (p. 15). In October 2001, 81% of Democrats thought it very important to reduce the spread of nuclear weapons; by July 2004 that number had declined to 63% (p. 23). This finding perhaps owed something to the administration's rationale of stopping Saddam Hussein's further nuclear development. While 60% of the sample said that preventive war was often or sometimes justified, 44% of Democrats thought so (p. 30). While 29% of the sample thought that the administration had gone too far in restricting civil liberties in the war on terror, 43% of definite Kerry voters thought so (p. 32). Thus, in a variety of ways, Democrats appear less concerned than the general population with the issues that drive the Bush foreign policy agenda and more critical of its elements. Here again, "yes, but" may well prove to be a less effective message than "everything that can be legally done."

These are not novel findings, and that is precisely the point. In a period when America is clearly a target of terrorists who want to catastrophically harm this country, most Americans wish to be protected.[49] The question that arises from these data is whether the Democratic Party and its allies are out of step with the general public.

Senate and House Democrats have waged a relentless battle against the Bush administration's foreign policies. Every once in a while one of their members makes a public statement that cuts through the public's dislike of partisan byplay and makes an impression, but not in a way that would be particularly helpful for the Democrats. Early on, Senator Kennedy labeled the Iraq War a "fraud" that was "made up in Texas," and alleged that "missing funds" are "being shuffled all around to these political leaders in all parts of the world, bribing them to send in troops."[50] Other Democratic Party leaders, activists, and pundits have been less constrained.

Examples are not hard to find. On July 14, 2005, Senator Dick Durbin (D-Il) compared the U.S. treatment of prisoners held at Guantanamo to the behavior of "Nazis, Soviets in their Gulags, or another mad regime—Pol Pot."[51] Dean compared Iraq to Vietnam and said the "idea that we're going to win the war in Iraq is an idea which is just plain wrong."[52] And finally, Pelosi called for the President to immediately start to withdraw American troops from Iraq and went on to say that she believed that a majority of the Democratic caucus clearly supports this position.[53]

It can be argued that these members are the most prominent voices of the Democratic Party on foreign policy, but they are not the only ones. It is true that there are exceptions, but they only underscore the general applicability of the rule. Senator Joseph Lieberman has publicly supported the President's policy in Iraq,[54] but in doing so has made many enemies in his party,[55] and as a result lost his Democratic primary fight against an avowedly antiwar candidate.[56]

Thus, given its unrelenting antagonism to the Bush administration's policies concerning the war on terror and in the startling statements of some of its most senior party leaders, it is not surprising that Democratic Party is not viewed favorably when it comes to protecting the United States. According to data reported by Al From and Mark Penn to the Democratic Leadership

Council, "the Republicans still hold the advantage on every national security issue we tested: Republicans led the Democrats by 40% to 36% on questions about which party can keep the country safe, 45% to 40% on which party can be trusted on national security, and 48% to 38% on which party can be trusted more to fight terrorism." That memo concludes with the stark warning that "in shaping alternative policies—particularly on national security, terrorism and Iraq—Democrats have to be very careful to avoid reinforcing the negative stereotype that has cost us so much in the last two national elections."[57]

A New Generation of Democratic Neocons?

The first generation of neocons started political life as strong defense Democrats. Intellectually, that group gathered around Henry "Scoop" Jackson (D-WA), a strong supporter of national defense and of containing the Soviet Union during the Cold War. The Democratic Party migrated leftward on defense issues during the 1960s, the presidential candidacy of George McGovern in 1972, and thereafter. Whether it was the migration of their party leftward, their own movement rightward, or a combination of both, neocons as individuals and as a group found themselves political orphans in the Democratic Party.

Some members and supporters of the Democratic Party have been quite clear that they have a "national security problem." George Packer, no supporter of the Bush administration, writing in the *New Yorker* about the Democratic Party's failure to be seen as seriously concerned with national security has characterized the dilemma as follows:

> The two complementary tendencies that doomed his [Kerry's] effort on Iraq have characterized Democrats since the war on terrorism began: on one side, the urge to take cover under Republican policies in order not to be labeled weak; on the other, a rigid opposition that invokes moral principle but often leads to the very results it seeks to prevent. Neither posture shows a willingness to grapple with the world as it is, to do the hard work of imagining a foreign policy for the post-September-11th era. [58]

That failure to more completely understand the nature of the 9/11 experience for most Americans and its implications for the Democrats is well captured in another *New Yorker* article on "toughness." In it Senator Biden was asked what advice he would have given John Kerry. He replied, "I would say to John, 'Let me put it to you this way. The Lord Almighty, or Allah, whoever, if he came to every kitchen table in America and said, Look, I have a Faustian bargain for you, you choose. I will guarantee to you that I will end all terror threats against the United States within the year, but in return for that there will be no help for education, no help for Social Security, no help for health care. What do you do?' My answer, Biden said, 'is that seventy-five percent of the American people would buy that bargain'." Asked whether Democrats have a seriousness or toughness problem, John Kerry had another view, "Look, the answer is, we have to do an unbranding." By this he meant that the Democrats had to do a better job of selling to the American people what he believed was already true—that the Democrats are every bit as serious on the security issue as Republicans. "We have to brand more effectively. It's marketing."[59]

Not all Democrats are "dovish" on national security issues. Joseph Lieberman (D-CT) and Joe Biden (D-DE) in the Senate and Ike Skelton (D-MS) and Jane Harman (D-CA) in the House are strong national security Democrats, however, they and their Congressional allies are in the minority of the party. Things are somewhat different in the world of Democratic-leaning think tanks and pundits.

Peter Beinart, a senior editor at the *New Republic*, has written, "Three years after September 11 brought the United States face-to-face with a new totalitarian threat, liberalism has still not 'been fundamentally reshaped' by the experience." Further, he argues, "there is little liberal passion to win the struggle against Al Qaeda."[60] Beinart traces the national security splits in the Democratic Party back through the beginnings of the Cold War anticommunism. He believes that it is possible for the left to embrace the global fight against Islamic extremism without sacrificing, and perhaps even advancing, their progressive views. However, he offers no specific theoretical rationales or policy prescriptions other than investing in international institutions.[61]

Fighting Words: New Democratic Thinking?

That rationale and policy development work has been done elsewhere. John Podesta, Bill Clinton's former Chief of Staff, heads the Center for American Progress, a progressive think tank. That center's chief contribution to a revised Democratic national security policy consists of two strategy documents. One entitled "Strategic Redeployment" has four elements: "military realignment that restores a realistic deployment policy for our active and reserve forces and moves troops to specific hot spots in the struggle against global terrorist networks or brings them home to rebuild; a global communications campaign to counter misinformation and hateful ideologies; new regional diplomatic initiatives; and smarter support for Iraq's renewal and reconstruction."[62] It is worth noting that the last three of these four items are already policies of the Bush administration, although one might certainly argue that more could be done, and better.

Replacing the Bush Doctrine: With What?

The question that must be asked of any new Democratic national security policy, or indeed any new framework or doctrine, is how well it addresses the fundamental post-9/11 security questions raised at the beginning of this chapter. Do the new possible Democratic national security strategies or other "grand theories" provide a reasonable alternative to the Bush Doctrine? What specifically do they put in its place?

The first suggestion put forward by the Center for American Progress seems to be a form of "off-shore balancing," a policy advocated by Steven Walt and also Christopher Layne.[63] In essence, this grand strategy would require the United States to reduce its military footprint worldwide, and to intervene only in cases of "overt aggression" against our "vital interests," while leaving the stability of most areas to "local actors." That would, it is argued, "reassure" our friends and foes alike of our "benign intentions."[64]

One problem with this is policy is that while the citizens of many countries disagree with American policies and in some cases are angry with them, it does not necessarily follow that they want less American presence. What they want is an American presence that supports their views of what ought to be done in one or another situation. Needless to say, designing American foreign policy on the basis of what others would have us do to advance their interests would, in a number of circumstances, be very imprudent. Moreover, it is just as likely that the U.S. will garner criticism for doing too little (defined by others' expectations) as for doing too much.

Perhaps more importantly, there is little guarantee that a smaller footprint will "reassure" more countries. On the contrary, states located in dangerous neighborhoods might be made quite anxious. Would Japan or South Korea prefer more autonomy to deal with China and North Korea? Who will be our "local actor" (read proxy) in the Middle East? Iraq? Not likely. Israel? That would very likely escalate regional tensions, not defuse them. And why would Israel be willing to be our proxy in the Middle East or Japan in the Far East?

Finally, how would our enemies read our disengagement? Would they be "reassured" about our benign intentions? That is most unlikely. The Saddam Husseins of the world see withdrawal and hesitation as weakness.[65] The only reassurance such a stance brings is to affirm that the United States lacks the will that underlies staying power.[66] Far from leading to a more hospitable world, such a posture invites threatened allies to accommodate and make their own peace with our enemies. In so doing they can hardly, at the same time, be counted upon to be our regional proxies.

The second Center for American Progress national security strategy paper is entitled "Integrated Power."[67] Like its counterpart discussed above, this paper too includes a substantial amount of criticism of Bush personally and his policies,[68] coupled with faint praise.[69] The core of "integrated power" is a strategy that entails using both hard and soft power rather than replying exclusively on either one.[70] If this strikes you as somewhat simplistic, you are not alone. No American president has ever relied on one of these to the exclusion of the other. In reality, the term seems to serve as a rather large umbrella under which to place an extensive list of policy proposals.

The stated goals of the strategy are to protect the American people, prevent conflict, and lead vital alliances and institutions. For these national security Democrats, preemption is in, prevention is out.[71] If an attack against the United States is imminent, we can respond before it happens. However, "if there is no evidence that an attack is imminent, no country has the right the launch an attack or wage a preventive war on another sovereign country."[72] This strategy does reserve the right to intervene militarily in other sovereign countries, under the "responsibility to protect" doctrine when "regimes are failing to protect their own people."[73] However, this puts the strategy in the curious position of allowing the United States to intervene militarily in sovereign countries to protect others, but not to intervene in order to protect Americans. It is also contradicted by its stated policy toward Iran's nuclear ambitions: "The leaders in Tehran…must also understand that any attempt to use or transfer nuclear weapons or their key components would result in decisive military action."[74] Really? Does that mean that if Iran helps another country master the complexity of "peaceful" but dual use nuclear technology, we will attack them?

Overall, "Integrated Power" is extremely ambitious regarding America's purposes. It has sections on spreading and supporting democracy (we should), environmental policies, energy use policy, international economic growth, poverty, nuclear proliferation, alliance building, and international institutional commitments, among others. This long list of policy initiatives combines traditional liberal institutionalism abroad with traditional liberal democratic policies at home. We should support democracy, but not impose it. We should increase our foreign aid and commit ourselves to international institutions and agreements (what to do about "cheaters" is not addressed). We should make more use of renewable energy sources, modernize our electric grid, and make use of nuclear power.

This democratic think tank document also appears to favor "selective engagement."[75] However, the document does not attempt to make or justify the hard trade-offs that presidents must make. The small sampling above hardly exhausts the long list of policy initiatives to be found in the document. Its extensive ambitions bring to mind Colin Dueck's accurate observation that "one major criticism of selective engagement…is that such a strategy seems to invite abuse through the proliferation of foreign policy commitments."[76] "Integrated Power" surpasses that concern by adding domestic policy to the list, and then multiplies large commitments even before the policy is enacted. For liberal internationalists the era of big government is not over, and that goes doubly in the arena of foreign policy.

Iraq: Liberal Interventionist Rollback?

Tough talk is the hallmark of "progressive" national security doctrine. Iran and North Korea are to be put on notice that the United States is "prepared to use force," or "would" use it. However, being prepared to use force is not the same as actually using it, and policy pronouncements from progressive think tanks are neither binding nor necessarily relevant to any future Democratic president. The purpose of such documents is to develop a muscular set of Democratic positions on national security, while maintaining liberal Democrats' traditional attitudes toward allies and international institutions and treaties. It is extremely difficult to reconcile these positions. In order to protect American national security interests, it may be necessary to abandon or downplay the internationalism stance that forms the basic pillar of their foreign policy stance.

One gets a better sense of the actual level of comfort with and willingness to use force among so-called liberal hawks by looking at their position on Iraq. The picture here is decidedly mixed. There is no doubt that some Democrats were as forceful as their neoconservative counterparts in making the case of the need to invade Iraq and topple Saddam Hussein. Perhaps the most forcefully argued brief for invasion was put forward by former CIA analyst Kenneth Pollack, whose book is a knowledgeable, thoughtful, and well-argued case for invasion.[77]

He was not the only one. A number of commentators and analysts with strong liberal or Democratic credentials like Paul Berman, Thomas Friedman, Fred Kaplan, Fareed Zakaria, Andrew Sullivan, Christopher Hitchens, and Michael Ignatieff, to name a few, all argued in favor of this application of the Bush Doctrine. Most did so because they favored the export of democracy, a key liberal project. Most were not primarily motivated by a concern with Hussein's interest in acquiring WMDs or in dominating the region.[78] In short, they supported the war on humanitarian, not national security, grounds. Hussein's dangerousness was beside the point.

Not surprisingly therefore, the tough aftermath of the initial military victory soured these liberal hawks into highly qualifying their original support.[79] Pollack argues that he had "opposed both the timing and manner of the actual war as the Bush administration pursued it." Ignatieff dismisses the humanitarian intervention as a "fantasy." Kaplan questions whether Bush is "reckless or clueless" and reminds others that he really should not be commenting in a debate about post-invasion second thoughts, "because I changed my mind before the war began."[80] Berman is relieved to be able to recall that even while championing the invasion he was cautioning against the President's "rhetoric, ignorance, and Hobbesian brutishness," and declaring himself "'terrified' at the dangers [Bush] was courting."

Friedman believes, "it was still the right war and still has a decent chance to produce a decent outcome." Yet elsewhere, he says, "Iraq is a terrible mess because of the criminal incompetence of the Bush national security team."[81] Zakaria also thinks "the war was worth it,"[82] but elsewhere he titles a piece on the President's Iraq policy, "A Vision and Little Else."[83] How he reconciles those two statements is unclear. Even Hitchens, supporting the invasion, criticized the administration's "near-impeachable irresponsibility in the matter of postwar planning in Iraq."[84]

It is hard to know what to make of these and similar reversals, intense ambivalence, and savage characterizations of the occupation. Former supporters are clearly distraught at the brutal toughness of the insurgency, the resulting carnage, and the difficulties of implementing their favored democracy project. In some respects their earlier expectations seem as rosy as the administration's, which they criticize for excessive optimism. Many of the issues on which they disparage the President (e.g., troop numbers, "de-Ba'athification," and sectarian splits) were not the result of thoughtless blunders. Rather, they were tough choices with many, sometimes conflicting, elements on each side. We won't know for some time how seriously the possibility of civil war, ethnic or regional partition, and other issues were debated or forseen. As Lawrence Kaplan argues, "It's not so easy to disentangle problems blamed on defects of implementation from the very ideas today's war critics were championing only yesterday."[85]

I do not anticipate any substantial migration of liberal internationalists into the neocon club. Historically, the original Democratic core of that group was driven by a view that their country faced grave danger, and they organized to do something about it.[86] They were patriots in the very fundamental sense of that word. They, like their fellow Americans, had affection for and appreciation of this country—its way of life, institutions, and fellow citizens. They also felt a strong commitment to and responsibility for the country, and felt that it faced grave danger during the Cold War. Yet, at the time, a number of their fellow Democrats saw nothing wrong with Henry Wallace and identified and aligned themselves with the great socialist experiment taking place in the Soviet Union. Their successors in the 1960s also said, when pressed, that they loved this country, but they showed little affection and appreciation of it as it stood facing these fundamental challenges.

Their view, vocally expressed in their support of identity politics, was that the United States trampled on its many minorities as it had on countries worldwide. The highest form of patriotism, therefore, was to acknowledge and counter what they saw as the racist and militaristic nature of the country. That is the historical political center of gravity of the left wing of the Democratic Party, in both mild and less nuanced form. It is also the political birthplace of national security hawks.

James Mann has written elsewhere that "in the 1990s, the Democrats became progressively more willing to support the use of military force. Mann sees the 1991 Persian Gulf War as a turning point. Yet in the run-up to the war, the overwhelming majority of Senate Democrats opposed military action to reverse Saddam Hussein's invasion of Kuwait. Several predicted that war against Iraq would return large numbers of Americans in body bags. After

Operation Desert Storm ended with relatively few American casualties, some Democrats began to reconsider."[87] However, it seems clear in retrospect after the Second Iraq War that Mann's sighting of a Democratic "turning point" was premature. His observation nonetheless raises another interesting point.

Most discussions of aversion to American casualties focus on the public's intolerance of war deaths. Mann delves into whether the two parties differ in their tolerance for the fact that deaths are often, if not always, among the consequences of major military missions. Here, too, the question of whose expectations were violated is raised. Did the Democratic leadership agree to the second Iraq invasion expecting a quick, low-cost outcome that mirrored the first? Like their liberal hawk allies in the world of pundit analysis, they seemed unprepared for the brutal carnage campaign that developed.

Were they pressured to agree to Hussein's removal out of fear of being labeled "soft," as George Packer argued? If so, their support was thin and politically driven, rather than genuinely felt as an important strategic matter. Here, the Democratic Party has its own "hearts and mind" dilemma. It knows what it needs to do, but its heart (the political center of gravity of its core constituents) isn't in it.

As noted, many Democratic hawks supported the Iraq War in 2003 primarily on humanitarian rather than national security grounds. If you fight a war of choice for a secondary reason and the war becomes costly and difficult, one response is to acknowledge making a bad choice. Another is to defend your judgment by questioning that of others.

As a result of the difficult and wrenching Iraqi occupation, liberal hawks are unlikely to support any future military action against a dangerous adversary unless the latter is caught on tape handing over nuclear materials to our avowed enemies. Even then they are more likely to support quick regime change imposed from without than face the difficulties of democratic transformation, especially if that would involve further tough combat.

The Democratic leadership's center of gravity, and its behavior before the first Gulf War and after the second, make it hard to envision that it will substantially join the Republicans in future Iraqs. The most recent Democratic Party statement on national security, "Real Security," does not subscribe to the Bush Doctrine's vision that there is a broad global threat that sees the United States engaged in a long dangerous struggle. There is no mention of preemptive action or of democracy.[88] Consequently, the development of a bipartisan national security consensus, paralleling the one reached during the Cold War, seems unlikely. Bush Doctrine Republicans, for better or worse, appear to be on their own.

In the Republican Party, the picture is somewhat different, but not enormously favorable. One man, George W. Bush, has singularly and determinedly driven the Doctrine. Agree with it or not, it is clear that the President not only holds the convictions that underlie his strategy, but embodies the psychological elements necessary to sustain it. He has both the convictions and the courage to pursue them through intense adversity. courage as well. He has persisted and paid a very high political cost for doing so, but has persevered nonetheless.

It is often said that Bush's legacy will depend on the outcome in Iraq. I think this is only partially true. His legacy will rest on, among other things, the fate of his Doctrine. Its continuation will depend on a successor who both sees the world as Bush does, and who acts on those views in the face of unrelenting criticism and deep international ambivalence. Expressing support for the worldview without being able or willing to act is like trying to run on one leg.

Bush's presidency is winding down, and 2008 will bring a new administration. A recent overview of the possible Republican contenders on the issue of foreign policy suggests that the Bush Doctrine has only one strong supporter among those likely to run in 2008.[89] —John McCain. The other Republican contenders like Chuck Hegel are more in tune with the premises of Democratic foreign policy perspectives.

On the democratic side, the 2006 midterm elections certainly have made "assertive realism," especially should it take the form of actual intervention, more difficult. Yet, it is also true that Democrats rejected the most vociferous anti-war candidate, John Murtha, for the position of Majority leader in favor of Steny Hoyer, who does not favor quick withdrawal from Iraq. In the event that the situation in Iraq is somewhat resolved, one way or another, by the presidential election season of 2008, it is quite possible the "tough talk" will be the order of the day for presidential candidates. It would be one of the supreme ironies of modern politics if the Democratic presidential nominee felt to the need to rhetorically defend the tough terms inherent in the Bush Doctrine; while the Republican nominee, whose party is almost synonymous with strong national security, campaigned on a kinder, gentler foreign policy.

Notes

My thanks to Peter Suedfeld, Gerhard Alexander, and Nick Petaludis for their comments on this chapter. Research support for this chapter was also provided by a City University of New York Research Award (No: 68018-00-37). I wish to thank the anonymous external reviewers for their comments.

Endnotes

1. The two were: "The End of the Bush Revolution: Democratization, Unilateralism, and preemption in American Foreign Policy," and "Offensive Realism, Global Jihadi Networks, and the Power of Preemption." All quotes from those two panels are from my verbatim notes.
2. Department of Defense, "Quadrennial Defense Review Report," February 6, 2006, 21, http://www.defenselink.mil/pubs/pdfs/QDR20060203.pdf.

3. When Ehud Olmert, now the Prime Minister of Israel, was asked what he had learned from his predecessor Ariel Sharon, he replied, "I learned many things... as he [Sharon] said, 'What you see from here [as prime minister] is not what you see from there [not being prime minister].'" "A Conversation Ehud Olmert Interim Israeli Prime Minister," *Washington Post*, April 9, 2006, B04.

4. *Washington Post*, September 14, 2005, A31.

5. Dana Milbank, "Bush Says Kerry Will Allow Foreign Vetoes," *Washington Post*, October 3, 2004, A08.

6. Robert Jervis, *American Foreign Policy in a New Era* (New York: Routledge, 2005), 4. I hasten to add a personal note here: I have the highest respect for Professor Jervis' thoughtfulness and work, even though he and I clearly have some substantive differences.

7. Coalition for a Realistic Foreign Policy, http://www.realisticforeignpolicy.org.

8. Hans J. Morgenthau, *Politics Among Nations: The Struggle for Power and Peace*, 4th ed. (New York: Knopf, 1967), 4-14.

9. John Mearsheimer, "The Rise of China Will Not Be Peaceful at All," *The Australian*, November 18, 2005. See also John Mearsheimer, *The Tragedy of Great Power Politics* (New York: Norton, 2002), 21-22, 31-39.

10. Gideon Rose, "Neoclassical Realism and Theories of Foreign Policy," *World Politics* 51 (1998): 144-172.

11. Robert O. Keohane and Lisa L. Martin, "The Promise of Institutional Theory," *International Security* 20 (1995), 39-51; see also, Charles A. Kupchan and Clifford A. Kupchan, "The Promise of Collective Security," *International Security* 20 (1995), 52-61.

12. John Mearsheimer, "The False Promise of International Institutions," *International Security*, 19 (1994/95), 5-49.

13. Stephen M. Walt, *Taming American Power: The Global Response to U.S. Primacy* (New York: Norton, 2005).

14. Anne-Marie Slaughter, "Comment on Walt," *Boston Review* (February/March 2005), http://bostonreview.net/ndf.html#Interest.

15. Ibid.

16. Kenneth N. Waltz, *Theory of International Politics* (Reading, MA: Addison-Wesley, 1979).

17. Robert O. Keohane, "Theory of World Politics," in *Neorealism and Its Critics*, ed. Robert O. Keohane (New York: Columbia University Press, 1986).

18. The classic formulation and analysis of these issues remains Robert Jervis, *Perception and Misperception in International Politics* (Princeton, NJ: Princeton University Press, 1976).

19. See John H. Herz, "Idealist Internationalism and the Security Dilemma," *World Politics*, 2 (1950): 157-180; Robert Jervis, "Cooperation Under the Security Dilemma," *World Politics*, 30 (1978): 167-214.

20. Lawrence Freedman, *Deterrence* (Cambridge, UK: Polity Press, 2004), 32-42.

21. Robert Jervis, *American Foreign Policy in a New Era*.

22. On Bush's deep emotional attachment to the country, see Stanley A. Renshon, "The World According to George W. Bush: Good Judgment or Cowboy Politics," in *Good Judgment in Foreign Policy: Theory and Research*, eds. Stanley A. Renshon and Deborah Welch Larson (Lantham, MD: Rowman & Littlefied, 2003), 279-280.

23. Richard K. Betts, "Power, Prospects, and Priorities: Choices for Strategic Change," *Naval War College Review* (Winter 1997).

24. Charles A. Kupchan, "After Pax Americana: Benign Power, Regional Integration, and the Sources of Stable Multipolarity," *International Security* 23 (1998): 40.

25. James Kurth, "American Strategy in the Global Age," *Naval War College Review* (Winter 2000).

26. Eugene Gholz, Daryl G. Press, and Harvey M. Sapolsky, "Come Home, America," *International Security* 21 (1997), 6, 8.

27. Robert Jervis, "U.S. Grand Strategy: Mission Impossible," *Naval War College Review* (Summer 1998) [italics added].

28. Both possibilities are discussed in Stephen M. Walt, *The Origins of Alliances* (Ithaca, NY: Cornell, 1987).

29. Keir A. Lieber and Gerard Alexander, "Waiting for Balancing: Why the World Is Not Pushing Back," *International Security* 30 (2005), 109.

30. Jervis, *American Foreign Policy*, 31. Among those doing so are T.V. Paul, "Soft Balancing in the Age of U.S. Primacy," *International Security* 30 (2005): 46-71; Robert Pape," Soft Balancing Against the United States," *International Security* 30 (2005): 7-45; and William C. Brooks and William C. Wohlforth, "Hard Times for Soft Balancing," *International Security* 30 (2005): 72-108.

31. Walt, *Taming American Power*.

32. Here Walt seems to adapt the position of Randall l. Schweller, "Bandwagoning for Fun and Profit: Bringing the Revisionist State Back In," *International Security* 19 (1994), 72-107.

33. Doug Struck, "Arrests Shake Image of Harmony: Muslims in Canada Brace for a Backlash After Foiled Bomb Plot," *Washington Post*, June 5, 2006, A10.

34. The quotes that follow are drawn from M. Elaine Bunn, "Preemptive Action: When, How, and to What Effect?" *Strategic Forum* 200 (July 2003): 6-7.

35. John Shaw, "Startling His Neighbors, Australian Leader Favors First Strikes," *New York Times*, December 2, 2002, A11.

36. LOI n° 2003–73 du 27 janvier 2003 relative à la programmation militaire pour les années 2003 à 2008 (1), section 2.3.1 [translation: law number 2003-73, January 27, 2003, concerning military programming for the years 2003 to 2008, paragraph 2.3.1], see also Ariane Benard, "Chirac Hints at Nuclear Reply to State-Supported Terrorism," *New York Times*, January 20, 2006, A8.

37. "Ishiba: Japan to 'Counterattack' if N. Korea Prepares to Attack," *Yomiuri Shimbun/Daily Yomiuri*, January 25, 2003.

38. James Brooke, "Japanese Official Wants Defense Against Missiles Expanded," *New York Times,* April 17, 2003, A13.

39. Shailagh Murray, "A Senate Maverick Acts to Force an Issue," *Washington Post*, March 15, 2006, A01.

40. A recent report by the House Democratic Judiciary Committee staff recommended the creation of a Special Select Committee of the Congress to report back to Congress on what the report characterizes as, "charges clearly [rising] to the level of impeachable offences." According to the Democrats there is a prima facie case that the "President, Vice-president, and other members of the administration violated a number of federal laws, including (1) Committing a Fraud against the United States; (2) Making False Statements to Congress; (3) The War Powers Resolution;

(4) Misuse of government Funds; federal Laws and International Treaties prohibiting torture and cruel, inhuman, and degrading treatment; federal laws concerned retaliating against witnesses and other individuals; and federal laws and regulations concerning leaking and other misuse of intelligence." See "The Constitution in Crisis: The Downing Street Minutes and Deception, Manipulation, Torture, Retribution, and Coverups in the Iraqi War," Investigative Status Report of the House Judiciary Committee Democratic Staff, Washington, DC, December 20, 2005, http://www.house.gov/judiciary_democrats/iraqrept122005/finalreport.pdf.

41. See, for example, Jennifer K. Elsea and Kenneth Thomas, "Guantanamo Detainees: *Habeas Corpus* Challenges in Federal Court," Congressional Research Service, Washington, DC, September 7, 2005, http://www.fas.org/sgp/crs/natsec/RL33180.pdf.

42. Evan Thomas and Daniel Klaidman, "Full Speed Ahead," *Newsweek*, January 9, 2006.

43. Neil A. Lewis, "Appeals Court Rejects U.S. Bid to Transfer Terror Suspect," *New York Times*, December 21, 2005. The full decision barring the move of the case of Jose Padilla to criminal courts may be found at http://news.findlaw.com/hdocs/docs/padilla/padhanft122105ord.pdf.

44. Pew Research Center, "The Dean Activists: Their Profile and Prospects," April 6, 2005, 3, http://people-press.org/reports/pdf/240.pdf.

45. Ibid.

46. Ibid., 5.

47. Ibid., 28.

48. Pew Research Center, "Foreign Policy Attitudes Now Driven by 9/11," August 18, 2004.

49. A December 28, 2005 Rasmussen poll found that 64% of the public (and 51% of Democrats) said that the National Security Agency ought to be allowed to intercept telephone conversations between terror suspects in other countries and people living in the United States. Available at http://www.rasmussenreports.com/2005/NSA.htm.

50. Dana Bash," Kennedy's 'Texas' remarks stirs GOP," *CNN*, September 18, 2003.

51. Congressional Record, June 14, 2005, S6594. Available at (http://durbin.senate.gov/gitmo.cfm.

52. "Dean: U.S. Won't Win in Iraq," WOAI; *San Antonio News*, December 4, 2005. The complete interview can be heard at http://cctvimedia.clearchannel.com/woai/deanint.mp3.

53. Liz Sidoti, "Pelosi Calls for Withdrawal From Iraq," Associated Press, November 30, 2005.

54. Joe Lieberman, "Our Troops Must Stay," *Wall Street Journal*, November 29, 2005, A18.

55. Shailagh Murray, "Lieberman Wins Republican Friends, Democratic Enemies for Support of War," *Washington Post*, December 10, 2005, A01

56. Dan Baltz," Lieberman Loss Could Be a Party Watershed," *Washington Post*, August 6, 2006, A01.

57. Al From and Mark Penn, "A Chance to Rebuild Our Democratic Majority: If We Will Take It," Democratic Leadership Council Memo, December 18, 2005, http://www.dlc.org/ndol_ci.cfm?kaid=86&subid=84&contentid=253656.

58. George Packer, "A Democratic World: Can Liberals Take Foreign Policy Back from the Republicans?," *New Yorker*, February 16/23, 2004; see also, James Mann, "Think Globally: Just How Many Elections Do Democrats Have to Lose Before They Deal with Their Foreign Policy Problem," *American Prospect*, November 21, 2004.

59. Both quotes are drawn from Jeffrey Goldberg, "The Unbranding," *New Yorker*, March 21, 2005. For a plea that Democrats exercise more "message management," see Matthew Yglesias, "Message Management," *American Prospect*, December 13, 2005.

60. Peter Beinart, "A Fighting Faith: An Argument for a New Liberalism," *The New Republic*, December 12, 2004. For some skeptical responses to his argument from fellow liberals, see Joshua Micah Marshall, "Talking Points Memo," December 9, 2004 (http://www.talkingpointsmemo.com/); John B. Judis, "Purpose Driven," *The New Republic Online*, December 12, 2004; and Kevin Drum, "Political Animal," *Washington Monthly*, December 2, 2004.

61. Peter Beinart, "Don't Be a Control Freak (Ask for Help)," *Washington Post*, June 11, 2006, B05; see also, Peter Beinart, *The Good Fight: Why Liberals—and Only Liberals Can Win the War on Terror and Make America Great Again* (New York: HarperCollins, 2006).

62. Lawrence Korb and Brian Katulis, "Strategic Redeployment: A Progressive Plan for Iraq and the Struggle Against Violent Extremists," Center for American Progress, September 29, 2005, http://www.americanprogress.org/atf/cf/{E9245FE4-9A2B-43C7-A521-5D6FF2E06E03}/redeployment.pdf.

63. Walt, *Taming American Power*; see also, Christopher Layne, "From Preponderance to Offshore Balancing: America's Future Grand Strategy," *International Security* 22 (1997): 86-124; Christopher Layne, "Offshore Balancing Revisited," *Washington Quarterly* (Spring 2002): 233-248; and Christopher Layne, *The Peace of illusions: American Grand Strategy from 1940 to the Present* (Ithaca, NY: Cornell University Press, 2006).

64. Ibid., 240-247.

65. Daryl Press has argued recently that in crisis circumstances during the Cold War and before whether a country had made threats it did not follow through on had little impact on whether they were taken seriously when the next major threat arose. On the other hand, a variety of America's more recent enemies have keyed in on the fact that Press accepts that America is casualty-sensitive. Press argues that the important distinction here is between fighting effectively and keeping commitments. He concludes, "quitting after taking a small number of casualties, may send signals about a country's power." Is this not a credibility signal that other countries take into account? See Daryl G. Press, *Calculating Credibility: How Leaders Assess Military Threats* (Ithaca, NY: Cornell University Press, 2005), 157.

66. Gary Rosen, "Bush and the Realists," *Commentary* (September 2005): 34.

67. Lawrence J. Korb and Robert O. Boorstin, "Integrated Power: A National Security Strategy for the 21st Century," Center for American Progress, June 2005.

68. There is talk of the President's "simplistic world view," criticizing him for having "developed virtually no concrete plan to achieve his goal," and castigating him for "weakening our military, draining our treasury and severely damaging our global power and influence." Ibid., ii-v.

69. "The U.S. has made *some* progress in safeguarding the homeland [but] homeland security is not the priority it should be." Ibid., 41 [italics added]. What trade-offs would have to be made between doing "everything" and doing what's needed is not spelled out.

70. Ibid., ii.

71. For the distinctions between the two and some answers to the question of why leaders choose these options, see Jonathan Renshon, *Why Leaders Choose War: The Psychology of Prevention* (Greenport, CT: Preager, 2006).

72. Korb and Boorstin, "Integrated Power," 18.

73. Ibid., 20.

74. Ibid., 38 [italics added]. Along similar lines another progressive Democratic foreign policy think tank has this to say about North Korea, "we will maintain a red line—making clear that if North Korea resumes production of nuclear weapons, the United States would be prepared to use force to protect its interests." See "Progressive Internationalism: A Democratic National Security Policy," October 30, 2003, 13. Just what "our interests" are in this case, how we would get South Korean or international institutions to agree to a military strike, or how we would avoid a second general land war in Korea are left unspecified.

75. Robert J. Art, *A Grand Strategy for America* (Ithaca, NY: Cornell University Press, 2000).

76. Colin Dueck, "New Perspectives on American Grand Strategy," *Survival* 28 (2004): 209.

77. Kenneth J. Pollack, *The Threatening Storm: The Case for Invading Iraq* (New York: Random House, 2002).

78. Cf. "I never did think that Saddam's weapons were sufficient grounds for war. I even said so here, in *Slate*, before the war." See Paul Berman, "Liberal Hawks Reconsider the Iraq War," *Slate*, January 12, 2005. (http://www.slate.com/id/2093620/entry/2093641/).

79. Paul Berman, Thomas Friedman, Christopher Hitchens, Fred Kaplan, George Packer, Kenneth M. Pollack, Jacob Weisberg, and Fareed Zakaria, "Liberal Hawks" in Slate, "Liberal Hawks Reconsider…

80. Fred Kaplan, "Liberal Hawks"

81. Thomas L. Freidman, "Hunting the Tiger," *New York Times*, October 21, 2004

82. Fareed Zakaria, "Liberal Hawks Reconsider"

83. *Newsweek*, September 13, 2004.

84. Christopher Hitchens, "Liberal Hawks Reconsider…"

85. Lawrence F. Kaplan, "Disillusioned, but Accountable," *The New Republic*, October 22, 2004.

86. James Mann, *Rise of the Vulcans: The History of Bush's War Cabinet* (New York: Viking, 2004).

87. James Mann, "A Party Still Trying to Figure It Out." *Washington Post*, May 23, 2004, B01.

88. "Real Security: The Democratic Plan to Protect American and Restore Our Leadership in the World," March 29, 2006, Congress, Second Session, http://democrats.senate.gov/pdfs/RealSecurity_web.pdf. See also Fred Hiatt, "Democrats' Narrow Vision," *Washington Post*, April 3, 2006, A19.

89. Joshua Kurlantzick, "After the Bush Doctrine: The Fight for Republican Foreign Policy," *The New Republic*, February 13, 2006. The article neglects to mention Rudy Guiliani a strong contenter for the GOP 2008 nomination and a Bush Doctrine supporter.

13

The Bush Doctrine in Perspective

PETER SUEDFELD

Many books end with an attempt to summarize, integrate, critique, or recreate the gist of the chapters that went before. I will not attempt to do that: it would be almost impossible to do so with such a diverse set of topics and viewpoints. Instead, I shall consider the five aspects of the Bush Doctrine with which we began—thoughts and musings that have certainly been influenced by the experts who contributed to the book. Parenthetically, Stanley Renshon and I hope that, no matter either the reader's original or current opinion of President George W. Bush, the Doctrine, or the administration's strategies, those opinions and their underlying knowledge have also been affected in some way by reading the book.

"Try to Remember the Kind of September...."[1]

To begin, we might consider just why the Bush Doctrine was promulgated. Billions of people around the world, and many even in America, are no longer able to reexperience the overwhelming shock and horror of watching the mass murders of 9/11 over and over again.[2] We recall the sights and the sounds, but the emotions have leached out of the memories unless we make an effort to revive them—and perhaps not even then.[3] Just as one example, consider the amazing survey result, cited in this book, that a measurable portion of the U.S. public believes that overthrowing a foreign government is unacceptable under *any* circumstances.

This exsanguination of memory makes it difficult now to appreciate the pain and outrage that Bush and his compatriots felt in the aftermath of the atrocity. It is no wonder that immediately after the terrorist attacks both the leader and the constituents needed a response that would be commensurate with the stimulus, and that could be delivered without delay, nuance, or self-doubt. President Bush, experiencing the emotions of the day and the stress of having to determine and lead that response, had the right personality, cognitive structure, and attitudes to take on that role; and almost all the people, even many of his leading political opponents, vigorously supported his answers.

From the Local to the Global

It is easy, and mistaken, to see the Bush Doctrine only in the restricted context of the trauma of 9/11. It is, indeed, a conceptual underpinning for the specific decisions that followed the attacks; but its aspirations are much higher and its reach is much longer. It is, in effect, the latest in a two-century series of pronouncements by American presidents that have reiterated their commitment to spreading and safeguarding democracy and freedom outside their own borders: first, in the Americas, then with a focus on Europe, and now globally. One might consider these expanding areas of concern and protection as growing along with America's strength and standing in the international system, and with the advances in military, commercial, and personal transportation and communication that have sequentially reduced and almost eliminated the functional distance between the United States and every other nation.

The globalization of markets, battlefields, and neighborhoods calls for a globalized political philosophy and strategy. The implications of this globalization have been presented in the series of speeches and documents produced by the President and his administration that are now subsumed under the shorthand title, the Bush Doctrine. The Bush team has rarely equaled the ringing inspiration of John F. Kennedy's "Let every nation know, whether it wishes us well or ill, that we shall pay any price, bear any burden, meet any hardship, support any friend, oppose any foe to assure the survival and the success of liberty"[4]—but the message is very similar indeed, and much more specific.

Let us now look at the five aspects of the Bush Doctrine as they were outlined in the first chapter.

1. American Preeminence

To the extent that the Bush Doctrine asserts that the economic and military power of the United States is greater than that of any other nation in the world, one can hardly argue the point. The real source of acrimony, both in the U.S. and abroad, seems to be that President Bush is unapologetic and straightforward about this fact and what it implies. Although he has recently modified his tone (to the extent of expressing regret in some cases), his challenge, "Bring it on," responding to a comment about his swagger with "In Texas, we call that 'walking'," and his lack of deference to people and nations who are accustomed to think of themselves as experts (academics, media commentators, UN devotees, the politicians of "Old Europe," et al.)—all these acts have evoked the cries of cowboy crudity and *hubris*. The low approval figures cited in this book, mostly directed at Bush himself, show how widespread this resentment is. Particularly interesting is the fact that many Europeans in fact agree with major tenets of the war on terrorism while rejecting the man who leads it.

To a great extent, it seems, this disrespect and disapproval is a reaction to Bush's style. It is reminiscent of the storm of scorn when President Ronald Reagan referred to the Soviet Union as the "Evil Empire." Most people, especially those who lived within that empire's sway, agreed with the characterization; but there was a widespread tacit agreement to pretend otherwise. Things have not changed much in the past few decades.

This pattern of resentment also explains the glee with which many critics emphasize the imperfections of how the Bush Doctrine has been carried out, usually ignoring or downplaying the successes. Many liberals who argue that Western nations, above all the U.S., should have intervened in Rwanda and should now intervene in Darfur also maintain that deposing Saddam Hussein was a bad idea. After all, it has led to instability—as though the stability enforced by a cruel and murderous thug and the minority religious faction to which he belonged had been a good thing. The post-overthrow violence and criminality, the looting of museums, and the bombings of markets and mosques have been perpetrated by Iraqis and their imported jihadist allies, but the coalition seems to be getting all the blame.

Among the more interesting accusations are the "error" of disbanding Hussein's army and firing its officers as well as Ba'ath Party civilian administrators, and the failure to predict the sectarian violence that we and the Iraqi population are now facing. Should the Allies have continued the *Wehrmacht*, the German General Staff, and Nazi officials after the fall of Hitler? Many did return to office, but usually only after being cleared of war crimes.[5] The eruption of internecine violence that had been suppressed by a dictator or at least a strong central government has historical precedents, for example, in the Indian subcontinent and, more recently, in ex-Yugoslavia; but there are also precedents in the opposite direction, as in most of the former Soviet bloc. It may indeed be the case that the Bush administration was too optimistic in assuming that freedom and democracy would trump religious and ethnic hatred in Iraq—an optimism totally compatible with the Bush Doctrine's goal of spreading democracy as a way of spreading peace.

At the same time, the President is now also being blamed for recognizing the limits of American power. Why did he order the attack on Iraq, but not North Korea or Iran? One wonders what the critics would be saying had he attacked either or both of those countries, much less if he did so now. The combination of circumstances that has kept the latter countries, dangerous as they are, from military intervention, defines the problems of exerting America's supremacy in arms: threats to allies, opposition from other major nations, tactical problems in identifying and destroying crucial targets, and the already troublesome overcommitment of U.S. armed forces. If and when North Korea and Iran develop a nuclear arsenal, and the vehicles with which to deliver it, many Western complainers may wish for the leadership of an unflinching defender of their values and nations.

The negative reaction to the Bush Doctrine may illustrate the dangers of eponymy and assumed authority. Referring to the national security strategy using the name of the President as an adjective and a noun that implies a set of authoritative rules may arouse "reactance": the natural resistance to a perceived assumption of authority and preeminence.[6] Perhaps the worldwide and domestic reaction would have been more benign had the strategy been called "Suggested Guidelines for Advancing Global Peace and Freedom."

2. Assertive Realism: Deterrence and Retaliation vs. Prevention and Preemption

Before 9/11, the American heartland had been safe from large-scale attack by foreigners since the War of 1812. Unlike many Europeans, Asians, and Africans, Americans considered their country invulnerable to such events. The surprise attack on Pearl Harbor in 1941—a remote outpost that was governed by, but was not part of, the United States—evoked official and popular reactions that were as rapid, absolute, and simple as anything that followed the surprise attacks on New York and Washington. There was no vocal dissent from declaring war, suspending many civil rights, forcibly relocating a large number of citizens whose loyalty was suspect merely because of their national origin, greatly widening compulsory military service, converting industry to producing weapons and ammunition, and so on.

In the post-World War II period, the reasonably even distribution of power and influence between the American and Soviet blocs and the deterrence strategy of Mutual Assured Destruction was apparently[7] successful in preventing a major war between the two primary protagonists, although it certainly did not ward off many wars among proxies and protégés of the two.

As several of our contributors have pointed out, deterrence may no longer be as effective as in the past. It may still apply to attacks when the origin of the attack can be clearly identified, and when the offense is of a kind that makes an all-out counterstrike seem symmetrical. But the world has changed since 1945. There has, for example, been a turnaround in the acceptance of casualties. In the aftermath of the Vietnam War, the American and allied publics seem to have decided that war can, and should, be bloodless; the shibboleth of "our boys coming home in body bags" and the daily recital of the number of dead and wounded, without consideration of why the soldiers are there and what they are accomplishing, is a potent weapon of antiwar propaganda. Furthermore, its power is something that enemies count on: we have seen a reference to Saddam Hussein's belief that his army could absorb many casualties but that the United States was too weak-willed to continue fighting after losses. Sadly, current opinion polls seem to bear this out; fortunately, the administration has so far stood firm against the Vietnam syndrome.

Public aversion is not only to death and injury on our own side. Western forces, at least, are now supposed to minimize civilian casualties ("collateral damage") even on enemy soil—not much of a concern when cities were being bombed or when street fighting was going on in Europe. In fact, they are expected to limit even enemy military losses. During the final phase of Gulf War I, there was an outcry when U.S. forces continued to attack the Iraqi withdrawal from Kuwait, as though a retreating (but not surrendered) enemy should be immune from further violence. One can only wonder what Napoleon, Wellington, Grant, Eisenhower, or Zhukov would have thought of that novel principle of war.

Employing massive deterrence under such rules of engagement is difficult, especially against enemies who fight under completely different rules. How can you deter suicide-murder bombers? If you must avoid civilian casualties, how can you deter enemies who hide among civilians? Deterrence still has its place (the ending of Libya's nuclear program may be one example) but its place seems nowhere near as prominent as during the Cold War.

If deterrence is so difficult, can we avoid the guilt of starting wars by maintaining a strong second-strike capability? The Bush administration seems to have understood a principle that is consonant with both loss aversion and historical experience. People whose territory has been the site of many battles know this, but Americans seem to have forgotten the lessons of the 1860s and many Europeans those of the 1940s: if there has to be a war, it is better to fight it on someone else's soil than on your own. There may be military difficulties, such as longer supply lines, but keeping the devastation of battle out of your homeland is a better idea than waiting to be attacked and then retaliating. This is especially true if the initial attack may cause severe damage and casualties, as could be the case, for example, in a terrorist atrocity using biological, chemical, nuclear, or radiological materials.

That seems to leave prevention and preemption. One can certainly argue the abstract ethics of going to war to head off an anticipated attack, whether in the immediate or the remote future; several chapters in this book have reviewed such arguments. For the people who are actually responsible for making the decision, however, the matter of abstract ethics is secondary (if that). More important is the supreme duty of safeguarding the country and the people, which requires the dispassionate calculation of possible gains and losses, or benefits and costs, emanating from alternative strategies. The shorthand formula for assessing risks is to look at the probability of each outcome in interaction with its potential cost or benefit. These calculations are affected by a number of variables, including a general human aversion to loss; that is, people are more eager to avoid losses than to achieve gains.[8]

The issue, of course, is does there have to be a war? Is there a real danger of being attacked? The costs of a false negative (assuming that there is no danger when in reality there is one) have to be weighed against the costs of a false positive (assuming that there is a danger when in reality there is none). And, as always, decisions must be evaluated in terms of what was known at the time, not what is known now. The Bush administration seems to have been mistaken in regard to Iraq, relying on and perhaps exaggerating the consensus of intelligence agencies worldwide about Hussein's WMD programs; this is what we know now, but not then. Recall the 1973 attack on Israel, whose leaders accepted a negative that turned out to be false (concluding that the massing of Egyptian forces near border areas was a training exercise). In the ensuing war against both Egypt and Syria (which were aided by nine other Arab states), Israel suffered several thousand casualties (including 2,400 dead) and the shattering of its myth of military invulnerability.

What guidelines should there be for solving future conundrums of this sort? Understanding more about the cultures and politics of potential antagonists, and about the personality of their leaders, would certainly help. Examples of relevant analyses are given in some of our chapters, and many others are in the social science literature. Similarly, there is no shortage of advice on decision making and risk assessment from a variety of academic disciplines[9] as well as from practical experience. Historical analogies are a common, albeit sometimes misleading, source of suggestions,[10] as are case studies of how decisions can go wrong.[11] We will probably not know for decades how the Bush administration goes about such tasks;[12] no doubt imperfectly, as do all decision-making groups, but apparently with clarity as to the primary goal of protecting America.

3 and 4. Strategic Stand-Apart Alliances and Selective Multilateralism: If You're Not With Us, You're Against Us (Or, at Least, We'll Ignore You)

The Bush administration's view toward allies, potential allies, ex-allies, quasi-allies, and pseudo-allies (be they individuals, nations, or supranational organizations) is mixed. On the one hand, official statements acknowledge that the United States can be friends with those who disagree on some specific issue, such as the war in Iraq or the Bush Doctrine; on the other, it is clear that the face the President turns toward them is not friendly. As we have seen, his feelings toward those who are only nominal allies but actual opponents are similar to his feelings toward out-and-out enemies.

The position outlined in the Bush Doctrine asserts the overwhelming importance of the war on terror, but the actual policy is more nuanced. Regardless of the President's personal attitudes, he and his officials have continued their attempts to obtain cooperation from such recalcitrant partners as France, Germany, the People's Republic of China, and Russia, as well as from the United Nations. They may have underestimated the strength of motives that militate against cooperation, both emotional—envy, nostalgia, anti-Americanism, anti-Semitism, anticapitalism—and pragmatic—deals for cheap oil, markets for weapons and other illicit goods, appeasement to avoid attack, pandering to Muslim immigrants and citizens, straight-out corruption. Not everyone agrees that the war on terrorism is paramount, important, or even real; even in U.S. publications, the phrase is frequently preceded by "so-called," or surrounded by the quotation marks of suspicion or superciliousness.

Under such conditions, picking one's allies is clearly more sensible than assuming common goals (much less common methods for reaching the goals). If indeed "selective multilateralism is perceived as unilateralism," as one of our contributors proposes, we should consider whether the perception or the reality is more important. How can the U.S. be *non*selectively multilateral when its motives, priorities, and aims are not shared by its potential allies and in fact are incompatible with some? It has not yet reached the level of accepting that other countries, or combinations of countries, should have veto power over its own foreign and defense policy, where, for example, military action is deemed illegal or at least illegitimate unless approved by the UN or NATO (a widespread assumption in Canada).

Besides the issues of defense and terrorism, the Bush administration has been castigated for its unilateralism in not underwriting the Kyoto Accord (which was left hanging at the end of the Clinton administration, as well as by many First World nations, and has been strongly criticized by a host of scientists and economists); not submitting American officials and soldiers to possible politically motivated persecution by the International Criminal Tribunal; and going ahead with the antimissile defense system (is it really a provocation to defend yourself against nuclear attack?). At the same time, it has a better record in curbing pollution than pro-Kyoto Canada (among others), continues to provide the major portion of the UN's budget, and contributes more in disaster relief and foreign aid than anyone else. Does it get credit for these policies? Are they irrelevant vis-à-vis the Bush Doctrine? The international opinion polls suggest that this is indeed the case. Why?

5. Democratic Transformation: Can We, Should We, Trust the People Everywhere?

Is the Bush Doctrine's principle, that democracy is both desirable in itself and because it leads to peace, wrong? Is democracy indeed always to be preferred to the alternatives? Churchill had claimed that this was so[13]; but some Western observers have noted that such optimism may be unwarranted in some cases.

Unfortunately, contemporary exceptions of this kind seem to be concentrated mostly in those nations where democracy may create more regimes that are inimical and dangerous to America, that is, where free elections can produce, and have produced, Islamist and even Islamist terrorist governments. In Egypt and Algeria, fundamentalist religious rule would have been established had it not been for military rejection of the popular vote; in Iran (where the election was certainly not free, but it was at least contested), a radical warmonger, who believes in an impending apocalypse followed by triumphant Islam, won against an opponent who, if not a moderate, was at least not as extreme; in the Palestinian territories, an unquestionably terrorist "party" won control of the government from a group that was willing to make at least temporary compromises to obtain at least temporary peace. We don't know who would win free elections in Saudi Arabia, Syria, Libya, the Emirates,

Pakistan, and other authoritarian but nontheocratic Muslim countries, but it is highly unlikely that the vote would go to tolerant, open-minded, freedom-loving admirers of the West. More likely it would be one man (literally), one vote, one time—and thereafter, the Koran, as interpreted by fundamentalist clergymen, would dictate both domestic and foreign policy.

Here is a dilemma for President Bush, the Bush Doctrine, and for all those who extol democracy. Do we still support it if its outcome is likely to be more totalitarian states replacing authoritarian ones, more terrorism against us and our allies, more enemies who possess nuclear weapons, more incitement of Muslims in Western countries to turn traitor and of Muslims everywhere to turn murderer? This is a contingency that the "no wars between democracies" camp has not sufficiently appreciated and that the Bush Doctrine ignores.

This may be another appropriate place to argue for more study and better understanding of cultural differences. The interaction between religion, tradition, and newly installed democracy is likely to differ across groups and as a function of strategy. For example, in countries that have experienced democracy in the past, and that may share traditions and histories that value individualism, democracy may be easily accepted. Elsewhere, without such experiences and values, it may have to take hold gradually, under an armed security umbrella, and even then with occasional setbacks. If we could tell which strategy would be needed where, we might be able to foster both democracy and peace.

A Balance Sheet

On balance, the national defense strategy enunciated by the Bush administration seems to have things more right than not. It *is* important to guard Western countries and Western values against terrorist attacks; when deterrence is impractical and retaliation can occur only after we suffer serious damage, it *is* appropriate to attack first; it *is* sensible to pick our friends, to chart our own course considering the "decent opinions of mankind" but not necessarily following them or making policy by opinion poll; and it *is* in keeping with America's traditions to try to encourage democracy and individual freedom.

At the same time, the Doctrine is not flawless. The power to guard is not limitless, forecasting attacks is by no means a precise science, ignoring the opinions of non-friends can be dangerous, and new democracies may be hostile even if they last (which they may not).

As to the future of the Bush Doctrine, we agree with several of our contributors that given the existence of terrorism and the continuing complexities that must be considered in dealing with it, the Doctrine—perhaps in modified form, or at least modified phrasing—will continue to shape America's policies. It may eventually be absorbed into an expanded version, just as its eponymous predecessors have been, perhaps extending democracy and mutual defense to Earth's outposts elsewhere.

Endnotes

1. *The Fantasticks*, book and lyrics by Tom Jones, music by Harvey Schmidt.
2. In this discussion, I ignore those who rejoice in any event that hurts the United States, and those who whenever this happens blame the victim: the searchers for "root causes," who always find the cause to be something that America has done wrong. Regrettably, many of these analysts are Americans and, too many of them, American academics; see, e.g., David Horowitz, *The Professors: The 101 Most Dangerous Academics in America* (Washington, DC: Regnery, 2006).
3. About the evanescent nature of event-related emotions, see, e.g., Daniel T. Gilbert and Jane E. J. Ebert, "Decisions and Revisions: The Affective Forecasting of Changeable Outcomes," *Journal of Personality and Social Psychology* 82 (2002): 503-514.
4. John F. Kennedy's Inaugural Address, January 20, 1961, http://www.quotedb.com/speeches/john-f-kennedy-inaugural-address.
5. General George S. Patton was relieved as Commander of the Third Army and Military Governor of Bavaria partly because, speaking to a group of reporters (as reported in the *New York Times*, September 24 1945), he said that "in general, far too much fuss has been made regarding denazification of Germany; that this Nazi thing is just like a Democratic and Republican election fight, and that the best hope for the future lies in showing the German people what grand fellows we are." Quoted in a secret memorandum from General Marshall to General Eisenhower, September 24 1945, http://72.14.203.104/search?q=cache:BNR6y_tUH2EJ:www.marshallfoundation.org/vol5Chap3.pdf+%22george+s.+patton%22+denazification+quotes&hl=en&gl=ca&ct=clnk&cd=10&client=frefox-a. Patton also told reporters that he intended to use former Nazi Party officials in administering Bavaria.
6. Jack W. Brehm, *A Theory of Psychological Reactance* (New York: Academic Press, 1966).
7. "Apparently," because the causal attribution is not subject to empirical test. It may be that even without MAD, no great-power war would have occurred. Cf. Philip E. Tetlock and Aaron Belkin, eds. *Counterfactual Thought Experiments in World Politics* (Princeton, NJ: Princeton University Press, 1996).
8. Rose McDermott, *Risk-Taking in International Politics: Prospect Theory in American Foreign Policy* (Ann Arbor: University of Michigan Press, 2001).
9. For example, Katrin Borcherding, Oleg I. Larichev, and David M Messick, eds., *Contemporary Issues in Decision Making* (Amsterdam: North Holland, 1990); Daniel Kahneman, Paul D. Slovic, and Amos Tversky, eds., *Judgment Under Uncertainty: Heuristics and Biases* (New York: Cambridge University Press, 1982); Donald A. Sylvan and James F. Voss *Problem Representation in Foreign Policy Decision Making* (New York: Cambridge University Press, 1998); Yaacov Y.I. Vertzberger, *The World in Their Minds: Information Processing, Cognition, and Perception in Foreign Policy Decisionmaking* (Stanford, CA: Stanford University Press, 1990).
10. See Yuen F. Khong, *Analogies at War: Korea, Munich, Dien Bien Phu, and the Vietnam Decisions of 1965* (Princeton, NJ: Princeton University Press, 1992).
11. For example, Irving L. Janis, *Groupthink: Psychological Studies of Policy Decisions and Fiascoes* (Boston: Houghton Mifflin, 1982).

12. Many details of the Kennedy decision-making team's deliberations during the Cuban Missile Crisis of 1962 have only very recently come to light, more than forty years after the event.

13. "Indeed, it has been said that democracy is the worst form of government except all those other forms that have been tried from time to time." Sir Winston Churchill, *Hansard*, November 11, 1947, http://www.quotationspage.com/quote/24926.html.

Contributors

GERARD ALEXANDER is an associate professor of politics at the University of Virginia in Charlottesville. He is author of *The Sources of Democratic Consolidation* (Cornell University Press, 2002) and articles on democratic transitions, democratic consolidation, and the rule of law in the *Journal of Theoretical Politics, Comparative Political Studies*, and the *Revista Española de Ciencia Política*. He has written about the democratization in post-9/11 American foreign policy in *Policy Review*, the *National Interest*, the *Brown Journal of World Affairs*, the *Weekly Standard*, and the *Claremont Review of Books*. He is working on a book project on U.S. national security policy, one part of which appears in *International Security* (2005).

WILLIE CURTIS is an associate professor of political science at the United States Naval Academy, focusing on nuclear deterrence theory, nuclear strategy, international security policy, and peacekeeping and peace operations. He is a consultant to the Department of Defense, Commission on Roles and Missions of the Armed Forces regarding peace operations; and a member of the advisory board, Center for National Security Law Institute, at the University of Virginia School of Law in Charlottesville. He is a contributor to *Maneuvering in the Gray Zone: The Gap between Traditional Peacekeeping and Warfighting: Peacemaking, Peace-Enforcement, and Post-Conflict Peace-Building* (National Defense University Press, 1994) and numerous journal articles on conflict, deterrence, and strategic defense.

DOUGLAS C. FOYLE is an associate professor of government at Wesleyan University in Middleton, Connecticut, where he specializes in the area of international relations and American foreign policy. His book, *Counting the Public In: Presidents, Public Opinion, and Foreign Policy* (Columbia University Press, 1999), examined the public's influence on American foreign policy decision making since World War II. In addition, he has published articles in *International Studies Quarterly, International Journal of Public Opinion Research*, and the *International Studies Review*. He is currently working on a book project entitled *Politics Beyond the Water's Edge: The Electoral Incentive and American Foreign Policy Decision Making*, which examines how presidents adjust their foreign policies during election campaigns.

RAJIV JHANGIANI is currently earning his PhD in social psychology at the University of British Columbia in Vancouver. His research interests include the responses of civilian populations to terrorist attacks and natural disasters, as well as elite decision making and ethnopolitical conflict. He is the winner of the Tara Nash Award for Outstanding Contributions to the Department of Psychology, A Research Associate Simons Centre for Disarmament & Non-proliferation Research Liu Institute for Global Issues, University of British Columbia; as well as the recipient of the Roberta Sigel Award for presenting the best student paper at the Scientific Meetings of the International Society of Political Psychology.

JACK S. LEVY is Board of Governors' Professor of Political Science at Rutgers University in New Brunswick, New Jersey. He is author of *War in the Modern Great Power System, 1495–1975* (University Press of Kentucky, 1983) and of numerous articles and book chapters. He received the American Political Science Association's Helen Dwight Reid Award for the best dissertation in international relations in 1975–76, and the Distinguished Scholar Award from the Foreign Policy Analysis Section of the International Studies Association (2000). He is president of the Peace Science Society (International) for 2005–2006, and president of the International Studies Association for 2007–2008.

ALEXANDER MOENS is a professor of political science at Simon Fraser University in Vancouver, British Columbia. He teaches American foreign policy and the political and security relations between Europe and North America. He is the author of *The Foreign Policy of George W. Bush: Values, Strategy, Loyalty* (Ashgate, 2004), as well as *Foreign Policy Under Carter: Testing Multiple Advocacy Decision Making* (Westview Press, 1990). He has served in the Policy Planning Staff of Canada's Foreign Affairs Department and has been a visiting fellow at the National Defense University in Washington, DC. He is also a researcher with the Council for Canadian Security in the 21st Century, and a Fellow of the Canadian Defense & Foreign Affairs Institute. In 2002, he was appointed Senior Fellow in American Policy at the Fraser Institute in Vancouver.

JERROLD M. POST is a professor of psychiatry, political psychology, and international affairs and director of the Political Psychology Program at George Washington University in Washington, DC. He was the founding director of the Center for the Analysis of Personality and Political Behavior at the Central Intelligence Agency, an interdisciplinary behavioral science unit that provided assessments of foreign leadership and decision making for the President and other senior officials. His books include *When Illness Strikes the Leader: The Dilemma of the Captive King* (Yale University Press, 1993); *Political Paranoia: The Psychopolitics of Hatred* (Yale University Press, 1997); *The Psychological Evaluation of Political Leaders: With Profiles of Saddam Hussein and William Jefferson Clinton* (University of Michigan Press, 2003); *Know Thy Enemy: Profiles of Adversary Leaders and Their Strategic Cultures* (with Barry Schneider, DIANE Publishing, 2004), and most recently *Leaders and Their*

Followers in a Dangerous World: The Psychology of Political Behavior (Cornell University Press, 2004). His book, *The Mind of the Terrorist,* will be published by Palgrave/Macmillan in 2007.

JONATHAN RENSHON is a doctoral student in the Government Department at Harvard University, focusing on international relations theory, national security, and foreign policy decision making. He holds a master's degree in international relations from the London School of Economics and Political Science. He has served on the editorial board of the *Millennium Journal of International Studies.* He recently received the White Fellowship for excellence in government studies from Wesleyan University in Middleton, Connecticut. His book, *Why Leaders Choose War: The Psychology of Prevention,* has been published this year by Preager. He is the author (with Daniel Kahneman) of "The Hawk Bias," *Foreign Policy* (2007).

STANLEY A. RENSHON is a professor of political science at the City University of New York, and a certified psychoanalyst. He has published over ninety professional articles and twelve books in the fields of political psychology, presidential politics, and international relations. His book on the Clinton presidency, *High Hopes: The Clinton Presidency and the Politics of Ambition* (New York University Press, 1996), won the 1997 American Political Science Association's Richard E. Neustadt Award for the best book published on the presidency. It was also the winner in 1998 of the National Association for the Advancement of Psychoanalysis' Gradiva Award for the best published work in the category of biography. He is at work on a book entitled *The Bush Doctrine and the Future of American National Security* (New Haven, CT: Yale University Press, 2008 forthcoming).

PETER SUEDFELD is Dean Emeritus of Graduate Studies and Professor Emeritus of Psychology at the University of British Columbia in Vancouver. His more than 230 publications focus on how people cope with challenging and dangerous situations. He is a pioneer in applying content analytic techniques to archival materials produced by political and military leadership elites facing critical decisions; survivors of extreme trauma (e.g., the Holocaust); people in challenging environments such as space and the polar regions; and ordinary citizens experiencing political, economic, and personal crises. He is a Fellow of the Royal Society of Canada (the National Academy of Arts and Sciences); the recipient of the Donald O. Hebb Award, the Canadian Psychological Association's highest award for scientific contributions; the National Science Foundation's Antarctica Service Medal; the Zachor Award for contributions to Canadian society; and the International Society of Political Psychology's Harold D. Lasswell Award for distinguished scientific contributions.

JANICE GROSS STEIN is Belzberg Professor of Conflict Management and Negotiation in the Department of Political Science and the director of the

Munk Centre for International Studies at the University of Toronto. Her books include *Getting to the Table: The Processes of International Prenegotiation* (Johns Hopkins University Press, 1989), *Choosing to Co-Operate: How States Avoid Loss* (Johns Hopkins University Press, 1993); as contributer, *We All Lost the Cold War* (Princeton University Press, 1994), *Powder Keg in the Middle East: The Struggle for Gulf Security,* Rowman & Littlefield, 1995), and *Knowledge Networks: Collaborative Innovation in International Learning* (University of Toronto Press, 2001). Her most recent book, *The Cult of Efficiency* (House of Anansi, 2003), was nominated for the Shaughnessy Cohen Prize in Political Writing by the Canadian Political Science Association for the Donald Smilie Prize, and for the Pearson Readers' Choice Book Award. She is a Fellow of the Royal Society of Canada and an Honorary Foreign Member of the American Academy of Arts and Science.

PHILIP E. TETLOCK is Mitchell Professor of Leadership, Haas School of Business, University of California, Berkeley, and also holds an appointment as professor of political science. He has published nine books, including, most recently, *Expert Political Judgment: How Good Is It? How Can We Know?* (Princeton University Press, 2005). He is also the author of over 185 journal articles and book chapters. He received two early career awards and has also won the American Association for the Advancement of Science Prize for Behavioral Science Research, the Woodrow Wilson Book Award, The Nevitt Sanford Award for Distinguished Professional Contributions to Political Psychology, and the National Academy of Sciences Award for Behavioral Research Relevant to the Prevention of War.

MARVIN ZONIS is Professor Emeritus, the Graduate School of Business, the University of Chicago. At Chicago's Graduate School of Business, he consults to corporations and professional asset management firms throughout the world, helping them to identify, assess, and manage their political risks in the changing global environment. He was educated at Yale University, the Harvard Business School, the Massachusetts Institute of Technology, where he received a PhD in political science, and the Chicago Institute for Psychoanalysis, where he received psychoanalytic training. His books include *The Kimchi Matters: Global Business and Local Politics in a Crisis-Driven World* (Agate, 2003), *The Eastern European Opportunity* (Wiley, 1992), *Majestic Failure: The Fall of the Shah* (University of Chicago Press, 1998), *Khomeini, the Islamic Republic of Iran, and the Arab World* (Center for Middle Eastern Studies, Harvard University, 1987), and *The Political Elite of Iran* (Princeton University Press, 1971).

Name Index

Subject Index